A Retrospective Bibliography
of American Demographic History
from Colonial Times to 1983

Recent Titles in
Bibliographies and Indexes in American History

A Retrospective Bibliography of American Demographic History from Colonial Times to 1983

Compiled by
David R. Gerhan and Robert V. Wells

Bibliographies and Indexes in American History, Number 10

Greenwood Press
New York • Westport, Connecticut • London

Library of Congress Cataloging-in-Publication Data

Gerhan, David R.
    A retrospective bibliography of American demographic history from
colonial times to 1983 / compiled by David R. Gerhan and Robert
V. Wells.
        p.   cm.—(Bibliographies and indexes in American history,
    ISSN 0742-6828 ; no. 10)
    Includes indexes.
    ISBN 0-313-23130-3 (lib. bdg. : alk. paper)
    1. United States—Population—History—Bibliography.
    2. Demography—United States—History—Bibliography.   I. Wells,
Robert V., 1943-   . II. Title. III. Series.
Z7165.U5G43   1989
[HB3505]
016.3046'0973—dc19   88-32348

British Library Cataloguing in Publication Data is available.

Library of Congress Catalog Card Number: 88-32348
ISBN: 0-313-23130-3
ISSN: 0742-6828

First published in 1989

Greenwood Press, Inc.
88 Post Road West, Westport, Connecticut 06881

Printed in the United States of America

The paper used in this book complies with the
Permanent Paper Standard issued by the National
Information Standards Organization (Z39.48-1984).

10 9 8 7 6 5 4 3 2 1

Contents

Preface

Modern American demographic history emerged as a clearly defined discipline in the middle of the 1960s, when John Demos, Philip Greven, Jr., and Kenneth Lockridge introduced scholars on this side of the Atlantic to some of the new techniques of research and results that French and English demographers and historians had pioneered in the 1950s. Slowly at first, but then with increasing speed, historians began to realize the full value of demographic information to their studies, whether they were working on matters of population or more indirectly related subjects. In recent years, what began as a trickle is now well on the way to a flood. In spite of this, there is no work that provides a guide to American demographic history. The only bibliography to demographic history in general, T.H. Hollingsworth's, Historical Demography (Ithaca, N.Y., Cornell University Press, 1969), is almost twenty years old; even more to the point, it had fewer than ten citations to works on America. Thus, a guide to the literature on American demographic history would be of considerable use to a wide variety of scholars.

The literature produced in the last ten years is large, and shows no sign of slowing. There is, however, a significant body of material produced before demographic history became popular that is still useful to scholars today. Some of it was written with demographic questions in mind; other studies emerged from other interests, and the authors might be quite surprised to find their work of value to demographic historians. In addition, scholars interested in topics such as immigration often had little interest in urbanization, childbearing, or life expectancy. As a result, bibliographies of books on a specific topic often are full of references to similar material, but they seldom cite works that are related in more subtle and complex ways. One of the main purposes of this guide is to make it easy to find works on a wide variety of topics, published in a number of books and journals not normally consulted by historians or even available to those who work at smaller institutions. The second goal is to introduce scholars to a range of topics sufficient to acquaint anyone studying any aspect of American demographic history with the complexities of the subject as a whole.

The number of works that are potential candidates for this guide is extremely large, considering the literature produced both before the 1960s and in recent years. As a result, we have placed some limits on what to include, and how best to organize the guide. The rapid rate of increase in publications in demographic history, and all its subspecialties, in recent years, coupled with a scholarly literature that dates back to the colonial period on some topics has led to the decision to provide this guide in two companion volumes. The first emphasizes the early literature and includes studies published before 1983. The companion volume will cover the most recent works.

Our explanation of the choices we made in assembling the first guide begins with a brief history of the evolution of the project. The core of the bibliography was assembled in the early 1970s when Wells was gathering the material that was synthesized in <u>Revolutions in Americans' Lives</u> (Westport, Connecticut, Greenwood Press, 1982). Much of the work was done while he was a fellow at Harvard's Charles Warren Center for Study in American History in 1974-1975. In the absence of appropriate indexes, this meant hours going through the rich collection of specialized history journals in Widener Library. Greenwood was reluctant to publish the initial bibliography of about 1500 items as part of the book but suggested the creation of a separate guide.

If this was a guide to historical demography, concerned only with the size of past populations and how they got to be that way, the question of what to include would be easy to answer. Demographic history, however, includes not only the basic patterns of population, but also the study of such things as family patterns and the social, economic, and political consequences of demographic trends. In addition, the hard quantitative data of population cannot be fully understood without reference to the values people attach to their behavior. As a result, this guide presents a comprehensive introduction to most of the topics that can legitimately be considered to fall within the purview of demographic history, broadly defined.

In all, this volume includes 3,840 separate citations (a few of which are duplicates when a work was of such scope as to require mention in more than one place). As we compiled and verified citations and tracked down leads, we have made a special effort to incorporate numerous interesting and useful studies published in a variety of out of the way places. Readers will find many appropriate articles published in state and local historical journals. These are often overlooked and are not always accessible in smaller libraries. Similarly, journals devoted to special topics such as medicine, migration, or geography have been combed for relevant studies. A look at the list of abbreviations of journal titles will demonstrate how widely we ranged in our search. In spite of our efforts, experience suggests that we have missed some studies that deserve to be included, but not many. Thus, we have provided a comprehensive, but not complete guide.

Three conscious decisions limited what can be found in these pages. First, the state and local history journals are full of first-person accounts of migration, marriage, family matters and other topics that can shed light on all kinds of demographic affairs. Diaries, letters, and memoirs abound, but we have chosen not to include these types of materials. We have, however, cited many studies that are based on these sources. Second, twentieth-century academic journals have been used sparingly. For example, sociological journals have been publishing on population and family for years. In most cases the material was on current matters, but by now works done in the 1930s on differential fertility, for example, are of historic value for both the data and the attitudes expressed. Nonetheless, we have left such studies out of this guide unless they had an originally intended historical orientation; that is they were concerned with changes over a significant amount of time. Finally, as mentioned above, this volume emphasizes material published before demographic history became a clearly defined field. Studies from this period are often overlooked because indexers were not concerned with demographic topics. In addition, this volume includes works published before 1983, the time when Revolutions in Americans' Lives appeared. A second volume will pick up at 1983, and will provide access to the recent flood of material.

The overall organization of the guide reflects its origins as part of Revolutions in Americans' Lives, so users of this work might want to examine that in order to understand how we think some of these materials relate to demographic history as a whole. The subdivisions in the various chapters are also influenced by the topics in the book. Nonetheless, an effort has been made to keep the material sufficiently free of our judgment on matters of detail so that others should be able to follow their own interests.

To provide some indication of the general outlines of a given field and how it fits with other areas, we have provided commentary at the start of each section of each chapter. When there are studies that are the obvious places to start they have been noted. The goal of this commentary is to offer help in selection at a level somewhere between annotation--that might not do full justice to the material-- and complex bibliographic essays --that could not include all the studies that we thought ought to be mentioned.

The Guide is simple to use. It is broken up into six chapters, and each of them has been subdivided into appropriate topics. The Table of Contents presents this in considerable detail. The first chapter is divided into four broad topics that provide various types of background materials. The first section treats the subject of formal demography for those readers who may not be familiar with the terms and techniques of the discipline. Some attention has been paid to the most important theories for historical work. Historical demography has its own techniques and a body of basic literature that deserve attention. This, along with works on the population of the Old World and the New, just before Columbus, makes up the second section. American demographic history receives third notice with general surveys, readers, and basic sources being noted.

Because this bibliography pays attention to values and communication, the last part has citations that bear on these topics and the ways in which we interpret the demographic events that happen to us.

Birth, death, marriage, and migration are all major influences on the way populations grow and change. We have chosen to start our survey of these fields in Chapter Two with marriage and childbearing, if only because life begins with birth. In addition, the study of fertility control in the past has provided one of the closest links between formal demography and demographic history. The nineteenth century marked major declines in childbearing in the United States; hence, the material here has been divided chronologically into the periods before, during, and after that change. "Early America" refers to the time before 1800, the "Nineteenth Century" runs from 1800 to 1920, and the "Twentieth Century" covers 1920 to the present. In the first section, the materials have been divided into marriage, duration of marriage and remarriage, childbearing, and illegitimacy and bridal pregnancy. Most of these studies have a common methodological underpinning, family reconstitution, a technique much like genealogy. The studies of the great change of the nineteenth century are generally based on the federal censuses of the time and are not strictly comparable to those of the earlier period. There are a few exceptions, mostly published at the start of this century. After listing the works on marriage and divorce (a topic new to this period), we turn to childbearing. There are enough studies, with enough differences, to consider general as well as white, black, regional, ethnic, and occupational differences in fertility. This is especially important because not all Americans experienced the change at the same time. The next section includes studies that seek to explain how and why the change took place, from the perspective both of those who lived through it and of modern scholars seeking to understand the motives and techniques involved. Material on the recent past is limited and basically describes how the earlier declines continued or were altered. The "baby boom" after World War II is perhaps the most important event of this time. This is one area where the sociological journals provide a valuable alternative resource.

The third chapter, on health and death, is organized somewhat differently, reflecting the fact that much of this literature was produced by two quite different groups, medical historians and demographers. The first category includes a number of works that range widely over time and subject. The section on levels of mortality in the various periods discusses rather specific evidence on death rates and life expectancy. It is both possible and desirable to separate the distinct experiences of Blacks and Indian Americans. The causes of health and death are important in understanding levels of mortality. In general, studies on this topic survey such things as the standard of living, medical practice, the state of public health, efforts to improve health, and options available to those who did not want to seek care from regular physicians. Readers should keep in mind that, although Americans actively sought to improve their life chances from the seventeenth century and began to live better and longer by 1750, doctors could not actually do much to prevent illness until 1880 and could not cure many people before 1920. This point has special importance for the last section, because Americans and their doctors have often had uneasy relationships with each other. Some of these attitudes are discussed in studies listed in the fourth part. Other topics included there are insurance, perspectives on death and dying, and the ways in which the highly personal experience with death could take on public import.

No topic in American demographic history has received more attention than the various aspects of migration: international, westward, and to the cities. Much of this work has been done by historians, though geographers and sociologists have also made major contributions. Such studies vary in scope from sweeping surveys to detailed portraits of local communities. A common theme throughout, is how America became a pluralistic society, from the earliest years of settlement. Although the nineteenth century saw over thirty million people move to this country, with great differences in language, religion, and skills, the theme of pluralism is one that dates from the seventeenth century. The materials on the English colonies demonstrate regional differences that the colonists themselves recognized. The fact that French and Spanish colonies, with their own particular patterns, were eventually incorporated into the United States has received note. Because America was already inhabited when the Europeans first arrived, it is important to examine what the settlement and expansion of whites meant to the Indians. Readers may want to refer to the materials on the pre-Columbian populations in Chapter One.   Cities played a major role in American society from the start, and became even more important in the nineteenth century, so the section on urbanization has been set off from the other studies.   If migration is the most popular topic in demographic history, then the nineteenth century is the period of preference.   Readers will note that several of the subsections here contain over two hundred citations. International immigration is one such area.   Interestingly, the subject of emigration has received only a small fraction of the note that immigration has.

Internal migration is a complex subject requiring at least six subheadings.   General studies examine large numbers of people over large areas.   A major theme of American scholarship in the last two decades has been the rapid movement of people within the country, often associated with social mobility.   These studies of population turnover frequently share common methods and common questions and may be the most coherent body of literature in this guide. Although the studies of turnover generally focus on a given location, there are numerous other works that also shed light on local patterns in states, counties, and towns.   Both Blacks and Indians have their own unique history of migration and each has been treated separately.   The sixth part of internal migration lists studies on the wide variety of factors that encouraged people to move and shaped their choice of destination.   These works examine motivating forces that range from the highly personal and subjective, to institutions that promoted migration, to technological changes that made the process easier.

Although it could be considered part of internal migration, urbanization has been given separate attention here, partly because of the size of the literature, and partly because the field is recognized as standing alone.   One group of studies looks at urban history as a general process, while a second approach is to write biographies of particular places.   These latter can be histories of a community, or may explore economic, political, or social events in a city.

Historical studies of the twentieth century are rarer, though some of the works cited under the nineteenth century carry over into the recent past.   Only three categories have been used for the period after 1920:   international migration, local

and regional, and urbanization.   Of these, the field of
international migration has the most significant new theme,
in view of newly enacted laws limiting immigration, which
combined with economic factors, are profoundly altering the
characteristics of recent arrivals.   Suburbanization emerged
as an important theme in urban history during this period, as
well.   A few works examine recent migration to the
"Sunbelt".

The last two chapters go beyond the traditional confines of
demographic history.   Chapter Five looks at the interaction
of families and demographic events.   After an opening section
on theories of the family and studies that look at families
over long periods, the chapter focuses on the three periods
that we have used before.   Each section includes works that
examine the internal structures of families and the relations
among the various members.   The importance of age, gender,
and race in shaping behavior are common concerns.   In
addition, the ways families function as units of production
and consumption, as exercisers of power, and as the primary
building blocks of society are common topics for family
historians and as such receive special mention.   Such
interactions with society exemplify how basic demographic
events, that are often located within families, can have an
effect on broader patterns.   Readers should note that the
demographic revolutions of the nineteenth century generated
a heated debate on what the changes meant for family life,
and whether such changes ought to be encouraged, opposed,
or left alone.   Many of the issues that appeared first in the
nineteenth-century debate on values are still with us today in
forms only slightly modified by experience.

The last chapter is difficult to describe.   Anyone who wishes
to understand how population can affect economic, political,
and social arrangements must read widely in this material.   It
is, however, difficult to divide the general topics of
economics, politics, and society into more specific categories
without separating works that can be usefully read together.
Since most titles are reasonably self-explanatory, we have
left readers to pick and choose on their own.   Suffice it to
say that the range of subjects is great and could probably be
expanded beyond the works cited here.   Many of the studies
listed in earlier chapters, and especially the one on
migration, also shed light on the topics covered here.

In each section of each chapter items are numbered sequentially, starting with a number ending in zero. Thus, the number of entries in each section is easily determined. Remember, in subtracting the end number from the start to allow for the fact that the series starts with a zero and not a one. These numbers can be used to locate any specific citation. The Table of Contents directs users to the entry numbers corresponding to major subject categories. In addition, we have provided three indexes: author, geographic, and major subject groups not indicated in the Table of Contents (for example, ethnic, nationality, occupational, age, gender, or religious).

Abbreviations

Journal titles throughout the bibliography have been abbreviated, with a few exceptions. Titles cited only once or twice have been given in full. Titles of only one word have not been shortened.

AAAPSS	Annals of the American Academy of Political and Social Science
AAASM	American Academy of Arts and Sciences, Memoirs
AAG	Annals of the Association of American Geographers
AASP	American Antiquarian Society. Proceedings
AgH	Agricultural History
AHQ	Alabama Historical Quarterly
AHR	American Historical Review
AI	Annals of Iowa
AJ	Amerasia Journal
AJA	American Jewish Archives
AJH	American Jewish History

AJHQ	American Jewish Historical Quarterly
AJLH	American Journal of Legal History
AJS	American Journal of Sociology
AkHQ	Arkansas Historical Quarterly
AMH	Annals of Medical History
APSP	American Philosophical Society. Proceedings
AQ	American Quarterly
AR	Alabama Review
ArH	Journal of Arizona History
ArW	Arizona and the West
AS	American Studies
ASAJ	American Statistical Association, Journal
ASAT	Actuarial Society of America Transactions
ASR	American Sociological Review
AW	American West
BHM	Bulletin of the History of Medicine
CH	Chicago History
CHQ	California Historical Quarterly
CHR	Catholic Historical Review
CHSB	Cincinnati Historical Society. Bulletin
CHSQ	California Historical Society Quarterly (later CHQ)
CM	The Colorado Magazine

CO	Chronicles of Oklahoma
CWH	Civil War History
DJMT	Dialogue: a Journal of Mormon Thought
EcHR	Economic History Review
EEH	Explorations in Economic History
EICH	Essex Institute Historical Collections
FCHQ	Filson Club Historical Quarterly
FHQ	Florida Historical Quarterly
FS	Feminist Studies
GHQ	Georgia Historical Quarterly
GPQ	Great Plains Quarterly
GR	Geographical Review
HB	Human Biology
HEQ	History of Education Quarterly
HHR	Hawaii Historical Review
HJWM	Historical Journal of Western Massachusetts
HM	Historical Methods
HSSCQ	Historical Society of Southern California Quarterly
IASSP	Indiana Academy of the Social Sciences. Proceedings
IH	Indian History
IJH	Iowa Journal of History
IJHP	Iowa Journal of History and Politics

IJWS	International Journal of Women's Studies
IMH	Indiana Magazine of History
IMHQ	Indiana Medical History Quarterly
IMR	International Migration Review
ISHSJ	Illinois State Historical Society Journal
ISSQ	Indiana Social Studies Quarterly
IY	Idaho Yesterdays
JAC	Journal of American Culture
JAEH	Journal of American Ethnic History
JAH	Journal of American History
JAS	Journal of American Studies
JEH	Journal of Economic History
JES	Journal of Ethnic Studies
JFH	Journal of Family History
JHMAS	Journal of the History of Medicine and Allied Sciences
JIH	Journal of Interdisciplinary History
JMF	Journal of Marriage and the Family
JMsH	Journal of Mississippi History
JNH	Journal of Negro History
JPC	Journal of Popular Culture
JSDH	Journal of San Diego History
JSH	Journal of Social History

JSouH	Journal of Southern History
JSpH	Journal of Sport History
JUH	Journal of Urban History
JW	Journal of the West
KH	Kansas History
KHQ	Kansas Historical Quarterly
KHSR	Kentucky Historical Society Register
LbH	Labor History
LH	Louisiana History
LHQ	Louisiana Historical Quarterly
LS	Louisiana Studies
MA	Mid-America
MdH	Maryland Historian
MH	Michigan History
MHM	Maryland Historical Magazine
MHSC	Massachusetts Historical Society Collections, 1st Series
MHSP	Massachusetts Historical Society, Proceedings
MMFQ	Milbank Memorial Fund Quarterly
MnH	Minnesota History
MoHR	Missouri Historical Review
MoHSB	Missouri Historical Society Bulletin
MQ	Mississippi Quarterly

MVHR	Mississippi Valley Historical Review (later JAH)
MWR	Monthly Weather Review
NCHR	North Carolina Historical Review
NDH	North Dakota History
NDHQ	North Dakota Historical Quarterly
NDQ	North Dakota Quarterly
NEQ	New England Quarterly
NEHGR	New England Historical and Genealogical Register
NH	Nebraska History
NHSQ	Nevada Historical Society Quarterly
NJH	New Jersey History
NMHR	New Mexico Historical Review
NOQ	Northwest Ohio Quarterly
NYH	New York History, also known as New York State Historical Association. Proceedings
OAHQ	Ohio Archeological and Historical Quarterly (later OhHQ)
OH	Ohio History
OhHQ	Ohio Historical Quarterly
OHQ	Oregon Historical Quarterly
PA	Pioneer America
PacH	Pacific Historian
PAH	Perspectives in American History
PAS	Polish American Studies

PH	Pennsylvania History
PHR	Pacific Historical Review
PMHB	Pennsylvania Magazine of History and Biography
PNQ	Pacific Northwest Quarterly
PS	Population Studies
PSQ	Political Science Quarterly
RAF	Revue d'histoire de l'Amerique Francaise
RHR	Radical History Review
RIH	Rhode Island History
SAQ	South Atlantic Quarterly
SB	Social Biology
SCHGM	South Carolina Historical and Geneological Magazine
SCHM	South Carolina Historical Magazine
SCQ	Southern California Quarterly
SDH	South Dakota History
SouS	Southern Studies
SPHQ	Swedish Pioneer Historical Quarterly
SSH	Social Science History
SSJ	Social Science Journal
SSQ	Social Science Quarterly
SWHQ	Southwestern Historical Quarterly
SWHR	Southwestern Historical Review (later SWHQ)

THQ   Tennessee Historical Quarterly

UHQ   Utah Historical Quarterly

VH   Vermont History

VMHB   Virginia Magazine of History and Biography

WestHQ   Western Historical Quarterly

WHQ   Washington Historical Quarterly (later PNQ)

WMH   Wisconsin Magazine of History

WMQ   William and Mary Quarterly, 3rd Series

WPHM   Western Pennsylvania Historical Magazine

WSJHQ   Western States Jewish Historical Quarterly

WVH   West Virginia History

A Retrospective Bibliography
of American Demographic History
from Colonial Times to 1983

1
Introduction and General Background

Demography-General

The materials is this chapter fall into one of two categories. The first are those which serve to acquaint beginners with some of the basic questions, methods, and findings of demography and demographic history. The second are those which provide overviews of sufficient breadth so as to make them unsuitable for other parts of the bibliography.

General Introduction

These studies provide good places to find out what demography is all about. Freedman, Heer, and Wrong are relatively short. Thomlinson is an excellent textbook of some size. The remaining materials explore more specialized topics.

1000. Freedman, Ronald, ed. Population: the Vital Revolution. (Garden City, New York, Anchor Books, 1964)

1001. Hauser, Philip Morris, ed. The Population Dilemma. (Englewood Cliffs, New Jersey, Prentice-Hall, 1963)

1002. Hauser, Philip Morris and Otis Dudley Duncan, eds. The Study of Population: an Inventory and Appraisal. (Chicago, University of Chicago Press, 1959)

1003. Heer, David M. Society and Population. (Englewood Cliffs, New Jersey, Prentice-Hall, 1968)

1004. Scientific American. Special issue on "The Human Population", issue 231, September, 1974.

1005. Thomlinson, Ralph. Population Dynamics: Causes and Consequences of World Demographic Change. 2nd ed. (New York, Random House, 1976)

1006. United Nations. Department of Economic ond Social Affairs. The Determinants and Consequences of Population Trends: New Summary of Findings on Interaction of Demographic, Economic, and Social Factors. 2 vols. (New York, United Nations, 1973-1978)

1007. Wrong, Dennis Hume. Population and Society. 3rd ed. (New York, Random House, 1967)

Technical Manuals

These books include some of the best definitions of demographic terms and demonstrations of how to calculate basic demographic measures. Barclay is the shortest, primarily because the other two provide selected descriptive, demographic statistics.

1020. Barclay, George W. Techniques of Population Analysis. (New York, Wiley, 1958)

1021. Bogue, Donald Joseph. Principles of Demography. (New York, Wiley, 1969)

1022. Shryock, Henry S. The Methods and Materials of Demography. 2 vols. (Washington, U.S. Bureau of the Census, 1973)

Theory and Population

Students of American demographic history need to be aware of some of the broader issues and theories that shape demography. Although there are other theories, those here have special ties to American materials. Malthus, for example, based some of his assumptions about population growth on American data before 1800. Transition theory, probably the dominant paradigm today, is concerned with whether the third world can repeat the experience of the west. American demographic history suggests that transition theory is, in fact, historically flawed and needs to be re-examined. Vinovskis and Wells make this point. There are also several works here that touch on what it is that defines the "modern" world and makes it different from the past. Given the demographic changes of the past two centuries, this is an important topic for students of population to keep in mind. The essay and book by Brown are helpful for the American experience. Wrigley's essay distinguishes among modernization, urbanization, and industrialization.

1030. Brown, Richard D. "Modernization and the Modern Personality in Early America, 1600-1865: a Sketch of a Synthesis." JIH 2 (Winter, 1972), 201-228.

1031. Brown, Richard D. Modernization: the Transformation of American Life, 1600-1865. (New York, Hill and Wang, 1976)

1032. Caldwell, John C. "Toward a Restatement of Demographic Transition Theory." Population and Development Review 2 (September-December, 1976), 321-366.

1033. Coale, Ansley J. "The Demographic Transition." In International Population Conference, Liege, 1973. International Population Conference/International Union for the Scientific Study of Population. (Liege. IUSSP, 1973), 53-72.

1034. Coale, Ansley J. "Population and Economic Development." In Philip Morris Hauser, ed. The Population Dilemma. (Englewood Cliffs, New Jersey, Prentice-Hall, 1963), 46-69.

1035. Coale, Ansley J. and Edgar Hoover. Population Growth and Economic Development in Low-Income Countries: a Case Study of India's Prospects. (Princeton, Princeton University Press, 1958)

1036. Habakkuk, H.J. Population Growth and Economic Development Since 1750. (New York, Humanities Press, 1972)

1037.   el-Hamamsy, Laila Shukri.   "Belief Systems and Family-Planning in Peasant Societies." In Harrison Brown and Edward Hutchings, Jr.; eds.   Are our Descendants Doomed? Technological Change and Population Growth.   (New York, Viking Press, 1972), 335-357.

1038.   Hareven, Tamara K.   "Modernization and Family History: Perspectives on Social Change." Signs 2 (Autumn, 1976), 190-206.

1039.   Inkles, Alex and Daniel H. Smith.   Becoming Modern: Individual Change in Six Developing Countries.   (Cambridge, Massachusetts, Harvard University Press, 1974)

1040.   Malthus, Thomas Robert.   An Essay on The Principle of Population, as it Affects the Future Improvement of Society.   (London, J.Johnson, 1798)

1041.   Malthus, Thomas Robert.   An Essay on the Principle of Population; or, a View of its Past and Present Effects on Human Happiness: with an Inquiry into our Prospects Respecting the Future Removal or Mitigation of the Evils which it Occasions.   6th Ed. (London, J. Murray, 1826)

1042.   Meadows, Donella H., et.al.   The Limits to Growth; a Report for the Club of Rome's Project on the Predicament of Mankind.   (New York, New American Library, 1972)

1043.   Vinovskis, Maris A.   Demographic History and the World Population Crisis.   (Worcester, Massachusetts, Clark University Press, 1976)

1044.   Wells, Robert V.   "Family History and Demographic Transition." JSH 9 (Fall, 1975), 1-19.

1045.   Wrigley, Edward Anthony.   "The Process of Modernization and Industrial Revolution in England." JIH 3 (1972), 225-260.

1046.   Zelinsky, Wilbur.   "The Hypothesis of the Mobility Transition." GR 61 (April, 1971), 219-249.

Historical Demography

Historical demography has its own sources and methods different from those of regular demography. This section introduces readers to technical manuals, some general readers with selections of recent work, and some background to American demographic history.

Manuals and Guides

These works explore some of the ways to derive demographic data from sources not amenable to the techniques outlined in the technical manuals listed above. Hollingsworth offers numerous bibliographic citations (but almost nothing on America) and discussions of findings, whereas Wrigley is more a how-to-do-it book, with a focus on English sources. Wrigley contains the best discussion of family reconstitution outside the French manuals written by Louis Henry and others. Neither is strong on migration, an important American topic, and both are dated. Methods for studying migration are often discussed in the works included in Chapter IV under Part B, 1800-1920.

1100. Hollingsworth, Thomas Henry. Historical Demography. (Ithaca, New York, Cornell University Press, 1969)

1101. Williagan, J. Dennis and Katherine A. Lynch. Sources and Methods of Historical Demography. (New York, Academic Press, 1982)

1102. Wrigley, Edward Anthony, ed. An Introduction to English Historical Demography from the Sixteenth to the Nineteenth Century. (New York, Basic Books, 1966)

Readers and Surveys

The primary focus of these studies is European. They are useful for understanding the origins of certain issues in demographic history and for placing American materials in a wider context. Glass and Eversley is a classic collection. Surveys and readers treating American topics are listed below starting with item 1200.

1110.   Glass, David   Victor and D.E.C. Eversley, eds. Population in History; Essays in Historical Demography. (Chicago, Aldine Publishing Company, 1965)

1111.   Glass, David Victor and Roger Revelle, eds. Population and Social Change. (New York, Crane, Russak, 1972)

1112. Lee, Ronald Demos, ed. Population Patterns in the Past. (New York, Academic Press, 1977)

1113. Tilly, Charles, ed. Historical Studies of Changing Fertility. (Princeton, Princeton University Press, 1978)

1114. Wrigley, Edward Anthony. Population and History. (New York, McGraw-Hill, 1969)

The Context of American Demographic History

The studies included in the three parts of this section help to set the background for the establishment of England's colonies in America. The Atlantic World explores Old World patterns of population and trade and the nature of colonization outside North America. Pre-Columbian Indians and the Columbian Contact lists works treating the demographic disaster that eliminated many of the first Americans after 1492. English background is intended to shed light on when and why the English settled where they did.

The Atlantic World: 1300-1800

European and African population patterns during the period of exploration and settlement in the New World are discussed in many of these works. In addition, the books by Josephy and Washburn provide information on the nature of Indian society.   Dunn's and Sanchez-Albornoz's works offer demographic comparisons for other areas of the New World. These works are informative and readable, and can be used to open up a fuller literature.

1120. Braudel, Fernand. The Structures of Everyday Life: The Limits of the Possible. 2nd edition. Translated by Sian

Reynolds. Volume 1 of Civilization and Capitalism, 15th-18th Century. (New York, Harper and Row, 1981)

1121.   Davidson, Basil.   Africa in History; Themes and Outlines. New, revised edition. (New York, Macmillan, 1974)

1122. Davidson, Basil. The African Genius; an Introduction to African Cultural and Social History.   (Boston, Little, Brown, 1969)

1123. Davies, Kenneth Gordon. The North Atlantic World in the Seventeenth Century.   (Minneapolis, University of Minnesota Press, 1974)

1124. Dunn, Richard S. Sugar and Slaves; the Rise of the Planter Class in the English West Indies, 1624-1713. (Chapel Hill, University of North Carolina Press, 1972)

1125.   Hance, William Adams.   Population, Migration, and Urbanization in Africa.   (New York, Columbia University Press, 1970)

1126. Jones, Dorothy V. License for Empire: Colonialism by Treaty in Early America.   (Chicago, University of Chicago Press, 1982)

1127. Josephy, Alvin M.   The Indian Heritage of America. (New York, Knopf, 1968)

1128.   Kilson, Martin L. and Robert I. Rotberg, eds.   The African   Diaspora: Interpretive   Essays.   (Cambridge, Massachusetts, Harvard University Press, 1976)

1129.   Klein, Herbert S.   The Middle Passage: Comparative Studies in the Atlantic Slave Trade. (Princeton, New Jersey, Princeton University Press, 1978)

1130.   Lamar, Howard and Leonard Thompson, eds.   The Frontier in   History: North America and Southern Africa Compared. (New Haven, Connecticut, Yale University Press, 1981)

1131.   Langer, William L.   "American Foods and Europe's Population Growth, 1750-1850." JSH 8 (Winter, 1975), 51-66.

1132. Porter, H.C. The Inconstant Savage: England and the North American Indian, 1500-1660. (London, Duckworth, 1979)

1133. Sanchez-Albornoz, Nicolas. The Population of Latin America; a History. (Berkeley, University of California Press, 1974)

1134. United Nations. Department of Economic and Social Affairs. "History of World Popualtion Growth." In its The Determinants and Consequences of Population Trends: New Summary of Findings on Interaction of Demographic, Economic, and Social Factors. 2 vols. (New York, United Nations, 1973-1978), v.1, 10-32.

1135. Washburn, Wilcomb E. The Indian in America. (New York, Harper and Row, 1975)

1136. Ziegler, Philip. The Black Death. (New York, John Day Co., 1969)

Pre-Columbian Indians and the Columbian contact

The size of the American population before 1492, and the scale of the demographic disaster after is a subject of heated debate. These works include many of the major, recent contributions,reflecting a variety of different positions. Crosby (1142) is one of the least technical and most readable of the studies. It also discusses the more positive results of expanding world-wide food supplies. Readers may also wish to refer to sections on Indian mortality in Chapter III.

1140. Cook, Sherburne Friend and Woodrow Borah. Essays in Population History: Mexico and the Caribbean. 2 vols. (Berkeley, University of California Press, 1971, 1974)

1141. Cook, Sherburne Friend. "The Significance of Disease in the Extinction of the New England Indians." HB 45 (September, 1973), 485-508.

1142. Crosby, Alfred W., Jr. The Columbian Exchange: Biological and Cultural Consequences of 1492. (Westport, Connecticut, Greenwood Press, 1972)

1143. Crosby, Alfred W., Jr. "Virgin Soil Epidemics as a Factor in the Aboriginal Depopulation in America." WMQ 33 (April, 1976), 289-299.

1144. Curtin, Philip D. "Epidemiology and the Slave Trade." PSQ 83 (June, 1968), 190-216.

1145. Deneven, William M., ed. The Native Population of the Americas in 1492. (Madison, University of Wisconsin Press, 1976)

1146. Dobyns, Henry F. "Estimating Aboriginal American Population: an Appraisal of Techniques with a New Hemispheric Estimate." Current Anthropology 7 (October, 1966), 395-416. (Comments and references cited, 425-449).

1147. Heizer, Robert Fleming and Albert B. Elsasser. The Natural World of the California Indians. (Berkeley, University of California Press, 1980)

1148. Jacobs, Wilbur R. "The Fatal Confrontation: Early Native-White Relations on the Frontiers of Australia, New Guinea, and America--a Comparative Study." PHR 41 (August, 1971), 283-310.

1149. Jacobs, Wilbur R. "The Tip of an Iceberg: Pre-Columbian Indian Demography and Some Implications for Revisionism." WMQ 31 (January, 1974), 123-132.

1150. Jennings, Francis, "The Widowed Land." In his The Invasion of America: Indians, Colonialism, and the Cant of Conquest. (Chapel Hill, University of North Carolina Press, 1975), 15-31.

1151. Lafitan, Joseph Francois. Customs of the American Indians Compared with the Customs of Primitive Times. Translated and edited by William N. Fenton and Elizabeth L. Moore. 2 vols. (Toronto, Champlain Society, 1974-1977)

English background

The volume by Wrigley and Schofield on English population during the colonial period is clearly the place to start when studying the actual human resources available for settlement in England's American colonies.   Campbell is valuable in terms of what the English thought they had to work with, and what those ideas meant for policies for or against migration.   Wrigley's article and Laslett's book are classic studies that are still worth reading.   Bridenbaugh and Stone, and Laslett too, discuss more general social disorder that may have contributed to a desire to emigrate.   See also the first section of Chapter IV.

1160.   Blanchard, Ian.   "Population Change, Enclosure, and the Early Tudor Economy."   EcHR 23 (December, 1970), 427-445.

1161.   Bridenbaugh, Carl.   Vexed and Troubled Englishmen, 1590-1642. (New York, Oxford University Press, 1968)

1162.   Campbell, Mildred.   "'Of People Either Too Few or Too Many'; the Conflict of Opinion on Population and its Relation to Emigration."   In William Appleton Aiken and Basil Dukes Henning, eds.   Conflict in Stuart England, Essays in Honour of Wallace Notestein.   (New York, New York University Press, 1960), 169-201.

1163.   Cornwall, Julian.   "English Population in the Early Sixteenth Century."   EcHR 23 (April, 1970), 32-44.

1164.   Hollingsworth, Thomas Henry.   "The Demography of the British Peerage."   PS 18 (November, 1964), supplement.

1165.   Laslett, Peter.   The World We Have Lost.   (New York, Scribner, 1966)

1166.   Stone, Lawrence.   The Crisis of the Aristocracy, 1558-1641.   (Oxford, Clarendon Press, 1965)
1167.   Wrigley, Edward Anthony.   "Family Limitation in Pre-Industrial England."   EcHR 19 (April, 1966), 82-109.

1168.   Wrigley, Edward Anthony, and R.S. Schofield.   The Population History of England, 1541-1871; a Reconstruction. (Cambridge, Massachusetts, Harvard University Press, 1981)

American Demographic History

Studies listed here are generally sufficiently broad in scope so as to preclude mention in the topical chapters. Readers unfamiliar with any aspect of American demographic history should start here.

General Surveys and Readers

Demographers Thompson and Whelpton wrote one of the first surveys of American demographic history, concentrating on the national period. The two books by the Taeubers offer more recent demographers' perspectives. Nugent and Wells provide overviews that link population patterns to broader historical events. Readers edited by Hareven and Vinovskis, separately and together, contain excellant examples of shoter, more specialized studies that cover many topics.

1200. Cassedy, James H. American Medical and Statistical Thinking, 1800-1860. (Cambridge, Massachusetts, Harvard University Press, 1984)

1201. Cassedy, James H. Demography in Early America; Beginnings of the Statistical Mind, 1600-1800. (Cambridge, Massachusetts, Harvard University Press, 1969)

1202. Cohen, Patricia Cline. A Calculating People; The Spread of Numeracy in Early America. (Chicago, University of Chicago Press, 1982)

1203. Easterlin, Richard Ainley. "The American Population." In Lance Edwin Davis, et al. American Economic Growth: an Economist's History of the United States. (New York, Harper and Row, 1972), 121-183.

1204. Engerman, Stanley L. "Some Economic and Demographic Comparisons of Slavery in the United States and the British West Indies." EcHR 29 (May, 1976), 258-275.

1205. Engerman, Stanley L. and Eugene D. Genovese, eds. Race and Slavery in the Western Hemisphere: Quantitative Studies. (Princeton, New Jersey, Princeton University Press, 1975)

1206. Gibson, Campbell. "The Contribution of Immigration to United States Population Growth: 1790-1970." IMR 9 (Summer, 1975), 157-177.

1207. Greenwald, William I. "The Ante-Bellum Population, 1830-1860." MA 36 (July, 1954), 176-189.

1208. Greven, Philip J., Jr. "Historical Demography and Colonial America." WMQ 24 (July, 1967), 438-454.

1209. Hareven, Tamara K., ed. Transitions: the Family and the Life Course in Historical Perspective. (New York, Academic Press, 1978)

1210. Hareven, Tamara K. and Maris A. Vinovskis, eds. Family and Population in Nineteenth-Century America. (Princeton, New Jersey, Princeton University Press, 1978)

1211. Hoetink, H. Slavery and Race Relations in the Americas: Comparative Notes on their Nature and Nexus. (New York, Harper and Row, 1973)

1212. McClelland, Peter D. and Richard J. Zeckhauser. Demographic Dimensions of the New Republic: American Interregional Migration, Vital Statistics, and Manumissions, 1800-1860. (Cambridge, England, Cambridge University Press, 1982)

1213. Nash, Gary B. Red, White, and Black, the Peoples of Early America. (Englewood Cliffs, New Jersey, Prentice-Hall, 1974)

1214. Nugent, Walter. Structures of American Social History. (Bloomington, Indiana University Press, 1981)

1215. Olson, James Stuart. The Ethnic Dimension in American History. (New York, St. Martin's Press, 1979)

1216. Potter, James. "The Growth of Population in America, 1700-1870." In David Victor Glass and David Edward Charles Eversley, eds. Population in History. (Chicago, Aldine Publishing Company, 1965), 631-688.

1217. Russo, David J. Families and Communities: a New View of American History. (Nashville, Tennessee, American Association for State and Local History, 1974)

1218. Smith, Daniel Scott. "A Perspective on Demographic Methods and Effects in Social History." WMQ 39 (July, 1982), 442-468.

1219. Swierenga, Robert P. "The New Rural History: Defining the Parameters." GPQ 1 (Fall, 1981), 211-223.

1220. Swierenga, Robert P. "Theoretical Perspectives on the New Rural History: from Environmentalism to Modernization." AgH 56 (July, 1982), 495-502.

1221. Taeuber, Conrad, and Irene B. Taeuber. The Changing Population of the United States. (New York, Wiley, 1958)

1222. Taeuber, Irene Barnes and Conrad Taeuber. People of the United States in the Twentieth Century. (Washington, D.C., U.S. Bureau of the Census, 1971)

1223. Thompson, Warren Simpson. "The Demographic Revolution in the United States." AAAPSS 262 (March, 1949), 62-69.

1224. Thompson, Warren Simpson, and P.K. Whelpton. Population Trends in the United States. (New York, McGraw-Hill. 1933)

1225. Vinovskis, Maris A. Studies in American Historical Demography. (New York, Academic Press, 1979)

1226. Wells, Robert V. The Population of the British Colonies in America Before 1776: a Survey of Census Data. (Princeton, New Jersey, Princeton University Press, 1975), Chapter One, 3-44.

1227. Wells, Robert V. Revolutions in Americans' Lives: A Demographic Perspective on the History of Americans, Their Families, and Their Society. (Westport, Connecticut, Greenwood Press, 1982)

1228. Wells, Robert V. Uncle Sam's Family: Issues in and Perspectives on American Demographic History. (Albany, State University of New York Press, 1985)

1229.   Wessel, Thomas R.   "Agriculture, Indians, and American History." AgH 50 (January, 1976), 9-20.

1230. Williamson, Jeffrey G. "Migration to the New World: Long Term Influences and Impact." EEH 11 (Summer, 1974), 357-389.

1231. Worcester, Donald E. "The Significance of the Spanish Borderlands to the United States."   WestHQ 7 (January, 1976), 5-18.

Sources

Several kinds of materials are listed here. Greene and Harrington and the Census Bureau publication(1264) contain data for the period before 1776. Several atlases offer maps of the population, as does Sutherland. A number of studies discuss the reliability and avialibility of census data. Items 1268-1274 provide an indepth survey of the American population in 1972, with comments on the past and future. The Census Bureau guidebooks(1263 and 1275) indicate the riches available in state and federal censuses. Unfortunately, there is no equivalent for church records, the second major source of data.

1250.   Cappon, Lester Jesse, ed.   Atlas of Early American History: The Revolutionary Era, 1760-1790. (Princeton, New Jersey, Princeton University Press. 1976)

1251.   Chapman, Anne W.   "Inadequacies of the 1848 Charleston Census." SCHM 81 (January, 1980), 24-34.

1252.   Cummings, John.   The Permanent Census Bureau: a Decade of Work." ASAJ 13 (December, 1913), 605-638.

1253.   Daniels, Roger.   "The Bureau of the Census and the Relocation of the Japanese-Americans: a Note and a Document." AJ 9 (1982), 101-106.

1254. Friis, Herman Ralph. A Series of Population Maps of the Colonies and the United States, 1625-1790. (New York, American Geographical Society, 1940)

1255.   Greene, Evarts Boutell and Virginia D. Harrington. American Population before the Federal Census of 1790. (New York, Columbia University Press, 1932)

1256. Hays, Samuel P. "History and Genealogy: Patterns of Change and Prospects for Cooperation." Prologue 7 (Spring, 1975), 39-43.

1257.   Holt, W. Stull.   The Bureau of the Census: Its History, Activities and Organization.   (Washington, The Brookings   Institution,   1929).   No.   53   in   the   Service Monographs of the United States Government.

1258.   Okamura, Raymond Y.   "The Myth of Census Confidentiality." AJ 8 (Fall/Winter, 1981), 111-120.

1259.   Paullin, Charles Oscar.   Atlas of the Historical Geography of the United States. (Washington, D.C., Carnegie Institution, 1932)

1260.   Sale, Randall D. and Edwin D. Karn.   American Expansion: a Book of Maps. (Homewood, Illinois, Dorsey Press, 1962)

1261.   Smith, Daniel Scott.   "The Estimates of Early American Historical Demographers: Two Steps Forward, One Step Back, What Steps in the Future?"   HM 12 (Winter, 1979), 24-38.

1262. Sutherland, Stella Helen. Population Distribution in Colonial America.   (New York, Columbia University Press, 1936)

1263.   U.S. Bureau of the Census. Bureau of the Census Catalog   of   Publications: 1790-1972.   (Washington,   D.C., Government Printing Office, 1974)

1264. U.S. Bureau of the Census. A Century of Population Growth, from the First Census of the United States to the Twelfth, 1790-1900. (Washington, D.C., Government Printing Office, 1909)

1265. U.S. Bureau of the Census. Historical Statistics of the United States, Colonial Times to 1970. (Washington, D.C., Government Printing Office, 1976)

1266. U.S. Bureau of the Census. Statistical Abstract of the United States. (Washington, D.C., Government Printing Office, 1937-)

1267. U.S. Bureau of the Census. Statistical Atlas, Twelfth Census of the United States, Taken in the Year 1900. (Washington, D.C., U.S. Census Office, 1903)

1268. U.S. Commission on Population Growth and the American Future. Aspects of Population Growth Policy. Edited by Robert Parke, Jr., and Charles F. Westoff. (Washington, D.C., Government Printing Office, 1972)

1269. U.S. Commission on Population Growth and the American Future. Demographic and Social Aspects of Population Growth. Edited by Charles F. Westoff and Robert Parke, Jr. (Washington, D.C., Government Printing Office, 1972)

1270. U.S. Commission on Population Growth and the American Future. Economic Aspects of Population Change. Edited by Elliot R. Morss and Ritchie H. Reed. (Washington, D.C., Government Printing Office, 1972)

1271. U.S. Commission on Population Growth and the American Future. Governance and Population: the Governmental Implications of Population Change. Edited by A.E. Keir Nash. (Washington, D.C., Government Printing Office, 1972)

1272. U.S. Commission on Population Growth and the American Future. Population and the American Future; the Report. (Washington, D.C., Government Printing Office, 1972)

1273. U.S. Commission on Population Growth and the American Future. Population, Distribution, and Policy. Edited by Sara Miles Mazie. (Washington, D.C., Government Printing Office, 1972)

1274. U.S. Commission on Population Growth and the American Future. Population Resources and the Environment.

Edited by Ronald G. Ridker. (Washington, D.C., Government Printing Office, 1972)

1275.   U.S. Library of Congress.   Census Library Project. State Censuses: an Annotated Bibliography of Censuses of Population Taken after the Year 1790 by States and Territories of the United States.   Prepared by Henry J. Dubester.   (Washington, D.C., Government Printing Office, 1948)

1276.   U.S. Library of Congress.   Census Library Project. Catalog of United States Census Publications, 1790-1945. Prepared   by   Henry   J.   Dubester.   (Washington,   D.C., Government Printing Office, 1950)

1277.   Willcox, Walter F.   "The Development of the American Census Office Since 1890."   PSQ 29 (September, 1914), 438-459.

Population and the Personal:
The Central Life Events

A full understanding of demographic history involves not only how population developes, but also how we interpret the changes. These studies offer insights into the importance of birth, death, marriage, and migration beyond the most obvious. They also emphasize the role culture plays in determining the patterns of these events and how we explain them.

1300.   Ames, Kenneth L.   "Material Culture as Non-Verbal Communication: a Historical Case Study."   JAC 3 (Winter, 1980), 619-641.

1301.   Bernard,   Jessie   Shirley.   The   Sex   Game: Communications Between the Sexes. (Englewood, New Jersey, Prentice-Hall, 1968)

1302.   Bryson, Reid A. and Thomas J. Murray. Climates of Hunger: Mankind   and   the   World's   Changing   Weather. (Madison, University of Wisconsin Press, 1977)

1303. Chapple, Eliot Dismore. Culture and Biological Man: Explorations in Behavioral Anthropology. (New York, Holt, Rinehart, and Winston, 1970)

1304. Fawcett, James T., ed. Psychological Perspectives on Population. (New York, Basic Books, 1973)

1305. Ford, Clellan Stearns and Frank A. Beach. Patterns of Sexual Behavior. (New York, Harper, 1951)

1306. Forer, Lucille K. The Birth Order Factor; how your Personality is Influenced by your Place in the Family. (New York, D. McKay, 1976)

1307. Geertz, Clifford. The Interpretation of Cultures: Selected Essays. (New York, Basic Books, 1973)

1308. Glick, Paul C. American Families. (New York, Wiley, 1957)

1309. Glick, Paul C. and Robert Parke, Jr. "New Approaches in Studying the Life Cycle of the Family." Demography 2 (1965), 187-202.

1310. Hall, Edward Twitchell. The Hidden Dimension. (Garden City, New York, Doubleday, 1966)

1311. Hall, Edward Twitchell. The Silent Language. (Garden City, New York, Doubleday, 1959)

1312. Journal of Social Issues 30, no. 4 (1974), "Population Policy and the Person, Congruence or Conflict?" Special issue on population policy.

1313. Kammen, Michael. "Changing Perceptions of the Life Cycle in American Thought and Culture." MHSP 91 (1979), 35-66.

1314. LaBarre, Weston. The Human Animal. (Chicago, University of Chicago Press, 1954)

1315. Lansing, John B. and Leslie Kish. "Family Life Cycle as an Independent Variable." ASR 22 (October, 1957), 512-519.

1316.   Senn, Milton J.E. and Claire Hartford, eds.   The Firstborn: Experiences of Eight American Families. (Cambridge, Massachusetts, Harvard University Press, 1968)

2
Marriage and Fertility

Although marriage and fertility can be studied independently, they have been linked in this bibliography, partly because marriage has frequently been a license to begin childbearing, and partly because many of the historical studies of one frequently contain significant amounts of material on the other. Users will note that the subdivisions for each of the three chronological periods are different. This reflects the availability of evidence, the nature of the sources and the techniques used to exploit them, and the primary historical problems of each period.

Early America

The primary concern of many of the studies in this section is to explain the unusually large families that were common in the eighteenth century, if not before. In general, the weight of the evidence suggests that marriage patterns were as important as the absolute level of childbearing in determining the level of fertility. Note the definite bias toward white populations in the English colonies.

Marriage

Most of the studies here are concerned with first marriages. They ask about the age at first marriage, how many people never married, and who chose the marriage partners. The works by Howard and Monahan are classic works which range well beyond colonial America. Both are definitely dated, and Howard has a clear idealogical slant. Although the article by Wells includes material from other studies, students will find additional data on marriage in the items listed under Childbearing.

2000. Brouwer, Merle G. "Marriage and Family Life among Blacks in Colonial Pennsylvania." PMHB 99 (July, 1975), 368-372.

2001. Gallman, James M. "Determinants of Age at Marriage in Colonial Perquimans County, North Carolina." WMQ 39 (January, 1982), 176-191.

2002. Howard, George E. A History of Matrimonial Institutions; Chiefly in England and the United States... 3 vols. (Chicago, University of Chicago Press, 1904)

2003. Monahan, Thomas Patrick. The Pattern of Age at Marriage in the United States. 2 vols. (Philadelphia, Printed by Stephenson Brothers, 1951)

2004. Norton, Susan L. "Marital Migration in Essex County, Massachusetts, in the Colonial and Early Federal Periods." JMF 35 (August, 1973), 406-418.

2005. Rubinger, Catherine. "Marriage and the Women of Louisbourg." Dalhousie Review 60 (Autumn, 1980), 445-461.

2006. Smith, Daniel Scott. "Parental Power and Marriage Patterns: an Analysis of Historical Trends in Hingham, Massachusetts." JMF 35 (August, 1973), 419-428.

2007. Wells, Robert V. "Quaker Marriage Patterns in a Colonial Perspective." WMQ 29 (July, 1972), 415-442.

Duration of Marriage and Remarriage

How long marriages lasted and how rapidly and often remarriage occurred will have an obvious effect on levels of childbearing. Although these works bear on this topic, most of them were written out of a concern with the roles of men and women within families, and the place of families within society.   Students interested in the questions about property, power, and permissiveness raised in these works will also want to consult many of the studies of colonial families cited in Chapter Five.

2010. Cott, Nancy F. "Divorce and the Changing Status of Women in Eighteenth-Century Massachusetts." WMQ 33 (October, 1976), 586-614.

2011. Cott, Nancy F. "Eighteenth-Century Family and Social Life Revealed in Massachusetts Divorce Records." JSH 10 (Fall, 1976), 20-43.

2012. Faragher, John Mack. "Old Women and Old Men in Seventeenth-Century Wethersfield, Connecticut." Women's Studies 4 (1976), 11-31.

2013. Grigg, Susan. "Toward a Theory of Remarriage: a Case Study of Newburyport at the Beginning of the Nineteenth Century." JIH 8 (Autumn, 1977), 183-220.

2014.   Keyssar,   Alexander.   "Widowhood   in Eighteenth-Century Massachusetts: a Problem in the History of the Family." PAH 8 (1974), 83-119.

2015. Lantz, Herman R. Marital Incompatibility and Social Change in Early America. (Beverly Hills, California, Sage Publications, 1976)

2016.   Meehan,   Thomas   R.   "'Not Made out of Levity;' Evolution of Early Divorce in Early Pennsylvania." PMHB 92 (October, 1968), 441-464.

Childbearing

Most of these works make use of genealogies or family reconstitution for demographic purposes to explore the average size of colonial families. Because of this, they are not directly comparable with materials on the American population after 1800 listed below, which are based on census data. Many of the earlier works included here were written out of a concern with the effects of late-nineteenth century immigration on the fertility of the descendants of earlier European settlers. Several more recent studies (Osterud and

Fulton, Temkin-Greener and Swedlund, and Wells) present evidence for family limitation long before immigration. Freeman's article contains a valuable discussion of the limits of genealogies as sources. Lotka's essay is important as one of the first studies to use stable population analysis, a powerful tool commonly used by current demographers. Scholten is concerned with customs surrounding childbirth, and does not offer new data on actual levels of childbearing.

2020.   Bailey, William B.   "A Statistical Study of the Yale Graduates, 1701-1792."   Yale Review 16 (February, 1907-1908), 400-426.

2021.   Bash, Wendell Hubbard.   Factors Influencing Family and Community Organization in a New England Town, 1730-1940.   (Unpublished Ph.D. Dissertation, Harvard University, 1941)

2022.   Crum, Frederick S.   "The Decadence of the Native American Stock; a Statistical Study of Genealogical Records." ASAJ 14 (1916-1917), 215-222.

2023.   Englemann, George J.   "The Increasing Sterility of American Women."   Journal of the American Medical Association 37 (1901), 891-897.

2024.   Freeman, Bettie C.   "Fertility and Longevity in Married Women Dying after the End of the Reproductive Period." HB 7 (1935), 392-418.

2025.   Hall, G. Stanley and Theodate L. Smith.   "Marriage and Fecundity of College Men and Women."   Pedagogical Seminary 10 (1903), 275-314.

2026.   Harper, Roland M.   "A Statistical Study of a Typical Southern Genealogy."   Journal of Heredity 25 (September, 1934), 363-370.

2027.   Higgs, Robert and H. Louis Stettler, III.   "Colonial New England Demography: a Sampling Approach."   WMQ 27 (April, 1970), 282-294.

2028.   Jones, Carl E.   "A Genealogical Study of Population." ASAJ 16 (December, 1918), 201-219.

2029.   Kulikoff, Allan.   "A 'Prolifick' People: Black Population Growth in the Chesapeake Colonies, 1700-1790." SouS 16 (Winter, 1977), 391-428.

2030.   Lotka, Alfred J.   "The Size of American Families in the Eighteenth-Century."   ASAJ 22 (1927), 154-170.

2031.   Osterud, Nancy and John Fulton.   "Family Limitation and Age at Marriage: Fertility Decline in Sturbridge, Massachusetts, 1730-1850."   PS 30 (November, 1976), 481-494.

2032.   Sage, David.   A Statistical Study of the Genealogical Records of New England.   (Unpublished M.A. Thesis, Clark University, 1917)

2033.   Schnucker, Robert V.   "Elizabethan Birth Control and Puritan Attitudes."   JIH 5 (Spring, 1975), 655-667.

2034.   Scholten, Catherine M.   "'On the Importance of the Obstetrick Art':   Changing Customs of Childbirth in America, 1760-1825."   WMQ 34 (July, 1977), 426-445.

2035.   Temkin-Greener, Helena and A.C. Swedlund.   "Fertility Transition in the Connecticut Valley: 1740-1850."   PS 32 (March, 1978), 27-41.

2036.   Wells, Robert V.   "Family Size and Fertility Control in Eighteenth-Century America: a Study of Quaker Families." PS 25 (March, 1971), 73-82.

Illegitimacy and Bridal Pregnancy

These are topics that have not been explored extensively, partly because most childbearing in early America occurred within marriage.   Smith and Hindus provide significant quantitative data and range widely over time.   Wells studies legal matters and the importance early Americans gave to stable and well-ordered families.

2050.   Smith, Daniel Scott and Michael S. Hindus. "Premarital Pregnancy in America, 1640-1971:   an Overview and Interpretation."   JIH 5 (Spring, 1975), 537-540.

2051. Wells, Robert V. "Illegitimacy and Bridal Pregnancy in Colonial America." In Peter Laslett, et al., eds. Bastardy and its Comparative History: Studies in the History of Illegitimacy and Marital Nonconformism in Britain, France, Germany, Sweden, North America, Jamaica, and Japan. (Cambridge, Massachusetts, Harvard University Press, 1980), 349-361.

The Nineteenth Century

The nineteenth century was a period of major demographic changes in American history. Perhaps none was more dramatic than the decline in fertility which saw levels of childbearing reduced by fifty percent or more between 1800 and 1920. Marriage patterns were more stable during this period, although the last three decades saw the emergence of new trends in divorce that became pronounced after 1920.

Marriage and Divorce

Given the importance of marriage in determining the onset of childbearing, we know surprisingly little about the age at which men and women married in the nineteenth century. The studies listed here are primarily concerned with attitudes and values, as they relate to the choice of marriage partners and the willingness to consider divorce when a marriage was causing conflict. The most abundant quantitative material is in the book by Monahan cited under Early America; additional evidence is present in the genealogy-based studies of fertility discussed above. The works on the choice of marriage partners focus either on intermarriage among ethnic groups (Bernard is the best such study) or on the relative power of parents and children in making the decision (Gorden and Bernstein is of interest here). Smith's article on Hingham entered earlier is also important. Three of the most important studies of divorce are those by Davis, May, and O'Neill.

2060. Bernard, Richard M. The Melting Pot and the Altar: Marital Assimilation in Early Twentieth-Century Wisconsin. (Minneapolis, University of Minnesota Press, 1980)

2061. Campbell, Eugene E. and Bruce L. Campbell. "Divorce among Mormon Polygamists: Extent and Explanations." UHQ 46 (Winter, 1978), 4-23.

2062. Censer, Jane Turner. "'Smiling through her Tears': Ante-Bellum Southern Women and Divorce." AJLH 25 (January,1981), 24-47.

2063. Davis, Kingsley. "The American Family in Relation to Demographic Change." In U.S. Commission on Population Growth and the American Future. Demographic and Social Aspects of Population Growth.
Edited by Charles F. Westoff and Robert Parke, Jr. (Washington, D.C. Government Printing Office, 1972)

2064. Gordon, Michael and M. Charles Bernstein. "Mate Choice and Domestic Life in the Nineteenth-Century Marriage Manual." JMF 32 (November, 1970), 665-674.

2065. Griswold, Robert L. Family and Divorce in California, 1850-1890: Victorian Illusions and Everyday Realities. (Albany, State University of New York Press, 1982)

2066. Hardaway, Roger D. "Prohibiting Interracial Marriage: Miscegenation Laws in Wyoming." Annals of Wyoming 52 (Spring, 1980), 55-60.

2067. Johnson, Guion Griffis. "Courtship and Marriage Customs in Ante-Bellum North Carolina." NCHR 8 (1931), 384-402

2068. Littlefield, Daniel F., Jr., and Lonnie E. Underhill. "Divorce
Seeker's Paradise: Oklahoma Territory, 1890-1897." ArW 17 (Spring, 1975), 21-34.

2069. Martin, Edeen. "Frontier Marriage and the Status Quo." Westport Historical Quarterly 10 (March, 1975), 99-108.

2070. May, Elaine Tyler. Great Expectations: Marriage and Divorce in Post-Victorian America. (Chicago, University of Chicago Press, 1980)

2071. May, Elaine Tyler. "The Pressure to Provide: Class, Consumerism, and Divorce in Urban America, 1880-1920." JSH 12 (Winter, 1978), 180-193.

2072. Miller, Darlis A. "Cross-Cultural Marriages in the Southwest: the New Mexico Experience, 1846-1900." NMHR 57 (October, 1982), 335-358.

2073. O'Neill, William L. Divorce in the Progressive Era. (New Haven, Yale University Press, 1967)

2074. Stetson, Dorothy M. and Gerald C. Wright, Jr. "The Effects of Laws on Divorce in American States." JMF 37 (August, 1975), 537-547.

2075. Swagerty, William R. "Marriage and Settlement Patterns of Rocky Mountain Trappers and Traders." WestHQ 11 (April, 1980), 159-180.

2076. Tolnay, Stewart E. and Avery M. Guest. "Childlessness in a Transitional Population: the United States at the Turn of the Century." JFH 7 (Summer, 1982), 200-219.

2077. Vinovskis, Maris A. "Marriage Patterns in Mid-Nineteenth-Century New York: a Multivariate Analysis." JFH 3 (1978), 51-61.

Childbearing

The materials on the nineteenth-century revolution in childbearing are divided into three categories. The first includes general studies, primarily of the white population. The second focuses on the fertility of blacks. More narrowly defined studies of particular occupational or ethnic groups and specific places comprise the third.

General and white

Most of these works make use of census materials to calculate very general levels of childbearing, and so are not strictly comparable to family-oriented studies. They seek not only to chronical the decline in fertility but also to explain it.   The book by Coale and Zelnik is technically sophisticated, but is least concerned with explainaing the change. Of the others, Yasuba is the classic starting point. Books by Forster and Tucker, Haines, Lindert, and Vinovskis all work within the same framework, looking at economic opportunity, urbanization, and education as possible causes for the decline in fertility. Vinovskis' study of Massachusetts offers the best review of the major questions involved, and is also the most concerned with values. Wertz and Wertz is quite different from the others in that it is a history of childbirth which emphasizes medical and family themes.

2080. Coale, Ansley J. and Melvin Zelnick. New Estimates of Fertility and Population in the United States; a Study of Annual White Births from 1855 to 1960 and of Completeness of Ennumeration in the Censuses from 1880 to 1960. (Princeton, New Jersey, Princeton University Press, 1963)

2081. Forster, Colin and G.S.L. Tucker. Economic Opportunity and White American Fertility Ratios, 1800-1860. (New Haven, Connecticut, Yale University Press, 1972)

2082. Haines, Michael R. "Fertility and Marriage in a Nineteenth-Century Industrial City: Philadelphia, 1850-1880." JEH 40 (March, 1980), 151-158.

2083. Haines, Michael. Fertility and Occupation: Population Patterns in Industrialization. (New York, Academic Press, 1979)

2084. Hastings, Donald W. and J. Gregory Robinson. "Incidence of Childlessness for United States Women, Cohorts Born 1891-1945." SB 21 (Summer, 1974), 178-184.

2085. Laidig, Gary L., Wayne A. Schutjer, and C. Shannon Stokes. "Agricultural Variation and Human Fertility in Antebellum Pennsylvania." JFH 6 (Summer, 1981), 195-204.

2086. Leasure, J. William. "La Baisse de la Fecondite aux Etats-Unis de 1800 a 1860." Population (1982), 607-622.

2087. Lindert, Peter H. Fertility and Scarcity in America. (Princeton, New Jersey, Princeton University Press, 1978)

2088.   Schapiro, Morton Owen.   "Land Availability and Fertility in the United States, 1760-1870."   JEH   42 (September, 1982), 577-600.

2089.   Shergold, Peter R.   "The Walker Thesis Revisited: Immigration and White American Fertility, 1800-1860." Australian Economic History Review 14 (September, 1974), 168-189.

2090. Tolnay, Stewart E., Stephen N. Graham, and Avery M. Guest.   "Own-Child Estimates of U.S. White Fertility, 1886-1899." HM 15 (Summer, 1982), 127-138.

2091. Vinovskis, Maris A.   Fertility in Massachusetts from the Revolution to the Civil War.   (New York, Academic Press, 1981)

2092.   Vinovskis, Maris A.   "Socio-economic Determinants of Interstate Fertility Differentials in the United States in 1850 and 1860." JIH 6 (Winter, 1976), 375-396.

2093. Wertz, Richard W. and Dorthy C. Wertz.   Lying-in: a History of Childbirth in America.   (New York, The Free Press, 1977)

2094.   Yasuba, Yasukichi.   Birth Rates of the White Population in the United States, 1800-1860: an Economic Study. (Baltimore, Johns Hopkins Press, 1962)

Black

Until about 1880, black fertility remained unaffected by the changes occurring in the white population.   In the last century, however, the trends in black and white fertility have been remarkably similar, even though levels have been different.   One reason why black childbearing has received separate attention is that scholars such as Farley and Cutright and Shorter have argued that the late onset of decline reflects a distinct black experience in American life, and that even when fertility fell it was for different reasons. Coale and Rives, McFalls and Masnick, and Meeker offer the most direct challenges to this view, seeing blacks as late-comers to birth control (along with some whites) who eventually behaved much as white Americans.   Engerman's essay includes an excellent survey of much of this debate.

2100.   Coale, Ansley J. and Norfleet W. Rives, Jr.   "A Statistical Reconstruction of the Black Population of the United States, 1880-1970." Population Index 39 (January, 1973), 3-36.

2101.   Cody, Cheryll Ann.   "A Note on Changing Patterns of Slave Fertility in the South Carolina Rice District, 1735-1865." SouS 16 (1977), 457-463.

2102.   Cutright, Phillips and Edward Shorter.   "The Effects of Health on the Completed Fertility of Nonwhite and White U.S. Women Born Between 1867 and 1935." JSH 13 (1979), 191-217.

2103.   Eblen, Jack Ericson.   "Growth of the Black Population in Antebellum America, 1820-1860." PS 26 (July, 1972), 273-289.

2104.   Eblen, Jack Ericson.   "New Estimates of the Vital Rates of the United States Black Population During the Nineteenth Century." Demography 11 (May, 1974), 301-319.

2105.   Engerman, Stanley L.   "Black Fertility and Family Structure in the U.S., 1880-1940." JFH 2 (Summer, 1977), 117-138.

2106.   Farley, Reynolds.   "The Demographic Rates and Social Institutions of the Nineteenth-Century Negro Population: a Stable Population Analysis." Demography 2 (1965), 386-398.

2107.   Holland, C.G.   "The Slave Population on the Plantation of John C. Cohoon, Jr., Nansemond County, Virginia, 1811-1863: Selected Demographic Characteristics." VMHB 80 (July, 1972), 333-340.

2108.   Klein, Herbert S., and Stanley L. Engerman.   "Fertility Differentials Between Slaves in the United States and the British West Indies: a Note on Lactation Practices and their Possible Implications." WMQ 35 (April, 1978), 357-74.

2109.   Lowe, Richard G. and Randolph B. Campbell.   "The Slave-Breeding Hypothesis: a Demographic Comment on the 'Buying'and 'Selling' States." JSouH 42 (August, 1976), 401-412.

2110. McFalls, Joseph A., Jr. "Impact of VD on the Fertility of the U.S. Black Population, 1880-1950." SB 20 (March, 1973), 2-19.

2111. McFalls, Joseph A., Jr., and George S. Masnick. "Birth Control and the Fertility of the U.S. Black Population, 1880-1980." JFH 6 (Spring, 1981), 89-106.

2112. Meeker, Edward. "Freedom, Economic Opportunity, and Fertility: Black Americans, 1860-1910." Economic Inquiry 15 (1977), 397-412.

2113. Zelnick, Melvin. "Fertility of the American Negro in 1830 and 1850." PS 20 (July, 1966), 77-83.

By occupation, ethnicity, or locality

The works listed here focus on segments of the white population, sometimes because of a special interest in a particular group such as the Amish, Mormons, or Lutherans, and sometimes because more detailed studies can resolve some of the problems of explanation encountered in more general works. The articles by Easterlin and by Hareven and Vinovskis are especially interesting in their technical and interpretive sophistication. Several of the genealogical studies done before World War II, cited above under Early American Childbearing, also provide more detailed evidence about the onset of fertility control in the nineteenth century.

2120. Bash, Wendell Hubbard. "Changing Birth Rates in Developing America: New York State, 1840-1875." MMFQ 41 (April, 1963), 161-182.

2121. Bloomberg, Susan E., et al. "A Census Probe into Nineteenth-Century Family History: Southern Michigan, 1850-1880." JSH 5 (Fall, 1971), 26-45.

2122. Easterlin, Richard Ainley. "Factors in the Decline of Farm Family Fertility in the United States: some Preliminary Research Results." JAH 63 (December, 1976), 600-614.

2123. Easterlin, Richard Ainley. "Population Change and Farm Settlement in the Northern United States." JEH 36 (March, 1976), 45-75.

2124. Eaton, Joseph W. and Albert J. Mayer. "The Social Biology of Very High Fertility among the Hutterites; the Demography of a Unique Population." HB 25 (September, 1953), 206-264.

2125. Graebner, Alan. "Birth Control and the Lutherans--the Missouri Synod as a Case Study." JSH 2 (Summer, 1969), 303-332.

2126. Haines, Michael R. "Fertility, Marriage, and Occupation in the Pennsylvania Anthracite Region, 1850-1880." JFH 2 (Spring, 1977), 28-55.

2127. Hareven, Tamara K. and Maris A. Vinovskis. "Marital Fertility, Ethnicity, and Occupation in Urban Families: an Analysis of South Boston and the South End in 1880." JSH 8 (Spring, 1975), 69-93.

2128. Hareven, Tamara K. and Maris A. Vinovskis. "Patterns of Childbearing in Late Nineteenth-Century America: the Determinants of Marital Fertility in Five Massachusetts Towns in 1880." In their Family and Population in Nineteenth-Century America. (Princeton, New Jersey, Princeton University Press, 1978)

2129. Kantrow, Louise. "Philadelphia Gentry: Fertility and Family Limitation Among an American Aristocracy." PS 34 (1980), 21-30.

2130. Leet, Don R. "The Determinants of the Fertility Transition in Antebellum Ohio." JEH 36 (June, 1976), 359-378.

2131. Leet, Don R. "Interrelationships of Population Destiny, Urbanization, Literacy, and Fertility." EEH 14 (October, 1977), 388-401.

2132. Mineau, G.P., L.L. Bean, and M. Skolnick. "Mormon Demographic History II: The Family Life Cycle and Natural Fertility." PS 33 (1979), 429-446.

2133. Modell, John. "An Ecology of Family Decisions: Suburbanization, Schooling, and Fertility in Philadelphia, 1880-1920." JUH 6 (August, 1980), 397-417.

2134. Modell, John. "Family and Fertility on the Indian Frontier, 1820." AQ 23 (December, 1971), 615-634.

2135. Skolnick, M., L. Bean, D. May, V. Arbon. K. DeNevers, and P. Cartwright.   "Mormon Demographic History. I. Nuptiality and Fertility of Once-Married Couples." PS 32 (1978), 5-19.

2136. Smith, Elmer L.   Studies in Amish Demography. (Harrisonburg,   Virginia,   Research   Council   of   Eastern Mennonite College, 1960)

2137. Smith, James E. and Phillip R. Kunz. "Polygyny and Fertility in Nineteenth-Century America." PS 30 (November, 1976), 465-480.

2138. Steckel, Richard H.   "Antebellum Southern White Fertility: a Demographic and Economic Analysis." JEH 40 (June, 1980), 331-350.

2139. Uhlenberg, Peter R. "A Study of Cohort Life Cycles: Cohorts of Native Born Massachusetts Women, 1830-1920." PS 23 (November, 1969), 407-420.

2140.   Wilcox, Jerry and Hilda H. Golden.   "Prolific Immigrants and Dwindling Natives?:   Fertility Patterns in Western Massachusetts, 1850 and 1880."   JFH 7 (Fall, 1982), 265-288.

Birth Control: Motive and Technique

The evidence from the studies on childbearing makes it clear that the nineteenth-century decline was from conscious choice.   Thus, it is of interest to know how and why fertility was controlled.   We can divide the relevant writings into those produced at the time, and those of historians working today.

Nineteenth-century writing

These works generally include both discussions of birth control techniques and considerations of whether the use of those techniques was appropriate.   Knowlton and Owen are early   advocates   of   family   limitation;   Foote   provides   an interesting, later perspective, especially because of his emphasis on women's concerns. Lewis and Storer were leading opponents. Curiously, much of the opposition literature provided explicit information on how births could be controlled.

2150. Allen, N. "Changes in Population." Harper's New Monthly Magazine 38 (December, 1868-May, 1869), 386-392.

2151. Ashton, James. The Book of Nature, Containing Information for Young People who Think of Getting Married, on the Philosophy of Procreation and Sexual Intercourse; Showing how to Prevent Conception and to Avoid Childbearing.... (New York, Ashton, 1860)

2152. Bergeret, Louis Francois Etienne. The Prevention Obstacle; or Conjugal Onanism. Translated from the Third French Edition. (New York, Turner and Mignard, 1870)

2153. Billings, John Shaw. "The Diminishing Birth-Rate in the United States." Forum 15 (June, 1893), 467-477.

2154. Cook, Nicholas Francis. Satan in Society. (Cincinnati, C.F. Vent, 1871)

2155. Dubois, Jean. Marriage Physiologically Discussed. 2nd ed. Translated by William Greenfield. (New York, 1839)

2156. Foote, Edward Bond. The Radical Remedy in Social Science; or Borning Better Babies through Regulating Reproduction by Controlling Conception. (New York, Murray Hill Publishing Company, 1886)

2157. Gardner, Augustus Kinsley. Conjugal Sins Against the Laws of Life and Health and the Effect upon the Father, Mother and the Child. (New York, J.S. Redfield, 1870)

2158. Knowlton, Charles. The Fruits of Philosophy; or the Private Companion of Young Married People. 2nd ed. (Boston, 1833)

2159. Lewis, Dio. Chastity; or our Secret Sins. (Philadelphia, G. Maclean, 1874)

2160.   Mauriceau, A.M.   The Married Woman's Private Medical Companion. (New York, 1847)

2161. Owen, Robert Dale. Moral Physiology; or a Brief and Plain Treatise on the Population Question. 2nd ed. (New York, Wright and Owen, 1831)

2162.   Reproductive control; or a Rational Guide to Matrimonial Happiness; ... by an American Physician. (Cincinnati, 1855)

2163. Soule, J. Science of Reproduction and Reproductive Control. (Cincinnati, Ohio, 1856)

2164. Storer, Horatio Robinson. Why Not? a Book for Every Woman. (New York, Arno Press, 1974; repr. of Boston, Lee and Shepard, 1868)

2165. Storer, Horatio Robinson. and Franklin Fiske Heard. Criminal Abortion: its Nature, its Evidence, and its Law. (New York, Arno Press, 1974; repr. of Boston, Little, Brown, 1868)

2166. Van de Warker, Ely. The Detection of Criminal Abortion, and a Study of Foeticidal Drugs. (Boston, J. Campbell, 1872)

Historical studies

Of these works, Himes is the classic work on the techniques known to Americans, and numerous other peoples as well. Cirillo, Kennedy, Nissenbaum, and Williams and Williams approach more general issues through the study of a major advocate of birth control. There are no comparable biographies of leading opponents such as Horatio Storer or Anthony Comstock. Gordon and Reed offer wide-ranging explorations into personal and public debates on birth control, from widely divergent perspectives. Barker-Benfield, Haller and Haller, and Yates have a distinct slant toward medical matters and the attitudes of doctors. Abortion was a major concern in the nineteenth century; this is the specific focus of Mohr and Sauer, with the former concentrating on legal efforts to outlaw the practice.

2170. <u>Abortion in Nineteenth-Century America</u>. (New York, Arno Press, 1974)

2171. Barker-Benfield, Graham J. "The Spermatic Economy: a Nineteenth-Century View of Sexuality." <u>FS</u> 1 (Summer, 1972), 45-74.

2172. Bush, Lester E., Jr. "Birth Control among Mormons: Introduction to an Insistent Question." <u>DJMT</u> 10 (Autumn, 1976), 12-44.

2173. Cirillo, Vincent J. "Edward Foote's Medical Common Sense: an Early American Comment on Birth Control." <u>JHMAS</u> 25 (July, 1970), 341-345.

2174. Gordon, Linda. "The Politics of Population: Birth Control and the Eugenics Movement." <u>Radical America</u> 8 (July-August, 1974), 61-98.

2175. Gordon, Linda. "Voluntary Motherhood: The Beginnings of Feminist Birth Control Ideas in the United States." In Mary S. Hartman and Lois Banner, eds. <u>Clio's Consciousness Raised</u>. (New York, Harper and Row, 1974), 54-71.

2176. Gordon, Linda. <u>Women's Body, Women's Rights: a Social History of Birth Control in America</u>. (New York, Grossman, 1976)

2177. Haller, John S., Jr. and Robin M. Haller. <u>The Physican and Sexuality in Victorian America</u>. (Urbana, University of Illinois Press, 1974)

2178. Himes, Norman Edwin. <u>Medical History of Contraception</u>, rev.ed. (New York, Schocken Books, 1970)

2179. Kennedy, David M. <u>Birth Control in America: the Career of Margaret Sanger</u>. (New Haven, Yale University Press, 1970)

2180. LaSorte, Michael A. "Nineteenth Century Family Planning Practices." <u>Journal of Psychohistory</u> 4 (Fall, 1976), 163-184.

2181. Mohr, James C. Abortion in America: the Origins and Evolutions of National Policy, 1800-1900. (New York, Oxford University Press, 1977)

2182. Nissenbaum, Stephen Willner. Careful Love: Sylvester Graham and the Emergence of Victorian Sexual Theory in America, 1830-1840. (Unpublished Ph.D Dissertation, University of Wisconsin, 1968)

2183. Reed, James. From Private Vice to Public Virtue: The Birth Control Movement and American Society since 1830. (New York, Basic Books, 1978)

2184. Sauer, R. "Attitudes to Abortion in America, 1800-1973." PS 28 (March, 1974), 53-67.

2185. Smith Daniel Scott. "Family Limitation, Sexual Control, and Domestic Feminism in Victorian America." In Mary S. Hartman and Lois Banner, eds. Clio's Consciousness Raised. (New York, Harper and Row, 1974), 119-136.

2186. Useem, John. "Changing Economy and Rural Security in Massachusetts." AgH 16 (1942), 29-40.

2187. Vinovskis, Maris A. Demographic History and the World Population Crisis. (Worchester, Massachusetts, Clark University, 1976)

2188. Williams, Doone and Greer Williams. Every Child a Wanted Child: Clarence James Gamble, M.D., and His Work in the Birth Control Movement. Edited by Emily P. Flint. (Boston, The Francis A. Countway Library of Medicine, 1978)

2189. Yates, Wilson. "Birth Control Literature and the Medical Profession in Nineteenth-Century America." JHMAS 31 (January, 1976), 42-54.

The Twentieth Century: 1920 to the Present

The relative paucity of titles in this section by no means reflects the amount of literature actually available. Numerous studies of marriage and fertility in sociological and demographic journals have been omitted for several reasons. In an effort to conserve space, we have included here works that are historical in that they consciously cover long run trends, instead of detailing patterns revealed by recent data. Thus, a study in 1940 on fertility from 1935 to 1939 would be excluded, but a synthesis using that work, covering a longer period, would not.   The two books by Conrad and Irene Taeuber in Chapter I, American Demographic History, provide extensive syntheses of what we know about marriage and fertility up to 1960; recent journal literature and government statistical yearbooks can fill in the later years.

Marriage and Divorce

Material on marriage ages and proportions marrying can be easily located.   These studies are concerned more with changing values attached to marriage in general and to the age at which marriage was expected to occur.

2200.   Bernard, Richard M.   The Melting Pot and the Altar: Marital Assimilation in Early Twentieth-Century Wisconsin. (Minneapolis, University of Minnesota Press, 1980)

2201.   Blumberg, Paul M. and P.W. Paul.   "Continuities and Discontinuities in Upper-Class Marriages."   JMF 37 (1975), 63-77.

2202.   Elder, Glen H., Jr., and Richard C. Rockwell.   "Marital Timing in Women's Life Patterns."   JFH 1 (Autumn, 1976), 34-53.

2203.   Glick, Paul C. and Arthur J. Norton.   "Marrying, Divorcing, and Living Together in the U.S. Today." Population Bulletin 32 (October, 1977)

2204.   Glick, Paul C. and Arthur J. Norton.   "Perspectives on the Recent Upturn in Divorce and Remarriage."   Demography 10 (August, 1973), 301-314.

2205.   Hirschman, Charles and Judah Matras.   "A New Look at the   Marriage Market and Nuptiality Rates, 1915-1958," Demography 8 (November, 1971), 549-569.

2206.   May, Elaine Tyler.   Great Expectations: Marriage and Divorce in Post-Victorian America.   (Chicago, University of Chicago Press, 1980)

2207.   Modell, John.   "Normative Aspects of American Marriage   Timing since World War II."   JFH 5 (Summer, 1980), 210-234.

2208.   Modell, John, Frank F. Furstenberg, Jr., and Douglas Strong.   "The Timing of Marriage in the Transition to Adulthood: Continuity and Change, 1860-1975."   In John Demos and Sarane Spence Boocock, eds.   Turning Points: Historical and Sociological Essays on the Family.   (Chicago, University of Chicago Press, 1978; supplement to AJS 84), S120-S150.

2209.   Seligson, Marcia.   The Eternal Bliss Machine: America's Way of Wedding.   (New York, Morrow, 1973)

Childbearing

The works included here are an eclectic lot.   Several include studies of the Amish and Mormons that can be used in conjunction with similar works on the same groups in the nineteenth century.   Blake is valuable on what size families Americans claim to want.   Easterlin is the principal student of the American baby boom, the major deviation from the long-run decline in fertility from 1800 to the present.   The books by Westoff and others are all part of a general project sponsored by Princeton's Office of Population Research on changes in childbearing over time, and continued differences in levels of fertility among various groups of Americans since World War II.   They are concerned with values and use survey research instead of census data.

2210.   Blake, Judith.   "Can We Believe Recent Data on Birth Expectations in the United States?"   Demography 11 (February, 1974), 25-44.

2211.   Clifford, William B., II.   "Modern and Traditional Value Orientations and Fertility Behavior: a Social Demographic Study."   Demography 8 (February, 1971), 37-48.

2212.   Cross, Harold E. and Victor A. McKusick.   "Amish Demography."   SB 17 (1970), 83-101.

2213. Defronzo, James. "Cross-Sectional Areal Analyses of Factors Affecting Marital Fertility: Actual versus Relative Income." JMF 38 (November, 1976), 669-676.

2214. Easterlin, Richard Ainley. The American Baby Boom in Historical Perspective. (New York, National Bureau of Economic Research, 1962)

2215. Easterlin, Richard Ainley. "On the Relation of Economic Factors to Recent and Projected Fertility Changes." Demography 3 (1966), 131-153.

2216. Ericksen, Julia A., Eugene P. Ericksen, John P. Hostetter and Gertrude E. Huntington. "Fertility Patterns and Trends Among the Old Order Amish." PS 33 (1979), 255-276.

2217. Glick, Paul C. "A Demographer Looks at American Families." JMF 37 (February, 1975), 15-26.

2218. Grabill, Wilson H., Clyde V. Kiser, and Pascal K. Whelpton. The Fertility of American Women. (New York, Wiley, 1958)

2219. Kiser, Clyde Vernon, Wilson H. Grabill, and Arthur A. Campbell. Trends and Variations in Fertility in the United States. (Cambridge, Massachusetts, Harvard University Press, 1968)

2220. Lindert, Peter H. Fertility and Scarcity in America. (Princeton, New Jersey, Princeton University Press, 1978)

2221. Sanderson, Warren. "The Fertility of American Women since 1920." JEH 30 (March, 1970), 271-272.

2222. Spicer, Judith C. and Susan O. Gustavus. "Mormon Fertility Through Half a Century: Another Test of the Americanization Hypothesis." SB 21 (1974), 70-76.

2223. Sweetser, Frank L. and Paavo Piepponen. "Postwar Fertility Trends and their Consequences in Finland and the United States." JSH 1 (Winter, 1967), 101-118.

2224. Westoff, Charles F. Family Growth in Metropolitan America. (Princeton, New Jersey, Princeton University Press, 1961)

2225. Westoff, Charles F., Robert G. Potter, Jr., and Phillip C. Sagi. The Third Child; a Case Study in the Prediction of Fertility. (Princeton, New Jersey, Princeton University Press, 1963)

2226. Westoff, Charles F. and Raymond H. Potvin. College Women and Fertility Values. (Princeton, New Jersey, Princeton University Press, 1967)

2227. Westoff, Charles F. and Norman B. Ryder. The Contraceptive Revolution. (Princeton, New Jersey, Princeton University Press, 1977)

2228. Westoff, Leslie Aldrich and Charles F. Westoff. From Now to Zero: Fertility, Contraception, and Abortion in America. (Boston, Little, Brown, 1971)

2229. Whelpton, Pascal K., Arthur A. Campbell, and John E. Patterson. Fertility and Family Planning in the United States. (Princeton, New Jersey, Princeton University Press, 1966)

3
Health and Death

The materials included in this chapter go beyond any narrow demographic concern with death rates, life expectancy, and causes of death and their impact on the growth of population. Likewise, they cover more than the often limited focus of much of medical history on great doctors, quaint or innovative practices, and epidemics. After an opening section that contains a number of important general works, the remainder of this chapter is divided into three major parts. The first contains works that provide information about the absolute levels of mortality at various times in various places. The second incorporates a good deal of medical history, along with other materials which shed light on both what made people get sick and die, and what contributed to health and well-being. The responses of individuals to epidemics, their expectations about health, and the attitudes doctors had about their patients and diseases are among the values and attitudes that interact with overall patterns of mortality. The final major division of this chapter provides references to these and related matters. Note that chronological subdivisions exist under two of the three topical areas. This is the reverse of Chapter Two, where three major periods were subdivided topically.

General Studies

The works listed here include a number of major studies that provide students with wide-ranging introductions to topics developed in detail below. The book by Dublin, Lotka, and Spiegelman is perhaps the best place to start a review of general mortality trends and how to understand various kinds of quantitative material. It is clearly a work of demography, and pays little attention to the personal and subjective side of matters of life and death. Richard Shryock's books on medicine and society in America are of equal importance in that they raise a number of important questions about how and why Americans went about trying to improve their health. Omran's essay is the most theoretical in its emphasis, although the various essays in Levitt and Numbers and in Reverby and Rosner can, in combination, provide a good sense of various themes and approaches. It is evident from the titles which of the other works to consult if one is interested in more limited questions of diet, drugs, drink, public health, and health reforms. More detailed studies of many of these topics are cited below, especially under nineteenth-century causes of health and death. Farley's book contains valuable materials on the black population, but is not limited to the topics of interest here.

3000. Bell, Alexander Graham. The Duration of Life and Conditions Associated with Longevity. (Washington, D.C, Genealogical Record Office, 1918)

3001. Bordley, James, III, and A. McGehee Harvey. Two Centuries of American Medicine, 1776-1976. (Philadelphia, Saunders, 1976)

3002. Camp, Charles. "Food in American Culture: a Bibliographic Essay." JAC 2 (Fall, 1979), 559-570.

3003. Courtwright, David T. Dark Paradise: Opiate Addiction in America before 1940. (Cambridge, Massachusetts, Harvard University Press, 1982)

3004. Dublin, Louis Israel and Alfred J. Lotka. "The History of Longevity in the United States." HB 6 (1934), 43-86.

3005. Dublin, Louis Israel, Alfred J. Lotka, and Mortimer Spiegelman. Length of Life: a Study of the Life Tables. revised ed. (New York, Ronald Press, 1949)

3006. Duffy, John. A History of Public Health in New York City, 1625-1966. 2 vols. (New York, Russell Sage Foundation, 1968-1974)

3007. Farley, Reynolds. Growth of the Black Population; a Study of Demographic Trends. (Chicago, Markham Publishing Company, 1971)

3008. Hooker, Richard J. Food and Drink in America: a History. (Indianapolis, Bobbs-Merrill, 1981)

3009. Kramer, Howard D. "The Beginnings of the Public Health Movement in the United States." BHM 21 (1947), 352-376.

3010. Levenstein, Harvey. "The New England Kitchen and the Origins of Modern American Eating Habits." AQ 32 (Fall, 1980), 369-386.

3011. Levitt, Judith and Ronald Numbers, eds. Sickness and Health in America: Readings in the History of Medicine and Public Health. (Madison, University of Wisconsin Press, 1978.)

3012. Morgan, H. Wayne. Drugs in America: a Social History, 1800-1980. (Syracuse, Syracuse University Press, 1981)

3013. Omran, Abdel R. "Epidemiologic Transition in the United States: the Health Factor in Population Change." Population Bulletin 32 (May, 1977).

3014. Reverby, Susan and David Rosner, eds. Health Care in America: Essays in Social History. (Philadelphia, Temple University Press, 1979)

3015. Roemer, Milton I. "Government's Role in American Medicine--a Brief Historical Survey." BHM 18 (1945), 146-168.

3016. Shryock, Richard H. Medical Licensing in America, 1650-1965. (Baltimore, John Hopkins Press, 1967)

3017. Shryock, Richard H. Medicine and Society in America 1660-1860. (New York, New York University Press, 1960)

3018. Shryock, Richard H. Medicine in America; Historical Essays. (Baltimore, Johns Hopkins Press, 1966)

3019. Shryock, Richard H. "The Origins and Significance of the Public Health Movement in the United States." AMH ns1 (November, 1929), 645-665.

3020. Sokoloff, Kenneth L. and Georgia C. Villaflor. "The Early Achievement of Modern Stature in America." SSH 6 (Fall, 1982), 453-482.

3021.   Strezze, M. Sue.   "Historical Observations on Nutrition." Studies in Popular Culture 2 (Spring, 1979), 46-58.

3022.   Weintraub, Linda.   "The American Still Life: a Document of the American Diet, 1800-Present." JAC 2 (Fall, 1979), 463-479.

3023.   Whorton, James C.   Crusaders for Fitness: The History of American Health Reformers.   (Princeton, New Jersey, Princeton University Press, 1982.)

Levels of Mortality

It is necessary to establish actual levels of mortality and sickness in order to understand the causes of health and death and how people interpreted them. This is easier said than done since records of disease and mortality vary widely in completeness and in the terms they use. Revolutions in life expectancy and health care that began in the 1880s have profoundly altered the ways by which we think about disease and measure mortality. Thus, records from before 1880 frequently require what amounts to translation before they can be subjected to manipulation and interpretation. Some scholars are more adept at this than others.

Early America

Perhaps the most important point to note here is that the chronological divisions used here may be less appropriate for mortality than for other demographic trends and events in American history. Recent evidence suggests that conditions in the seventeenth century were much worse (at least for whites) than in the eighteenth century. By 1750, however, if not before, patterns emerged that remained relatively constant until the 1880s. In addition to time, mortality conditions varied significantly by place, over both long and short distances.

General

Although many of these studies imply a focus on the American population in general, only Dunn's article offers any significant evidence on blacks, and it barely fits the time period. Material on Indians is in the next section. The works cited here can be divided into those published in the late-eighteenth and early-nineteenth centuries, and those published after 1900. The early works, especially those written by Barton, Ramsey, and Wigglesworth provide a good sense of the data available and perceptions at the time. Of the recent studies, students should read the works of Earle, Rutman and Rutman, Vinovskis, and Walsh and Menard for the best introductions to the major techniques and interpretations. Works on childbearing, duration of marriage, and family life in other parts of the bibliography contain scattered, but often not very rigorous or systematic references to mortality levels and their consequences.

3040.   Barton, William.   "Observations on Progress of Population and the Probabilities of the Duration of Human Life in the United States of America." American Philosophical Society, Transactions 3 (1793), 25-62.

3041. Bills of Mortality in AAASM 1 (1785), 546-550, 565; 2, pt. 2 (1804), 62-70; MHSC 1 (1792), 116; 4 (1795), 19; 9 (1801), 147, 168-169, 235-241; and various late eighteenth-century magazines and newspapers.

3042. Cates, Gerald L. "'The Seasoning': Disease and Death among the First Colonists of Georgia." GHQ 64 (Summer, 1980), 146-158.

3043. Currie, William. An Historical Account of the Climates and Diseases of the United States of America. (Philadelphia, Printed by T. Dobson, 1792)

3044. Duffy, John. "Eighteenth-Century Carolina Health Conditions." JSouH 3 (August, 1952), 289-302.

3045. Dunn, Richard S. "A Tale of Two Plantations; Slave Life at Mesopotamia in Jamaica and Mount Airy in Virginia, 1799 to 1828." WMQ 34 (January, 1977), 32-65.

3046. Earle, Carville. "Environment, Disease, and Mortality in Early Virginia." In Thad W. Tate and David L. Ammerman, eds. The Chesapeake in the Seventeenth Century: Essays on Anglo-American Society and Politics. (Chapel Hill, University of North Carolina Press, 1979), 96-125.

3047. Estes, J. Worth. "'As Healthy a Place as Any in America': Revolutionary Portsmouth, New Hampshire." BHM 50 (Winter, 1976), 536-552.

3048. Gallman, James M. "Mortality among White Males: Colonial North Carolina." SSH 4 (Summer, 1980), 295-316.

3049. Gould, Alice. "The Longevity of Grandparents." Eugenical News 12 (1927), 166-171, 175-178.

3050. Holyoke, Edward. "On Meteorological Observations and Bills of Mortality." AAASM 2, pt. 2 (1804), 58-61.

3051. Kupperman, Karen Ordahl. "Apathy and Death in Early Jamestown." JAH 66 (June, 1979), 24-40.

3052. Lockwood, Rose Ann. "Birth, Illness, and Death in 18th-Century New England." JSH 12 (Fall, 1978), 111-128.

3053. Meindl, R. S. and A. C. Swedlund. "Secular Trends in Mortality in the Connecticut Valley, 1700-1850." HB 49 (September, 1977), 389-414.

3054. Morris, Edward B. "The Mortality Experience of Yale Graduates." ASAT 10 (1907-1908), 230-252.

3055. Nichols, Walter S. "An Investigation of the Mortality Prevailing among the American Clergy in its Relation to Other Classes of the Population and its Bearings on a New Standard Table of Mortality." ASAT 19 (1918), 67-78.

3056. Norton, Susan L. "Population Growth in Colonial America: a Study of Ipswich, Massachusetts." PS 25 (November, 1971), 433-452.

3057. Ramsay, David. A Review of the Improvement, Progress, and State of Medicine in the XVIIIth Century. (Charleston, Printed by W. P. Young, 1801)

3058. Rea, Robert R. "'Graveyard for Britons,' West Florida, 1763-1781." FHQ 47 (April, 1969), 345-364.

3059. Richards, Harry A. "A Study of New England Mortality." ASAJ 11 (December, 1909), 636-646.

3060. Russell, Frances E. and E. L. Lucia. "A Comparison of the Mortality in a New England Colonial Town with that of Modern Times." American Journal of Hygiene 9 (1929), 513-528.

3061. Rutman, Darrett Bruce and Anita Rutman. "Of Agues and Fevers: Malaria in the Early Chesapeake." WMQ 33 (January, 1976), 31-60.

3062. Smith, Daniel Blake. "Mortality and Family in the Colonial Chesapeake." JIH 8 (Winter, 1978), 403-427.

3063. Vinovskis, Maris A. "Mortality Rates and Trends in Massachusetts Before 1860." JEH 32 (March, 1972), 184-218.

3064. Vinovskis, Maris A. "The 1789 Life Table of Edward Wigglesworth." JEH 31 (September, 1971), 570-590.

3065. Walsh, Lorena S. and Russell R. Menard. "Death in the Chesapeake: Two Life Tables for Men in Early Colonial Maryland." MHM 69 (Summer, 1974), 211-227.

3066. Warden, David Bailie. A Statistical, Political, and Historical Account of the United States of North America. 3 vols. (Edinburgh, Printed for A. Constable and Co.; Philadelphia, T. Wardle, 1819), vol. 1, chapter 7.

3067. Webster, Noah. A Brief History of Epidemic and Pestilential Diseases. 2 vols. (Hartford, Printed by Hudson and Goodwin, 1799)

3068.   Wells, Robert V.   A Demographic Analysis of Some Middle Colony Quaker Families of the Eighteenth Century. (Unpublished Ph.D. Dissertation, Princeton University, 1969), chapter 6.

3069.   Wertenbaker, Thomas Jefferson.   The First Americans, 1607-1690. (New York, Macmillan, 1927)

3070.   Wigglesworth, Edward.   "A Table Showing the Probability of the Duration, the Decrement, and the Expectation of Life, in the States of Massachusetts and New Hampshire...." AAASM 2, pt. 2 (1791), 131-135.

3071. Wigglesworth, Edward. "Observations on the Longevity of the Inhabitants of Ipswich and Hingham, and Proposals for Ascertaining the Value of Estates Held for Life, and the Reversion of Them." AAASM 1 (1785), 565-568.

Indian

These works carry forth the themes of Indian depopulation which are discussed extensively in studies cited in Chapter One, and provide a bridge to similar efforts on the nineteenth century. Note that four of these five studies are for tribes and locations west of the Mississippi.

3080.   Dobyns, Henry F.   "Indian Extinction in the Middle Santa Cruz River Valley, Arizona." NMHR 38 (April, 1963), 163-181.

3081.   Duffy, John.   "Smallpox and the Indians in the American Colonies." BHM 25 (1951), 324-341.

3082.   Jackson, Robert H.   "Epidemic Disease and Population Decline in the Baja California Missions, 1697-1834." SCQ 63 (Winter, 1981), 308-346.

3083.   Simmons, Marc.   "New Mexico's Smallpox Epidemic of 1780-1781." NMHR 41 (October, 1966), 319-326.

3084.   Unrau, William E.   "The Depopulation of the Dhegia-Siouan Kansa Prior to Removal." NMHR 48 (October, 1973), 313-328.

The Nineteenth Century

The nineteenth century probably should be divided about 1870 or 1880 in terms of patterns of mortality. Prior to that time, conditions were much as they had been in the eighteenth century. The half century before 1920 saw major improvements, brought about primarily by preventive medicine. Doctors' abilities to actually cure people emerged relatively recently.

General

As a whole, the studies cited in this section have a certain tension. On the one hand, there are works that attempt to determine overall levels of mortality in nineteenth-century America; on the other hand, numerous histories of epidemics describe episodes of unusually high mortality that might strike on a local, regional, or national level. Although much remains to be done before we have a full understanding of mortality levels in the nineteenth century, students have a variety of useful works for partial answers to their questions. The articles by Condran, Cheney, and Crimmins are extremely interesting both for what they tell us about absolute levels of mortality, and for their sophisticated analyses of when and how changes occurred. Dalton, Jacobson, and Jaffe and Lourie are still useful efforts to gauge life expectancy before the Civil War, though one should also read Vinovskis' critique of Jacobson. Haines and Higgs provide important quantitative evidence, along with discussions of techniques, sources, and issues. Vinovskis' article on mortality in Massachusetts cited under Early America and his book on fertility should also be consulted. Meeker's article on improving health deserves reading also.

Of the numerous works on epidemics, several stand out. The books by Crosby on influenza, Duffy on yellow fever, and Rosenberg on cholera describe not only the extraordinary demographic effects of epidemics, but also consider the social context of these spectacular events. Ackernecht's study of malaria is also important, but differs somewhat in that he focuses on an endemic illness, with somewhat lower case fatality rates. Interestingly, there is no major work on tuberculosis, the major killer of the period. Students interested in particular episodes of high mortality should be able to isolate relevant articles easily; otherwise a wide-ranging selection is desireable to provide a good sense of the varied impact epidemics could have on a given community. Time, place, class, and disease gave every local epidemic a unique history.

3100.   Ackernecht, Erwin Heinz.   Malaria in the Upper Mississippi Valley, 1760-1900.   Baltimore: Johns Hopkins Press, 1945.

3101. Aldrich, Mark. "Determinants of Mortality among New England Cotton Mill Workers during the Progressive Era." JEH 42 (December, 1982), 847-863.

3102. Armstrong, John M. "The Asiatic Cholera in St. Paul." MnH 14 (1933), 288-302.

3103.   Baird, Nancy D.   "Asiatic Cholera: Kentucky's First Public Health Instructor." FCHQ 48 (October, 1974), 327-341.

3104.   Baker, Thomas H.   "Yellowjack: The Yellow Fever Epidemic of 1878 in Memphis, Tennessee."   BHM 42 (May-June, 1968), 241-264.

3105.   Barret, James T.   "Cholera in Missouri."   MoHR 55 (July, 1961), 344-354.

3106.   Brill, Robert E.   "The Sabbath-Day Summer: Madison, Indiana, and the 1849 Cholera Epidemic."   IMHQ 8 (September, 1982), 3-16.

3107.   Capers, Gerald M., Jr.   "Yellow Fever in Memphis in the 1870's." MVHR 24 (March, 1938), 483-502.

3108.   Carrigan, Jo Ann.   "Yellow Fever in New Orleans, 1853: Abstractions and Realities." JSouH 25 (August, 1959), 339-355.

3109.   Condran, Gretchen A. and Rose A. Cheney. "Mortality Trends in Philadelphia: Age- and Cause-Specific Death Rates 1870-1930." Demography 19 (1982), 97-124.

3110.   Condran, Gretchen A. and Eileen Crimmins.   "A Description and Evaluation of Mortality Data in the Federal Census: 1850-1900." HM 12 (Winter, 1979), 1-23.

3111.   Condran, Gretchen A. and Eileen Crimmins-Gardner.
"Public Health Measures and Mortality in U.S. Cities in the
Late Nineteenth Century." Human Ecology 6 (1978), 27-54.

3112.   Crosby, Alfred W., Jr.   Epidemic and Peace, 1918.
(Westport, Connecticut, Greenwood Press, 1976)

3113.   Crutcher, Charlotte.   "Asiatic Cholera in Jonesboro,
1873."   THQ 31 (Spring, 1972), 74-76.

3114.   Dalton, Mary.   "Mortality in New York City a Century
and a Quarter Ago."   HB 6 (1934), 87-97.

3115.   Doherty, William T.   "A West Virginia County's
Experiences with the 1918 Influenza Epidemic."   WVH 38
(January, 1977), 136-140.

3116.   Dollar, Clyde D.   "The High Plains Smallpox Epidemic
of 1837-38."   WHQ 8 (January, 1977), 15-38.

3117.   Doyle, John E.   "The Epidemic Cholera in Springfield,
1832 and 1849."   HJWM 3 (Fall, 1974), 1-14.

3118.   Duffy, John.   Sword of Pestilence: The New Orleans
Yellow Fever Epidemic of 1853.   (Baton Rouge, Louisiana
State University Press, 1966)

3119.   Everett, Donald E.   "The New Orleans Yellow Fever
Epidemic of 1853."   LHQ 33 (October, 1950),   380-405.

3120.   Farilie, Margaret C.   "The Yellow Fever Epidemic of
1888 in Jacksonville."   FHQ 19 (1940), 95-108.

3121.   Forman, Jonathan.   "The First Cholera Epidemic in
Columbus, Ohio (1833)."   AMH 6 (1934), 410-426.

3122.   Galishoff, Stuart.   "Cholera in Newark, New Jersey."
JHMAS 25 (October, 1970), 438-448.

3123.   Galishoff, Stuart.   "Newark and the Great Influenza
Pandemic of 1918."   BHM 43 (May-June, 1969), 246-258.

3124.   Galishoff, Stuart.   "Newark and the Great Polio
Epidemic of 1916."   NJH 94 (Summer-Autumn, 1976), 101-111.

3125.   Gersuny,   Carl.   "New   England   Mill   Casualties, 1890-1910." NEQ 52 (December, 1979), 467-482.

3126.   Griswold   del   Castillo,   Richard.   "Health   and   the Mexican   Americans   in   Los   Angeles,   1850-1887."   Journal of Mexican American History 4 (1974), 19-27.

3127.   Haggard,   J.   Villasana.   "Epidemic   Cholera   in   Texas, 1833-1834." SWHQ 40 (1937), 216-230.

3128.   Haines,   Michael   R.   "Mortality   in   Nineteenth   Century America: Estimates   From   New   York   and   Pennsylvania   Census Data, 1865 and 1900." Demography 14 (1977), 311-332.

3129.   Haines,   Michael   R.   and   Roger   C.   Avery.   "The American   Life   Table   of   1830-1860:   an   Evaluation."   JIH   11 (Summer,   1980), 73-95.

3130.   Hall, Don Alan and Ruth A. Hall.   "The Plague of New Elizabeth." IMH 70 (September, 1974), 197-228.

3131.   Higgs, Robert.   "Cycles and Trends of Mortality in 18 Large American Cities, 1871-1900." EEH 16 (1979), 381-408.

3132.   Higgs, Robert.   "Mortality in Rural America, 1870-1920: Estimates and Conjectures." EEH 10 (Winter, 1973), 177-196.

3133.   Higgs,   Robert   and   David   Booth.   "Mortality Differentials Within Large American Cities in 1890."   Human Ecology 7 (1979), 353-370.

3134.   Hutchens,   Kathryn   S.   "The   Indianapolis   Influenza Epidemic of 1918." IMHQ 5 (December, 1979), 4-14.

3135.   Irey, Thomas R.   "Soldiering, Suffering, and Dying in the Mexican War." JW 11 (April, 1982), 285-298.

3136.   Jacobson,   Paul   H.   "Cohort   Survival   for   Generations since 1840." MMFQ 42 (July, 1964), 36-53.

3137.   Jacobson,   Paul   H.   "An   Estimate   of   the   Expectation   of Life   in   the   United   States   in   1850."   MMFQ   35   (1957), 197-201.

3138.   Jaffe, A.J. and W.I. Lourie, Jr.   "An Abridged Life Table for the White Population of the United States in 1830." HB 14 (1942), 352-371.

3139.   Kanter, David Morris.   "The Invisible Monster: Investigations into the 1833 Cholera Epidemic in Southern Indiana." IMHQ 4 (December, 1978), 4-17.

3140.   Katz, Robert S.   "Influenza 1918-1919:   a Study in Mortality." BHM 48 (Fall, 1974), 416-422.

3141.   Lane, Roger.   Violent Death in the City: Suicide, Accident, and Murder in Nineteenth-Century Philadelphia. (Cambridge, Massachusetts, Harvard University Press, 1979)

3142.   Langtry, David A.   "The 1832 Epidemic of Asiatic Cholera in New Haven, Connecticut." JHMAS 25 (October, 1970), 449-476.

3143.   Legan, Marshall Scott.   "Mississippi and the Yellow Fever Epidemics of 1878-1879," JMsH 33 (1971), 199-218.

3144.   McLear, Patrick E.   "The St. Louis Cholera Epidemic of 1849." MoHR 63 (January, 1969), 171-181.

3145.   McShane, Kevin C.   "The 1918 Kansas City Influenza Epidemic." MoHR 63 (October, 1968), 55-70.

3146.   Meeker, Edward.   "The Improving Health of the United States, 1850-1915." EEH 9 (Summer, 1972), 353-374.

3147.   Melzer, Richard.   "A Dark and Terrible Moment: the Spanish Flu Epidemic of 1918 in New Mexico." NMHR 57 (July, 1982), 213-236.

3148.   Merrill, Tennis I. Underwood.   "The Year of the Smallpox." MoHSB 31 (April, 1975), 206-209.

3149.   Nichols, Roger L.   "Scurvy at Cantonment Missouri, 1819-1820." NH 49 (Winter, 1968), 333-347.

3150.   Partin, Robert.   "Alabama's Yellow Fever Epidemic of 1878." AR 10 (January, 1957), 31-51.

3151.   Pearce, George F.   "Torment of Pestilence: Yellow Fever Epidemics in Pensacola."   FHQ 56 (April, 1978), 448-472.

3152.   Powers, Ramon S. and Gene Younger.   "Cholera and the Army in the West: Treatment and Control in 1866 and 1867."   Military Affairs 39 (April, 1975), 49-54.

3153.   Powers, Ramon S. and Gene Younger.   "Cholera on the Plains: the Epidemic of 1867 in Kansas."   KHQ 37 (1971), 351-393.

3154.   Pyle, Gerald F.   "The Diffusion of Cholera in the United States in the Nineteenth Century."   Geographic Analysis 1 (1969), 59-75.

3155.   Richmond, C.   "Diseases Prevalent in the Early Settlement of Kokomo."   IMHQ 5 (June, 1979), 12-16.

3156.   Rosenberg, Charles E.   The Cholera Years, the United States in 1832, 1849 and 1866.   (Chicago, University of Chicago Press, 1962)

3157.   Sigerist,   Henry   E.   "Problems   of Historical-Geographical Pathology."   BHM 1 (1933), 10-18.

3158.   Smith, Delores.   "Northwestern Ohio's Cholera Years: 1849-1854."   NOQ 47 (Spring, 1975), 60-69.

3159.   Smith, John David.   "The Health of Vermont's Civil War Recruits."   VH 43 (Summer. 1975), 185-192.

3160.   Stickle, Douglas F.   "Death and Class in Baltimore: the Yellow Fever Epidemic of 1800."   MHM 74 (September, 1979), 282-299.

3161.   Strong, Wendell M.   "Mortality among Graduates of the Yale   Divinity School, 1825-1872."   ASAT 9 (1905-1906), 139-142.

3162.   Vinovskis, Maris A. "The Jacobson Life Table of 1850: a Critical Reexamination from a Massachusetts Perspective." JIH 8 (Spring, 1978), 703-724.

3163.   Walls, Edwina.   "Observations on the New Orleans Yellow-Fever Epidemic, 1878." LH 23 (Winter, 1982), 60-67.

3164.   Walters, Karen A.   "McLean County and the Influenza Epidemic of 1918-1919." ISHSJ 74 (Summer, 1981), 130-144.

3165.   Waring, Joseph Ioor.   "The Yellow Fever Epidemic of Savannah in 1820, with a Sketch of William Coffee Daniell." GHQ 52 (December, 1968), 398-404.

3166.   Wolfe, Robert J.   "Alaska's Great Sickness, 1900:   an Epidemic of Measles and Influenza in a Virgin Soil Population." APSP 126 (April 8, 1982), 91-121.

3167.   Wolley, Ivan   "The 1918 'Spanish Influenza' Pandemic in Oregon." OHQ 64 (1963), 246-258.

Black and slave

Many of the materials on black mortality in the nineteenth century focus on the period before 1865, when the Thirteenth Amendment brought an end to slavery.   General bad helath, poor medical care, and bad diet have been used to explain low life expectancy among blacks, though the three are not easily separated.   Students should start their study of these matters with the books by Kiple and King, and Savitt.   In addition to these studies, the book by Farley cited in the first section of this chapter is very important, especially for the post-emancipation period.   Given the debate over the effects of illness and mortality on black fertility, readers should also refer to that material, especially the articles by Eblen and Farley.

3180.   Cohn, Raymond L. and Richard A. Jensen.   "Mortality Rates and the Slave Trader."   In James H. Soltow, ed. Essays in Economic and Business History: Selected Papers from the Economic and Business Historical Society, 1979. (East Lansing, Division of Research,   Graduate School of Business Administration, Michigan State University, 1981), 17-26.

3181.   Johnson, Michael P.   "Smothered Slave Infants: Were Slave Mothers at Fault?"   JSouH 47 (November, 1981), 493-520.

3182. Kiple, Kenneth E. and Virginia H. King. Another Dimension to the Black Diaspora: Diet, Disease and Racism. (Cambridge, England, Cambridge University Press, 1981)

3183. Kiple, Kenneth and Virginia H. Kiple. "The African Connection: Slavery, Disease, and Racism." Phylon 41 (September, 1980), 211-222.

3184. Kiple, Kenneth and Virginia H. Kiple. "Black Tongue and Black Men: Pellagra and Slavery in the Antebellum South." JSouH 43 (August, 1977), 411-428.

3185. Kiple, Kenneth and Virginia H. Kiple. "Black Yellow Fever Immunities, Innate and Acquired, as Revealed in the American South." SSH 1 (Summer, 1977), 419-436.

3186. Kiple, Kenneth E. and Virginia H. Kiple. "Slave Child Mortality: some Nutritional Answers to a Perennial Puzzle." JSH 10 (Spring, 1977), 284-309.

3187. Lee, Anne S. and Everett S. Lee. "The Health of Slaves and the Health of Freedmen: a Savannah Study." Phylon 38 (June, 1977), 170-180.

3188. Legan, Marshall Scott. "Disease and the Freedmen in Mississippi during Reconstruction." JHMAS 28 (July, 1973), 257-267.

3189. Margo, Robert A. and Richard H. Steckel. "The Heights of American Slaves: New Evidence on Slave Nutrition and Health." SSH 6 (Fall, 1982), 516-538.

3190. Meeker, Edward. "Mortality Trends of Southern Blacks, 1850-1910: some Preliminary Findings." EEH 13 (January, 1976), 13-42.

3191. Savitt, Todd L. Medicine and Slavery: the Diseases and Health Care of Blacks in Antebellum Virginia. (Urbana, University of Illinois Press, 1978)

3192. Steckel, Richard H. "Slave Height Profiles from Coastwise Manifests." EEH 16 (1979), 363-380.

3193. Steckel, Richard H. "Slave Mortality: Analysis of Evidence from Plantation Records." SSH 3 (1979), 86-114.

3194.   Swados, Felice.   "Negro Health on Ante Bellum Plantations." BHM 10 (1941), 460-472.

3195.   Torchia, Marion M.   "Tuberculosis among American Negroes: Medical Research on a Racial Disease, 1830-1950." JHMAS 32 (July, 1977), 252-279.

Indian

There are relatively few citations here and no truly outstanding studies. This may reflect an overwhelming focus on Indian mortality before 1700, poor sources, small populations, or a lack of interest. What little is available carries on themes from studies of earlier periods.

3200.   Allen, Virginia R. "Agency Physicians to the Southern Plains Indians, 1868-1900." BHM 49 (Fall, 1975), 318-330.

3201.   Allen, Virginia R.   "The White Man's Road: the Physical and Psychological Impact of Relocation on the Southern Plains Indians." JHMAS 30 (April, 1975), 148-163.

3202.   Cook, Sherburne Friend.   "The Epidemic of 1830-1833 in California and Oregon." University of California Publications in American Archaeology and Ethnology 43 (1955), 303-325.

3203.   Dunn, Adrian R.   "A History of Old Fort Berthhold." NDH 30 (October, 1963), 157-236.

3204.   Howard, R. Palmer and Virginia E. Allen.   "Stress and Death in the Settlement of Indian Territory." CO 54 (Fall, 1976), 352-359.

3205.   Martin, Calvin.   "Wildlife Diseases as a Factor in the Depopulation of the North American Indian." WestHQ 7 (January, 1976), 47-62.

3206.   Salmon, Roberto Mario.   "The Disease Complaint at Bosque Redondo (1864-1868)." IH 9 (Summer, 1976), 2-7.

3207.   Sarafian, Winston L.   "Smallpox Strikes the Aleuts." Alaska Journal 7 (Winter, 1977), 46-49.

3208.   Valle, Rosemary K.   "James Ohio Pattie and the 1827-1828 Alta California Measles Epidemic."   CHSQ 52 (Spring, 1973), 28-36.

Recent

Given the almost overwhelming amount of material on twentieth-century levels of mortality available in government publications and sociology and demography journals, all that has been included here are a handful of more historically oriented studies.   The general studies cited at the start of this chapter and in Chapter One provide abundant data.

3250.   Brown, D. Clayton.   "Health of Farm Children in the South, 1900-1950."   AgH 53 (January, 1979), 170-187.

3251.   Iskrant, Albert P. and Paul V. Joliet.   Accidents and Homicide.   (Cambridge, Massachusetts, Harvard University Press, 1968)

3252.   Kitagawa, Evelyn M.   and   Philip   M.   Hauser. Differential   Mortality   in   the   United   States: A   Study   of Socioeconomic   Epidemiology.   (Cambridge,   Massachusetts, Harvard University Press, 1973)

3253.   Savitt, Todd L.   "Invisible Malady: Sickle Cell Anemia in America, 1910-1970."   National Medical Association Journal 73 (August, 1981), 739-746.

3254.   Shin, Eui Hang.   "Black-White Differentials in Infant Mortality in the South, 1940-1970."   Demography 12 (1975), 1-19.

Causes of Death and Health

Levels of mortality are the result of a combination of factors, some which contributed to sickness and death, and some which produce health and well-being.   Unfortunately, it is not always easy to sort out the contribution of any one factor.   Medical care, for example, can contribute to health, but it can also lead to death if it is based on faulty premises.   Bleeding is obviously a dangerous treatment. Similarly, diet can contribute both to health and death.

When a number of factors interact to produce a given level of mortality or to change an old pattern, it can be hard to sort out the precise contribution of each. This section of the bibliography presents material relating to the determinants of death and health subdivided into categories that reflect both the main changes of the time and the interests of later historians.

Early America

Studies of the causes of health and death in early America that go beyond descriptions of quaint or outlandish practices are rare. Not only are sources scattered, but they are also difficult to use because the people of the time had dramatically different understandings of causes of health and death than we do today, and so recorded evidence and observations that frequently need translation, even if they are relevant.

General conditions

Although epidemics often are not the principle determinants of mortality, they frequently attract the attention of the people exposed to them, who then produce records used by historians. Duffy is the leading student of epidemics in early America. Agriculture and diet are important topics on the positive side. Bidwell and Falconer, and McMahon offer excellent starting places on this topic.

3300. Bidwell, Percy Wells and John I. Falconer. History of Agriculture in the Northern United States 1620-1860. (Washington, D.C., The Carnegie Institution, 1925)

3301. Blake, John Ballard. Public Health in the Town of Boston, 1630-1822. (Cambridge, Massachusetts, Harvard University Press, 1959)

3302. Blanton, Wyndham Bolling. "Epidemics, Real and Imaginary, and Other Factors Influencing Seventeenth Century Virginia's Population." BHM 31 (September-October, 1957), 454-462.

3303. Caulfield, Ernest. "Some Common Diseases of Colonial Children."   Publications of the Colonial Society of Massachusetts 35 (1942-1946), 4-65.

3304. Caulfield, Ernest. "A True History of the Terrible Epidemic, Vulgarly Called the Throat Distemper, as it Occured in His Majesty's New England Colonies Between 1735 and 1740." Yale Journal of Biology and Medicine 11 (1939), 219-272; 277-335.

3305. Day, Clarence Albert. A History of Maine Agriculture, 1604-1860. (Orono, Maine, Printed at the University Press, 1954)

3306. Duffy, John. Epidemics in Colonial America. (Baton Rouge, Louisiana State University Press, 1953)

3307. Duffy, John. "Yellow Fever in Colonial Charleston." SCHGM 52 (October, 1951), 189-197.

3308. McMahon, Sarah F. "A Comfortable Subsistence: the Changing Composition of Diet in Rural New England, 1620-1840." WMQ 42 (January, 1985), 26-65.

3309. McMahon, Sarah F. "Provisions Laid up for the Family: Toward a History of Diet in New England, 1650-1860." HM 14 (Winter, 1981), 4-21.

3310. Savitt, Todd L. "Smothering and Overlaying of Virginia Slave Children: a Suggested Explanation." BHM 49 (Fall, 1975), 400-404.

3311. Williams, William H. America's First Hospital: the Pennsylvania Hospital, 1751-1841. (Wayne, Pennsylvania, Haverford House, 1976)

Medical practice

The best studies of medical practice in early America are the works by Shryock listed in the first section of this chapter. Most of the works listed here focus on a particular colony or a specific issue such as smallpox inoculation. The latter topic, and Cotton Mather's efforts to introduce inoculation, are certainly major themes in the medical history of early America. However, the story may be less important from the demographic point of view because overall mortality remained high.

3320.   Beall,   Otho   T.,   Jr.   "Cotton   Mather,   the   First Significant   Figure   in   American   Medicine."   BHM   26 (March-April, 1952), 103-166.

3321.   Bell,   Whitfield   J.,   Jr.   "Medical   Practice   in   Colonial America."   BHM 31 (September-October, 1957), 442-453.

3322. Blanton, Wyndham Bolling. Medicine in Virginia in the Eighteenth Century. (Richmond, Garrett and Massie, 1931)

3323.   Diller,   Theodore.   "Pioneer   Medicine   in   Western Pennsylvania."   AMH   8   (June-September,   1926),   141-154, 292-324.

3324.   Estes,   J.   Worth.   Hall   Jackson   and   the   Purple Foxglove: Medical   Practice   and   Research   in   Revolutionary America, 1760-1820.   (Hanover, New Hampshire, University Press of New England, 1979)

3325. Jarcho, Saul. "A Papal Physician and the Sanitation of New York City." BHM 52 (Fall, 1978), 410-418.

3326. Kestigan, Mark C. "Early Medical Care in Deerfield." HJWM 7 (June, 1979), 5-14.

3327.   Morris,   James   Polk.   "Smallpox   Inoculation   in   the American Colonies, 1763-1783." MdH 8 (Spring, 1977), 47-58.

3328.   Sigerist,   Henry   E.   "American   Spas   in   Historical Perspective." BHM 11 (1942), 133-147.

3329. Sigerist, Henry E. "The Philosophy of Hygiene." BHM 1 (1933), 323-331.

3330. Waring, Joseph Ioor. "James Killpatrick and Small Pox Inoculation in Charlestown." AMH n.s. 10 (1938), 301-308.

3331.   Waring,   Joseph   Ioor.   "St.   Philip's   Hospital   in Charlestown   in   Carolina;   Medical   Care   of   the   Poor   in Colonial Times." AMH n.s. 4 (1932), 283-289.

The Nineteenth Century

The materials in this section have been divided into four broad groups. A large and impressive literature on the public health movement receives first attention, not only because of its quality and quantity, but also because preventive medicine was the source of improvements which occurred after 1870. Reformers in the nineteenth century advocated a variety of specific changes to improve the health of the public. Studies of these specific reforms and their advocates are the second category. Medical practice was subject to major changes during this period, and actually began to help people in the last few decades. Section three, then, is what might be termed medical history. The fourth part reviews a large literature on the many options from which Americans chose when they wanted to avoid the care of regular doctors.

Public health movement

The works cited here are generally of high quality and are important to understanding nineteenth-century Americans' efforts for a better life. Rosenkrantz is probably the best place to start, along with Duffy's study of New York City cited in the first section of this chapter. Readers should pay special attention to the politics involved in public health reform. These connections are frequently best observed in sharply focussed works such as those by Cain, Ellis, Galishoff, Kramer, Melosi, Rosen, and Waserman. The works on specific reforms and reforms cited next are also valuable.

3350. Cain, Louis P. Sanitation Strategy for a Lakefront Metropolis: the Case of Chicago. (DeKalb, Northern Illinois Univeristy Press, 1978)

3351. Cain, Louis P. The Search for an Optimum Sanitation Jurisdiction: the Metropolitan Sanitary District of Greater Chicago; a Case Study. (Essays in Public Works History, 10) (Chicago, Public Works Historical Society, 1980)

3352. Campbell, Harry J. "The Congressional Debate over the Seaman's Sickness and Disability Act of 1798: the Origins of the Continuing Debate on the Socialization of American Medicine." BHM 48 (Fall, 1974), 423-426.

3353.   Cavins, Harold M.   "The National Quarantine and Sanitary Conventions of 1857 and 1860 and the Beginnings of the American Public Health Association."   BHM 13 (1943), 404-426.

3354.   Cohen, Abby.   "Public Health and Preventive Medicine in Providence, 1913."   RIH 36 (May, 1977), 54-63.

3355.   Corn, Jacqueline Karnell.   "Community Responsibility for Public Health: the Impact of Epidemic Disease and Urban Growth on Pittsburgh."   WPHM 59 (July, 1976), 319-339.

3356.   Cumberland, William H.   "Epidemic! Iowa Fights the Spanish Influenza."   Palimpsest 62 (January/February, 1981), 26-32.

3357.   Davenport, Francis Garvin.   "John Henry Ranch and Public Health in Illinois, 1877-1891."   ISHSJ 50 (Autumn, 1957), 277-293.

3358.   Duffy, John.   "Hogs, Dogs, and Dirt; Public Health in Early Pittsburgh."   PMHB 87 (July, 1963), 294-305.

3359.   Duffy, John.   "Nineteenth Century Public Health in New York and New Orleans: a Comparison."   LH 15 (Fall, 1974), 325-337.

3360.   Ellis, John H.   "Memphis Sanitary Revolution, 1880-1890."   THQ 23 (March, 1964), 59-72.

3361.   Galishoff, Stuart.   Public Health in Newark, 1832-1918. (Unpublished Ph.D. Dissertation, New York University, 1969)

3362.   Galishoff, Stuart.   Safeguarding the Public Health: Newark, 1895-1918. (Westport, Connecticut, Greenwood Press, 1975)

3363.   Gallison, Gordon.   "Louisana: Pioneer in Public Health." LH 4 (Summer, 1963), 207-232.

3364.   Hopkins, Richard J.   "Public Health in Atlanta: the Formative Years, 1865-1879."   GHQ 53 (September, 1969), 287-304.

3365.   Jamieson, Duncan R.   "Cities and the AMA: the American Medical Association's First Report on Public Hygiene." MdH 8 (Spring, 1977), 23-32.

3366. Kleinschmidt, Earl E. "The Sanitary Reform Movement in Michigan." MH 26 (1942), 373-401.

3367.   Kramer, Howard D.   "Agitation for Public Health Reform in the 1870's." JHMAS 3 (1948), 473-488; 4 (1949), 75-89.

3368.   Kramer, Howard D.   "Early Municipal and State Boards of Health." BHM 24 (1950), 503-529.

3369. Kramer, Howard D. "The Germ Theory and the Early Public Health Program in the United States." BHM 22 (1948), 233-247.

3370.   McGee, N.W.   "State Administration of Public Health in Iowa." IJHP 31 (1933), 163-210.

3371.   Melosi, Martin V.   Garbage in the Cities: Refuge, Reform, and the Environment, 1880-1980.   (College Station, Texas A&M University Press, 1981)

3372.   Melosi, Martin V., ed.   Pollution and Reform in American Cities, 1870-1930.   (Austin, University of Texas Press, 1980)

3373.   Romanofsky, Peter.   "'To One Common End': the United States Public Health Service and the Missouri Child Hygiene Movement, 1919-1921."   BHM 52 (Summer, 1978), 251-265.

3374. Rosen, George, ed. "Politics and Public Health in New York City (1838-1842)." BHM 24 (1950), 441-461.

3375. Rosenkrantz, Barbara Gutmann. Public Health and the State: Changing Views in Massachusetts, 1842-1936. (Cambridge, Massachusetts, Harvard University Press, 1972)

3376.   Schoonover, Shirley G.   "Alabama Public Health Campaign, 1900-1919." AR 28 (July, 1975), 218-233.

3377. Waserman, Manfred. "The Quest for a National Health Department in the Progressive Era." BHM 49 (Fall, 1975), 353-380.

3378. Zimmerman, Jane. "The Formative Years of the North Carolina Board of Health, 1877-1893." NCHR 21 (1944), 1-34.

Reforms

Readers' interests in particular places or reforms will mean that few will want or need to explore all or most of these works. It is important, however, to keep in mind the numerous specific health reforms advocated in the nineteenth century which make it difficult to assess the precise impact of any one change. Condran's works cited in the section on levels of mortality in the nineteenth century are models of how to demonstrate the importance of a specific reform.

3380. Armstrong, Thomas F. "Nor for 'Barter and Speculation': a Comparative Study of Antebellum Virginia Urban Water Supply." SouS 18 (Fall, 1979), 304-319.

3381. Bell, Whitfield J., Jr. "Dr. James Smith and the Public Encouragement for Vaccination for Smallpox." AMH 3rd series, 2 (1940), 500-517.

3382. Bellows, Barbara. "'Insanity Is the Disease of Civilization': the Founding of the South Carolina Lunatic Asylum." SCHM 82 (July, 1981), 263-272.

3383. Bennett, Merrill K. and Rosamond H. Pierce. "Change in the American National Diet, 1879-1959." Food Research Institute Studies 2 (May, 1961), 95-119.

3384. Berger, Michael L. "The Influence of the Automobile on Rural Health Care, 1900-1929." JHMAS 28 (October, 1973), 319-335.

3385. Berliner, Howard S. "New Light on the Flexner Report: Notes on the AMA-Carnegie Foundation Background." BHM 51 (Winter, 1977), 603-609.

3386. Betts, John R. "American Medical Thought on Exercise as the Road to Health, 1820-1860." BHM 45 (March-April, 1971), 138-158.

3387.   Braeman, John.   "Albert J. Beveridge and the First National Child Labor Bill."   IMH 60 (March, 1964), 1-36.

3388.   Bruce, Janet.   "Of Sugar and Salt and Things in the Cellar and Sun: Food Preservation in Jackson County in the 1850's."   MoHR 75 (July, 1981), 417-447.

3389.   Burris, Evadene A.   "Frontier Food."   MnH 14 (1933), 378-392.

3390.   Cain, Louis P.   "The Creation of Chicago's Sanitary Dictrict and Construction of the Sanitary and Ship Canal."   CH 8 (Summer, 1979), 98-110.

3391.   Cain, Louis P.   "Unfouling the Public's Nest: Chicago's Sanitary Diversion of Lake Michigan Water."   Technology and Culture 15 (October, 1974), 594-613.

3392.   Cassedy, James H.   "The 'Germ of Laziness' in the South, 1900-1915:   Charles Wardell Stiles and the Progressive Paradox."   BHM 45 (March-April, 1971), 159-169.

3393.   Cassedy, James H.   "Muckraking and Medicine: Samuel Hopkins Adams."   AQ 16 (Spring, 1963), 85-99.

3394.   Cavallo, Dominick.   Muscles and Morals: Organized Playgrounds and Urban Reform, 1880-1920.   (Philadelphia, University of Pennsylvania Press, 1981)

3395.   Dain, Norman.   Clifford W. Beers: Advocate for the Insane.   (Pittsburgh, University of Pittsburgh Press, 1980)

3396.   Dale, Edward Everett.   "The Food of the Frontier."   ISHSJ 40 (1947), 38-61.

3397.   Davidson, Elizabeth Huey.   "The Child-Labor Problem in North Carolina, 1883-1903."   NCHR 13 (1936), 105-121.

3398.   Davidson, Elizabeth Huey.   "Child-Labor Reforms in North Carolina since 1903."   NCHR 14 (1937), 109-134.

3399.   Davidson, Elizabeth Huey.   "Early Development of Public Opinion Against Southern Child Labor."   NCHR 14 (1937), 230-250.

3400. Duffy, John. "School Vaccination: the Precursor to School Medical Inspection." JHMAS 33 (July, 1978), 344-355.

3401. Ellis, John and Stuart Galishoff. "Atlanta's Water Supply, 1865-1918." MdH 8 (Spring, 1977), 5-22.

3402. English, Peter C. Shock, Physiological Surgery, and George Washington Crile: Medical Innovation in the Progressive Era. (Westport, Connecticut, Greenwood Press, 1980)

3403. Gagliardo, Domenico. "A History of Kansas Child-Labor Legislation." KHQ 1 (1932), 379-401.

3404. Galishoff, Stuart. "Drainage, Disease, Comfort, and Class: a History of Newark's Sewers." Societas 6 (Spring, 1976), 121-138.

3405. Gignilliat, John L. "Pigs, Politics, and Protection: the European Boycott of American Pork, 1879-1891." AgH 35 (January, 1961), 3-12.

3406. Glassberg, David. "The Design of Reform: the Public Bath Movement in America." AS 20 (Fall, 1979), 5-21.

3407. Goldfield, David R. "The Business of Health Planning: Disease Prevention in the Old South." JSouH 42 (November, 1976), 557-570.

3408. Grinder, Robert Dale. "The War Against St. Louis's Smoke, 1891-1924." MoHR 69 (January, 1975), 191-205.

3409. Grossberg, Michael. "Guarding the Altar: Physiological Restrictions and the Rise of State Intervention in Matrimony." AJLH 26 (July, 1982), 197-226.

3410. Haber, Carole. "The Old Folks at Home: the Development of Institutionalized Care for the Aged in Nineteenth-Century Philadelphia." PMHB 101 (April, 1977), 240-257.

3411. Harkins, Michael J. "Public Health Nuisances in Omaha, 1870-1900." NH 56 (Winter, 1975), 471-492.

3412.   Herget, James E.   "Taming the Environment: the Drainage District in Illinois." ISHSH 71 (May, 1978), 119-132.

3413.   Hildreth, Peggy Bassett.   "Early Red Cross: the Howard Association of New Orleans; 1837-1878." LH 20 (Winter, 1979), 49-75.

3414.   Hochheiser, Sheldon.   "The Evolution of U.S. Food Color Standards, 1913-1919."   AgH 55 (October, 1981), 385-391.

3415.   Huch, Ronald K.   "'Typhoid' Truelsen, Water, and Politics in Duluth, 1896-1900."   MnH 47 (Spring, 1981), 189-199.

3416.   Hunt, Marion and Olin Fellow.   "Women and Childsaving: St. Louis Children's Hospital, 1879-1979." MoHSB 36 (January, 1980), 65-79.

3417.   Hilliard, Sam B.   "Pork in the Ante-Bellum South: the Geography of Self-Sufficiency."   AAG 59 (September, 1969), 461-480.

3418.   Jones, Alton D.   "The Child Labor Reform Movement in Georgia." GHQ 49 (December, 1965), 396-417.

3419.   Kane, R. James.   "Populism, Progressivism, and Pure Food." AgH 38 (July, 1964), 161-166.

3420.   Keuchel, Edward F.   "Chemicals and Meat: the Embalmed Beef Scandal of the Spanish-American War." BHM 48 (Summer, 1974), 249-264.

3421.   Kirkland, Edward C.   "'Scientific Eating':   New Englanders Prepare and Promote a Reform, 1873-1907." MHSP 86 (1974), 28-52.

3422.   Leavitt, Judith W.   "The Wasteland: Garbage and Sanitary Reform in the Nineteenth-Century American City." JHMAS 35 (October, 1980), 431-452.

3423.   Leikund, Morris C.   "An Episode in the History of Smallpox Vaccination in New Hampshire." BHM 7 (1939), 671-686.

3424. MacGaffey, Edward. "A Pattern for Progress: The Minnesota Children's Code." MnH 41 (Spring, 1969), 229-236.

3425. Marcus, Alan I. "The Strange Career of Municipal Health Initiatives: Cincinnati and City Government in the Early Nineteenth Century." JUH 7 (November, 1980), 3-29.

3426. Meyer, Karl Friedrich. Disinfected Mail. (Holton, Kansas, Gossip Printery, 1962)

3427. Moyers, David M. "From Quackery to Qualification: Arkansas Medical and Drug Legislation, 1881-1909." AkHQ 35 (Spring, 1976), 3-26.

3428. Mullen, Pierce C. "Bitterroot Enigma: Howard Taylor Ricketts and the Early Struggle against Spotted Fever." Montana 32 (Winter, 1982), 2-13.

3429. Nissenbaum, Stephen. Sex, Diet, and Debility in Jacksonian America: Sylvester Graham and Health Reform. (Westport, Connecticut, Greenwood Press, 1980)

3430. Numbers, Ronald L. Prophetess of Health: a Study of Ellen G. White. (New York, Harper and Row, 1976)

3431. O'Connell, James C. "Chicago's Quest for Pure Water." Essays in Public Works History 1 (June, 1976), 1-19.

3432. Peterson, Jon A. "The Impact of Sanitary Reform upon American Urban Planning, 1840-1890." JSH 13 (Fall, 1979), 83-103.

3433. Phaneuf, Margaret M. "Sanitation and Cholera: Springfield and the 1866 Epidemic." HJWM 8 (January, 1980), 26-36.

3434. Pisani, Donald J. "The Polluted Truckee: a Study in Interstate Water Quality, 1870-1934." NHSQ 20 (Fall, 1977), 151-166.

3435. Pittman, Walter. "Chemical Regulation in Mississippi: the State Laboratory (1882-   )." JMsH 41 (May, 1979), 133-153.

3436.   Roemer, Milton I. and Barbara Faulkner.   "The Development of Public Health Services in a Rural County: 1838-1949." JHMAS 6 (1951), 22-43.

3437.   Rosen, George.   "The Efficiency Criterion in Medical Care, 1900-1920: an Early Approach to an Evaluation of Health Service." BHM 50 (Spring, 1976), 28-44.

3438.   Rosen,   George.   "The Medical Aspects of the Controversy over Factory Conditions in New England, 1840-1850." BHM 15 (1944), 483-497.

3439.   Rosenberg, Charles E.   "On the Study of American Biology and Medicine: Some Justifications."   BHM 38 (July-August, 1964), 364-376.

3440. Schultz, Stanley K. and Clay McShane. "To Engineer the Metropolis: Sewers, Sanitation, and City Planning in Late-Nineteenth-Century America."   JAH 65 (September, 1978), 389-411.

3441. Tarr, Joel Arthur. "The Separate vs. Combined Sewer Problem: a Case Study in Urban Technology Design Choice." JUH 5 (May, 1979), 308-339.

3442. Temin, Peter. Taking your Medicine: Drug Regulation in the United States. (Cambridge, Massachusetts, Harvard University Press, 1980)

3443. Thompson, Kenneth. "Irrigation as a Menace to Health in California: a Nineteenth-Century View." GR 59 (April, 1969), 195-214.

3444.   Tierno, Mark J.   "The Search for Pure Water in Pittsburgh: the Urban Response to Water Pollution, 1893-1914." WPHM 60 (January, 1977), 26-36.

3445. Walker, William O., III. Drug Control in the Americas. (Albuquerque, University of New Mexico Press, 1981)

3446.   Waserman, Manfred J.   "Henry L. Coit and the Certified Milk Movement in the Development of Modern Pediatrics." BHM 46 (1972), 359-390.

3447. Whorton, James C. Before Silent Spring: Pesticides and Public Health in pre-DDT America. (Princeton, New Jersey, Princeton University Press, 1974)

3448. Whorton, James C. "Insecticide Spray Residues and Public Health: 1865-1938." BHM 45 (May-June, 1971), 219-241.

3449. Whorton, James C. "Muscular Vegetarianism: the Debate over Diet and Athletic Performance in the Progressive Era." JSpH 8 (Summer, 1981), 58-75.

3450. Williams, Marilyn Thornton. "Philanthropy in the Progressive Era: the Public Baths of Baltimore." MHM 72 (Spring, 1977), 118-131.

3451. Wolfe, Margaret Ripley. "The Agricultural Experiment Station and Food and Drug Control: Another Look at Kentucky Progressivism, 1898-1916." FCHQ 49 (October, 1975), 323-338.

3452. Wolfe, Margaret Ripley. Lucius Polk Brown and Progressive Food and Drug Control: Tennessee and New York City, 1908-1920. (Lawrence, Regents Press of Kansas, 1978)

3453. Wosh, Peter J. "Sound Minds and Unsound Bodies: Massachusetts Schools and Mandatory Physical Training." NEQ 55 (March, 1982), 39-60.

3454. Young, James Harvey. "Botulism and the Ripe Olive Scare of 1919-1920." BHM 50 (Fall, 1976), 372-391.

Medical practice

The studies included here generally fall into one of three types: biographies of doctors (generally major figures); histories of particular, and often peculiar, forms of treatment; and studies of the profession in general, ranging from education to medical societies, licensing, and philosophy. Readers may also want to consult the works on health care options and attitudes and health care in conjunction with works listed here.

3470. Atwater, Edward C. "The Medical Profession in a New Society, Rochester, New York, 1811-1860." BHM 47 (May-June, 1973), 221-235.

3471. Atwater, Edward C. "The Physicians of Rochester, N.Y., 1860-1910: a Study in Professional History, Part II." BHM 51 (Spring, 1977), 93-106.

3472. Ayer, Hugh M.. "Nineteenth Century Medicine." IMH 48 (September, 1952), 233-254.

3473. Baird, W. David. Medical Education in Arkansas, 1879-1978. (Memphis, Tennessee, Memphis State University Press, 1979)

3474. Bogdan, Janet C. "Care or Cure? Childbirth Practices in Nineteenth-Century America." FS 4 (June, 1978), 92-99.

3475. Bonner, Thomas Neville. "German Doctors in America--1887-1914: Their Views and Impressions of American Life and Medicine." JHMAS 14 (January, 1959), 1-17.

3476. Bonner, Thomas Neville. The Kansas Doctor: a Century of Pioneering. (Lawrence, University of Kansas Press, 1959)

3477. Brieger, Gert H. "Therapeutic Conflicts and the American Medical Profession in the 1860's." BHM 41 (May-June, 1967), 215-222.

3478. Bryan, Leon S., Jr. "Blood-Letting in American Medicine, 1830-1892." BHM 38 (1964), 516-529.

3479. Buley, R. Carlyle. "Pioneer Health and Medical Practices in the Old Northwest Prior to 1840." MVHR 20 (March, 1934), 497-520.

3480. Cangi, Ellen Corwin. "Patrons and Proteges: Cincinnati's First Generation of Women Doctors, 1875-1910." CHSB 37 (Summer, 1979), 89-114.

3481. Clapesattle, Helen. "Health and Medicine in Rochester, 1855-1870." MnH 20 (1939), 221-242.

3482.   Dale, Edward Everett.   "Medical Practices on the Frontier." IMH 43 (1947), 307-328.

3483. Drachman, Virginia G. "Gynecological Instruments and Surgical Decisions at a Hospital in Late Nineteenth-Century America." JAC 3 (Winter, 1980), 660-672.

3484. Duffy, John. "Anglo-American Reaction to Obstetrical Anesthesia." BHM 38 (1964), 32-44.

3485.   Duffy, John.   "Medical Practice in the Ante-Bellum South." JSouH 25 (February, 1959), 53-72.

3486.   Eberson, Frederick.   "A Great Purging-Cholera or Calomel?" FCHQ 50 (April, 1976), 28-35.

3487.   Eckman, James.   "Anglo-American Hostility in American Medical Literature of the Nineteenth Century." BHM 9 (1941), 31-71.

3488. Fleming, Donald Harnish. William H. Welch and the Rise of Modern Medicine. (Boston, Little Brown, 1954)

3489. Foster, Gaines M. "The Limitations of Federal Health Care for Freedmen, 1862-1868." JSouH 48 (August, 1982), 349-372.

3490. Grob, Gerald N. Edward Jarvis and the Medical World of Nineteenth-Century America. (Knoxville, University of Tennessee Press, 1978).

3491. Haller, John S., Jr. American Medicine in Transition, 1840-1910. (Urbana, University of Illinois Press, 1981)

3492.   Hand, Wayland D.   "Measuring and Plugging: the Magical Containment and Transfer of Disease." BHM 48 (Summer, 1974), 221-233.

3493.   Harstad, Peter T.   "Sickness and Disease on the Wisconsin Frontier." WMH 43 (Winter, 1959, and Summer, 1960), 83-96, 203-220, 253-263.

3494. Hasson, Gail S. "Health and Welfare of Freedmen in Reconstruction Alabama." AR 35 (April, 1982), 94-110.

3495.   Hollander, Russell.   "Mental Health Policy in Washington Territory, 1853-1875."   PNQ 71 (October, 1980), 152-161.

3496.   Jones, Russel M.   "American Doctors in Paris, 1820-1861: a Statistical Profile."   JHMAS 25 (April, 1970), 143-157.

3497.   Kaufman, Martin.   "The Admission of Women to Nineteenth-Century American Medical Societies."   BHM 50 (Summer, 1976), 251-260.

3498.   Kaufman, Martin.   American Medical Education: The Formative Years, 1765-1910.   (Westport, Connecticut, Greenwood Press, 1976)

3499.   Kaufman, Martin.   "How Prospective Doctors Spent their Days: Medical Student Life at the University of Vermont, 1854-1900."   VH 43 (Fall, 1975), 274-291.

3500.   Kaufman, Martin.   The University of Vermont College of Medicine.   (Hanover, New Hampshire, University of Vermont College of Medicine, 1979)

3501.   Kleinschmidt, Earl E.   "Major Problems in Sanitation and Hygiene in Michigan, 1850-1900."   MH 28 (1944), 420-445.

3502.   Kleinschmidt, Earl E.   "Pioneer Health: Prevailing Diseases and Hygienic Conditions in Early Michigan."   MH 25 (1941), 57-99.

3503.   Kraus, Michael.   "American and European Medicine in the Eighteenth Century."   BHM 8 (1940), 679-695.

3504.   Landis, H.R.M.   "The Reception of Koch's Discovery in the United States."   AMH n.s. 4 (1932),   531-537.

3505.   Larkey, Sanford W. and Janet B. Kondelka.   "Medical Societies and Civil War Politics."   BHM 36 (January-February, 1962), 1-12.

3506.   Lovejoy, David B., Jr.   "The Hospital and Society: the Growth of Hospitals in Rochester, New York, in the Nineteenth Century."   BHM 49 (Winter, 1975), 536-55.

3507. McDonell, Katherine Mandusic. "Women and Medicine in Early Nineteenth-Century Indiana." IMHQ 6 (June, 1980), 3-4.

3508. Miller, Keith L. "Planning, Proper Hygiene, and a Doctor: the Good Health of the English Settlement." ISHSJ 71 (1978), 22-29.

3509. Moes, Robert J. "Smallpox Immunization in Alta California: a Story Based on Jose Estrada's 1821 Postscript." SCQ 61 (Summer, 1979), 125-158.

3510. Morantz, Regina Markell and Sue Zschoche. "Professionalism, Feminism, and Gender Roles: a Comparative Study of Nineteenth-Century Medical Therapeutics." JAH 67 (December, 1980), 568-588.

3511. Morrell, Joseph R. "Medicine of the Pioneer Period in Utah." UHQ 23 (April, 1955), 127-144.

3512. Neisuler, Jeanette. "Medicine in Early Schenectady." NYH 36, i.e. New York State Historical Association. Proceedings 53 (1955), 385-403.

3513. Numbers, Ronald L., ed. The Education of American Physicians: Historical Essays. (Berkeley, University of California Press, 1980)

3514. Parsons, Gail Pat. "Equal Treatment for All: American Medical Remedies for Male Sexual Problems, 1850-1900." JHMAS 32 (January, 1977), 55-71.

3515. Patton, James W. "Facets of the South in the 1850's." JSouH 23 (February, 1957), 3-24.

3516. Petersen, William John. "Diseases and Doctors in Pioneer Iowa." IJH 49 (April, 1951), 97-116.

3517. Phifer, Edward W. "Certain Aspects of Medical Practice in Ante-Bellum Burke County." NCHR 36 (January, 1959), 28-46.

3518. Riznick, Barnes. Medicine in New England, 1790-1840. 2nd ed. (Sturbridge, Massachusetts, Old Sturbridge Village, 1969)

3519.   Riznick, Barnes.   "The Professional Lives of Early Nineteenth-Century New England Doctors."   JHMAS 19 (January, 1964), 1-16.

3520.   Rosenberg, Charles E.   "The American Medical Profession: Mid-Nineteenth Century." MA 44 (July, 1962), 163-171.

3521.   Sahli, Nancy.   "A Stick to Break our Heads with: Elizabeth Blackwell and Philadelphia Medicine."   PH 44 (October, 1977), 335-347.

3522.   Savitt, Todd L.   "The Use of Blacks for Medical Experimentation and Demonstration in the Old South." JSouH 48 (August, 1982), 331-348.

3523. Shryock, Richard H. "Public Relations of the Medical Profession   in   Great   Britain   and   the   United   States: 1600-1870." AMH n.s. 2 (May, 1930), 308-339.

3524. Shryock, Richard H.   "Medical Practice in the Old South." SAQ 29 (April, 1930), 160-178.

3525.   Splitter, Henry W.   "Health in Southern California, 1850-1900." JW 8 (1969), 526-558.

3526.   Takaki, Ronald.   "Aesculapius was a White Man: Antebellum Racism and Male Chauvinism at Harvard Medical School." Phylon 39 (June, 1978), 128-134.

3527. Thompson, Kenneth. "Early California and the Causes of Insanity." SCQ 58 (Spring, 1976), 45-62.

3528.   Ward, Patricia Spain.   "The American Reception of Salvarsan." JHMAS 36 (January, 1981), 44-62.

3529.   Warner, John Farlez.   "'The Nature-Trusting Heresy': American Physicians and the Concept of the Healing Power of Nature in the 1850's and 1860's." PAH 11 (1977-1978), 289-324.

3530.   Wendler, Marilyn Van Voorhis.   "Doctors and Diseases on the Ohio Frontier." OH 89 (Spring, 1980), 222-240.

3531. Whitten, David O. "Medical Care of Slaves: Louisiana Sugar Region and South Carolina Rice District." SouS 16 (Summer, 1977), 153-180.

3532. Whorton, James C. "'Athlete's Heart': the Medical Debate over Athleticism, 1870-1920." JSpH 9 (Spring, 1982), 30-52.

3533. Whorton, James C. "The Hygiene of the Wheel: an Episode in Victorian Sanitary Science." BHM 52 (Spring, 1978), 61-88.

3534. Wirtschafter, Jonathan Dine. "The Genesis and Impact of the Medical Lobby: 1898-1906." JHMAS 13 (January, 1958), 15-49.

Health care options

Before regular doctors could actually help anyone, and when they often did much damage, many Americans sought cures and relief from a variety of sources. The works listed here demonstrate just how wide-ranging the options were. Readers with a general interest in this topic should start with Young because of the range of themes he addresses and the number of specific alternatives he mentions.

3550. Baur, John E. "The Health Seeker in the Westward Movement, 1830-1900." MVHR 46 (1959), 91-110.

3551. Breeden, James O. "Thompsonianism in Virginia." VMHB 82 (April, 1974), 150-180.

3552. Bush, Lester E., Jr. "Mormon Elders' Wafers: Images of Mormon Virility in Patent Medicine Ads." DJMT 10 (Autumn, 1976), 89-93.

3553. Clapesattle, Helen. "When Minnesota Was Florida's Rival." MnH 35 (March, 1957), 214-221.

3554. Fuller, Robert C. Mesmerism and the American Cure of Souls. (Philadelphia, University of Pennsylvania Press, 1982)

3555. Hand, Wayland D. "The Folk Healer: Calling and Endowment." JHMAS 26 (July, 1971), 263-275.

3556.   Hardman, Nicholas P.   Shucks, Shocks, and Hominy Blocks: Corn as a Way of Life in Pioneer America.   (Baton Rouge, Louisiana State University Press, 1981)

3557.   Jones, Louis C.   "Practitioners of Folk Medicine." New York Academy of Medicine. Bulletin 23 (1949), 480-493.

3558.   Kleinschmidt, Earl E.   "Metorological, Topographical, and Climatological Studies of Early Michigan Sanitarians." BHM 11 (1942), 161-173.

3559.   Kobrin, Frances E.   "The American Midwife Controversy: a Crisis of Professionalization."   BHM 40 (July-August, 1966), 350-363.

3560.   Litoff, Judy Barrett.   "Forgotten Women: American Midwives at the Turn of the Twentieth Century."   Historian 40 (February, 1978), 235-251.

3561.   Long, Esmond R.   "Weak Lungs on the Santa Fe Trail." BHM 8 (1940), 1040-1054.

3562.   McHugh, Christine.   "Phrenology: Getting your Head Together in Ante-Bellum America."   Midwest Quarterly 23 (Autumn, 1981), 65-77.

3563.   McNamara, Brooks.   "Health or Money Restored: the Great Era of the Indian Medicine Show."   AW 12 (March, 1975), 10-13.

3564.   Meeks, Harold A.   "Stagnant, Smelly, and Successful: Vermont's Mineral Springs."   VH 47 (Winter, 1979), 5-20.

3565.   Morrissey, Charles T.   "Inspiration and Perspiration: Vermont and the Thompsonian Cure for Illness: (I) Samuel Thompson and the Indian Remedies He Learned in Jericho, Vermont.'"   VH 44 (Fall, 1976), 222-224.

3566.   Park, Roberta J.   "'Embodied Selves':   the Rise and Development of Concern for Physical Education, Active Games, and Recreation for American Women, 1776-1865." JSpH 5 (Summer, 1978), 5-41.

3567.   Piercy, Harry D.   "Shaker Medicines."   OAHQ 63 (October, 1954), 336-348.

3568. Poulsen, Richard C. "Some Botanical Cures in Mormon Folk Medicine: an Analysis." UHQ 44 (Fall, 1976), 379-388.

3569. Richmond, Phyllis Allen. "Some Variant Theories in Opposition to the Germ Theory of Disease." JHMAS 9 (July, 1954), 290-303.

3570. Risse, Guenter B., Ronald L. Numbers, and Judith Walzer Leavitt. Medicine without Doctors: Home Health Care in American History. (New York, Science History, 1977)

3571. Shafer, Henry Burnell. "Early Medical Magazines in America." AMH n.s. 7 (1935), 480-491.

3572. Shane, Karen D. "New Mexico: Salubrious El Dorado." NMHR 56 (October, 1981), 387-399.

3573. Shryock, Richard H. "Sylvester Graham and the Popular Health Movement, 1830-1870." MVHR 18 (September, 1931), 172-183.

3574. Smith, David C. and Anne E. Bridges. "The Brighton Market: Feeding Nineteenth-Century Boston." AgH 56 (January, 1982), 3-21.

3575. Stage, Sarah. Female Complaints: Lydia Pinkham and the Business of Women's Medicine. (New York, Norton, 1979)

3576. Teahan, John F. "Warren Felt Evans and Mental Healing: Romantic Idealism and Practical Mysticism in Nineteenth-Century America." Church History 48 (March, 1979), 63-80.

3577. Walsh, Anthony A. "Phrenology and the Boston Medical Community in the 1830's." BHM 50 (Summer, 1976), 261-273.

3578. Whiteside, Henry O. "The Drug Habit in Nineteenth-Century Colorado." CM 55 (Winter, 1978), 46-68.

3579. Wilson, Benjamin C. and Pat A. Wilson. "The Amazing Curative Powers of Black Home Remedies and other Elements of Folk Wisdom in Rural Southwestern Michigan." Negro History Bulletin 45 (October/November/December, 1982), 110-112.

3580.   Young, James Harvey.   American Self-Dosage Medicines: an Historical Perspective.   (Lawrence, Kansas, Coronado, 1974)

3581.   Young, James Harvey.   The Toadstool Millionaires: a Social History of Patent Machines in America Before Federal Regulation.   (Princeton, New Jersey, Princeton University Press, 1961)

Recent

Government statistical publications and general surveys of population describe recent trends in the causes of health and death.   Since 1920, the search for improvement has generally been much more successful.   Three major reminders of how much we continue to damage ourselves are the books by Carson, Jones, and Young.   They lend a cautionary note to an otherwise fairly positive story.

3600.   Antler, Joyce and Daniel M. Fox.   "The Movement Toward a Safe Maternity: Physican Accountability in New York City, 1915-1940."   BHM 50 (Winter, 1976), 569-595.

3601.   Bair, Barbara.   "'The Full Light of this Dawn': Congressman John Fogarty and the Historical Cycle of Community Mental Health Policy in Rhode Island."   RIH 41 (November, 1982), 128-138.

3602.   Brienes, Marvin.   "Smog Comes to Los Angeles."   SCQ 58 (Winter, 1976), 515-532.

3603.   Brown, E. Richard.   "Public Health in Imperialism: Early Rockefeller Programs at Home and Abroad."   American Journal of Public Health 66 (September, 1976), 897-903.

3604.   Brown, E. Richard.   Rockefeller Medicine Men: Medicine and Capitalism in America.   (Berkeley, University of California Press, 1979)

3605.   Carson, Rachel Louise.   Silent Spring.   (Boston, Houghton Mifflin, 1962)

3606. Dunlap, Thomas R. DDT: Scientists, Citizens, and Public Policy. (Princeton, New Jersey, Princeton University Press, 1981)

3607. Dusenberry, William Howard. "Foot and Mouth Disease in Mexico, 1946-1951." AgH 29 (April, 1955), 82-90.

3608. Ettling, John. The Germ of Laziness: Rockefeller Philanthropy and Public Health in the New South. (Cambridge, Harvard University Press, 1981)

3609. Golden, Janet and Eric C. Schneider. "Custody and Control: the Rhode Island State Hospital for Mental Diseases, 1870-1970." RIH 41 (November, 1982), 112-125.

3610. Harvey, A. McGehee. Science at the Bedside: Clinical Research in American Medicine, 1905-1945. (Baltimore, Johns Hopkins University Press, 1981)

3611. Jones, Bartlett C. "Prohibition and Eugenics, 1920-1933." JHMAS 18 (April, 1963), 158-172.

3612. Jones, Bartlett C. "A Prohibition Problem: Liquor as Medicine: 1920-1933." JHMAS 18 (October, 1963), 353-369.

3613. Jones, C. Clyde. "The Burlington Railroad's Swine Sanitation Trains of 1929." IJH 57 (January, 1959), 23-33.

3614. Jones, James H. Bad Blood: The Tuskegee Syphilis Experiment. (New York, Free Press, 1981)

3615. Judkins, Bennett M. "Occupational Health and the Developing Class Consciousness of Southern Textile Workers: the Case of the Brown Lung Association." MdH 13 (Spring/Summer, 1982), 55-71.

3616. McClary, Andrew. "Sunning for Health: Heliotherapy as Seen by Professionals and Popularizers, 1920-1940." JAC 5 (Spring, 1982), 65-68.

3617. Mail, Patricia D. "Hippocrates Was a Medicine Man: the Health Care of Native Americans in the Twentieth Century." AAAPSS No. 436 (March, 1978), 40-49.

3618. Pearlman, Michael. "Leonard Wood, William Muldoon and the Medical Profession: Public Health and Universal Military Training." NEQ 52 (September, 1979), 326-344.

3619. Pillard, Ellen. "Nevada's Treatment of the Mentally Ill, 1882-1961." NHSQ 22 (Summer, 1979), 83-99.

3620. Rosen, George. Preventive Medicine in the United States, 1900-1975: Trends and Interpretations. (New York, Science History Publications, 1975)

3621. Worster, Donald. "Hydraulic Society in California: an Ecological Interpretation." AgH 56 (July, 1982), 503-515.

3622. Young, James Harvey. The Medical Messiahs: a Social History of Health Quackery in Twentieth-Century America. (Princeton, New Jersey, Princeton University Press, 1967)

Values and Attitudes

Although the desires to improve health and lengthen life are two of the oldest and most universal human goals, the actual values and attitudes people have held regarding these matters have varied markedly. What one considers to be the cause of sickness has a major effect on the search for a cure. The material in this section is divided into four categories. Issues of public health frequently became entangled with local and occasionally national politics, either as matters of public policy in their own right or as a means to gain political advantage. A second way values matter concerns the attitudes doctors and patients have toward each other, and toward the illnesses that link them. The third group of studies focuses on the specific topic of the origin and development of health and life (or illness and death) insurance. The fourth group of studies examines cultural expectations about appropriate behavior by the dying and their survivors. Many of the studies listed above under nineteenth-century causes of death and health have material that relates to the first two categories here, even though the issues are not always addressed directly.

Public Response to Disease

One of the most obvious public responses to disease was when epidemic outbreaks of diseases such as smallpox or yellow fever became entangled in ongoing political or social controversy. Billias, Carrigan, Fox, Henderson, Leavitt, and Pernick are all valuable here. Rosen links medical thought to Jeffersonian ideals on a much more philosophical level. Economic concerns are studied by East, Ellis, Meeker, and Sigerist from a variety of perspectives. Two somewhat different works by Pattison and Riedesel look at what cemetaries tell us about public attitudes.

3650. Billias, George A. "Pox and Politics in Marblehead, 1773-1774." EIHC 92 (January, 1956), 43-58.

3651. Brewer, Paul W. "Voluntarism on Trial: St. Louis' Response to the Cholera Epidemic of 1849." BHM 49 (Spring, 1975), 101-122.

3652. Carrigan, Jo Ann. "Impact of Epidemic Yellow Fever on Life in Louisiana." LH 4 (Winter, 1963), 5-34.

3653. Carrigan, Jo Ann. "Privilege, Prejudice, and the Stranger's Disease in Nineteenth-Century New Orleans." JSouH 36 (November, 1970), 568-578.

3654. Ciocco, Antonio and Dorthy Perrott. "Statistics on Sickness as a Cause of Poverty: a Historical Review of U.S. and English Data." JHMAS 12 (January, 1957), 42-60.

3655. Claman, Gretchen. "A Typhoid Fever Epidemic and the Power of the Press in Denver in 1879." CM 56 (Summer/Fall, 1979), 143-160.

3656. Corn, Jacqueline Karnell. "Social Response to Epidemic Disease in Pittsburgh, 1872-1895." WPHM 56 (January, 1973), 59-70.

3657. Dewey, Frank L. "Thomas Jefferson's Law Practice: the Norfolk Anti-Inoculation Riots." VMHB 91 (January, 1983), 39-53.

3658. Drews, Robert S. "A History of the Care of the Sick Poor of the City of Detroit (1703-1855)." BHM 7 (1939), 759-782.

3659. Duffy, John. "Mental Strain and 'Overpressure' in the Schools: a Nineteenth-Century Viewpoint." JHMAS 23 (January, 1968), 63-79.

3660. Duffy, John. "Social Impact of Disease in the Late Nineteenth Century." New York Academy of Medicine. Bulletin 47 (July, 1971), 797-810.

3661. East, Dennis, II. "Health and Wealth: Goals of the New Orleans Public Health Movement, 1879-1884." LH 9 (Summer, 1968), 245-275.

3662. Ellis, John H. "Businessmen and Public Health in the Urban South During the Nineteenth Century: New Orleans, Memphis, and Atlanta." BHM 44 (May-June, 1970), 197-212; (July-August, 1970), 346-371.

3663. Fox, Daniel M. "Social Policy and City Politics: Tuberculosis Reporting in New York, 1889-1900." BHM 49 (Summer, 1975), 169-195.

3664. Friedman, Reuben. "The Influence of Immigration on the Incidence of Scabies in the United States." AMH 2 (1940), 393-400.

3665. Goldfield, David R. "The Business of Health Planning: Disease Prevention in the Old South." JSouH 42 (November, 1976), 557-570.

3666. Henderson, Patrick. "Smallpox and Patriotism: the Norfolk Riots, 1768-1769." VMHB 73 (October, 1965), 413-424.

3667. Kalisch, Philip A. "The Black Death in Chinatown: Plague and Politics in San Fransisco, 1900-1904." ArW 14 (Summer, 1972), 113-136.

3668. Kevles, Daniel J. "Genetics in the United States and Great Britain, 1890-1930: a Review with Speculations." Isis 71 (September, 1980), 441-455.

3669.   Leavitt, Judith W.   "Politics and Public Health: Smallpox in Milwaukee, 1894-1895."   BHM 50 (Winter, 1976), 553-568.

3670.   McClary, Andrew.   "Germs Are Everywhere: the Germ Threat as Seen in Magazine Articles, 1890-1920."   JAC 3 (Spring, 1980), 33-46.

3671.   Meeker, Edward.   "The Social Rate of Return on Investment in Public Health, 1880-1910."   JEH 34 (June, 1974), 392-419.

3672.   Pattison, William David.   "The Cemeteries of Chicago: a Phase of Land Utilization."   AAG 45 (September, 1955), 245-257.

3673.   Pernick, Martin S.   "Politics, Parties, and Pestilence: Epidemic Yellow Fever in Philadelphia and the Rise of the First Party System."   WMQ 29 (October, 1972), 559-586.

3674.   Remele, Larry.   "Sewage Disposal and Local Politics at Jamestown, 1926-1929: a Case Study in North Dakota Urban History."   NDH 49 (Spring, 1982), 22-29.

3675.   Riedesel, Gordon M.   "The Geography of Saunders County Rural Cemeteries from 1859."   NH 61 (Summer, 1980), 215-228.

3676.   Rosen, George.   "Patterns of Health Research in the United States, 1900-1960."   BHM 39 (1965), 201-221.

3677.   Rosen, George.   "Political Order and Human Health in Jeffersonian Thought."   BHM 26 (1952), 32-44.

3678.   Sigerist, Henry E.   "The Cost of Illness to the City of New Orleans in 1850."   BHM 15 (1944), 498-507.

3679.   Smith, Thomas G.   "Detaining the Insane: Detention Hospitals, Mental Health, and Frontier Politics in Alaska, 1910-1915."   PNQ 73 (July, 1982), 124-133.

3680.   Solis-Cohen, Rosebud T.   "The Exclusions of Aliens from the United States for Physical Defects."   BHM 21 (1947), 33-50.

3681.   Starr, Paul.   "Medicine, Economy and Society in Nineteenth-Century America."   JSH 10 (June, 1977), 588-607.

3682.   Tatge, Robert O.   "A Quarantine Quandary: Ship Fever and Yellow Fever in Providence, Rhode Island, 1797." American Neptune 40 (July, 1980), 192-210.

3683.   Vecoli, Rudolph J.   "Sterilization: a Progressive Measure?" WMH 43 (Spring, 1960), 190-202.

Attitudes and Health Care

Attitudes of the providers and recipients of health care toward each other and their understanding of the causes (and hence cures) of illness profoundly affect who does what to and for whom, and what expectations for success may be. Place of birth, sex, race, and social class are the principle factors that helped determine treatment.   Bullough, Donegan, Grob,   Haller,   Morantz,   Rosenberg,   and   Wood   offer particularly helpful insights into these matters.   Readers may also want to consult the works cited earlier under medical practice and health care options in the nineteenth century.

3700.   Bardell, Eunice B.   "German Immigrants and Health Care in Pioneer Milwaukee."   Milwaukee County Historical Society. Historical Messenger 33 (Autumn, 1977), 86-96.

3701.   Bonner, Thomas Neville.   "The Social and   Political Attitudes of Midwestern Physicians, 1840-1940:   Chicago as a Case History." JHMAS 8 (1953), 133-164.

3702.   Breeden, James O.   "Body Snatchers and Anatomy Professors: Medical   Education   in   Nineteenth-Century Virginia." VMHB 83 (July, 1975), 321-345.

3703. Bullough, Vern L. and Martha Vought.   "Homosexuality and its   Confusion with the 'Secret Sin' in Pre-Freudian America." JHMAS 28 (April, 1973), 143-155.

3704.   Bullough, Vern L. and Martha Vought.   "Women, Menstruation, and Nineteenth-Century Medicine."   BHM 47 (January-February, 1973), 66-82.

3705. Burnham, John C. "The Social Evil Ordinance-a Social Experiment in Nineteenth-Century St. Louis." MoHSB 27 (1971), 203-217.

3706. Cassedy, James H. "An Early American Hangover: the Medical Profession and Intemperance, 1800-1860." BHM 50 (Fall, 1976), 405-413.

3707. Corgan, James X. "Non-medical Functions of the Nashville Journal of Medicine and Surgery, 1851-1861." Tennessee Medical Association. Journal 70 (March, 1977), 168-170.

3708. Dain, Norman. Disordered Minds: the First Century of the Eastern State Hospital in Williamsburg, Virginia, 1766-1866. (Williamsburg, University Press of Virginia, 1971)

3709. Dain, Norman and Eric T. Carlson. "Social Class and Psychological Medicine in the United States, 1789-1824." BHM 30 (1959), 454-465.

3710. Donegan, Jane B. Women & Men Midwives: Medicine, Mortality, and Misogyny in Early America. (Westport, Connecticut, Greenwood Press, 1978)

3711. Edwards, Linden F. "Body Snatching in Ohio During the Nineteenth Century." OAHQ 59 (October, 1950), 329-351.

3712. Ewalt, Donald H. "Patients, Politics, and Physicians: the Struggle for Control of State Lunatic Asylum No. 1, Fulton, Missouri." MoHR 77 (January, 1983), 170-188.

3713. Fellman, Anita Clair and Michael Fellman. Making Sense of Self: Medical Advice Literature in Late Nineteenth-Century America. (Philadelphia, University of Pennsylvania Press, 1981)

3714. Fisher, William. "Physicans and Slavery in the Antebellum Southern Medical Journal." JHMAS 23 (January, 1968), 36-49.

3715. Fox, Richard W. So Far Disordered in Mind: Insanity in California, 1870-1930. (Berkeley, University of California Press, 1978)

3716.   Friedman, Lawrence J. and Arthur H. Shaffer. "History, Politics, and Health in Early American Thought: the Case of David Ramsay." JAS 13 (April, 1979), 37-56.

3717.   Gilman, Stuart C.   "Degeneracy and Race in the Nineteenth Century: the Impact of Clinical Medicine." JES 10 (Winter, 1983), 27-50.

3718.   Grob, Gerald N.   "Class, Ethnicity, and Race in American Mental Hospitals, 1830-1875." JHMAS 28 (July, 1973), 207-229.

3719.   Grob, Gerald N.   "Mental Illness, Indigency, and Welfare: the Mental Hospital in Nineteenth-Century America." In Tamara K. Hareven, ed. Anonymous Americans. (Englewood Cliffs, New Jersey, Prentice-Hall, 1971), 250-279.

3720.   Grob, Gerald N.   "The Social History of Medicine and Disease in America: Problems and Possibilities." JSH 10 (June, 1977), 391-409.

3721.   Haller, John S., Jr.   "The Physican Versus the Negro: Medical and Anthropological Concepts of Race in the Late Nineteenth Century." BHM 44 (March-April, 1970), 154-167.

3722.   Jordan, Weymouth Tyree.   "Plantation Medicine in the Old South." AR 3 (April, 1950), 83-107.

3723.   Kaufman, Martin and Leslie L. Hanawalt.   "Body Snatching in the Midwest." MH 55 (Spring, 1971), 23-40.

3724.   Litoff, Judy B.   American Midwives: 1860 to the Present. (Westport, Connecticut, Greenwood Press, 1978)

3725.   Lindenthal, Jacob Jay.   "Abi Gezunt: Health and the Eastern European Jewish Immigrant." AJH 70 (June, 1981), 420-441.

3726.   Mark, Gregory Yee.   "Racial, Economic and Political Factors in the Development of America's First Drug Laws." Issues in Criminology 10 (Spring, 1975), 49-72.

3727.   Morantz, Regina Markell.   "The Lady and her Physician." In Mary S. Hartman and Lois Banner, eds. Clio's

Consciousness Raised. (New York, Harper Colophon Books, 1974), 38-53.

3728. Morantz, Regina Markell. "Making Women Modern: Middle Class Women and Health Reform in 19th Century America." JSH 10 (Summer, 1977), 490-507.

3729. Rabinowitz, Howard N. "From Exclusion to Segregation: Health and Welfare Services for Southern Blacks, 1865-1890." Social Service Review 48 (September, 1974), 327-354.

3730. Rosenberg, Charles E. "And Heal the Sick: the Hospital and the Patient in the Nineteenth-Century America." JSH 10 (June, 1977), 428-447.

3731. Rosenberg, Charles E. "The Bitter Fruit: Heredity, Disease, and Social Thought in Nineteenth-Century America." PAH 8 (1974), 187-235.

3732. Rosenberg, Charles E. "Factors in the Development of Genetics in the United States: Some Suggestions." JHMAS 22 (January, 1967), 27-46.

3733. Sicherman, Barbara. "The Paradox of Prudence: Mental Health in the Gilded Age." JAH 62 (March, 1976), 890-912.

3734. Sicherman, Barbara. "The Uses of a Diagnosis: Doctors, Patients, and Neurasthenia." JHMAS 32 (January, 1977), 33-54.

3735. Smith-Rosenberg, Carroll and Charles Rosenberg. "The Female Animal: Medical and Biological Views of Women and her Role in Nineteenth-Century America." JAH 60 (September, 1973), 332-356.

3736. Thomas, Samuel J. "Nostrum Advertising and the Image of Woman as Invalid in Late Victorian America." JAC 5 (Fall, 1982), 104-112.

3737. Thompson, E. Bruce. "Reforms in the Care of the Insane in Tennessee, 1830-1850." THQ 3 (1944), 319-334.

3738. Tomes, Nancy. "The Domesticated Madman: Changing Concepts of Insanity at the Pennsylvania hospital, 1780-1830." PMHB 106 (April, 1982), 271-282.

3739. Torchia, Marion M. "The Tuberculosis Movement and the Race Question, 1890-1950." BHM 49 (Summer, 1975), 152-168.

3740. Tylor, Peter. "'Denied the Power to Choose the Good': Sexuality and Mental Defect in American Medical Practice, 1850-1920." JSH 10 (June, 1977), 472-489.

3741. Verbrugge, Martha H. "Women and Medicine in Nineteenth-Century America." Signs 1 (Summer, 1976), 957-972.

3742. Vogel, Morris J. The Invention of the Modern Hospital: Boston, 1870-1930. (Chicago, University of Chicago Press, 1980)

3743. Vogel, Morris J. and Charles E. Rosenberg, eds. The Therapeutic Revolution: Essays in the Social History of American Medicine. (Philadelphia, University of Pennsylvania Press, 1979)

3744. Walsh, Mary Roth. "Doctors Wanted: No Women Need Apply": Sexual Barriers in the Medical Profession, 1835-1975. (New Haven, Connecticut, Yale University Press, 1977)

3745. Wood, Ann Douglas. "'The Fashionable Diseases': Women's Complaints and their Treatment in Nineteenth-Century America." JIH 4 (Summer, 1973), 25-52.

Insurance

Most of these works focus on the years after 1900, when insurance became acceptable economically, politically, and philosophically. See Haller, Savitt, Stowe, and Terris for studies of early, but not very widespread efforts to develop insurance programs.

3750. Anderson, Odin W. "Health Insurance-the United States, 1910-1920." JHMAS 5 (1950), 363-396.

3751. Grant, H. Roger. "W.D. Vandiver and the 1905 Life Insurance Scandals." MoHSB 19 (1972), 5-19.

3752. Haller, John S., Jr. "Race, Mortality, and Life Insurance: Negro Vital Statistics in the Late Nineteenth Century." JHMAS 25 (July, 1970), 247-261.

3753. Long, Durward. "An Immigrant Co-operative Medicine Program in the South, 1887-1963." JSouH 31 (November, 1965), 417-434.

3754. Numbers, Ronald L. Almost Persuaded: American Physicians and Compulsory Health Insurance, 1912-1920. (Baltimore, Johns Hopkins Univeristy Press, 1978)

3755. Poen, Monte M. Harry S. Truman Versus the Medical Lobby: the Genesis of Medicine. (Columbia, University of Missouri Press, 1979)

3756. Savitt, Todd L. "Slave Life Insurance in Virginia and North Carolina." JSouH 43 (November, 1977), 583-600.

3757. Schwartz, Jerome L. "Early History of Prepaid Medical Care Plans." BHM 39 (September-October, 1965), 450-475.

3758. Stowe, Walter Herbert. "The Corporation for the Relief of Widows and Children of Clergymen." Historical Magazine of the Protestant Episcopal Church 3 (1934), 19-33.

3759. Terris, Milton. "An Early System of Compulsory Health Insurance in the United States, 1798-1884." BHM 15 (1944), 433-444.

3760. Viseltear, Arthur J. "Compulsory Health Insurance in California, 1915-1918." JHMAS 24 (April, 1969), 151-182.

3761. Zelizer, Viviana A. Rotman. Morals and Markets: the Development of Life Insurance in the United States. (New York, Columbia University Press, 1979)

Perspectives on Death

How Americans prepared for their own deaths and those of their family, and how the survivors managed afterward has produced some extraordinarily interesting studies on topics ranging from appropriate expressing of emotion to gravestone carving and cemetary layout. In the absence of a general synthesis, readers should start with one or more of the following, depending on their interest: Aries, Benes, Douglas, Ferrell, Jordan, Kubler-Ross, Saum, Stannard, and Vinovskis. Aries has little to say about America, but does provide a good general context.

3800. Aaron, Daniel. "The Etiquettee of Grief: a Literary Generation's Response to Death." Prospects 4 (1979), 197-213.

3801. Ames, Kenneth L. "Ideologies in Stone: Meanings in Victorian Gravestones." JPC 14 (Spring, 1981), 641-656.

3802. Aries, Phillippe. The Hour of Our Death. Translated by Helen Weaver. (New York, Alfred A. Knopf, 1981)

3803. Aries, Philippe. Western Attitudes toward Death from the Middle Ages to the Present. Translated by Patricia M. Ranum. (Baltimore, Johns Hopkins University Press, 1974)

3804. Benes, Peter. The Masks of Orthodoxy: Folk Gravestone Carving in Plymouth County, Massachusetts, 1689-1805. (Amherst, University of Massachusetts Press, 1977)

3805. Benes, Peter, ed. Puritan Gravestone Art: the Dublin Seminar for New England Folklife. Annual Proceedings, 1976. (Dublin, New Hampshire, Dublin Seminar for New England Folklife, jointly with Boston University, 1977)

3806. Chatfield, Penelope. "Wyuka: a 'Rural' Cemetery in Lincoln, Nebraska." NH 63 (Summer, 1982), 184-193.

3807. Douglas, Ann. "Heaven Our Home: Consolation Literature in the Northern United States, 1830-1880." AQ 26 (December, 1974), 496-515.

3808.   Elliott, Emory.   "The Development of the Puritan Funeral Sermon and Elegy: 1600-1750."   Early American Literature 15 (Fall, 1980), 151-164.

3809.   Farrell, James J.   Inventing the American Way of Death, 1830-1920.   (Philadelphia, Temple University Press, 1980)

3810.   Geselbracht, Raymond H.   "The Ghosts of Andrew Wyeth: the Meaning of Death in the Transcendental Myth of America."   NEQ 47 (March, 1974), 13-29.

3811.   Gribben, William.   "Divine Providence or Miasma?   The Yellow Fever Epidemic of 1822."   NYH 53, i.e. New York State Historical Association.   Proceedings 70 (1972), 283-298.

3812.   Jackson, Charles O.   "American Attitudes to Death."   JAS 11 (December, 1977), 297-312.

3813.   Jordan, Terry G.   "'The Roses so Red and the Lilies so Fair':   Southern Folk Cemeteries in Texas."   SWHQ 83 (January, 1980), 227-258.

3814.   Jordan, Terry G.   Texas Graveyards: a Cultural Legacy.   (Austin, University of Texas Press, 1982)

3815.   Kubler-Ross, Elizabeth.   On Death and Dying.   (New York, Macmillan, 1969)

3816.   Lancaster, R. Kent.   "Green Mount: the Introduction of the Rural Cemetery into Baltimore."   MHM 74 (March, 1979), 62-79.

3817.   More, William B. and Stephen C. Davies.   "The Art of Death: Nineteenth Century Tombstone Carving in Crawford County, Pennsylvania."   Journal of Erie Studies 7 (Fall, 1978), 54-72.

3818.   Naglack, James J.   "Death in Colonial New England."   HJWM 4 (Fall, 1975), 21-33.

3819.   Narrett, David W.   "Preparation for Death and Provision for the Living: Notes on New York Wills (1665-1760)."   NYH 57, i.e. New York State Historical Association.   Proceedings 74 (1976), 417-437.

3820.   Nelson, Malcolm A. and Diana Hume George. "'Grinning Skulls, Smiling Cherubs, Bitter Words.'" JPC 14 (Spring, 1981), 633-640.

3821.   Pickering, Samuel, Jr.   "The Grave Leads but to Paths of Glory: Deathbed Scenes in American Children's Books, 1800-1860." Dalhousie Review 59 (Autumn, 1979), 452-464.

3822.   Pike, Martha.   "In Memory of: Artifacts Relating to Mourning in Nineteenth-Century America." JAC 3 (Winter, 1980), 642-659.

3823.   Powers, Thomas.   "Learning to Die."   Harper's Magazine 242 (June, 1971), 72-80.

3824.   Roediger, David R.   "And Die in Dixie: Funerals, Death, and Heaven in the Slave Community, 1700-1865." Massachusetts Review 22 (Spring, 1981), 163-183.

3825.   Saum, Lewis O.   "Death in the Popular Mind of Pre-Civil War America." AQ 26 (December, 1974), 477-495.

3826.   Shneidman, Edwin S., ed.   Death: Current Perspectives. (Palo Alto, California, Mayfield Publishing Company, 1976)

3827.   Stannard, David E.   "Death and Dying in Puritan New England." AHR 78 (December, 1973), 1305-1330.

3828.   Stannard, David E.   "Death and the Puritan Child." AQ 26 (December, 1974), 456-476.

3829.   Stannard, David E., ed.   "Death in America." AQ 26 (December, 1974), whole issue.

3830.   Stannard, David E.   The Puritan Way of Death: a Study in Religion, Culture, and Social Change. (New York, Oxford University Press, 1977)

3831.   Steele, Thomas J.   "The Death Cart: its Place among the Santos of New Mexico." CM 55 (Winter, 1978), 1-14.

3832.   Vinovskis, Maris A.   "Angels' Heads and Weeping Willows: Death in Early America." AASP 86 (1976), 273-302.

3833. Welch, Richard F. "Colonial and Federal New York and New Jersey Gravestones." <u>Journal of Long Island History</u> 17 (Winter, 1981), 4-29.

3834. Wells, Ronald V. "Dignity and Integrity in Dying (Insights from Early 19th Century Protestantism)." <u>Journal of Pastoral Care</u> 26 (1972), 99-107.

4
Migration, Pluralism, and Local Patterns

This chapter is the longest, by far, of any in the bibliography. This is explained partly by the fact that Americans have long been aware of the importance of international migration and westward expansion to their history, and so have been writing on these subjects for a long time. In addition, the variety of immigrants to and multiplicity of destinations in this continental nation has provided opportunities for numerous studies of particular groups and places. Even though migration of various sorts may have been most prominent in the nineteenth century, there has never been a time when it did not require attention. Unlike certain aspects of the history of fertility and mortality which require a degree of technical expertise, migration has been easier to study by means of more general historical skills.

In spite of the size of this chapter, it by no means exhausts the literature. Certain general categories of materials have been omitted almost entirely. For example, travelers' accounts (whether visitors or migrants), letters, diaries, and memoirs fill the pages of state and local historical publications, and have occasionally appeared as books. In the late-nineteenth and early-twentieth centuries, many communities produced local histories that contain information on the origins of the earliest inhabitants, generally in the form of individual biographies. Many of the works cited here make use of these kinds of materials, and so at least some of them can be identified. Most of what is included here is the product of students and scholars studying migration as it affected groups rather than individuals. The authors are more often observers than participants.

Although we have divided the studies here into some categories that appear to be rather specific, the themes in the chapter heading are not always conceptually clear or easily separated. Migration, for example, involves movement to the United States from other countries, and the movement within the country from one rural area to another, and from country to city. The complex variety of local patterns that have resulted from these different migrant streams are worth study in their own right, and with regard to how different combinations produced a fragmented, or pluralistic society, instead of a homogeneous culture. Although many of the works included here offer insights into the consequences of migration and pluralism, readers interested in such issues will want to refer also to Chapter Six.

Early America

Although migration has frequently been seen as a major theme for nineteenth-century historians, students of earlier centuries can not ignore it. Migration played an important role in the emerging American societies before 1800, and many of the patterns that were important between 1800 and 1920 are discernible earlier. The works here are divided into four categories. The first includes works on the English colonies in North America that became the original United States. The second set of studies are for French and Spanish settlements that were eventually incorporated into the United States. Studies of Indian migrations both independent of and in interaction with Europeans comprise the third group. The presence of cities in some colonies, but not in others, and the importance of rural to urban migration after 1800 make urbanization an important fourth topic.

Migration and Settlement: The English Colonies

To try to divide international from internal migration, local studies from more general works, or the movement of blacks from whites makes little or no sense in this period either historically or historio- graphically. Nonetheless, it is possible to identify several broad issues that provide some common links among some of these works. Who the migrants were and why they moved are common concerns. The degree to which English or European culture was transferred to or transformed by America has interested historians for a century or more. Studies of individual communities are a third group, although the focus on a particular place and time is frequently linked with the broader issues just mentioned, as well as with matters of family life which will be considered in Chapter Five.

Without intending to slight the contribution of the other studies, a number of specific titles deserve mention here as important places to start. The books by Hansen, Maldwyn Jones, and Wittke are important, if somewhat dated syntheses of the immigrant experience. All go well beyond the colonial period. New England towns have often been studied for their own sake and as detailed examples of some of the broader processes at work. Some of the best include studies by Allen, Bissell, Breen and Foster, Demos, Grant, Greven, Gross, Haller, D. Jones, Lockridge, Powell, Rutman, and Zuckerman. Communities outside New England have recently received some attention by scholars such as Archdeacon, Earle, Lemon, Mitchell, Trewartha, White, and Wolf. The interest in who moved to America and why has generated a small, but important literature on indentured servants. Readers should begin with Campbell and A.E. Smith, and then turn to Galenson and Menard. The migration of blacks and their incorporation into American society are important parts of this story as is evident from works by Berlin, Boles, Craven, Curtin, Davis, Gemery and Hogendorn, Goodfriend, Greene, Menard, E.S. Morgan, P. Morgan, Nash, Wacker, and Wood. Learning to read the landscape for historical evidence is an important skill as is shown by Earle, Kniffen, Stilgoe, and Wacker.

4000. Alexander, John K. "The Philadelphia Numbers Game: an Analysis of Philadelphia's Eighteenth-Century Population." PMHB 98 (July, 1974), 314-324.

4001. Allen, David G. In English Ways: the Movement of Societies and the Transferal of English Local Law and

Custom to Massachusetts Bay in the Seventeenth Century.
(Chapel Hill, University of North Carolina Press, 1981)

4002. American Council of Learned Societies. Committee on
Linguistic and National Stocks in the Population of the
United States. Report of the Committee on Linguistic and
National Stocks in the United States. In American
Historical Association. Report for the Year 1931.
(Washington, D.C.: American Historical Association, 1932)

4003. Anderson-Green, Paula Hathaway. "The New River
Frontier Settlement on the Virginia-North Carolina Border,
1760-1820." VMHB 86 (October, 1978), 413-431.

4004. Arbuckle, Robert D. "John Nicholson and the
Pennslyvania Population Company." WPHM 57 (October,
1974), 353-385.

4005. Archdeacon, Thomas J. New York City, 1664-1710:
Conquest and Change. (Ithaca, New York, Cornell University
Press, 1976)

4006. Banks, Charles Edward. "English Sources of
Emigration to the New England Colonies in the Seventeenth
Century." MHSP 60 (1926-27), 366-373.

4007. Banks, Charles Edward. "The Topographical Sources
of English Emigration to the New England Colonies
1620-1650." New York Genealogical and Biographical Record
61 (January, 1930), 3-6.

4008. Berlin, Ira. "Time, Space, and the Evolution of
Afro-American Society on British Mainland North America."
AHR 85 (February, 1980), 44-78.

4009. Bickford, Christopher P. "The Lost Connecticut
Census of 1762 Found." Connecticut Historical Society
Bulletin 44 (April, 1979), 33-43.

4010. Bissell, Linda Anwers. "From One Generation to
Another: Mobility in Seventeenth-Century Windsor,
Connecticut." WMQ 31 (January, 1974), 79-110.

4011. Bjarnson, Donald Einar. "Swedish-Finnish Settlement in New Jersey in the Seventeenth Century." SPHQ 27 (October, 1976), 238-246.

4012. Boles, John B. Black Southerners, 1619-1869. (Lexington, University Press of Kentucky, 1983)

4013. Breen, Timothy Hall. "Transfer of Culture: Chance and Design in Shaping Massachusetts Bay, 1630-1660." NEHGR 132 (January, 1978), 3-17.

4014. Breen, Timothy Hall and Stephen Foster. "Moving to the New World: the Character of Early Massachusetts Immigration." WMQ 30 (April, 1973), 189-222.

4015. Butler, Lindley S. "The Early Settlement of Carolina: Virginia's Southern Frontier." VMHB 79 (January, 1971), 20-28.

4016. Campbell, Mildred. "English Emigration on the Eve of the American Revolution." AHR 61 (October, 1955), 1-20.

4017. Campbell, Mildred. "Social Origins of Some Early Americans."   In   James   Morton   Smith,   ed. Seventeenth-Century America. (Chapel Hill, University of North Carolina Press, 1959), 63-89.

4018. Canny, Nicholas P. "The Ideology of English Colonization: from Ireland to America." WMQ 30 (October, 1973), 575-598.

4019. Carroll, Kenneth L. "Quakerism on the Eastern Shore of Virginia." VMHB 74 (April, 1966), 170-189.

4020. Clemens, Paul G.E. "The Settlement and Growth of Maryland's Eastern Shore During the English Restoration." MdH 5 (Fall, 1974), 63-78.

4021. Cohen, David Steven. "How Dutch Were the Dutch of New Netherland?" NYH 62, i.e. New York State Historical Association. Proceedings 79 (January, 1981), 43-60.

4022. Coldham, Peter Wilson. "The 'Spiriting' of London Children to Virginia, 1648-1685." VMHB 83 (July, 1975), 280-287.

4023.   Coleman, Kenneth.   "The   Southern   Frontier:
Georgia's Founding and the Expansion of South Carolina."
GHQ 56 (Summer, 1972), 163-174.

4024.   Conover, Bettie Jones.   "British West Florida's
Mississippi Frontier Posts, 1763-1779."   AR 29 (July, 1976),
177-207.

4025.   Coulter, E. Merton.   "A List of the First Shipload of
Georgia Settlers." GHQ 31 (December, 1947), 282-288.

4026.   Crandall, Ralph J.   "New England's Second Great
Migration: the First Three Generations of Settlement,
1630-1700." NEHGR 129 (October, 1975), 347-360.

4027.   Crary, Catherine Snell.   "The Humble Immigrant and
the American Dream: Some Case Histories, 1746-1776."
MVHR 46 (June, 1959), 46-66.

4028.   Craven, Wesley Frank.   White, Red, and Black: the
Seventeenth Century Virginian. (Charlottesville, University
Press of Virginia, 1971)

4029.   Crow, Jeffrey J.   The Black Experience in
Revolutionary North Carolina. (Raleigh, North Carolina
Department of Cultural Resources, 1977)

4030.   Currer-Briggs, Noel.   "Similarity of Surnames in York
County, Virginia, and County Norfolk, England."   VMHB 78
(October, 1970), 442-446.

4031.   Curtin, Philip D.   The Atlantic Slave Trade: a
Census. (Madison, University of Wisconsin Press, 1969)

4032.   Daniels, Doris Groshen.   "Colonial Jewry: Religion,
Domestic, and Social Relations."   AJHQ 66 (March, 1977),
375-400.

4033.   Davis, Thomas J.   "New York's Long Black Line: a
Note   on   the   Growing   Slave   Population,   1626-1790."
Afro-Americans in New York Life and History 2 (January,
1978), 41-60.

4034.   DeJong, Gerald F.   The Dutch in America, 1609-1974.
(Boston, Twayne, 1975)

4035. Demos, John. "Families in Colonial Bristol, Rhode Island: an Exercize in Historical Demography." WMQ 25 (January, 1968), 40-57,

4036. Demos, John. "Notes on Life in Plymouth Colony." WMQ 22 (April, 1965), 264-286.

4037. Detweiler, Robert. "Was Richard Hakluyt a Negative Influence in the Colonization of Virginia?" NCHR 48 (October, 1971), 359-369.

4038. Diamond, Sigmund. "An Experiment in 'Feudalism': French Canada in the Seventeenth Century." WMQ 18 (January, 1961), 1-34.

4039. Diamond, Sigmund. "From Organization to Society: Virginia in the Seventeenth Century." AJS 63 (March, 1958), 457-475.

4040. Diamond, Sigmund. "Values as an Obstacle to Economic Growth: the American Colonies." JEH 27 (December, 1967), 561-575.

4041. Dunaway, Wayland Fuller. "The English Settlers in Colonial Pennsylvania." PMHB 52 (1928), 317-341.

4042. Dunaway, Wayland Fuller. "The French Racial Strain in Colonial Pennsylvania." PMHB 53 (1929), 322-342.

4043. Dunaway, Wayland Fuller. "Pennsylvania as an Early Distributing Center of Population." PMHB 55 (1931), 134-169.

4044. Earle, Carville V. The Evolution of a Tidewater Settlement System: All Hallow's Parish, Maryland, 1650-1783. (Chicago, University of Chicago, Department of Geography, 1975)

4045. East, Robert A. "Puritanism and New Settlement." NEQ 17 (June, 1944), 255-264.

4046. Ellis, David Maldwyn. Landlords and Farmers in the Hudson-Mohawk Region, 1790-1850. (Ithaca, New York, Cornell University Press, 1946)

4047. Ellis, David Maldwyn. "New York and Middle Atlantic Regionalism."   NYH 35, i.e. New York State Historical Association. Proceedings 52 (January, 1954), 3-13.

4048. Ellis, David Maldwyn. "The Yankee Invasion of New York, 1783-1850." NYH 32, i.e. New York State Historical Association. Proceedings 49 (1951), 3-17.

4049. Flowers, Carl, Jr. "The Wofford Settlement on the Georgia Frontier." GHQ 61 (Fall, 1977), 258-267.

4050. Fusell, G.E. "Social and Agrarian Background of the Pilgrim Fathers." AgH 7 (1933), 183-202.

4051. Galenson, David W. "British Servants and the Colonial Indenture System in the Eighteenth Century." JSouH 44 (February, 1978), 41-66.

4052. Galenson, David W. White Servitude in Colonial America: an Economic Analysis. (Cambridge, England, Cambridge University Press, 1981)

4053. Gehrke, William H. "The Beginnings of the Pennsylvania-German Element in Rowan and Cabarrus Counties, North Carolina." PMHB 58 (1934), 342-369.

4054. Gemery, Henry A. "Emigration from the British Isles to the New World, 1630-1700: Inferences from Colonial Populations." Research in Economic History 5 (1980), 179-232.

4055. Gemery, Henry A. and Jan S. Hogendorn, eds. The Uncommon Market: Essays in the Economic History of the Atlantic Slave Trade. (New York, Academic Press, 1979)

4056. Goldenberg, Joseph A., Eddie D. Nelson, and Rita Y. Fletcher. "Revolutionary Ranks: an Analysis of the Chesterfield Supplement." VMHB 87 (April, 1979), 182-189.

4057. Goodfriend, Joyce D. "Burghers and Blacks: The Evolution of a Slave Society at New Amsterdam." NYH 59, i.e. New York State Historical Association. Proceedings 76 (April, 1978), 125-144.

4058. Graham, Ian Charles Cargill. Colonists from Scotland: Emigration to North America, 1707-1783. (Ithaca, New York, Cornell University Press, 1956)

4059. Grant, Charles S. Democracy in the Connecticut Frontier Town of Kent. (New York, Columbia University Press, 1961)

4060. Greene, Lorenzo Johnston. The Negro in Colonial New England; 1620-1776. (New York, Columbia University Press, 1942)

4061. Greven, Philip J., Jr. Four Generations: Population, Land, and Family in Colonial Andover, Massachusetts. (Ithaca, New York, Cornell University Press, 1970)

4062. Gross, Robert A. The Minutemen and their World. (New York, Hill and Wang, 1976)

4063. Haller, William, Jr. The Puritan Frontier: Town-Planting in New England Colonial Development, 1630-1660. (New York, Columbia University Press, 1951)

4064. Hammon, Neal O. "Pioneers in Kentucky, 1773-1775." FCHQ 55 (July, 1981), 268-283.

4065. Hansen, Marcus Lee. The Atlantic Migration, 1607-1860. (Cambridge, Massachusetts, Harvard University Press, 1940)

4066. Heavner, Robert O. "Indentured Servitude: the Philadelphia Market, 1771-1773." JEH 38 (September, 1978), 701-713.

4067. Hecht, Irene W.D. "The Virginia Muster of 1624/5 as a Source for Demographic History." WMQ 30 (January, 1973), 65-92.

4068. Higgins, Ruth Loving. Expansion in New York with Especial Reference to the Eighteenth Century. (Columbus, Ohio, Ohio State University, 1931)

4069. Higgins, W. Robert. "Charleston: Terminus and Entrepot of the Colonial Slave Trade." In Martin L. Kilson and Robert I. Rotberg, eds. The African Diaspora;

Interpretive Essays. (Cambridge, Massachusetts, Harvard University Press, 1976), 114-131.

4070. Hoyt, Edward A. "Naturalization under the American Colonies: Signs of a New Community." PSQ 67 (June, 1952), 248-266.

4071. Inikori, J.E. "Measuring the Atlantic Slave Trade: an Assessment of Curtin and Anstey." Journal of African History 17 (1976), 197-223.

4072. Jones, Douglas Lamar. Village and Seaport: Migration and Society in Eighteenth-Century Massachusetts. (Hanover, New Hampshire, University Press of New England, 1981)

4073. Jones, Maldwyn Allen. American Immigration. (Chicago, University of Chicago Press, 1960)

4074. Karinen, Arthur Eli. "Maryland Population: 1631-1730: Numerical and Distributional Aspects." MHM 54 (December, 1959), 365-407.

4075. Kenney, Alice P. "The Albany Dutch: Loyalists and Patriots." NYH 42, i.e. New York State Historical Association. Proceedings 59 (1961), 331-350.

4076. Kenney, Alice P. "Dutch Patricians in Colonial Albany." NYH 49, i.e. New York State Historical Association. Proceedings 66 (1968), 249-283.

4077. Kenney, Alice P. "Patricians and Plebeians in Colonial Albany." De Halve Maen 45, no. 1 (1970), 7-8, 14; 45, no. 2 (1971), 9-11, 13; 45 no. 3 (1970), 9-11; 45, no. 4 (1971), 13-14; 46, no. 1 (1971), 13-15.

4078. Kirchner, Walther. "Emigration: some Eighteenth Century Considerations." Comparative Studies in Society and History 5 (1962-1963), 346-356.

4079. Kirchner, Walther. "Emigration to Russia." AHR 55 (April, 1950), 552-566.

4080. Klein, Herbert S. "Slaves and Shipping in Eighteenth-Century Virginia." JIH 5 (Winter, 1975), 383-412.

4081.   Klein, Milton M.   "New York in the American Colonies: A New Look."   NYH 53, i.e. New York State Historical Association. Proceedings 70 (1972), 132-156.

4082.   Klein, Milton M.   "Shaping the American Tradition: The Microcosm of Colonial New York."   NYH 59, i.e. New York Historical Association. Proceedings 76 (1978), 173-197.

4083.   Klepp, Susan.   "Five Early Pennslyvania Censuses." PMHB 106 (October, 1982), 483-514.

4084.   Kniffen, Fred.   "Folk Housing: Key to Diffusion." AAG 55 (1965), 549-577.

4085.   Kniffen, Fred and Henry Glassie.   "Building in Wood in the Eastern United States: a Time-Place Perspective." GR (January, 1966), 40-66.

4086.   Kolb, Avery E.   "Early Passengers to Virginia: When Did They Really Arrive?"   VMHB 88 (October, 1980), 401-414.

4087.   Lee, R. Alton.   "A Note on Early Immigration Restriction."   JES 4 (Fall, 1976), 103-104.

4088.   Lefler, Hugh T.   "Promotional Literature of the Southern Colonies." JSouH 33 (February, 1967), 3-25.

4089.   Lemon, James T.   The Best Poor Man's Country: a Geographical Study of Early Southeastern Pennsylvania. (Baltimore, Johns Hopkins University Press, 1972)

4090.   Littlefield, Daniel C.   "Plantations, Paternalism, and Profitability: Factors Affecting African Demography in the Old British Empire." JSouH 47 (May, 1981), 167-182.

4091.   Littlefield, David C.   Rice and Slaves: Ethnicity and the Slave Trade in Colonial South Carolina.   (Baton Rouge, Louisiana State University Press, 1981)

4092.   Lockridge, Kenneth A.   "Land, Population, and the Evolution of New England Society, 1630-1790."   Past and Present no. 39 (April, 1968), 62-80.

4093. Lockridge, Kenneth A. A New England Town; the First Hundred Years, Dedham, Massachusetts, 1636-1736. (New York, Norton, 1970)

4094. Lockridge, Kenneth A. "The Population of Dedham, Massachusetts, 1636-1736." EcHR 19 (August, 1966), 318-344.

4095. Lydon, James G. "New York and the Slave Trade, 1700-1774." WMQ 35 (April, 1978), 375-394.

4096. McDonald, Forrest and Ellen Shapiro McDonald. "The Ethnic Origins of the American People, 1790." WMQ 37 (1980), 179-199.

4097. McManis, Douglas R. Colonial New England: a Historical Geography (New York, Oxford University Press, 1975)

4098. Mellor, George R. "Emigration from the British Isles to the New World, 1765-1775." History n.s. 40 (1955), 68-83.

4099. Menard, Russell R. "Five Maryland Censuses, 1700-1712: a Note on the Quality of the Quantities." WMQ 37 (October, 1980), 616-626.

4100. Menard, Russell R. "From Servant to Freeholder: Status Mobility and Property Accumulation in Seventeenth-Century Maryland." WMQ 30 (January, 1973), 37-64.

4101. Menard, Russell R. "The Maryland Slave Population, 1658 to 1730: a Democratic Profile of Blacks in Four Counties." WMQ 32 (January, 1975), 29-54.

4102. Merwick, Donna. "Becoming English: Anglo-Dutch Conflict in the 1670's in Albany, New York." NYH 62, i.e. New York State Historical Association. Proceedings 79 (1981), 389-414.

4103. Merwick, Donna. "Dutch Townsmen and Land Use: a Spatial Perspective on Seventeenth-Century Albany, New York." WMQ 37 (January, 1980), 53-78.

4104. Miller, J. Virgil. "Amish Mennonites in Northern Alsace and the Palatinate in the Eighteenth Century and

e

Their Connection with Immigrants to Pennsylvania."
<u>Mennonite Quarterly Review</u> 50 (October, 1976), 272-280.

4105.   Mitchell, Robert D.   <u>Commercialism and Frontier:</u>
<u>Perspectives on the Early Shenandoah Valley</u>.
(Charolottesville, University of Virginia, 1977)

4106.   Mitchell, Robert D.   "Content and Context:
Tidewater Characterictics in the Shenandoah Valley." <u>MdH</u> 5
(Fall, 1974), 79-92.

4107.   Moller, Herbert.   "Sex Composition and Correlated
Culture Patterns of Colonial America." <u>WMQ</u> 2 (April, 1945),
113-153.

4108.   Mood, Fulmer.   "Studies in the History of American
Settled Areas and Frontier Lines: 1625-1790." <u>AgH</u> 26
(January, 1952), 16-34.

4109.   Morgan, Edmund S.   <u>American Slavery, American</u>
<u>Freedom</u>. (New York, Norton, 1975)

4110.   Morgan, Edmund S.   "Headrights and Head Counts: A
Review Article." <u>VMHB</u> 80 (July, 1972), 361-371.

4111.   Morgan, Philip D.   "Work and Culture: the Task
System and the World of Lowcountry Blacks, 1700 to 1880."
<u>WMQ</u> 39 (October, 1982),
563-599.

4112.   Morris, Richard.   "Urban Population Migration in
Revolutionary America: the Case of Salem, Massachusetts,
1759-1799." <u>JUH</u> 9 (November, 1982), 3-30.

4113.   Morrison, Charles.   "Early Land Grants and Settlers
along Patterson Creek." <u>WVH</u> 40 (Winter, 1979), 164-199.

4114.   Nash, Gary B.   "The New York Census of 1737:   a
Critical Note on the Integration of Statistical and Literary
Sources." <u>WMQ</u> 36 (July, 1979), 428-435.

4115.   Nash, Gary B.   "Slaves and Slaveowners in Colonial
Philadelphia." <u>WMQ</u> 30 (April, 1973), 223-256.

4116. Nash, Gary B. "Up from the Bottom in Franklin's Philadelphia." Past and Present, No. 77 (November, 1977), 57-83.

4117. Nash, Gary B. and Billy G. Smith. "The Population of Eighteenth-Century Philadelphia." PMHB 99 (July, 1975), 362-368.

4118. Newton, A.P. "The Great Emigration, 1618-1648." In Rose, John Holland. et al., eds. The Cambridge History of the British Empire, volume 1. (Cambridge, The University Press, 1929), 136-182.

4119. Parish, John Carl. The Persistence of the Westward Movement and Other Essays. (Berkeley, University of California Press, 1943)

4120. Porter, Frank W., III. "From Backcountry to County: the Delayed Settlemnt of Western Maryland." MHM 70 (Winter, 1975), 329-349.

4121. Powell, Sumner Chilton. Puritan Village: the Formation of a New England Town. (Middletown, Connecticut, Wesleyan University Press, 1963)

4122. Pryde, George S. "Scottish Colonization in the Province of New York." NYH 16, i.e. New York State Historical Association. Proceedings 33 (1935), 138-157.

4123. Rink, Oliver A. "The People of New Netherland: Notes on Non-English Immigration to New York in the Seventeenth Century." NYH 62, i.e. New York State Historical Association. Proceedings 79 (1981), 5-42.

4124. Risch, Erna. "Immigrant Aid Societies Before 1820." PMHB 60 (January, 1936), 15-33.

4125. Robinson, W. Stitt, Jr. "Indian Education and Missions in Colonial Virginia." JSouH 18 (May, 1952), 152-168.

4126. Rosenberry, Lois (Kimball) Mathews. The Expansion of New England; the Spread of New England Settlement and Institutions to the Mississippi River, 1620-1865. (Boston, Houghton Mifflin, 1909)

4127.   Rothermund, Dietmar.   "The German Problem of Colonial Pennsylvania." PMHB 84 (January, 1960), 3-21.

4128.   Rutman, Darrett B. and Anita H. Rutman.   "'More True and Perfect Lists': the Reconstruction of Censuses for Middlesex County, Virginia, 1668-1704." VMHB 88 (January, 1980), 37-74.

4129.   Ryan, Dennis P.   "Landholding Opportunity, and Mobility in Revolutionary New Jersey." WMQ 36 (October, 1979), 571-592.

4130.   Sandler, Philip.   "Earliest Jewish Settlers in New York." NYH 36, i.e. New York State Historical Association. Proceedings 53 (1955), 39-50.

4131.   Scofield, Edna.   "The Origin of Settlement Patterns in Rural New England." GR 28 (October, 1938), 652-663.

4132.   Simler, Lucy. "The Township: the Community of the Rural Pennsylvania." PMHB 106 (January, 1982), 41-68.

4133.   Smith, Abbot Emerson.   Colonists in Bondage: White Servitude and Convict Labor in America, 1607-1776. (Chapel Hill, University of North Carolina Press, 1947)

4134.   Smith, Billy G.   "Death and Life in a Colonial Immigrant City: a Demographic Analysis of Philadelphia." JEH 37 (December, 1977), 863-889.

4135.   Smith, Daniel Scott.   "The Demographic History of Colonial New England." JEH 32 (March, 1972), 165-183.

4136.   Smith, Daniel Scott. Population, Family, and Society in Hingham, Massachustees, 1635-1880. (Unpublished Ph.D. Dissertation, Berkeley, University of California, 1973)

4137.   Starr, J. Barton.   "Campbell Town: French Huguenots in British West Florida." FHQ 54 (April, 1976), 532-547.

4138.   Stilgoe, John R.   Common Landscapes of America, 1580 to 1845. (New Haven, Yale University Press, 1982)

4139.   Stillwell,   Lewis.   "Migration   from   Vermont (1776-1860)." Proceedings of the Vermont Historical Society 5 (1937), 63-246.

4140.   Stout, Harry S.   "The Morphology of Remigration: New England University Men and their Return to England, 1640-1660." JAS 10 (August, 1976), 151-172.

4141.   Stout, Harry S.   "University Men in New England, 1620-1660: a Demographic Analysis."   JIH 4 (Winter, 1974), 375-400.

4142.   Strauss, Felix F.   "A Brief Survey of Protestantism in Archepiscopal Salzburg and the Emigraton of 1732." GHQ 43 (March, 1959), 28-59.

4143.   Swedlund, Alan C.   "Population Growth and Settlement Pattern in Franklin and Hampshire Counties, Massachusetts, 1650-1850." American Antiquity 40 (1975), 22-33.

4144.   Trewartha, Glenn T.   "Types of Rural Settlement in Colonial America." GR 36 (October, 1946), 568-596.

4145.   Tully,   Alan.   "Englishmen   and   Germans: National-Group Contact in Colonial Pennslyvania, 1700-1755." PH 45 (July, 1978), 237-256.

4146.   Vaughan, Alden T.   "Blacks in Virginia: a Note on the First Decade." WMQ 29 (July, 1972), 469-478.

4147.   Vaughan, Alden T.   "'Expulsion of the Salvages': English Policy and the Virginia Massacre of 1622." WMQ 35 (January, 1978), 57-84.

4148.   Villaflor, Georgia C. and Kenneth L. Sokoloff. "Migration in Colonial America: Evidence from the Militia Muster Rolls." SSH 6 (Fall, 1982), 539-570.

4149. VonHippel, Wolfgang. "Emigration from Wurtemberg in the 18th and 19th Centuries."   Immigration History Newsletter 13 (May, 1981), 8-11.

4150.   Wacker, Peter O.   Land and People: a Cultural Geography of Preindustrial New Jersey Origins and

Settlement   Patterns.   (New   Brunswick,   N.J.,   Rutgers
University Press, 1975)

4151.   Wagman, Morton.   "The Rise of Pieter Classen
Wyckoff: Social Mobility on the Colonial Frontier." NYH
53, i.e. New York State Historical Association. Proceedings
70 (1972), 5-24.

4152.   Walne, Peter.   "Emigrants from Hertfordshire
1630-1640: Some Correction and Additions." NEHGR 132
(January, 1978), np.

4153.   Walsh, Lorena S.   "The Historian as Census Taker:
Individual Reconstitution and the Reconstruction of Censuses
for a Colonial Chesapeake County." WMQ 38 (April, 1981),
242-260.

4154.   Waterhouse, Richard.   "Reluctant Emigrants: the
English Background of the First Generation of the New
England Puritan Clergy." Historical Magazine of the
Protestant Episcopal Church 44 (December, 1975), 473-488.

4155.   Waters, John J.   The Otis Family in Provincial and
Revolutionary Massachusetts.   (Chapel Hill, University of
North Carolina Press, 1968)

4156.   Waters, John J.   "Patrimony, Succession, and Social
Stability: Guilford, Connecticut, in the Eighteenth Century."
PAH 10 (1976), 129-160.

4157.   Wax, Darold D.   "Black Immigrants: the Slave Trade
in Colonial Maryland." MHM 73 (Spring, 1978), 30-45.

4158.   Wax, Darold D.   "Negro Import Duties in Colonial
Pennsylvania." PMHB 97 (January, 1973), 22-44.

4159.   Wax, Darold D.   "Negro Import Duties in Colonial
Virginia: a Study of British Commercial Policy and Local
Public Policy." VMHB 79 (January, 1971), 29-44.

4160.   Wax, Darold D.   "'A People of Beastly Living':
Europe, Africa, and the Atlantic Slave Trade." Phylon 41
(March, 1980), 12-24.

4161. White, Donald W. "Census Making and Local History: in Quest of the People of a Revolutionary Village." Prologue 14 (Fall, 1982), 157-168.

4162. White, Philip L. Beekmantown, New York: Forest Frontier to Farm Community. (Austin, University of Texas Press, 1979)

4163. Williams, Linda K. "East Florida as a Loyalist Haven." FHQ 54 (April, 1976), 465-478.

4164. Wittke, Carl Frederick. We Who Built America: the Saga of the Immigrant. New York, Prentice-Hall, 1939)

4165. Wokeck, Marianne. "The Flow and the Composition of German Immigration to Philadelphia, 1727-1775." PMHB 105 (July, 1981), 249-278.

4166. Wolf, Jacquelyn H. "Patents and Tithables in Proprietary North Carolina, 1663-1729." NCHR 56 (July, 1979), 263-277.

4167. Wolf, Stephanie Grauman. Urban Village: Population, Community, and Family Structure in Germantown, Pennsylvania, 1693-1800. (Princeton, New Jersey, Princeton University Press, 1976)

4168. Wood, Peter H. Black Majority: Negroes in Colonial South Carolina from 1670 through the Stono Rebellion. (New York, Knopf, 1974)

4169. Woodmason, Charles. The Carolina Backcountry on the Eve of the Revolution; the Journal and other Writings of Charles Woodmason, Anglican Itinerant.   (Chapel Hill, University of North Carolina Press, 1953)

4170. Wright, J. Leitch, Jr. "Blacks in British East Florida." FHQ 54 (April, 1976), 425-442.

4171. Wright, Langdon G. "In Search of Peace and Harmony: New York Communities in the Seventeenth Century." NYH 61, i.e. New York State Historical Association. Proceedings 78 (Jan., 1980), 5-21.

4172. Wright, Martin. "The Antecedents of the Double-Pen House Type." AAG 48 (June, 1958), 109-117.

4173. Wurst, Klaus G. "German Mystics and Sabbatarians in Virginia, 1700-1764." VMHB 72 (July, 1964), 330-347.

4174. Zuckerman, Michael. Peaceable Kingdoms: New England Towns in the Eighteenth Century. (New York, Knopf, 1970)

Migration and Settlement: French and Spanish Colonies

The materials included here serve to remind us that some early French and Spanish settlements eventually became part of the United States. The titles indicate whether the focus is on Florida (St. Augustine), Louisiana, or the southwest (Texas, New Mexico, and Arizona). See the works by Charbonneau and Henripin for comparisons with Quebec; there are no comparable studies cited for the heart of the Spanish empire. Spanish penetration of California began in 1769, but that story is mostly nineteenth century, and so nothing is cited here. The work by Voorhies deserves mention as an extraordinary collection of by-and-large unexploited sources.

4200. Allain, Mathe. "L'Immigration Francaise en Louisiane, 1718-1721." RAF 28 (March, 1975), 555-564.

4201. Archibald, Robert. "Acculturation and Assimilation in Colonial New Mexico." NMHR 53 (July, 1978), 205-217.

4202. Archibald, Robert. "Canon de Carnue: Settlement of a Grant." NMHR 51 (October, 1976), 313-328.

4203. Bannon, John Francis. "The Spaniards and the Illinois Country, 1762-1800." ISHSJ 69 (May, 1976), 110-118.

4204. Charbonneau, Hubert. Vie et Mort de nos Ancetres: Etude Demographique. (Montreal, Universite de Montreal, 1975)

4205. Coker, William S. "Religious Censuses of Pensacola, 1796-1801." FHQ 61 (July, 1982), 54-63.

4206.   Conrad, Glenn R.   "L'Immigration Alsacienne en Louisiane, 1753-1759." RAF 28 (March, 1975), 565-577.

4207.   Corbett, Theodore G.   "Migration to a Spanish Imperial Frontier in the Seventeenth and Eighteenth Centuries: St. Augustine." Hispanic American Historical Review 54 (August, 1974), 414-430.

4208.   Corbett, Theodore G.   "Population Structure in Hispanic St. Augustine, 1629-1763." FHQ 54 (January, 1976), 263-284.

4209.   Crouch, Dora P., Daniel J. Garr and Axel I. Mundigo. Spanish City Planning in North America.   (Cambridge, Massachusetts, MIT Press, 1982)

4210.   Cutter, Donald C., trans.   "An Anonymous Statistical Report on New Mexico in 1765." NMHR 50 (October, 1975), 347-352.

4211.   Dart, Albert Laplace.   "Ship Lists of Passangers Leaving France for Louisiana, 1718-1724." LHQ 14 (1931), 516-520; 15 (1932), 68-77, 453-467; 21 (1938), 963-978.

4212.   Din, Gilbert C.   "Francisco Bouligny's 1778 Plans for Settlement in Louisiana." SouS 16 (Summer, 1977), 211-224.

4213.   Din, Gilbert C.   "Proposals and Plans for Colonization in Spanish Louisiana." LH 11 (Summer, 1970), 197-219.

4214.   Din, Gilbert C.   "Spain's Immigration Policy in Louisiana and the American Penetration, 1792-1803." SWHQ 76 (1973), 255-276.

4215.   Ditchy, Jay K.   "Early Census Tables of Louisiana." LHQ 13 (April, 1930), 205-229.

4216.   Dobyns, Henry F.   Spanish Colonial Tucson: a Demographic History. (Tucson, University of Arizona Press, 1976)

4217.   Dunkle, John Robert.   "Population Change as an Element in the Historical Geography of St. Augustine." FHQ 37 (July, 1958), 3-32.

4218. Engstrand, Iris Wilson. "Land Grant Problems in the Southwest: the Spanish and Mexican Heritage." NMHR 53 (October, 1978), 317-336.

4219. Everett, Donald E. "Free Persons of Color in Colonial Louisiana." LH 7 (Winter, 1966), 21-50.

4220. Garr, Daniel J. "A Rare and Desolate Land: Population and Race in Hispanic California." WestHQ 6 (April, 1975), 133-148.

4221. Gentilcore, Rocco Louis. "Vincennes and French Settlement in the Old Northwest." AAG 47 (September, 1957), 285-297.

4222. Gerlach, Russel L. Immigrants in the Ozarks: a Study in Ethnic Geography. (Columbia, University of Missouri Press, 1976)

4223. Gold, Robert L. "The Settlement of the East Florida Spaniards in Cuba, 1763-1766." FHQ 42 (January, 1964), 216-231.

4224. Hardy, James D., Jr. "The Transportation of Convicts to Colonial Louisiana." LH 7 (Summer, 1966), 207-220.

4225. Henripin, Jacques. La Population Canadienne au debut du XVIIIᵉ Siecle; Nuptualite, Fecondite, Mortalite Infantile. (Paris, Presses Universitaires de France, 1954)

4226. Henripin, Jacques and Yves Peron. "The Demographic Transition of the Province of Quebec." In David Victor Glass and Roger Revelle, eds. Population and Social Change. (New York, Crane, Russak, 1972), 213-231.

4227. Holmes, Jack D. L. "Alabama's Forgotten Settler: Notes on the Spanish Mobile District, 1780-1813." AHQ 33 (Summer, 1971), 87-97.

4228. Holmes, Jack D. L. "A New Look at Spanish Louisiana Census Accounts: the Recent Historiography of Antonio Acosta." LH 21 (Winter, 1980), 77-86.

4229. Igartua, Jose E. "Le Comportement Demographique des Marchands do Montreal vers 1760." RAF 33 (December, 1979), 427-445.

4230. John, Elizabeth Ann Harper. Storms Brewed in Other Men's Worlds: the Confrontation of Indians, Spanish, and French in the Southwest, 1540-1795. (College Station, Texas A&M University Press, 1975)

4231. Johnson, C. "Missouri-French Houses: some Relict Features of Early Settlement." PA 6 (July, 1974), 1-11.

4232. Jones, Oakah L., Jr. Los Paisanos: Spanish Settlers on the Northern Frontier. (Norman, University of Oklahoma Press, 1979)

4233. Kondert, Reinhart. "Germans in Louisiana: the Colonial Experience, 1720-1803." Yearbook of German-American Studies 16 (1981), 59-66.

4234. Kondert, Reinhart. "Les Allemands in Louisiane de 1721 a 1732." RAF 33 (June, 1979), 51-65.

4235. Lemieux, Donald J. "The Mississippi Valley, New France, and French Colonial Policy." SouS 17 (Spring, 1978), 39-56.

4236. Lockey, Joseph B., ed. "The St. Augustine Census of 1786; Translated from the Spanish with an Introduction and Notes." FHQ 18 (1939), 11-31.

4237. Maduell, Charles R., Jr. The Census Tables for the French Colony of Louisiana from 1699 through 1732. (Baltimore, Genealogical Pub. Co., 1972)

4238. Matter, Robert Allen. "Mission Life in Seventeenth-Century Florida." CHR 67 (July, 1981), 401-420.

4239. Mattison, Ray H. "Early Spanish and Mexican Settlements in Arizona." NMHR 21 (1946), 273-327.

4240. Nasatir, Abraham P. Borderland in Retreat: from Spanish Louisiana to the Far Southwest. (Albuquerque, University of New Mexico Press, 1976)

4241.   Rey, Agipeto.   "Missionary Aspects of the Founding of New Mexico." NMHR 23 (January, 1948), 22-31.

4242.   Simmons, Marc.   "Settlement Patterns and Village Plans in Colonial New Mexico." JW 8 (January, 1969), 7-20.

4243.   Strout, Clevy Lloyd.   "The Resettlement of Santa Fe, 1695: the Newly Found Muster Roll." NMHR 53 (July, 1978), 261-270.

4244.   Timmons, W.H.   "The Population of the El Paso Area-a Census of 1784." NMHR 52 (October, 1977), 311-316.

4245.   Tjarks, Alicia V.   "Comparative Demographic Analysis of Texas, 1777-1793." SWHQ 77 (January, 1974), 291-338.

4246.   Tjarks, Alicia V.   "Demographic, Ethnic and Occupational Strucure of New Mexico, 1790."   Americas 35 (July, 1978), 45-88.

4247.   Trewartha, Glenn T.   "French Settlement in the Driftless Hill Land." AAG 28 (1938), 179-200.

4248.   Usner, Daniel H., Jr.   "From African Captivity to American Slavery: the Introduction of Black Laborers to Colonial Louisiana." LH 20 (Winter, 1979), 25-48.

4249.   Viles, Jonas.   "Population and Extent of Settlement in Missouri Before 1804." MoHR 5 (July, 1911), 189-213.

4250.   Voorhies, Jacqueline K., trans.   "The Attakapas Post: the First Acadian Settlement." LH 17 (Winter, 1976), 91-96.

4251.   Voorhies, Jacqueline K., comp. Some Late Eighteenth Century   Louisianians: Census   Records,   1758-1796. (Lafayette, Louisiana, University of Southwestern Louisiana, 1973)

4252.   Wedel, Mildred Mott.   "The Benard de la Harpe Historiography on French Colonial Louisiana."   LS 13 (Spring, 1974), 9-67.

Migration and Settlement: Indians

Most of the works here discuss the migrations of Indians who lived beyond white control.   Sometimes, however, migration was influenced by contact with whites.   No one study provides a sense of the complex patterns that resulted as different groups of Indians and Europeans interacted with each other in different environments.   Meinig provides some interesting analytical perspectives in a study that goes well beyond 1800.

4300. Amsden, Charles. "Navaho Origins." NMHR 7 (1932), 193-209.

4301.   Campbell, Paul R. and Glenn W. La Fantasie. "Scattered to the Winds of Heaven--Narragansett Indians 1676-1880." RIH 37 (August, 1978), 66-83.

4302.   Clifton, James A.   The Prairie People: Continuity and Change in Potawatomi Indian Culture, 1665-1965. (Lawrence, Regents Press of Kansas, 1977)

4303.   Covington, James W.   "Migration of the Seminoles into Florida, 1700-1820." FHQ 46 (April, 1968), 340-357.

4304. Day, Gordon M. "The Indian as an Ecological Factor in the Northeastern Forest."   Ecology 34 (April, 1953), 329-346.

4305.   Forbes, Jack D.   "The Early Western Apache, 1300-1700." JW 5 (July, 1966), 336-354.

4306. Goodwin, Gary C. Cherokees in Transition: a Study of Changing Culture and Environment Prior to 1775. (Chicago, University of Chicago, Department of Geography, 1977)

4307.   Hudson, Charles.   The Southeastern Indians. (Knoxville, University of Tennessee Press, 1976)

4308. Kinnaird, Lawrence and Lucia B. Kinnaird. "Choctaws West of the Mississippi, 1766-1800." SWHQ 83 (April, 1980), 349-370.

4309.   Kupperman, Karen Ordahl.   Settling with the Indians: the Meeting of English and Indian Cultures in America, 1580-1640.   (Totowa, New Jersey, Rowman and Littlefield, 1980)

4310.   McIntire, Elliot G.   "Changing Patterns of Hopi Indian Settlement."   AAG 61 (September, 1971), 510-521.

4311.   Meinig, Donald W.   Southwest: Three Peoples in Geographical Change, 1600-1970.   (New York, Oxford University Press, 1971)

4312.   Merrell, James H.   "Cultural Continuity among the Piscataway Indians of Colonial Maryland."   WMQ 36 (October, 1979), 548-570.

4313.   Moodie, D.W. and Barry Kaye.   "The Northern Limit of Indian Agriculture in North America."   GR 59 (October, 1969), 513-529.

4314.   Porter, Frank W., III.   "A Century of Accommodation: the Nanticoke Indians in Colonial Maryland."   MHM 74 (June, 1979), 175-192.

4315.   Ronda, James P.   "'We Are Well as We Are':   an Indian Critique of Seventeenth-Century Christian Missions." WMQ 34 (January, 1977), 66-82.

4316.   Rostlund, Erhard.   "The Geographic Range of the Historic Bison in the   Southeast."   AAG 50 (December, 1960), 395-407.

4317.   Rostlund, Erhard.   "The Myth of a Natural Prairie Belt in Alabama: an Interpretation of Historical Record." AAG 47 (December, 1957), 392-411.

4318.   Russell, Howard S.   Indian New England before the Mayflower.   (Hanover, New Hampshire, University Press of New England, 1980)

4319.   Salmon, Roberto Mario.   "Frontier Warfare in the Hispanic Southwest: Tarahumara Resistance, 1649-1780." MA 58 (October, 1976), 175-185.

4320. Schroeder, Albert H. "Shifting for Survival in the Spanish Southwest." NMHR 43 (October, 1968), 291-310.

4321. Sheehan, Bernard W. Savagism and Civility: Indians and Englishmen in Colonial Virginia. (Cambridge, England, Cambridge University Press, 1980)

4322. Simmons, William S. "Conversion from Indian to Puritan." NEQ 52 (June, 1979), 197-218.

4323. Simmons, William S. "Cultural Bias in the New England Puritans' Perception of Indians." WMQ 38 (January, 1981), 56-72.

4324. Stewart, Omer C. "Ute Indians: before and after White Contact." UHQ 34 (Winter, 1966), 38-61.

4325. Vaughan, Alden T. "From White Man to Redskin: Changing Anglo-American Perception of the American Indian." AHR 87 (October, 1982), 917-953.

4326. Vaughan, Alden T. and Daniel K. Richter. "Crossing the Cultural Divide: Indians and New Englanders, 1605-1763." AASP 90 (April 16, 1980), 23-99.

4327. Waselkov, Gregory. "Prehistoric Agriculture in the Central Mississippi Valley." AgH 51 (July, 1977), 513-519.

4328. White, Richard. "The Winning of the West: the Expansion of the Western Sioux in the Eighteenth and Nineteenth Centuries." JAH 65 (September, 1978), 319-343.

Urbanization

Although cities were neither numerous nor large in early America, several places did emerge as centers of empire. In addition, the colonial towns anticipated the processes of urbanization that became much more important after 1820. Bridenbaugh's two books are full of information, but are conceptually dated. Reps' works contain an abundance of visual materials in terms of maps and drawings. Ernst and Merrows, and Rainbolt consider the absence of cities in the South. Daniels, Kross, and Rutman could have been included in the first section of this chapter, but have important things to say about the process and meaning of urbanization.

4350. Archer, John. "Puritan Town Planning in New Haven." Society of Architectural Historians. Journal 34 (May, 1975), 140-149.

4351. Bridenbaugh, Carl. Cities in Revolt: Urban Life in America, 1743-1776. (New York, Knopf, 1955)

4352. Bridenbaugh, Carl. Cities in the Wilderness: the First Century of Urban Life in America, 1625-1742. (New York, Ronald Press Company, 1938)

4353. Daniels, Bruce C. The Connecticut Town: Growth and Development, 1635-1790. (Middletown, Connecticut, Wesleyan University Press, 1979)

4354. Daniels, Bruce C. "Emerging Urbanism and Increasing Social Stratification in the Era of the American Revolution." West Georgia College Studies in the Social Sciences 15 (June, 1976), 15-30.

4355. Dill, Alonzo T., Jr. "Eighteenth-Century New Bern; a History of the Town and Craven County, 1700-1800." NCHR 22 (January, 1945), 1-21; (April, 1945), 152-175; (July, 1945), 293-319; (October, 1945), 460-489; 23 (January, 1946), 47-78; (April, 1946), 142-171; (July, 1946), 325-359; (October, 1946), 405-535.

4356. Ernst, Joseph A. and H. Roy Merrens. "'Camden's Turrets Pierce the Skies!': the Urban Process in the Southern Colonies During the Eighteenth Century." WMQ 30 (October, 1973), 549-574.

4357. Fries, Sylvia Doughty. The Urban Idea in Colonial America. (Philadelphia, Temple University Press, 1977)

4358. Kross, Jessica. The Evolution of an American Town: Newton, New York, 1642-1775. (Philadelphia, Temple University Press, 1983)

4359. MacLear, Anne Bush. Early New England Towns; a Comparative Study of their Development. (New York, Columbia University, 1908)

4360.   Maier, Pauline.   "Boston and New York in the Eighteenth Century." AASP 91 (October 21, 1981), 177-195.

4361. Price, Jacob M. "Economic Function and the Growth of American Port Towns in the Eighteenth Century." PAH 8 (1974), 121-186.

4362.   Rainbolt, John C.   "The Absence of Towns of Seventeenth-Century Virginia." JSouH 35 (August, 1969), 343-360.

4363. Reps, John W. Cities of the American West: a History of Frontier Urban Planning. (Princeton, New Jersey, Princeton University Press, 1979)

4364. Reps, John W. Tidewater Towns: City Planning in Colonial Virginia and Maryland. (Williamsburg, Virginia, Colonial Williamsburg Foundation, 1972)

4365. Reps. John W. Town Planning in Frontier America. (Princeton, New Jersey, Princeton University Press, 1969)

4366. Rosenwaike, Ira. "The Jews of Baltimore to 1810." AJHQ 64 (June, 1975), 291-320.

4367. Rutman, Darrett Bruce. "People in Process: the New Hampshire Towns of the Eighteenth Century." In Tamara K. Hareven, ed. Family and Kin in Urban Communities. (New York, New Viewpoints, 1977), 16-37.

4368.   Rutman, Darrett Bruce.   Winthrop's Boston: a Portrait of a Puritan Town, 1630-1649. (Chapel Hill, University of North Carolina Press, 1965)

4369.   Wood, Jerome H., Jr.   Conestoga Crossroads: Lancaster, Pennsylvania, 1730-1790.   (Harrisburg, Pennsylvania Historical and Museum Commission, 1979)

The Nineteenth Century

Materials on migration in the nineteenth century make up the largest single part of the whole bibliography. In fact, they exceed any other whole chapter. Three major types of migration have been used here to subdivide the works into more manageable units. Studies of inter-national migration are listed first, followed by works on internal migration, with the exception of those focusing on urbanization, which make up the third group. Readers should keep in mind that many Americans experienced all three types of movement during their lifetimes, or even in one move. Remember that Chapter Six contains additional material on the consequences of migration.

International Migration

Materials included here obviously touch on migrants who crossed national boundries. Most studies involve people arriving directly from Europe, though there are a handful of works that consider people who arrived from other countries in the New World. There are also a significant number of works on Asian immigrants, especially the Chinese. Emigration out of the United States receives separate attention.

Immigration and settlement

It is evident from the titles below that most of the studies on immigration concentrate on one group or one place, or even one group in one place. Scholars should be able easily to pick out what interests them, though all should keep in mind the extraordinary variety of patterns and experiences that resulted as different groups combined under circumstances altered by time and place. There was no single immigrant experience, nor were all communities affected equally. Several works provide good places to start for those approaching the subject for the first time. Taylor's text combined with Maldwyn Jones' work cited in the section on the English colonies provide excellent overviews and additional bibliography. Hansen's and Wittke's works, also cited earlier, are earlier syntheses that are still worth reading. Handlin's two quite different studies have had a major influence on a whole generation of scholars. The encyclopedia edited by Thernstrom, Orlov, and Handlin is an excellent source of information, but, understandably, lacks any systematic interpretation. Higham's book on nativism is a comprehensive account of the origins of immigration restriction that mark the years around 1920 as a major turning point in American history. Thistlewaite reminds us to view nineteenth-century American history from an international perspective. The works by Hvidt and Shepperson represent opposite ends of a spectrum of studies that start with quantitative materials and end up in literary sources. Chickering is not essential, but it is the first major study of what obviously became a very important topic.

4500. Alexander, June Granatir. "City Directories as 'Ideal' Censuses: Slovak Immigrants and Pittsburgh's Early Twentieth-Century Directories as a Test Case." WPHM 65 (July, 1982), 203-220.

4501. Alexander, June Granatir. "Staying Together: Chain Migration and Patterns of Slovak Settlement in Pittsburgh Prior to World War I." JAEH 1 (Fall, 1981), 56-83.

4502. Alexis, Gerhard T. "Sweden to Minnesota: Vilhelm Moberg's Fictional Reconstruction." AQ 18 (Spring, 1966), 81-94.

4503. Ander, O. Fritiof. "The Immigrant Church and the Patrons of Husbandry." AgH 8 (1934), 155-168.

4504. Andersen, Arlow W. The Norwegian-Americans. (Boston, Twayne, 1975)

4505. Appel, John J. "American Negro and Immigrant Experience: Similarities and Differences." AQ 18 (Spring, 1966), 95-103.

4506. Appel, John J. "Marion Dexter Learned and the German American Historical Society." PMHB 86 (1962), 287-318.

4507. Archdeacon, Thomas J. Becoming American: an Ethnic History. (New York, Free Press, 1983)

4508.   Bailey, Kenneth R.   "A Judicious Mixture: Negroes and Immigrants in the West Virginia Mines, 1880-1917." WVH 34 (January, 1973), 141-161.

4509.   Baily, Samuel L.   "The Italians and Organized Labor in the United States and Argentina: 1880-1910."   IMR 1 (Summer, 1966-1967), 56-66.

4510.   Barth, Gunther Paul.   "Chinese Sojourners in the West: the Coming." SCQ 46 (March, 1964), 55-68.

4511.   Barton, H. Arnold, ed.   Letters from the Promised Land: Swedes in America, 1840-1914.   (Minneapolis, University of Minnesota Press, 1975)

4512.   Barton, H. Arnold.   The Search for Ancestors: a Swedish-American Family Saga.   (Carbondale, Southern Illinois University Press, 1979)

4513.   Barton, Josef J.   Peasants and Strangers: Italians, Rumanians, and Slovaks in an American City, 1890-1950. (Cambridge, Massachusetts, Harvard University Press, 1975)

4514.   Baxter, Maurice G.   "Encouragement of Immigration to the Middle West During the Era of the Civil War." IMH 46 (1950), 25-38.

4515.   Belissary, C.G.   "Tennessee and   Immigration, 1865-1880." THQ 22 (September, 1948), 229-248.

4516.   Belk, Fred R.   "The Final Refuge: Kansas and Nebraska Migration of Mennonites from Central Asia after 1884." KHQ 40 (Autumn, 1974), 379-392.

4517.   Belk, Fred R.   "Migration of Russian Mennonites." Social Science 50 (Winter, 1975), 17-21.

4518.   Berger, Max.   "The Irish Emigrant and American Nativism as Seen by British Visitors, 1836-1860." PMHB 70 (April, 1946), 146-160.

4519.   Berlin, William S.   On the Edge of Politics: the Roots of Jewish Political Thought in America.   (Westport, Connecticut, Greenwood Press, 1978)

4520. Bernstein, Seth. "The Economic Life of the Jews in San Francisco during the 1860's as Reflected in the City Directories." AJA 27 (April, 1975), 70-77.

4521. Berthoff, Rowland T. British Immigrants in Industrial America, 1790-1950. (Cambridge, Massachusetts, Harvard University Press, 1953)

4522. Bjorklund, Elaine M. "Ideology and Culture Exemplified in Southwestern Michigan." AAG 54 (June, 1964), 227-241.

4523. Blackburn, George M. and Sherman L. Ricards. "The Chinese of Virginia City, Nevada: 1870." AJ 7 (1980), 51-71.

4524. Blegen, Theodore C. "The Competition of the Northwestern States for Immigrants." WMH 3 (September, 1919), 3-29.

4525. Blow, David J. The Establishment and Erosion of French-Canadian Culture in Winooski, Vermont, 1867-1900." VH 43 (Winter, 1975), 59-74.

4526. Bodnar, John E. Immigration and Industrialization: Ethnicity in an American Mill Town, 1870-1940. (Pittsburgh, University of Pittsburgh Press, 1977)

4527. Bodnar, John E. "Immigration and Modernization: the Case of Slavic Peasants in Industrial America." JSH 10 (Fall, 1976), 44-71.

4528. Bodnar, John E., Michael Weber, and Roger Simon. "Migration, Kinship, and Urban Adjustment: Blacks and Poles in Pittsburgh, 1900-1930." JAH 66 (December, 1979), 548-565.

4529. Bohme, Frederick, G. "The Portugese in California." CHSQ 35 (September, 1956), 233-252.

4530. Briggs, John W. An Italian Passage: Immigrants to Three American Cities, 1890-1930. (New Haven, Connecticut, Yale University Press, 1978)

4531.   Brister, Louis E.   "The Image of Arkansas in the Early German Emigrant Guidebook: Notes on Immigration." AkHQ 36 (Winter, 1977), 338-345.

4532.   Brodskii, R.M.   "Russkie Immigranty na Gavaiiakh (Russian Immigrants to the Hawaiian Islands)."   Novaia i Noveishaia Istoriia (no.3, 1981), 172-177.   (In Russian with English summary)

4533.   Brown, Kenny L.   "Peaceful Progress: an Account of the Italians of Krebs, Oklahoma."   CO 53 (Fall, 1975), 332-352.

4534.   Brown, Arthur J.   "The Promotion of Emigration to Washington, 1854-1909."   PNQ 36 (1945), 3-17.

4535.   Buckley, Frank.   "Thoreau and the Irish."   NEQ 13 (September, 1940), 389-400.

4536.   Burchell, Robert A.   "British Immigrants in Southern California, 1850-1870."   SCQ (Winter, 1971), 283-302.

4537.   Burchell, Robert A.   "The Gathering of a Community: the British-Born of San Francisco in 1852 and 1872."   JAS 10 (December, 1976), 279-312.

4538.   Burchell, Robert A.   The San Francisco Irish, 1848-1880.   (Berkeley, University of California Press, 1980)

4539.   Caldwell, Dan.   "The Negroization of the Chinese Sterotype in California."   SCQ 53 (Summer, 1971), 123-131.

4540.   Cardoso, Lawrence A.   Mexican Emigration to the United States, 1897-1931:   Socio-Economic Patterns. (Tuscon, University of Arizona Press, 1980)

4541.   Chickering, Jesse.   Immigration into the United States.   (Boston, Charles C. Little and James Brown, 1848)

4542.   Clark, Dennis.   The Irish in Philadelphia; Ten Generations of Urban Experience.   (Philadelphia, Temple University Press, 1973)

4543.   Clark, Dennis.   The Irish Relations: Trials of an Immigrant Tradition.   (Rutherford, New Jersey, Fairleigh Dickinson University Press, 1982)

4544.   Corbett, P. Scott and Nancy Parker Corbett.   "The Chinese in Oregon, c. 1870-1880."   OHQ 78 (March, 1977), 73-85.

4545.   Corwin, Arthur F., ed.   Immigrants--and Immigrants: Perspectives on Mexican Labor Migration to the United States. (Westport, Connecticut, Greenwood Press, 1978)
4546.   Cozzens, Arthur B.   "Conservation in German Settlements of the Missouri Ozarks."   GR 33 (April, 1943), 286-298.

4547.   Crockett, Norman L.   "A Study of Confusion: Missouri's Immigration Program, 1865-1916."   MoHR 57 (April, 1963), 248-260.

4548.   Curti, Merle Eugene and Kendall Birr.   "The Immigrant and the American Image in Europe, 1860-1914." MVHR 37 (September, 1950), 203-230.

4549.   Dahlie, Jorgen.   "Old World Paths in the New: Scandinavians Find Familiar Homes in Washington."   PNQ 61 (April, 1970), 65-71.

4550.   Daniels, Roger.   "Westerners from the East: Oriental Immigrants Reappraised."   PHR 35 (November, 1966), 373-384.

4551.   Danielson, Michael N.   The Politics of Exclusion. (New York, Columbia University Press, 1976)

4552.   Daskarolis, George P.   "San Francisco's Greek Colony: Evolution of an Ethnic Community, 1890-1945." California History 60 (Summer, 1981), 114-133.

4553.   Davis, Darrell H.   "The Finland Community, Minnesota."   GR 25 (July, 1935), 382-394.

4554.   DeJong, Gerald F.   "The Coming of the Dutch to the Dakotas."   SDH 5 (Winter, 1974), 20-51.

4555.   DeJong, Gerald F.   "Dutch Immigrants in New Jersey before World War I."   NJH 94 (Summer-Autumn, 1976), 69-88.

4556. DeMarco, William M. Ethnics and Enclaves: Boston's Italian North End. (Ann Arbor, Michagan, UMI Research, 1981)

4557. Dew, Lee A. "The J.L.C. & E.R.R. and the Opening of the 'Sunk Lands' of Northeast Arkansas." AKHQ 27 (Spring, 1968), 22-39.

4558. Dickinson, Joan Younger. "Aspects of Italian Immigration to Philadelphia." PMHB 90 (October, 1966), 445-465.

4559. Dobbert, G.A. "German-Americans Between Old and New Fatherland, 1870-1914." AQ 19 (Winter, 1967), 663-680.

4560. Dolan, Jay P. The Immigrant Church: New York's Irish and German Catholics, 1815-1865. (Baltimore, Johns Hopkins University Press, 1975)

4561. Dore, Grazia. "Some Social and Historical Aspects of Italian Emigration to America." JSH 2 (Winter, 1968), 95-122.

4562. DuFour, Clarence John. "The Russian Withdrawal from California." CHSQ 12 (September, 1933), 240-276.

4563. Dumke, Glenn S. "The Real Estate Boom of 1887 in Southern California." PHR 11 (December, 1942), 425-438.

4564. Dunlevy, James A. and Henry A. Gemery. "Economic Opportunity and the Responses of 'Old' and 'New' Migrants to the United States." JEH 38 (December, 1978), 901-917.

4565. Early, Frances H. "Mobility Potential and the Quality of Life in Working-Class Lowell, Massachusetts: the French Canadians ca. 1870." Labour/Le Travailleur 2 (1977), 214-228.

4566. Ehrlich, Richard L., ed. Immigrants in Industrial America, 1850-1920. (Charlottesville, University Press of Virginia, 1977)

4567. Eliopoulos, George T. "Greek Immigrants in Springfield, 1884-1944." HJWM 5 (Spring, 1977), 46-56.

4568. Ellis, David Maldwyn. "The Assimilation of the Welsh in Central New York." NYH 53, i.e. New York State Historical Association. Proceedings 70 (July, 1972), 299-333.

4569. Elson, Ruth Miller. Guardians of Tradition: American Schoolbooks of the Nineteenth Century. (Lincoln, University of Nebraska Press, 1964)

4570. Eltis, D. "The British Contribution to the Nineteenth-Century Transatlantic Slave Trade." EcHR 32 (May, 1979), 211-227.

4571. Engen, Arnfinn. "Emigration from Dovre, 1865-1914." Norwegian-American Studies 29 (1983), 210-252.

4572. Ernst, Robert. Immigrant Life in New York City, 1825-1863. (Port Washington, N.Y., I.J. Friedman, 1965, c1949)

4573. Essig, E.O. "The Russian Settlement at Ross." CHSQ 12 (1933), 191-209.

4574. Feingold, Henry L. Zion in America: the Jewish Experience from Colonial Times to the Present. (New York, Twayne, 1974)

4575. Feldstein, Stanley. The Land that I Show You: Three Centuries of Jewish Life in America. (Garden City, New York, Anchor/Doubleday, 1978)

4576. Fisher, Marvin. "The 'Garden' and the 'Workshop': Some European Conceptions and Preconceptions of America, 1830-1860." NEQ 34 (September, 1961), 311-327.

4577. Fite, Gilbert Courtland. "Daydreams and Nightmares: the Late Nineteenth-Century Agricultural Frontier." AgH 40 (October, 1966), 285-294.

4578. Fleming, Donald Harnish and Bernard Bailyn, eds. Dislocation and Emigration: the Social Background of American Immigration. Special issue of PAH 7 (1973).

4579. Flom, George T. "The Scandinavian Factor in the American Population." IJHP 3 (January, 1905), 57-91.

4580.   Fogarty,   Robert   S.   The   Righteous   Remnant: the
House of David.   (Kent, Ohio, Kent State University Press,
1981)

4581.   Fong,   Lawrence   Michael.   "Sojourners   and   Settlers:
the Chinese Experience in Arizona."   JArH 21 (Autumn,
1980), 227-256.

4582.   Fordyce,   Wellington   G.   "Immigrant   Colonies   in
Cleveland." OAHQ 45 (1936), 320-340.

4583.   Fordyce,   Wellington   G.   "Immigrant   Institutions   in
Cleveland." OAHQ 47 (1938), 87-103.

4584.   Friman,   Axel.   "Swedish   Emigration   to   North   America,
1820-1850." SPHQ 27 (July, 1976), 153-177.

4585.   Futrell,   Robert   Frank.   "Efforts   of   Mississippians   to
Encourage Immigration, 1865-1880."   JMsH 20 (April, 1958),
59-76.

4586.   Gallaway,   Lowell   E.,   Richard   K.   Vedder,   and   Vishwa
Shukla.   "The Distribution of the Immigrant Population in
the United States: an Economic Analysis."   EEH 11 (Spring,
1974), 213-226.

4587.   Garcia,   Mario   T.   Desert   Immigrants: the   Mexicans
of El Paso, 1880-1920.   (New Haven, Yale University Press,
1981)

4588.   Gartner,   Lloyd   P.   History   of   the   Jews   of   Cleveland.
(Cleveland,   Western   Reserve   Historical   Society/Jewish
Theological Seminary of America, 1978)

4589.   Gehrke,   William   H.   "The   Ante-Bellum   Agriculture   of
the Germans in North Carolina."   AgH 9 (1935), 143-160.

4590.   Giovinco,   Joseph.   "Democracy   in   Banking: the   Bank
of Italy and California's Italians."   CHSQ 47 (September,
1968), 195-218.

4591.   Gleason,   Philip.   "The   Melting   Pot: Symbol   of   Fusion
or Confusion?" AQ 16 (Spring, 1964), 20-46.

4592. Goering, Jacob D. and Robert Williams. "Generational Drift on Four Variables among the Swiss-Volhynian Mennonites in Kansas." Mennonite Quarterly Review 50 (October, 1976), 290-297.

4593. Golab, Caroline. Immigrant Destinations. (Philadelphia, Temple University Press, 1977)

4594. Gould, Charles F. "Portland Italians, 1880-1920." OHQ 77 (September, 1976), 238-260.

4595. Greene, Victor. For God and Country: the Rise of Polish and Lithuanian Ethnic Consciousness in America, 1860-1910. (Madison, State Historical Society of Wisconsin, 1975)

4596. Gurock, Jeffrey S. When Harlem Was Jewish, 1870-1930. (New York, Columbia University Press, 1979)

4597. Hale, Douglas. "European Immigrants in Oklahoma: a Survey." CO 53 (Summer, 1975), 179-203.

4598. Halick, Wasyl. "Ukrainian Farmers in the United States." AgH 10 (1936), 25-39.

4599. Hammersmith, Jack L. "West Virginia, the 'Heathen Chinee', and the 'California Conspiracy'." WVH 34 (April, 1973), 291-296.

4600. Handlin, Oscar. Boston's Immigrants, 1790-1880: a Study in Acculturation, rev. ed. (New York, Atheneum, 1969)

4601. Handlin, Oscar. The Uprooted: the Epic Story of the Great Migrations That Made the American People, 2nd ed. (Boston, Little Brown, 1973)

4602. Hansen, Marcus Lee. "Offical Encouragement of Immigration to Iowa." IJHP 19 (April, 1921), 159-195.

4603. Harnsberger, John L. and Robert P. Wilkins. "New Yeovil, Minnesota: a Northern Pacific Colony in 1873." ArW 12 (Spring, 1970), 5-22.

4604. Hedges, James Blaine. "Promotion of Immigration to the Pacific Northwest by the Railroads." MVHR 15 (September, 1928), 183-203.

4605. Heitman, Sidney, ed. Germans from Russia in Colorado. (Fort Collins, Colorado, Western Social Science Association, 1978)

4606. Heizer, Robert Fleming and Alan F. Almquist. The Other Californians: Prejudice and Discrimination under Spain, Mexico, and the United States to 1920. (Berkeley, University of California Press, 1971)

4607. Hendrickson, Gordon Olaf. Peopling the High Plains: Wyoming's European Heritage. (Cheyenne, Wyoming State Archives and Historical Department, 1977)

4608. Hennesey, James. American Catholics: a History of the Roman Catholic Community in the United States. (New York, Oxford University Press, 1981)

4609. Higham, John. "Origins of Immigration Restriction, 1882-1897: a Social Analysis." MVHR 39 (June, 1952), 77-88.

4610. Higham, John. Send These to Me: Jews and Other Immigrants in Urban America. (New York, Atheneum, 1975)

4611. Higham, John. Strangers in the Land: Patterns of American Nativism, 1860-1925, 2nd ed. (New York, Antheneum, 1965)

4612. Hoerder, Dick, ed. American Labor and Immigration History, 1877-1920's: Recent European Research. (Urbana, University of Illinois Press, 1983)

4613. Holt, Raymond M. "The Fruits of Viniculture in Orange County." HSSCQ 28 (1946), 7-33.

4614. Horsman, Reginald. Race and Manifest Destiny: the Origins of American Racial Anglo-Saxonism. (Cambridge, Massachusetts, Harvard University Press, 1981)

4615. Hummasti, P. George. "World War I and the Finns of Astoria, Oregon: the Effects of the War on an Immigrant Community." IMR 11 (Fall, 1977), 334-349.

4616. Hvidt, Kristian. Flight to America: the Social Background of 300,000 Danish Emigrants. (New York, Academic Press, 1975)

4617. Hyde, Stuart W. "The Chinese Sterotype in American Melodrama." CHSQ 34 (December, 1955), 357-367.

4618. Ichioka, Yuji. "Amerika Nadeshiko: Japanese Immigrant Women in the United States, 1900-1924." PHR 49 (May, 1980), 339-357.

4619. Irwin, Richard. "Changing Patterns of American Immigration." IMR 6 (Spring, 1972), 18-31.

4620. Iwata, Masakazu. "The Japanese Immigrants in California Agricutlure." AgH 36 (January, 1962), 25-37.

4621. Johnson, Hildegard Binder. "Factors Influencing the Distribution of the German Pioneer Population in Minnesota." AgH 19 (January, 1945), 39-57.

4622. Johnson, Hildegard Binder. "The Location of German Immigrants in the Middle West." AAG 41 (March, 1951), 1-41.

4623. Jones, Maldwyn A. Destination America. (New York, Holt, Rinehart and Winston, 1976)

4624. Jordan, Terry G. "The German Settlement of Texas after 1865." SWHQ 73 (October, 1969), 193-212.

4625. Juhnke, James C. A People of Two Kingdoms: the Political Acculturation of the Kansas Mennonites. (Newton, Kansas, Faith and Life, 1975)

4626. Kahan, Arcadius. "Economic Opportunities and Some Pilgrims' Progress: Jewish Immigrants from Eastern Europe in the U.S., 1890-1914." JEH 38 (March,1978), 235-251.

4627. Kantowicz, Edward R. "A Fragment of French Canada on the Illinois Prairies." ISHSJ 75 (Winter, 1982), 263-276.

4628. Karlin, Jules Alexander. "The Anti-Chinese Outbreaks in Seattle, 1885-1886." PNQ 39 (April, 1948), 103-130.

4629. Karni, Michael G. and Douglas J. Ollila, Jr. For the Common Good: Finnish Immigrants and the Radical Response to Industrial America. (Superior, Wisconsin, Tyomies Society, 1977)

4630. Kaups, Matti. "Finnish Place Names in Minnesota: a Study in Cultural Transfer." GR 56 (July, 1966), 377-397.

4631. Kedro, M. James. "Czechs and Slovaks in Colorado, 1860-1920." CM 54 (Spring, 1977), 93-125.

4632. Kessner, Thomas. The Golden Door: Italian and Jewish Immigrant Mobility in New York City, 1880-1915. (New York, Oxford University Press, 1977)

4633. Kohnova, Marie J. "The Moravians and their Missionaries-a Problem in Americanization." MVHR 19 (December, 1932), 348-361.

4634. Koop, P. Albert. "Some Economic Aspects of Mennonite Migration: with Special Emphasis on the 1870's Migration from Russia to North America." Mennonite Quarterly Review 55 (April, 1981), 143-156.

4635. Kroes, Rob, ed. American Immigration: its Variety and Lasting Imprint. (Amsterdam, Netherlands, Amerika Instituut, 1979)

4636. Kollmorgen, Walter M. "Immigrant Settlements in Southern Agriculture: a Commentary on the Significance of Cultural Islands in Agricultural History." AgH 19 (1945), 69-78.

4637. Kuznets, Simon Smith. "Immigration of Russian Jews to the United States: Background and Structure." PAH 9 (1975), 33-124.

4638. Larson, Gustive O. "The Story of the Perpetual Emigration Fund." MVHR 18 (September, 1931), 184-194.

4639. Leonard, Stephen J. "The Irish, English, and Germans in Denver, 1860-1890." CM 54 (Spring, 1977), 126-153.

4640. Linkh, Richard M. American Catholicism and European Immigrants (1900-1924). (Staten Island, New York, Center for Migration Studies, 1975)

4641. Luebke, Frederick C. "Ethnic Group Settlement on the Great Plains." WestHQ 8 (October, 1977), 405-430.

4642. Lyman, Stanford M. "Conflict and the Web of Group Affiliation in San Francisco's Chinatown, 1850-1910." PHR 43 (November, 1974), 473-499.

4643. McCaffrey, Lawrence J. The Irish Diaspora in America. (Bloomington, Indiana University Press, 1976)

4644. MacDonagh, Oliver. "The Irish Famine Emigration to the United States." PAH 10 (1976), 355-446.

4645. McDonald, Forrest and Grady McWhiney. "The Antebellum Southern Herdsman: a Reinterpretation." JSouH 41 (May, 1975), 147-166.

4646. McKee, Delber L. Chinese Exclusion Versus the Open Door Policy, 1900-1906: Clashes over China Policy in the Roosevelt Era. (Detriot, Wayne State University Press, 1977)

4647. McKee, Delber L. "'The Chinese Must Go!'; Commissioner General Powderly and Chinese Immigration, 1897-1902." PH 44 (January, 1977), 37-51.

4648. Martinelli, Phyllis Cancilla. "Italy in Phoenix." JArH 18 (Autumn, 1977), 319-340.

4649. Mathews, Glenna. "The Community Study: Ethnicity and Success in San Jose." JIH 7 (Autumn, 1976), 305-318.

4650. Meinig, Donald W. "The Mormon Culture Region: Strategies and Patterns in the Geography of the American West, 1847-1964." AAG 65 (June, 1965), 191-220.

4651. Merriam, Paul G. "The 'Other Portland': a Statistical Note on Foreign-Born, 1860-1910." OHQ 80 (Fall, 1979), 258-268.

4652. Meyer, Douglas K. "Immigrant Clusters in the Illinois Military Tract." PA 12 (May, 1980), 97-112.

4653. Miller, Kerby A., Bruce Boling, and David N. Doyle. "Emigrants and Exiles: Irish Cultures and Irish Emigration to North America, 1790-1922." Irish Historical Studies 22 (September, 1980), 97-125.

4654. Miller, Stuart Creighton. The Unwelcome Immigrant: the American Image of the Chinese, 1785-1882. (Berkeley, University of California Press, 1969)

4655. Miller, Randall M. "Immigrants in the Old South." Immigration History Newsletter 10 (November, 1978), 8-14.

4656. Miller, Randall M. and Thomas D. Marzik, eds. Immigrants and Religion in Urban America. (Philadelphia, Temple University Press, 1977)

4657. Modell, John. "Class or Ethnic Solidarity: the Japanese American Company Union." PHR 38 (May, 1969), 193-206.

4658. Modell, John. The Economics and Politics of Racial Accommodation: the Japanese of Los Angeles, 1900-1942. (Urbana, University of Illinois Press. 1977)

4659. Modell, John. "Tradition and Opportunity: the Japanese Immigrant in America." PHR 40 (May, 1971), 163-182.

4660. Moore, Deborah Dash. At Home in America: Second Generation New York Jews. (New York, Columbia University Pess, 1981)

4661. Morley, Charles, ed. "The Chinese in California, as Reported by Henryk Sienkiewicz." CHSQ 34 (1956), 301-316.

4662. Mormino, Gary R. and George E. Pozzetta. "Immigrant Women in Tampa: the Italian Experience, 1890-1930." FHQ 61 (January, 1983), 296-312.

4663. Mulder, William. "Image of Zion: Mormonism as an American Influence in Scandinavia." MVHR 43 (June, 1956), 18-38.

4664. Mulder, William. "Utah's Ugly Ducklings: a Profile of the Scandinavian Immigrant." UHQ 23 (July, 1955), 233-259.

4665. Murray, Elise. "French Experiments in Pioneering in Pennsylvania." PMHB 68 (April, 1944), 175-188.

4666. Murray, Stanley N. "Railroads and the Agricultural Development of the Red River Valley of the North, 1870-1890." AgH 31 (October, 1957), 57-66.

4667. Nadell, Pamela S. "The Journey to America by Steam: the Jews of Eastern Europe in Transition." AJH 71 (December, 1981), 269-284.

4668. Naess, Harold S., ed. Norwegian Influence on the Upper Midwest: Proceedings of an International Conference, University of Minnesota, Duluth, May 22-24, 1975. (Duluth, University of Minnesota, Continuing Education and Extension, 1976)

4669. Nelli, Humbert S. The Italians in Chicago, 1880-1930: a Study in Ethnic Mobility. (New York, Oxford University Press, 1976)

4670. Nelli, Humbert S. "Italians in Urban America: a Study in Ethnic Adjustment." IMR 1 (Summer, 1967), 38-55.

4671. Nelson, David P. "Ryssby: a Swedish Settlement." CM 54 (Spring, 1978), 184-199.

4672. Nielsen, George R. The Danish Americans. (Boston, Twayne, 1981)

4673. North, Hart H. "Chinese and Japanese Immigration to the Pacific Coast." CHSQ 28 (December, 1949), 343-350.

4674. Olson, John Alden. "Proselytism, Immigration, and Settlement of Foreign Converts to the Mormon Culture in Zion." JW 6 (April. 1967), 189-204.

4675. Orton, Lawrence D. Polish Detroit and the Kolasinski Affair. (Detroit, Wayne State University Press, 1981)

4676.   Pap, Leo.   The Portuguese-Americans.   (Boston, Twayne, 1981)

4677.   Parish, William Jackson.   "The German Jew and the Commercial Revolution in Territorial New Mexico, 1850-1900."   NMHR 35 (January, 1960), 1-29; 35 (April, 1960), 129-150.

4678.   Parker, Edna March.   "The Southern Pacific Railroad and Settlement in Southern California."   PHR 6 (1937), 103-119.

4679.   Patterson, Wayne.   "Sugar-Coated Diplomacy: Horace Allen and Korean Immigration to Hawaii, 1901-1905." Diplomatic History 3 (Winter, 1979), 19-38.

4680.   Pierce, Bessie Louise.   Civic Attitudes in American School Textbooks.   (Chicago, University of Chicago Press, 1930)

4681.   Pierson, George W.   "The M-Factor in American History."   AQ 14 (Summer, 1962), 275-289.

4682.   Pitkin, Thomas M.   Keepers of the Gate: a History of Ellis Island.   (New York, New York University Press, 1975)

4683.   Pitt, Leonard.   The Decline of the Californios: a Social History of the Spanish-Speaking Californians, 1846-1890.   (Berkeley, University of California Press, 1966)

4684.   Pozzetta, George E.   "Foreigners in Florida: a Study of Immigration Promotion, 1865-1910."   FHQ 53 (October, 1974), 164-180.

4685.   Procko, Bohdam P.   Ukranian Catholics in America: a History.   (Washington, University Press of America, 1982)

4686.   Prpic, George.   South Slavic Immigration in America. (Boston, Twayne, 1978)

4687.   Pursinger, Marvin Gavin.   "The Japanese Settle in Oregon: 1880-1920."   JW 5 (April, 1966), 251-262.

4688. Purvis, Thomas L. "The Ethnic Descent of Kentucky's Early Population: a Statistical Investigation of European and American Sources of Emigration, 1790-1820." KHSR 80 (Summer. 1982), 253-266.

4689. Qualey, Carlton C. "Some National Groups in Minnesota." MnH 31 (March, 1950), 18-32.

4690. Quinn, Larry D. "'Chink Chink Chinaman': the Beginnings of Nativism in Montana." PNQ 58 (April, 1967), 82-89.

4691. Rankin, Lois. "Detroit Nationality Groups." MH 23 (1939), 129-205.

4692. Raup, Hallock Floyd. "The Italian-Swiss in California." CHSQ 30 (December, 1951), 305-314.

4693. Ricards, Sherman L. and George M. Blackburn. "The Sydney Ducks: a Demographic Analysis." PHR 42 (February, 1973), 20-31.

4694. Rischin, Moses. The Promised City: New York's Jews, 1870-1914. (Cambridge, Massachusetts, Harvard University Press, 1962)

4695. Rockett, Ian R.H. "American Immigration Policy and Ethnic Selection: an Historical Overview." JES 10 (Winter, 1983), 1-26.

4696. Rogers, William Warren and Jeneane Kaiser. "From the Rhine to the Alabama: Hugo Lehmann Lures the Germans." AR 35 (January, 1982), 14-29.

4697. Rolle, Andrew F. The American Italians: their History and Culture. (Belmont, California, Wadsworth, 1972)

4698. Roske, Ralph J. "The World Impact of the California Gold Rush, 1849-1857." ArW 5 (Autumn, 1963), 187-232.

4699. Rowe, John. The Hard-Rock Men: Cornish Immigrants and the North American Mining Frontier. (New York, Barnes and Noble, 1974)

4700. Runblom, Harald and Hans Norman, eds. From Sweden to America: a History of the Migration. (Minneapolis, University of Minnesota Press, 1976)

4701. Russell, Horace H. "The Finnish Farmers in America." AgH 11 (1937), 65-79.

4702. Sallet, Richard. Russian-German Settlements in the United States. Trans. by Lavern J. Rippley and Armand Bauer. (Fargo, North Dakota Institute for Regional Studies, 1974)

4703. Sanders, James W. The Education of an Urban Minority: Catholics in Chicago, 1833-1965. (New York, Oxford University Press, 1977)

4704. Saxton, Alexander Plaisted. The Indispensable Enemy: Labor and the Anti-Chinese Movement in California. (Berkeley, University of California Press, 1971)

4705. Schell, Herbert S. "Offical Immigration Activities of Dakota Territory." NDHQ 7 (October, 1932), 5-24.

4706. Seager, Robert, II. "Some Denominational Reactions to Chinese Immigration to California, 1856-1892." PHR 28 (February, 1959), 49-66.

4707. Semmingsen, Ingrid. "Haugeans, Rappites, and the Emigration of 1825." Norwegian-American Studies 29 (1983), 3-42.

4708. Semmingsen, Ingrid. Norway to America: a History of the Migration. Trans. by Einar Haugen. (Minneapolis, University of Minnesota Press, 1978)

4709. Shepperson, Wilbur Stanley. "The Foreign-Born Response to Nevada." PHR 39 (February, 1970), 1-18.

4710. Shepperson, Wilbur Stanley. "The Immigrant in Nevada's Short Stories and Biographical Essays." NHSQ 13 (Fall, 1970), 3-16.

4711. Shepperson, Wilbur Stanley. "Immigrant Themes in Nevada Newspapers." NHSQ 12 (Summer, 1969), 5-46.

4712.   Shepperson, Wilbur Stanley.   "Thomas Rawlings and David Hoffman: Promoters of Western Virginia Immigration." WVH 15 (July, 1954), 311-320.

4713.   Shpall, Leo.   "Jewish Agricultural Colonies in the United States." AgH 24 (July, 1950), 120-146.

4714.   Simms, James Y., Jr.   "Impact of Russian Famine, 1891-1892, upon the United States."   MA 60 (October, 1978), 171-184.

4715.   Smith, Michael M.   "Beyond the Borderlands: Mexican Labor in the Central Plains, 1900-1930." GPQ 1 (Fall, 1981), 239-251.

4716.   Smith, Timothy L.   "Immigrant Social Aspirations and American Education: 1880-1930."   AQ 21 (Fall, 1969), 523-543.

4717.   Smith, Timothy L.   "Lay Initiative in the Relgous Life of American Immigrants, 1880-1950."   In Tamara K. Hareven, ed. Anonymous Americans. (Englewood Cliffs, New Jersey, Prentice Hall, 1971), 214-249.

4718.   Solomon, Barbara Miller.   Ancestors and Immigrants: a   Changing   New   England   Tradition.   (Cambridge, Massachusetts, Harvard University Press, 1956)

4719.   Sowell, Thomas.   Ethnic America: a History.   (New York, Basic Books, 1981)

4720.   Special issue on Asian-American history.   AJ 3 (Summer, 1975).

4721. Special issue on Asian Americans. PHR 43 (November, 1974).

4722.   Special issue on ethnicity in California.   CHQ 50 (September, 1971).

4723.   Spencer,   Joseph   Earle.   "The   Development   of Agricultural Villages in Southern Utah." AgH 14 (1940), 181-189.

4724. Spetter, Allan. "The United States, the Russian Jews, and the Russian Famine of 1891-1892." AJHQ 64 (March, 1975), 236-244.

4725. Spoehr, Luther W. "Sambo and the Heathen Chinee: Californians' Racial Sterotypes in the Late 1870's." PHR 42 (May, 1973), 185-209.

4726. Standart, M. Colette. "The Sonora Migration to California, 1848-1856: a Study in Prejudice." SCQ 58 (Fall, 1976), 333-357.

4727. Stipanovich, Joseph. "South Slav Settlements in Utah, 1890-1935." UHQ 43 (Spring, 1975), 155-171.

4728. Stipanovich, Joseph. The South Slavs in Utah: a Social History. (Saratoga, California, R and E Research Associates, 1975)

4729. Svalestuen, Andres A. "Emigration from the Community of Tinn, 1837-1907: Demographic, Economic, and Social Background." Norwegian-American Studies 29 (1983), 43-88.

4730. Swanson, Evadene Burris. "Italians in Cortland, New York." NYH 44, i.e. New York State Historical Association. Proceedings 61 (1963), 258-273.

4731. Swierenga, Robert P. and Harry S. Stout. "Dutch Immigration in the Nineteenth Century, 1820-1877: a Quantitative Overview." ISSQ 28 (Autumn, 1975), 7-34.

4732. Taylor, Philip A.M. The Distant Magnet: European Emigration to the United States of America. (New York, Harper and Row, 1971)

4733. Taylor, Philip A.M. "Mormons and Gentiles on the Atlantic." UHQ 24 (July, 1956), 195-214.

4734. Thernstrom, Stephan, Ann Orlov and Oscar Handlin, eds. Harvard Encyclopedia of American Ethnic Groups. (Cambridge, Massachusetts, Belknap Press of Harvard University, 1980)

4735.   Thistlewaite, Frank.   "Migration from Europe Overseas in the Nineteenth and Twentieth Centuries."   In International Congress in History, 11th, Stockholm, 1960, Reports and Papers. (Stockholm, Almqvist, 1961), v.5, 32-60

4736. Thomas, Howard. "The Welsh Came to Remsen." NYH 30, i.e. New York State Historical Association. Proceedings 47 (1949), 33-42.

4737. Tipton, Gary P. "Men out of China: Origins of the Chinese Colony in Phoenix." JArH 18 (Autumn, 1977), 341-356.

4738.   Tomasi, Silvano M.   Perspectives in Italian Immigration and Ethnicity: Proceedings of the Symposium held at Casa Italiana, Columbia University, May 21-23, 1976. (New York, Center for Migration Studies, 1977)

4739. Trescatheric, Bryn. "Furness Colony in England and Minnesota, 1872-1880." MnH 47 (Spring, 1980), 16-25.

4740.   Turk, Eleanor L.   "The Germans of Atchison, 1854-1859: Development of an Ethnic Community." KH 2 (Autumn, 1979), 146-156.

4741. Turney, Roberta Stevenson. "The Encouragement of Immigration in West Virginia, 1863-1871." WVH 12 (October, 1950), 46-60.

4742.   VanCleef, Eugene.   "The Finn in America." GR 6 (September, 1918), 185-214.

4743.   Vecoli, Rudolph J.   "European Americans: from Immigrants to Ethnics." IMR 6 (Winter, 1972), 403-434.

4744.   Vecoli, Rudolph J.   "Prelates and Peasants--Italian Immigrants and the Catholic Church." JSH 2 (Spring, 1969), 217-268.

4745.   Wakatsuki, Yasuo.   "Japanese Emigration to the United States, 1866-1924: a Monograph." PAH 12 (1979), 389-516.

4746.   Walsh, Victor A.   "Across 'The Big Wather': the Irish-Catholic Community of Mid-Nineteenth-Century Pittsburgh." WPHM 66 (January, 1983), 1-24.

4747.   Ward, David.   "The Emergence of the Central Immigrant Ghettoes in American Cities: 1840-1920." AAG 58 (June, 1968), 343-359.

4748.   Warner, Robert M. and Francis X. Blouin, Jr. "Documenting the Great Migrations and a Century of Ethnicity in America." American Archivist 39 (July, 1976), 319-328.

4749.   Weaver, Herbert.   "Foreigners in Ante-Bellum Mississippi." JMsH 16 (July, 1954), 151-163.

4750.   Weaver, Herbert.   "Foreigners in Ante-Bellum Savannah." GHQ 27 (March, 1953), 1-17.

4751.   Weaver, Herbert.   "Foreigners in the Ante-Bellum Towns of the Lower South." JSouH 13 (February, 1947), 62-73.

4752.   Wilcox, B.P.   "Anti-Chinese Riots in Washington." WHQ 20 (July, 1929), 204-211.

4753.   Wolfe, Margaret Ripley.   "Aliens in Southern Appalachia, 1900-1920: the Italian Experience in Wise County, Virginia." VMHB 87 (October, 1979), 455-472.

4754.   Wooster, Ralph A.   "Foreigners in the Principal Towns of Ante-Bellum Texas." SWHQ 66 (October, 1962), 208-220.

4755.   Wynne, Robert E. "American Labor Leaders and the Vancouver Anti-Oriental Riots."   PNQ 57 (October, 1966), 172-180.

4756.   Yans-McLaughlin, Virginia.   Family and Community: Italian Immigrants in Buffalo, 1880-1930. (Ithaca, New York, Cornell University Press, 1977)

4757.   Yans-McLaughlin, Virginia.   "A Flexible Tradition: South Italian Immigrants Confront a New Work Experience." JSH 7 (Summer, 1974), 429-445.

4758. Yasui, Barbara. "The Nikkei in Oregon, 1834-1940." OHQ 86 (September, 1975), 225-257.

4759. Zilinskas, Raymond. "Japanese at Turtle Bay, Lower California, 1915." SCQ 60 (Spring, 1978), 45-58.

Emigration

The relative handful of studies on those who became disenchanted with the United State and left is the result of both limited sources and interests. Some additional studies can be found on the topic in the section on international migration after 1920. The works by Norton and Peters are chronologically out of place by a few years, but fit better here than anywhere else. Technically speaking, at least some of the studies cited below under Indian migration could be included here. Whites who moved west more rapidly than the country's boundries might also be considered temporary emigrants.

4800. Axelrod, Bernard. "Historical Studies of Emigration from the United States." IMR 6 (Spring, 1972), 32-49.

4801. Caroli, Betty Boyd. Italian Repatriation from the United States, 1900-1914. (New York, Center for Migration Studies, 1973)

4802. Dyer, Brainerd. "The Persistence of the Idea of Negro Colonization." PHR 12 (March, 1943), 53-65.

4803. Friedman, Lawrence J. "Purifying the White Man's Country: the American Colonization Society Reconsidered, 1816-1840." Societas 6 (Winter, 1976), 1-24.

4804. Hale, Frederick. "Danish Immigrant Disillusionment in the Pacific Northwest." PNQ 71 (January, 1980), 15-23.

4805. Hardy, B. Carmon. "Cultural 'Encystment' as a Cause of the Mormon Exodus from Mexico in 1912." PHR 34 (November, 1965), 439-454.

4806. Hardy, B. Carmon. "The Trek South: How the Mormons Went to Mexico." SWHQ 73 (July, 1969), 1-16.

4807.   Knapp, Frank A., Jr.   "A New Source on the Confederate Exodus to Mexico: the Two Republics." JSouH 19 (August, 1953), 364-373.

4808.   Miller, Floyd J.   The Search for a Black Nationality: Black Emigration and Colonization.   (Urbana, University of Illinois Press, 1975)

4809.   Miller, Randall M.   "Georgia on their Minds: Free Blacks and the African Colonization Movement in Georgia." SouS 17 (Winter, 1978), 349-362.

4810.   Mutunhu, Tendai.   "The North Carolina Quakers and Slavery: the Emigration and Settlement of their Former Slaves in Haiti." Journal of African-Afro-American Affairs 4 (Spring, 1980), 54-67.

4811.   Naylor, Thomas H.   "The Mormons Colonize Sonora: Early Trials at Colonai Oaxaca."   ArW 20 (Winter, 1978), 325-342.

4812.   Norton, Mary Beth.   The British-Americans; the Loyalist Exiles in England, 1774-1789. (Boston, Little, Brown, 1972)

4813.   Norton, Mary Beth.   "The Fate of Some Black Loyalists of the American Revolution."   JNH 58 (October, 1973), 402-426.

4814.   Peters, Thelma.   "The Loyalist Migration from East Florida to the Bahama Islands." FHQ 40 (1961), 123-141.

4815. Redwine, Augustin. "Lovell's Mexican Colony." Annals of Wyoming 51 (Fall, 1979), 26-35.

4816.   Reynolds, Alfred W.   "The Alabama Negro Colony in Mexico, 1894-1896."   AR 5 (October, 1952), 243-268; 6 (January, 1953), 31-58.

4817. Sarna, Jonathan D. "The Myth of No Return: Jewish Return Migration to Eastern Europe, 1881-1914." AJH 71 (December, 1981), 256-268.

4818.   Schoonover,   Thomas.   "Misconstrued   Mission:
Expansionism and Black Colonization in Mexico and Central
America During the Civil War." PHR 49 (November, 1980),
607-620.

4819.   Seaton,   Douglas   P.   "Colonizers   and   Reluctant
Colonists: the New Jersey Colonization Society and the
Black Community, 1815-1848." NJH 96 (Spring-Summer, 1978),
7-22.

4820. Seraile, William. "Afro-American Emigration to Haiti
During the American Civil War."   Americas 35 (October,
1978), 185-200.

4821. Sharp, Paul F. "The American Farmer and the 'Last
Best West'." AgH 21 (1947), 65-75.

4822.   Shepard, R. Bruce.   "Diplomatic Racism: Canadian
Government and Black Migration from Oklahoma, 1905-1912."
GPQ 3 (Winter, 1983), 5-16.

4823.   Shepperson,   Wilbur   Stanley.   Emigration   and
Disenchantment: Portraits of Englishmen Repatriated from
the United States. (Norman, University of Okalahoma Press,
1965)

4824.   Simmons,   Charles   Willis.   "Racist   Americans in a
Multi-Racial Society: Confederate Exiles in Brazil." JNH 67
(Spring, 1982), 34-39.
4825.   Streifford, David M.   "The American Colonization
Society: an Application of Republican Ideology to Early
Antebellum Reform." JSouH 45 (May, 1979), 201-220.

4826.   Virtanen, Keijo.   Settlement or Return: Finnish
Emigrants (1860-1930) in the International Overseas Return
Migration Movement. (Turku, Finland, Migration Institute,
1979)

4827.   Weaver, Blanche Henry Clark.   "Confederate
Emigration to Brazil." JSouH 27 (February, 1961), 33-53.

4828. Winberry, John J. "Oklahoma Pioneers in Mexico: the
Chamal Colony." CO 56 (Spring, 1978), 145-157.

Internal Migration

Migration within the borders of the United States has received considerable attention on levels ranging from the continental to the local.   There are numerous ways this material could be subdivided to enhance the logic and convenience of research.   We have created six separate categories.   General studies is a combination of wide-ranging empirical and theoretical works, plus some pieces that do not fit elsewhere.   The questions of how often Americans moved in the nineteenth century and what that meant to themselves and their society has produced a sizeable body of material listed under population turnover.   Studies of local patterns make up the third category.   Local here means anything from the smallest community to states or even regions.   The studies of population turnover are local in focus and so should be referred to by anyone seeking works on a given place.   In general, there are few references to cities, because they are treated separately under urbanization.   Keep in mind, however, that urban biographies also study local patterns of population.   The migration of blacks and Indians are different enough from the white experience, and have a large enough literature to make up the fourth and fifth categories.   Works on the factors affecting why people moved and how they chose their destinations are included in the final section.   In general, these studies have little in terms of quantitative data on actual levels of migration.   Obviously, urbanization was part of internal migration.   Urban history, however, has become a subject of specialization with a large literature of its own, and so has received separate attention.

General studies

There is little that ties these works together other than a fairly general focus and the fact that they do not fit into one of the other categories.   A few, however, can justifiably be called general studies.   Billington and Webb reflect Americans' long interest in the west and the frontier and work within the tradition of Frederick Jackson Turner.   Several other titles also mention the frontier.   Gastil is a valuable work which seeks to define the parts that make up the whole of the United States.   Kuznets and Thomas is a classic in terms of data and method, with an emphasis quite different than Gastil.

4900. Abrahams, Roger D. "Moving in America." Prospects 3 (1977), 63-82.

4901. Allen, James P. "Changes in the American Propensity to Migrate." AAG 67 (December, 1977), 577-587.

4902. Bartlett, Richard A. The New Country: Social History of the American Frontier, 1776-1890. (New York, Oxford University Press, 1974)

4903. Billington, Ray Allen. Westward Expansion: a History of the American Frontier. 4th edition. (New York, Macmillan, 1974)

4904. Darroch, A. Gordon. "Migrants in the Nineteenth Century: Fugitives or Families in Motion?" JFH 6 (Fall, 1981), 257-277.

4905. Fite, Gilbert Courtland. "Flight from the Farm." NH 40 (September, 1959), 159-176.

4906. Gallaway, Lowell E. and Richard K. Vedder. "Mobility of Native Americans." JEH 31 (September, 1971), 613-649.

4907. Gastil, Raymond D. Cultural Regions of the United States. (Seattle, University of Washington Press, 1976)

4908. Hine, Robert V. Community on the American Frontier: Separate but not Alone. (Norman, University of Oklahoma Press, 1980)

4909. Kuznets, Simon Smith and Dorothy Swaine Thomas, eds. Population Redistribution and Economic Growth: United States, 1870-1950. 3 vols. (Philadelphia, American Philosophical Society, 1957-1964)

4910. Lebergott, Stanley. "Migration within the U.S., 1800-1960: Some New Estimates." JEH 30 (December, 1970), 839-847.

4911. Merk, Frederick. History of the Westward Movement. (New York, Knopf, 1978)

4912.   Miller, David Harry and Jerome O. Steffen.   The Frontier: Comparative Studies.   (Norman, University of Oklahoma Press, 1977)

4913.   Nash, Gerald D.   "The Census of 1890 and the Closing of the Frontier."   PNQ 71 (July, 1980), 98-100.

4914.   Parkerson, Donald H.   "How Mobile Were Nineteenth-Century Americans?"   HM 15 (Summer, 1982), 99-109.

4915.   Rohrbough, Malcolm J.   The Trans-Appalachian Frontier: People, Societies, and Institutions.   (New York, Oxford University Press, 1978)

4916.   Sharpless, John.   "Population Redistribution in the American Past: Empirical Generalizations and Theoretical Perspectives."   SSQ 61 (December, 1980), 401-417.

4917.   Steffen, Jerome O.   The American West: New Perspectives, New Dimensions.   (Norman, University of Oklahoma Press, 1979)

4918.   Steffen, Jerome O.   Comparative Frontiers: a Proposal for Studying the American West.   (Norman, University of Oklahoma Press, 1980)

4919.   Vedder, Richard K. and Lowell E. Gallaway. "Population Transfers and the Post-Bellum Adjustment to Economic Dislocation, 1870-1920."   JEH 40 (March, 1980), 143-149.

4920.   Webb, Walter Prescott.   The Great Plains.   (Boston, Ginn and Company, 1931)

4921.   Zelinsky, Wilbur.   "Changes in the Geographic Patterns of Rural Population in the United States, 1790-1960."   GR 52 (October, 1962), 492-524.

4922.   Zorbaugh, Grace S.M.   "Farm Background of Country Migrants to Iowa Industries."   IJHP 34 (July, 1936), 312-318.

Population turnover

The works here have several things in common. They all make use of censuses and/or city directories to trace individuals in an effort to find out how often people moved in the nineteenth century. Most are also concerned with possible connections between geographic and social mobility. Malin is the pioneer, along with Throne and Curti. Thernstrom applied the techniques to urban America, and provides an excellent summary in his book on Boston. Lathrop's study of Texas demonstrates a quite different way to use the censuses to get at many of the same questions. McDonald examines similar questions using biographies of Seattle's business elite.

4950. Barr, Alwyn. "Occupational and Geographic Mobility in San Antonio, 1870-1900."   SSQ 51 (September, 1970), 396-403.

4951. Bogue, Allan G. From Prairie to Corn Belt: Farming on the Illinois and Iowa Prairies in the Nineteenth Century. (Chicago, University of Chicago Press, 1963)

4952. Buettinger, Craig. "The Rise and Fall of Hiram Pearson: Mobility on the Urban Frontier." CH 9 (Summer, 1980), 112-117.

4953. Chudacoff, Howard P. Mobile Americans: Residential and Social Mobility in Omaha, 1880-1920. (New York, Oxford University Press, 1972)

4954. Coleman, Peter J. "Restless Grant County: Americans on the Move." WMH 46 (Autumn, 1962), 16-20.

4955. Connor, Seymour V. "A Statistical Review of the Settlement of the Peters Colony, 1841-1848." SWHQ 57 (July, 1953), 38-64.

4956. Curti, Merle Eugene. The Making of an American Community: a Case Study of Democracy in a Frontier Community. (Stanford, California, Stanford University Press, 1959)

4957. Davis, Rodney O. "Prairie Emporium: Clarence, Iowa, 1860-1900; a Study of Population Trends."   MA 51 (April, 1969), 130-139.

4958. Engerrand, Steven W.   "Black and Mulatto Mobility and Stability in Dallas, Texas, 1880-1910."   Phylon 29 (September, 1978), 203-215.

4959. Garver, Frank Harmon. "The Settlement of Woodbury County." IJHP 9 (July, 1911), 359-384.

4960. Gelfand, Mitchell B. "Jewish Economic and Residential Mobility in Early Los Angeles." WSJHQ 11 (July, 1979), 332-347.

4961. Gelfand, Mitchell B. "Progress and Prosperity: Jewish Social Mobility in Los Angeles in the Booming Eighties." AJH 68 (June, 1979), 408-433.

4962.   Griffen, Clyde.   "Making it in America: Social Mobility in   Mid-Nineteenth Century Poughkeepsie." NYH 51, i.e. New York State Historical Association. Proceedings 68 (1970), 479-499.

4963.   Heller, Charles F., Jr. and F. Stanley Moore. "Continuity in Rural Land Ownership: Western Kalamazoo County, Michigan, 1830-1861." MH 56 (Fall, 1972), 233-246.

4964.   Hertzberg, Steven.   "Unsettled Jews: Geographic Mobility in a Nineteenth-Century City." AJHQ 67 (December, 1977), 125-139.

4965.   Hopkins, Richard J.   "Occupational and Geographic Mobility in Atlanta, 1870-1896."   JSouH 34 (May, 1968), 200-213.

4966.   Kerr, Homer L.   "Migration into Texas, 1860-1880." SWHQ 70 (October, 1966), 184-216.

4967.   Lathrop, Barnes F.   "Migration into East Texas, 1835-1860."   SWHQ 52 (July, 1948), 1-31; (October, 1948), 184-208; (January, 1949), 325-348.

4968.   Lynch, Joseph P. "Blacks in Springfield, 1868-1880: a Mobility Study." HJWM 7 (June, 1979), 25-34.

4969. McDonald, Norbert. "The Business Leaders of Seattle, 1880-1910." PNQ 50 (1959), 1-13.

4970. McQuillan, D. Aidan. "The Mobility of Immigrants and Americans: a Comparison of Farmers on the Kansas Frontier." AgH 53 (July, 1979), 576-596.

4971. Malin, James C. "The Turnover of Farm Population in Kansas." KHQ 4 (1935), 339-372.

4972. Mann, Ralph. "The Decade after the Gold Rush: Social Structure in Grass Valley and Nevada City, California, 1850-1860." PHR (November, 1972), 484-504.

4973. Peterson, Richard H. "The Frontier Thesis and Social Mobility on the Mining Frontier." PHR 44 (February, 1975), 52-67.

4974. Reuss, Carl F. "The Pioneers of Lincoln County, Washington, a Study in Migration." PNQ 30 (1939), 51-65.

4975. Robbins, William G. "Opportunity and Persistence in the Pacific Northwest: a Quantitative Study of Early Roseburg, Oregon." PHR 39 (August, 1970), 279-296.

4976. Shepherd, Rebecca A. "Restless Americans: the Geographic Mobility of Farm Laborers in the Old Midwest, 1850-1870." OH 89 (Winter, 1980), 24-45.

4977. Silag, William. "Citizens and Strangers: Geographic Mobility in the Sioux City Region, 1860-1900." GPQ 2 (Summer, 1982), 168-183.

4978. Stephenson, Charles. "Tracing Those Who Left: Mobility Studies and the Soundex Indexes to the U.S. Census." JUH 1 (November, 1974), 73-84.

4979. Tank, Robert M. "Mobility and Occupational Structure on the Late-Nineteenth-Century Urban Frontier: the Case of Denver, Colorado." PHR 47 (May, 1978), 189-216.

4980. Thernstrom, Stephan. The Other Bostonians: Poverty and Progress in the American Metropolis, 1880-1970. (Cambridge, Massachusetts, Harvard University Press, 1973)

4981.   Thernstrom, Stephan.   Poverty and Progress: Social Mobility in a Nineteenth-Century City.   (Cambridge, Massachusetts, Harvard University Press, 1964)

4982.   Thernstrom, Stephan and Peter R. Knights.   "Men in Motion: Some Data and Speculations about Urban Population Mobility in Nineteenth-Century America."   In Tamara K. Hareven, ed. Anonymous Americans. (Englewood Cliffs, New Jersey, Prentice Hall, 1971), 17-47.

4983.   Throne, Mildred.   "A Population Study of an Iowa County in 1850." IJH 57 (October, 1959), 305-330.

4984.   Wiener, Jonathan M.   "Planter Persistence and Social Change: Alabama, 1850-1870."   JIH 7 (Autumn, 1976), 235-260.

4985.   Worthman, Paul B.   "Working Class Mobility in Birmingham, Alabama, 1800-1914." In Tamara K. Hareven, ed. Anonymous Americans. (Englewood Cliffs, New Jersey, Prentice-Hall, 1971)

Local patterns

The numerous studies included in this section vary widely in method, time period, geographic scale, and depth of analysis. Without knowing a reader's interests, it would be hard to select more than a handful of these works for general consumption. The overall impression is clearly that local patterns vary significantly, and so anyone who would generalize about internal migration must do so with this literature in mind. Note, also, that most of the works listed above under population turnover and below under urban biography also describe local patterns. What distinguishes these studies are an emphasis on describing the origins and growth of local population and a generally limited interest in broader theoretical issues. Many of the localities are rural. Although they are not necessarily required reading, the following are especially rewarding for students interested in the various possibilities of local history. William Bowen's book on the Willamette Valley is an extraordinarily sophisticated and detailed use of census records. Conzen, on Iowa, and Hareven, on New England, demonstrate the interaction of local and regional patterns, and the value of theoretical perspective.   Geographers Terry Jordan and Donald Meinig raise interesting questions that historians do not always consider.   Doyle's study of Jacksonville, Illinois, is an excellent example of what can be built on a foundation of demographic patterns.

5000.   Abbott, Richard H.   "Yankee Farmers in Northern Virginia, 1840-1860." VMHB 76 (1968), 56-63.

5001.   Adkins, Howard G.   "The Historical Geography of Extinct Towns in Mississippi."   Southern Quarterly 17 (Spring-Summer, 1979), 123-151.

5002.   Anderson, Hattie M.   "Missouri, 1804-1828: Peopling a Frontier State." MoHR 31 (1937), 150-180.

5003.   Anderson, Henry S.   "The Little Landers' Land Colonies: a Unique Agricultural Experiment in California." AgH 5 (1931), 139-150.

5004.   Angel, Marc D.   "Notes on the Early History of Seattle's Sephardic Community." WSJHQ 7 (October, 1974), 22-30.

5005.   Arrington, Leonard J.   "The Mormon Settlement of Cassia County, Idaho, 1873-1921." IY 23 (Summer, 1979), 36-46.

5006.   Arrington, Leonard J. and Davis Bitton. The Mormon Experience: a History of the Latter-Day Saints. (New York, Knopf, 1979)

5007.   Athearn, Robert G.   The Coloradans. (Alburquerque, University of New Mexico Press, 1976)

5008.   Bailey, Joanne Passet.   "The Settlement and Development of Perry Township, Wood County, and West Millgrove, Ohio: 1830-1870." NOQ 51 (Summer, 1979), 85-102.

5009.   Barnhart, John D.   "Sources of Southern Migration into the Old Northwest." MVHR 22 (1935), 49-62.

5010.   Barnhart,   John   D.   "Southern   Contributions   to   the Social   Order   of   the   Old   Northwest."   NCHR   17   (1940), 237-248.

5011.   Barnhart,   John   D.   "The   Southern   Influence   in   the Formation of Illinois." ISHSJ 32 (1939), 358-378.

5012.   Barron,   Hal   Seth.   "The   Case   for   Appalachian Demographic   History."   Appalachian   Journal   4 (Spring-Summer, 1977), 208-215.

5013.   Barrows,   Robert   G.   "The   Ninth   Federal   Census   of Indianapolis: a   Case   Study   in   Civic   Chauvinism."   IMH   73 (March, 1977), 1-16.

5014.   Bayor,   Ronald   H.   "Ethnic   Residential   Patterns   in Atlanta, 1880-1940." GHQ 64 (Winter, 1979), 435-447.

5015.   Beach,   Frank   L.   The   Transformation   of   California, 1900-1920:   the   Effects   of   the   Westward   Movement   on California's   Growth   and   Development   in   the   Progressive Period.   (Unpublished   Ph.D.   Dissertation,   University   of California, Berkeley, 1963)

5016.   Beezley,   William   H.   "Homesteading   in   Nebraska, 1862-1872." NH 53 (Spring, 1972), 59-75.

5017.   Bellamy,   Donnie   D.   "The   Persistency   of   Colonization in Missouri." MoHR 72 (October, 1977), 1-24.

5018.   Bennett,   Guy   Vernon.   "Eastward   Expansion   of Population from the Pacific Slope." WHQ 3 (1908), 115-123.

5019.   Benoit,   Virgil.   "Gentilly: a   French-Canadian Community   in   the   Minnesota   Red   River   Valley."   MnH   44 (Winter, 1975), 279-289.

5020.   Bergquist,   James   M.   "Tracing   the   Origins   of   a Midwestern   Culture: the   Case   of   Central   Indiana."   IMH   77 (March, 1981), 1-32.

5021.   Berthoff,   Rowland   T.   "The   Social   Order   of   the Anthracite   Region,   1825-1902."   PMHB   89   (July,   1965), 261-291.

5022.   Bitton, Davis.   "Peopling the Upper Snake: the Second Wave of Mormon Settlement in Idaho."   IY 23 (Summer, 1979), 47-52.

5023.   Black, Lloyd D.   "Middle Willamette Valley Population Growth."   OHQ 43 (1942), 40-55.

5024.   Blackburn, George M. and Sherman L. Ricards.   "A Demographic History of the West: Manistee County, Michigan, 1860."   JAH 57 (December, 1970), 600-618.

5025.   Blackburn, George M. and Sherman L. Ricards.   "A Demographic History of the West: Nueces County, Texas, 1850."   Prologue 4 (Spring, 1972), 3-20.

5026.   Boskin, Joseph.   "Associations and Picnics as Stabilizing Forces in Southern California."   CHSQ 44 (March, 1965), 17-26.

5027.   Bowen, Marshall.   "Migration to and from a Northern Wyoming Mormon Community, 1900 to 1925."   PA 9 (December, 1977), 208-227.

5028.   Bowen, William A.   "The Oregon Frontiersman: a Demographic View."   In Thomas Vaughn, ed., The Western Shore: Oregon Essays Honoring the American Revolution. (Portland, Oregon Historical Society, 1975), 181-196.

5029.   Bowen, William A.   The Williamette Valley: Migration and Settlement on the Oregon Frontier.   (Seattle, University of Washington Press, 1978)

5030.   Brandhorst, L. Carl.   "The North Platte Oasis: Notes on the Geography and History of an Irrigated District."   AgH 51 (January, 1977), 166-172.

5031.   Briggs, Harold E.   "The Great Dakota Boom, 1879 to 1886."   NDHQ 4 (January, 1930), 78-108.

5032.   Briggs, Harold E.   "The Settlement and Development of the Territory of Dakota, 1860-1870."   NDHQ 7 (1933), 144-149.

5033. Brumgardt, John R. and William David Putney. "San Salvador: New Mexican Settlement in Alta California." SCQ 59 (Winter, 1977), 353-364.

5034. Buice, David. "When the Saints Came Marching in: the Mormon Experience in Antebellum New Orleans, 1840-1855." LH 23 (Summer, 1982), 221-237.

5035. Burckel, Nicholas C., ed. Racine: Growth and Change in a Wisconsin County. (Racine, Wisconsin, Racine County Board of Supervisors, 1977)

5036. Burton, Orville Vernon and Robert C. McMath, Jr., eds. Class, Conflict, and Consensus: Antebellum Southern Community Studies. (Westport, Connecticut, Greenwood Press, 1982)

5037. Burton, Orville Vernon and Robert C. McMath, Jr., eds. Toward a New South? Studies in Post-Civil War Southern Communities. (Westport, Connecticut, Greenwood Press, 1982)

5038. Cape, Wilson. "Population Changes in the West North Central States, 1900-1930." NDHQ 6 (1932), 276-291.

5039. Camarillo, Albert. Chicanos in a Changing Society: from Mexican Pueblos to American Barrios in Santa Barbara and Southern California, 1848-1930. (Cambridge, Massachusetts, Harvard University Press, 1979)

5040. Carter, Gregg Lee. "Social Demography of the Chinese in Nevada: 1780-1880." NHSQ 18 (Summer, 1975), 72-89.

5041. Chenault, William W. and Robert C. Reinders. "The Northern-Born Community of New Orleans in the 1850's." JAH 51 (September, 1964), 232-247.

5042. Clark, Dan E. "The Movement to the Far West During the Decade of the Sixties." WHQ 17 (April, 1926), 105-113.

5043. Clark, Thomas C. Agrarian Kentucky. (Lexington, University Press of Kentucky, 1977)

5044.   Clawson,   Marion.   "What It Means to Be a Californanian." CHSQ 24 (1945), 139-161.

5045. Conner, Paul. "Patriarchy: Old World and New." AQ 17 (Spring, 1965), 48-62.

5046. Cohen, David Steven. The Ramapo Mountain People. (New Brunswick, New Jersey, Rutgers University Press, 1974)

5047. Connor, Seymour V. The Peters Colony of Texas; a History and Biographical Sketches of the Early Settlers. (Austin, Texas State Historical Association, 1959)

5048.   Conzen,   Michael P.   "Local Migration Systems in Nineteenth-Century Iowa." GR 64 (July, 1974), 339-361.

5049.   Corbett, Pearson Starr.   "Settling the Muddy River Valley." NHSQ 18 (Fall, 1975), 141-151.

5050.   Crozier, William L.   "A People Apart: a Census Analysis of the Polish Community of Winona, Minnesota, 1880-1905." PAS 38 (Spring, 1981), 5-22.

5051.   Current, Richard Nelson.   Northernizing the South. (Athens, University of Georgia Press, 1983)

5052. Davis, James Edward. Frontier America, 1800-1840: a Comparative Demographic Analysis of the Settlement Process. (Glendale, California, A.H. Clark Co. 1977)

5053. DeLeon, Arnoldo. They Called Them Greasers: Anglo Attitudes toward Mexicans in Texas, 1821-1900.   (Austin, University of Texas Press, 1983)

5054.   Demaree, L. Steven.   "Post-Civil War Immigration to Southwest Missouri, 1865-1873." MoHR 69 (January, 1975), 169-190.

5055.   Diettrich, Sigismond DeR.   "Florida's Human Resources." GR 38 (April, 1948), 278-288.

5056.   Doran, Michael F.   "Population Statistics of Nineteenth-Century Indian Territory."   CO 53 (Winter, 1975-1976), 492-515.

5057. Dormon, James H. "Aspects of Acadian Plantation Life in the Mid-Nineteenth Century: a Microcosmic View." LH 16 (Fall, 1975), 361-370.

5058. Douglas, Jesse S. "Origins of the Population of Oregon in 1850." PNQ 41 (April, 1950), 95-108.

5059. Doyle, Don Harrison. The Social Order of a Frontier Community: Jacksonville, Illinois, 1825-1870. (Urbana, University of Illinois Press, 1978)

5060. Dyer, Douglas D. "The Place of Origin of Florida's Population." AAG 42 (December, 1952), 283-294.

5061. Eblen, Jack Ericson. "An Analysis of Nineteenth-Century Frontier Population." Demography 2 (1965), 399-413.

5062. Eller, Ronald D. Miners, Millhands, and Mountaineers: Industrialization of the Appalachian South, 1880-1930. (Knoxville, University of Tennessee, 1982)

5063. Ellis, David Maldwyn. "The Yankee Invasion of New York, 1783-1850." NYH 32, i.e. New York State Historical Association. Proceedings 49 (1951), 3-17.

5064. Farmer, Margaret Pace. "The Plain Folk of Old Pike County." AR 33 (April, 1980), 83-91.

5065. Fite, Gilbert Courtland. "Agricultural Pioneering in Dakota: a Case Study." GPQ 1 (Summer, 1981),

5066. Flynt, J. Wayne. Dixie's Forgotten People: the South's Poor Whites. (Bloomington, Indiana University Press, 1979)

5067. Frazar, Thomas. "Pioneers from New England." OIIQ 83 (Spring, 1982), 37-52.

5068. Gallaway, B.P. "Population Trends in the Western Cross Timbers of Texas, 1890-1960: Economic Change and Social Balance." SWHQ 67 (January, 1964), 376-396.

5069.   Gallaway, B.P.   "Population Trends in the Western Cross Timbers of Texas, 1890-1960:   Growth and Distributation." SWHQ 65 (January, 1962), 333-347.

5070. Garonzik, Joseph. "The Racial and Ethnic Make-up of Baltimore Neighborhoods, 1850-1870." MHM 71 (Fall, 1976), 392-402.

5071.   Gates, Paul W.   "Homesteading in the High Plains." AgH 51 (January, 1977), 109-133.

5072.   Gates, Paul W.   "Large Scale Farming in Illinois, 1850 to 1870." AgH 6 (1932), 14-25.

5073.   Gerlach, Russell L.   "Population Origins in Rural Missouri." MoHR 71 (October, 1976), 1-21.

5074.   Gillette, John M.   "Study of Population Trends in North Dakota." NDHQ 9 (April, 1942), 179-193.

5075. Goldfield, David R. Cotton Fields and Skyscrapers: Southern City and Region, 1607-1980.   (Baton Rouge, Louisiana University Press, 1982)

5076.   Goldfield, David R.   Urban Growth in the Age of Sectionalism: Virginia, 1847-1861. (Baton Rouge, Louisiana University Press, 1977)

5077.   Gordon, Leon M., II.   "The Price of Isolation in Northern Indiana, 1830-1860." IMH 46 (June, 1950), 152-164.

5078.   Gottlieb, Amy Zahl.   "British Coal Miners: a Demographic Study of Braidwood and Streator, Illinois." ISHSJ 72 (August, 1979), 179-192.

5079. Gower, Calvin W. "Lectures, Lyceums and Libraries in Early Kansas, 1854-1864." KHQ 36 (1970), 175-182.

5080.   Greenberg, Stephanie W.   "Neighborhood Change, Racial Transistion, and Work Location: a Case Study of an Industrial City, Philadelphia, 1880-1930." JUH 7 (May, 1981), 267-314.

5081.   Greer,   Richard R.   "Origins of the Foreign-Born
Population of New Mexico During the Territorial Period."
NMHR 17 (1942), 281-287.

5082.   Griffin, William.   "The Computer and the Artisan: a
Demographic Study of Indiana Furniture Makers, 1850."
IASSP 8 (October, 1973), 121-126.

5083.   Guice, John D.W.   "Alabama Planters in the Rockies."
CM 53 (Winter, 1976), 1-47.

5084.   Hallberg,   Carl   V.   "Soperville: an   Immigrant
Community in Knox County." ISHSJ 74 (Spring, 1981), 51-57.

5085.   Halsell, Willie D.   "Migration into, and Settlement of,
LeFlore County, 1833-1876." JMsH (1947), 219-237.

5086.   Hannon,   Joan   Underhill.   "City   Size   and   Ethnic
Discrimination: Michigan Agricultural Implements and Iron
Working Industries, 1890." JEH 42 (December, 1982), 825-845.

5087.   Hansen, Klaus J.   Mormonism and the American
Experience. (Chicago, University of Chicago Press, 1981)

5088. Hareven, Tamara K. "Family Time and Industrial Time:
Family and Work in a Planned Corporation Town, 1900-1924."
JUH 1 (May, 1975), 365-389.

5089. Harper, Roland M.   "Ante-Bellum Census Enumerations
in Florida." FHQ 6 (July, 1927), 42-52.

5090.   Herscher,   Uri   D.   Jewish Agricultural Utopias in
America, 1880-1910. (Detroit, Wayne State University Press,
1981)

5091.   Hertzberg, Steven.   Strangers Within the Gate City:
the Jews of Atlanta, 1845-1915.   (Philadelphia, Jewish
Publication Society, 1978)

5092. Hewes, Leslie. "Early Suitcase Farming in the Central
Great Plains." AgH 51 (January, 1977), 23-37.

5093. Hine, Robert V. California's Utopian Colonies. (New
Haven, Connecticut, Yale University Press, 1966; repr. of San
Marino, California, Huntington Library, 1953)

5094. Hornbeck, David and Mary Tucey. "The Submergence of a People: Migration and Occupational Structure in California, 1850." PHR 46 (August, 1977), 471-484.

5095. Huertas, Thomas F. "Damnifying Growth in the Antebellum South." JEH 39 (March, 1979), 87-100.

5096. Humphrey, Effingham P., Jr. "'Gone West'-Kentuckians in California, 1856." FCHQ 50 (January, 1976), 58-59.

5097. Hunt, Rockwell D. "History of the California State Division Controversy." HSSCQ 13 (1924), 37-53.

5098. Hynek, Paul. "Demographic Study of Easthampton, Massachusetts, 1850-1870." HJWM 6 (Fall, 1977), 6-22.

5099. Jakle, John A. and James O. Wheeler. "The Changing Residential Structure of the Dutch Population in Kalamazoo, Michigan." AAG 59 (September, 1969), 441-460.

5100. Jenks, William L. "Michigan Immigration." MH 28 (January-March, 1944), 67-100.

5101. Johnson, Keach. "Iowa's Industrial Roots, 1890-1910." AI 44 (Winter, 1978), 163-190.

5102. Jones, Charles Edwin. "Disinherited or Rural? a Historical Case Study in Urban Holiness Religion." MoHR 66 (April, 1972), 395-412.

5103. Jordan, Terry G. "The Imprint of the Upper and Lower South on Mid-Nineteenth Century Texas." AAG 57 (December, 1967), 667-690.

5104. Jordan, Terry G. "Population Origins in Texas, 1850." GR 59 (January, 1969), 83-103.

5105. Jordan, Terry G. Trails to Texas: Southern Roots of Western Cattle Ranching. (Lincoln, University of Nebraska Press, 1981)

5106. King, G. Wayne. "The Emergence of Florence, South Carolina, 1853-1890." SCHM 82 (July, 1981), 197-209.

5107. Kinsey, Stephen D. "The Development of the Jewish Community of San Jose, California, 1850-1900, Chapter One." WSJHQ 7 (October, 1974), 70-87.

5108. Kinsey, Stephen D. "The Development of the Jewish Community of San Jose, California, 1850-1900, Chapter Two." WSJHQ 7 (January, 1975), 163-182.

5109. Kinsey, Stephen D. "The Development of the Jewish Community of San Jose, California, 1850-1900, Chapter Three." WSJHQ 7 (April, 1975), 264-273.

5110. Kirk, Gordon W., Jr. and Carolyn Tyirin Kirk. "Migration, Mobility and the Transformation of the Occupational Structure in an Immigrant Community: Holland, Michigan; 1850-1880." JSH 7 (Winter, 1974), 142-164.

5111. Knepler, Jane E. "Up and Out of the East End: the Irish in Springfield." Illinois Geographical Society. Bulletin 18 (July, 1976), 25-32.

5112. Kniffen, Fred. "The American Agricultural Fair: Time and Place." AAG 41 (March, 1951), 42-57.

5113. Kocolowski, Gary P. "Stabilizing Migration to Louisville and Cincinnati, 1865-1901." CHSB 37 (Spring, 1979), 23-48.

5114. Kousser, J. Morgan and James M. McPherson, eds. Region, Race, and Reconstruction: Essays in Honor of C. Vann Woodward. (New York, Oxford University Press, 1982)

5115. Lamb, Blaine. "Jews in Early Phoenix, 1870-1920." JArH 18 (Autumn, 1977), 299-318.

5116. Lang, Elfrieda Wilhelmina Henrietta. "An Analysis of Northern Indiana's Population in 1850." IMH 49 (March, 1953), 17-60.

5117. Lang, Elfrieda Wilhelmina Henrietta. "Irishmen in Northern Indiana Before 1850." MA 36 (July, 1954), 190-198.

5118. Lang, Elfrieda Wilhelmina Henrietta. "Ohioans in Northern Indiana Before 1850." IMH 49 (December, 1953), 391-404.

5119. Lang, Elfrieda Wilhelmina Henrietta. "Southern Migration to Northern Indiana Before 1850." IMH 50 (December, 1954), 349-356.

5120. Lang, Marvel. "Population Trends in Jasper County, Mississippi, 1833-1970: a Historical Geographical Perspective." JMsH 43 (November, 1981), 294-308.

5121. Larson, Albert J. "Northern Illinois as New England Extended: a Preliminary Report." PA 7 (January, 1975), 45-51.

5122. Laurie, Bruce, Theodore Hershberg and George Alter. "Immigrants and Industry: the Philadelphia Experience, 1850-1880." JSH (Winter, 1975), 219-248.

5123. Lawlis, Chelsea. "Changes in the Whitewater Valley, 1840-1850." IMH 44 (March, 1948), 69-82.

5124. Lawlis, Chelsea. "The Great Migration and the Whitewater Valley." IMH 43 (June, 1947), 125-139.

5125. Lawlis, Chelsea. "Migration to the Whitewater Valley, 1820-1830." IMH 43 (September, 1947), 225-239.

5126. Lawlis, Chelsea. "Population of the Whitewater Valley, 1850-1860." IMH 44 (June, 1948), 161-174.

5127. Lawlis, Chelsea. "Prosperity and Hard Times in the Whitewater Valley, 1830-1840." IMH 43 (December, 1947), 363-378.

5128. Lawlis, Chelsea. "Settlement of the Whitewater Valley, 1790-1810." IMH 43 (March, 1947), 23-40.

5129. Lecompete, Janet. Pueblo, Hardscrabble, Greenhorn: the Upper Arkansas, 1832-1865. (Norman, University of Oklahoma Press, 1978)

5130. Lorch, Fred W. "Iowa and the California Gold Rush of 1849." IJHP 30 (1932), 307-376.

5131. Love, Frank. "Poston and the Birth of Yuma: the Father of Arizona Invents a Story." JArH 19 (Winter, 1978), 403-416.

5132.   Lowery, Charles D.   "The Great Migration to the Mississippi Territory." JMsH 30 (August, 1968), 173-192.

5133.   Lynch, William O.   "The Westward Flow of Southern Colonists Before 1861." JSouH 9 (August, 1943), 303-327.

5134.   Lyon, William H.   "The Corporate Frontier in Arizona." ArH 9 (Spring, 1968), 1-17.

5135.   McIlvain, Josephine.   "Twelve Blocks: a Study of One Segment of Pittsburgh's South Side, 1880-1915." WPHM 60 (October, 1977).

5136.   McTigue, Geraldine.   "Patterns of Residence: Housing Distribution by Color in Two Louisiana Towns, 1860-1880." LS 15 (Winter, 1976), 345-388.

5137.   Madsen, Brigham D.   Gold Rush Sojourners in Great Salt Lake City, 1849 and 1850.   (Salt Lake City, University of Utah Press, 1983)

5138.   Malin, James C.   "Housing Experiments in the Lawrence Community, 1855." KHQ 21 (Summer, 1954), 95-121.

5139.   Mandle, Jay R.   "The Plantation States as a Sub-Region of the Post-Bellum South." JEH 34 (September, 1974), 733-738.

5140.   Manzo, Joseph.   "Sequent Occupance in Kansas City, Kan.--a Historical Geography of Strawberry Hill."   KH 4 (Spring, 1981), 247-254.

5141.   Marti, Donald B.   "The Puritan Tradition in a New England of the West." MnH 40 (Spring, 1966), 1-11.

5142.   Matthews, Glenna.   "An Immigrant Community in Indian Territory." LbH 23 (Summer, 1982), 374-394.

5143.   May, Dean L.   "People on the Mormon Frontier: Kanab's Families of 1874." JFH 1 (Winter, 1976), 169-192.

5144.   Meinig, Donald W.   "American Wests: Preface to a Geographical Interpretation." AAG 62 (1972), 159-184.

5145. Meinig, Donald W. The Great Columbia Plain; a Historical Geography. (Seattle, University of Washington Press, 1968)

5146. Meinig, Donald W. Imperial Texas: an Interpretive Essay in Cultural Geography. (Austin, University of Texas Press, 1969)

5147. Miller, Douglas T. "Immigration and Social Stratification in Pre-Civil War New York." NYH 49, i.e. New York State Historical Association. Proceedings 66 (1968), 157-168.

5148. Miller, Wallace Elden. The Peopling of Kansas. (Columbia, Ohio, Press of F.J. Herr, 1906)

5149. Mills, Gary B. The Forgotten People; Cane River's Creoles of Color. (Baton Rouge, Louisiana State University Press, 1977)

5150. Mock, S.D. "Effects of the 'Boom' Decade, 1870-1880, upon Colorado Population." CM 11 (1934), 27-34.

5151. Modell, John. "The Peopling of a Working-Class Ward: Reading, Pennsylvania, 1850." JSH 5 (Fall, 1971), 71-95.

5152. Nackman, Mark E. "Anglo-American Migrants to the West: Men of Broken Fortunes? The Case of Texas, 1821-1846." WestHQ 5 (October, 1974), 441-455.

5153. Nieuwenhuis, Nelson. "A New Colony in Northwest Iowa." Palimpsest 59 (November/December, 1978), 182-193.

5154. Norman, Hans. "Demographic Structures in Two Swedish Settlements in Wisconsin." In Ingrid Semmingsen and Per Seyersted, eds. Scando-Americana Papers on Scandinavian Emigration to the United States. (Oslo, American Institute, University of Oslo, 1980), 95-109.

5155. Ostergren, Robert C. "Geographic Perspectives on the History of Settlement in the Upper Middle West." Upper Midwest History 1 (1981), 27-39.

5156. Owsley, Frank L. "The Pattern of Migration and Settlement on the Southern Frontier." JSouH 11 (May, 1945), 147-176.

5157. Penman, John T. "Historic Choctaw Towns of the Southern Division." JMsH 40 (May, 1978), 133-141.

5158. Perejda, Andrew J. "Sources and Dispersal of Michigan's Population." MH 32 (December, 1948), 355-366.

5159. Petersen, William John. "Population Advance to the Upper Mississippi Valley, 1830-1860." IJHP 32 (1934), 312-353.

5160. Peterson, Charles S. "Utah's Regions, a View from the Hinterland." UHQ 47 (Spring, 1979), 103-109.

5161. Peterson, Charles S. "The Valley of the Bear River and the Movement of Culture Between Utah and Idaho." UHQ 47 (Spring, 1979), 194-214.

5162. Peterson, Richard H. The Bonanza Kings: the Social Origins and Business Behavior of Western Mining Entrepreneurs, 1870-1900. (Lincoln, University of Nebraska Press, 1977)

5163. Pitcaithley, Dwight. "Settlement of the Arkansas Ozarks: the Buffalo River Valley." AkHQ 37 (Autumn, 1978), 203-222.

5164. Posadas, Barbara M. "A Home in the Country: Suburbanization in Jefferson Township, 1870-1889." CH 7 (Fall, 1978), 134-149.

5165. Powell, William E. "European Settlement in the Cherokee-Crawford Coal Field of Southeastern Kansas." KHQ 41 (Summer, 1975), 150-165.

5166. Preyer, Norris W. "Why Did Industrialization Lag in the Old South?" GHQ 55 (Fall, 1971), 378-396.

5167. Raphael, Marc Lee. Jews and Judaism in a Midwestern Community: Columbus, Ohio, 1840-1975. (Columbus, Ohio Historical Society, 1979)

5168. Reinders, Robert C. "New England Influences on the Formation of Public Schools in New Orleans." JSouH 30 (May, 1964), 181-195.

5169. Riley, Glenda. "The Frontier in Process: Iowa's Trail Women as a Paradigm." AI 46 (Winter, 1982), 167-197.

5170. Rogers, Tommy W. "The Great Population Exodus from South Carolina, 1850-1860." SCHM 68 (January, 1967), 14-21.

5171. Rogers, Tommy W. "Migration from Tennessee During the Nineteenth Century: Origin and Destination of Tennessee Migrants, 1850-1860." THQ 27 (Summer, 1968), 118-122.

5172. Rogers, Tommy W. "Migration Patterns of Alabama's Population, 1850 and 1860." AHQ 28 (Spring-Summer, 1966), 45-50.

5173. Rogers, William Warren. "The Way They Were: Thomas Countians in 1860." GHQ 60 (Summer, 1976), 131-144.

5174. Rosenwaike, Ira. "The First Jewish Settlers in Louisville." FCHQ 53 (January, 1979), 37-44.

5175. Rosenwaike, Ira. "The Jews of Baltimore: 1810 to 1820." AJHQ 67 (December, 1977), 101-124.

5176. Rosenwaike, Ira. Population History of New York City. (Syracuse, New York, Syracuse University Press, 1972)

5177. Schmier, Louis. "The First Jews of Valdosta." GHQ 62 (Spring, 1978), 32-49.

5178. Schmitt, Robert C. Demographic Statistics of Hawaii: 1778-1965. (Honolulu, University of Hawaii Press, 1968)

5179. Schroeder, Walter A. "Spread of Settlement in Howard County, Missouri, 1810-1859." MoHR 63 (October, 1968), 1-37.

5180. Schwartz, Sally. "Cantwell's Bridge, Delaware: a Demographic and Community Study." Delaware History 19 (Spring-Summer, 1980), 20-38.

5181. Scott, Thomas A. "The Impact of Tennesse's Migrating Sons." THQ 27 (Summer, 1968), 123-141.

5182. Sherlock, Richard. "Mormon Migration and Settlement after 1875." Journal of Mormon History 2 (1975), 53-68.

5183. Sherow, James E. "Rural Town Origins in Southwest Reno County." KH 3 (Summer, 1980), 99-111.

5184. Shook, R.W. "Years of Transition: Victoria, Texas, 1880-1920." SWHQ 78 (October, 1974), 155-182.

5185. Shortridge, James R. "The Expansion of the Settlement Frontier in Missouri." MoHR 75 (October, 1980), 64-90.

5186. Shortridge, Wilson Porter. The Transition of a Typical Frontier; with Illustrations from the Life of Henry Hastings Sibley, Fur Trader.... (Menasha,Wisconsin, George Banta Publishing Company, 1922)

5187. Smith, Melvin T. "Forces that Shaped Utah's Dixie: Another Look." UHQ 47 (Spring, 1979), 110-129.

5188. Smith, R. Marsh. "Migration of Georgians to Texas, 1821-1870." GHQ 20 (1936), 307-325.

5189. Smith, Thomas H. The Mapping of Ohio. (Kent, Ohio, Kent State University Press, 1977)

5190. Smith, Warren I. "Land Patterns in Ante-Bellum Montgomery County, Alabama." AR 8 (July, 1955), 196-208.

5191. Special issue on borderlands. Social Science Journal 12 (October, 1975/January, 1976)

5192. Splitter, Henry W. "Education in Los Angeles: 1850-1900." HSSCQ 33 (June-December, 1951), 101-117, 226-244, 313-330.

5193. Stevens, J. Harold. "The Influences of New England in Michigan." MH 19 (1935), 321-353.

5194. Sutherland, Daniel E. "Looking for a Home: Louisiana Emigrants During the Civil War and Reconstruction." LH 21 (Fall, 1980), 341-359.

5195. Taber, Morris C. "New England Influence in South Central Michigan." MH 45 (December, 1961), 305-336.

5196. Taniguchi, Nancy Jacobus. "Rebels and Relatives: the Mormon Foundation of Spring Glen, 1878-1890." UHQ 48 (Fall, 1980), 366-378.

5197. Taylor, Joe Gray. Eating, Drinking, and Visiting in the South: an Informal History. (Baton Rouge, Louisiana State University Press, 1982)

5198. Thomason, Philip. "The Men's Quarter of Downtown Nashville." THQ 41 (Spring, 1982), 48-66.

5199. Toll, William. "Fraternalism and Community Structure on the Urban Frontier: the Jews of Portland, Oregon--a Case Study." PHR 47 (August, 1978), 369-403.

5200. Towle, Jerry C. "Changing Geography of Willamette Valley Woodlands." OHQ 83 (Spring, 1982), 67-87.

5201. Turner, Orasmus. "The Pioneer Settler upon the Holland Purchase, and his Progress." (Introduction by S. George Ellsworth) WestHQ 6 (October, 1975), 425-435.

5202. Vance, Maurice M. "Northerners in Late Nineteenth Century Florida: Carpetbaggers or Settlers." FHQ 38 (July, 1959), 1-14.

5203. Van Ravensway, Charles. The Arts and Architecture of German Settlements in Missouri: a Survey of a Vanishing Culture. (Columbia, University of Missouri Press, 1977)

5204. Vaughn, Thomas, ed. The Western Shore: Oregon Country Essays Honoring the American Revolution. (Portland, Oregon Historical Society, 1976)

5205. Vickery, Joyce Carter. Defending Eden: New Mexican Pioneers in Southern California, 1830-1890. (Riverside, University of California, Riverside/Riverside Museum Press, 1977)

5206. Visher, Stephen S. "Distribution of Birthplaces of Indianians in 1870." IMH 26 (June, 1930), 126-142.

5207. Visher, Stephen S. "Indiana's Population, 1850-1940; Sources and Dispersal." IMH 38 (March, 1942), 51-59.

5208. Waldrep, Christopher. "Immigration and Opportunity along the Cumberland River in Western Kentucky." KHSR 80 (Autumn, 1982), 392-407.

5209. Webb, Warren F. and Stuart A. Brody. "The California Gold Rush and the Mentally Ill." SCQ 50 (Spring, 1968), 43-50.

5210. Weber, David J. The Mexican Frontier; 1821-1846: the American Southwest under Mexico. (Albuquerque, University of New Mexico Press, 1982)

5211. Weber, Michael P. Social Change in an Industrial Town: Patterns of Progress in Warren, Pennsylvania, from Civil War to World War I. (University Park, Pennsylvania State University Press, 1976)

5212. White, Richard. Land Use, Environment, and Social Change: the Shaping of Island County, Washington. (Seattle, University of Washington Press, 1980)

5213. Wilhelm, Gene, Jr. "Folk Settlements in the Blue Ridge Mountains." Appalachian Journal 5 (Winter, 1978), 204-245.

5214. Wills, Morris W. "Sequential Frontiers: the Californian and Victorian Experience, 1850-1900." WestHQ 9 (October, 1978), 483-494.

5215. Wilson, Harold Fisher. "Population Trends in Northwestern New England, 1790-1830." GR 24 (April, 1934), 272-277.

5216. Winter, Robert. "Architecture on the Frontier: the Mormon Experiment." PHR 43 (February, 1974), 50-60.

5217. Winther, Oscar Osburn. "The Colony System of Southern California." AgH 27 (October, 1953), 94-103.

5218. Wooster, Ralph A. "Wealthy Texans, 1870." SWHQ 74 (July, 1970), 24-35.

5219. Young, Biloine Whiting. "On the Trail of the Cutlerite Settlers." MnH 47 (Fall, 1980), 111-113.

Black migration

Nineteenth-century migration patterns for black Americans were certainly different than those of whites. Prior to the end of slavery, most blacks had little choice about when and where they moved within the South. Freedom brought some choice, but only after 1890 was there any major movement out of the South and/or into cities. The years between 1890 and 1920 introduced new destinations for migrating blacks that had a significant effect on recent American history. These are some of the most important issues that can be traced in the studies cited here. Farley's study of urbanization of blacks should be used in conjuntion with his book on black population patterns, cited above under black fertility. Other works here that contain material on migration, but also much more, include those by Fogel and Engerman, Gutman, and Meier and Rudwick. Excellent general works on the post-1890 movement out of the South are those by Fligstein, Henri, and Johnson and Campbell. Mullin's book on slave resistance links length of residence in America to forms of rebellion, such as flight.

5250. Barr, Alwyn. Black Texans: a History of Negroes in Texas, 1528-1971. (Austin, Jenkins, 1973)

5251. Bellamy, Donnie D. "Free Blacks in Antebellum Missouri, 1820-1860." MoHR 67 (January, 1973), 198-226.

5252. Berry, Mary Frances and John W. Blassingame. Long Memory: the Black Experience in America. (New York, Oxford University Press, 1982)

5253. Bethel, Elizabeth Rauh. Promiseland: a Century of Life in a Negro Community. (Philadelphia, Temple University Press, 1981)

5254.   Bigham, Darrel E.   "The New History and Neglected Hoosiers: a Case Study of Blacks in Vanderburgh County, 1850-1880."   IASSP 12 (October, 1977), 88-96.

5255.   Bigham, Darrel E.   "Work, Residence, and the Emergence of the Black Ghetto in Evansville, Indiana, 1865-1900."   IMH 76 (December, 1980), 287-318.

5256.   Bingham, Alfred M.   "Squatter Settlements of Freed Slaves in New England."   Connecticut Historical Society. Bulletin 41 (July, 1976), 65-80.

5257.   Blassingame, John W.   Black New Orleans, 1860-1880. (Chicago, University of Chicago Press, 1973)

5258.   Boyd, Willis Dolmond.   "Negro Colonization in the Reconstruction Era, 1865-1870."   GHQ 40 (October, 1956), 360-382.

5259.   Bringhurst, Newell G.   Saints, Slaves, and Blacks: the Changing Place of Black People Within Mormonism. (Westport, Connecticut, Greenwood Press, 1981)

5260.   Camerota, Michael.   "Westfield's Black Community, 1755-1905."   HJWM 5 (Spring, 1976), 17-27.

5261.   Carlton, Robert L.   "Blacks in San Diego County: a Social Profile, 1850-1880."   JSDH 21 (Fall, 1975), 7-20.

5262.   Cox, Thomas C.   Blacks in Topeka, Kansas, 1865-1915: a Social History.   (Baton Rouge, Louisiana State University Press, 1982)

5263.   Crockett, Norman L.   The Black Towns.   (Lawrence, Regents Press of Kansas, 1979)

5264.   Curry, Leonard P.   The Free Black in Urban America, 1800-1850:   the Shadow of the Dream.   (Chicago, University of Chicago Press, 1981)

5265.   Daniels, Douglas Henry.   Pioneer Urbanities: a Social and Cultural History of Black San Francisco.   (Philadelphia, Temple University Press, 1980)

5266. DeGraaf, Lawrence B.   "The City of Black Angels: the Emergence of the Los Angeles Ghetto, 1890-1930." PHR 39 (August, 1970), 323-352.

5267. Engs, Robert Francis. Freedom's First Generation: Black Hampton, Virginia, 1861-1890. (Philadelphia, University of Pennsylvania Press, 1979)

5268. Ernst, William J. "Changes in the Slave Population of the Virginia Tidewater and Piedmont, 1830-1860: a Stable Population Analysis." Essays in History 19 (1975), 75-88.

5269. Farley, Reynolds. "The Urbanization of Negroes in the United States." JSH 1 (Spring, 1968), 241-258.

5270. Farrison, William E. "The Negro Population of Guilford County, North Carolina, Before the Civil War." NCHR 21 (October, 1944), 319-329.

5271. Fligstein, Neil. Going North: Migration of Blacks and Whites from the South, 1900-1950. (New York, Academic Press, 1981)

5272. Fogel, Robert William and Stanley L. Engerman. Time on the Cross: the Economics of American Negro Slavery. (Boston, Little Brown, 1974)

5273. Fogel, Robert William and Stanley L. Engerman. Time on the Cross: Evidence and Methods--a Supplement. (Boston, Little, Brown, 1974)

5274. George, Paul S. "Colored Town: Miami's Black Community, 1896-1930." FHQ 56 (April, 1978), 432-447.

5275. Goldin, Claudia Dale. Urban Slavery in the American South, 1820-1860: a Quantitative History. (Chicago, University of Chicago Press, 1976)

5276. Grenz, Suzanna M. "The Exodusters of 1879: St. Louis and Kansas City Responses." MoHR 73 (October, 1978), 54-70.

5277. Gutman, Herbert George. Slavery and the Numbers Game: a Critique of Time on the Cross. (Urbana, University of Illinois Press, 1975)

5278. Gutman, Herbert George. "The World Two Cliometricians Made: a Review-Essay of Time on the Cross." JNH 60 (January, 1975), 53-227.

5279. Hart, John Fraser. "The Changing Distribution of the American Negro." AAG 50 (1960), 242-266.

5280. Henri, Florette. Black Migration: Movement North, 1900-1920. (Garden City, New York, Anchor Press, 1975)

5281. Hershberg, Theodore. "Free Blacks in Antebellum Philadelphia: a Study of Ex-Slaves, Freeborn, and Socio-economic Decline." JSH 5 (Winter, 1971-72), 183-209.

5282. Hill, James L. "Migration of Blacks to Iowa, 1820-1960." JNH 66 (Winter, 1981-1982), 289-303.

5283. Irby, Charles C. "The Black Settlers on Saltspring Island in the Nineteenth Century." Phylon 35 (December, 1974), 368-374.

5284. Johnson, Daniel M. and Rex R. Campbell. Black Migration in America: a Social Demographic History. (Durham, North Carolina, Duke University Press, 1981)

5285. Karst, Frederick A. "A Rural Black Settlement in St. Joseph County, Indiana, Before 1900." IMH 74 (September, 1978), 252-267.

5286. Kellogg, John. "The Foundation of Black Residential Areas in Lexington, Kentucky, 1865-1887." JSouH 48 (February, 1982), 21-52.

5287. Kellogg, John. "Negro Urban Clusters in the Post-Bellum South." GR 67 (July, 1977), 310-321.

5288. Kotlikoff, Laurence J. and Anton J. Rupert. "The Manumission of Slaves in New Orleans, 1827-1846." SouS 19 (Summer, 1980), 172-181.

5289. Kusmer, Kenneth L. A Ghetto Takes Shape: Black Cleveland, 1870-1930. (Urbana, University of Illinois Press, 1976)

5290.   Lack, Paul D.   "An Urban Slave Community: Little Rock, 1831-1862."   AkHQ 41 (Autumn, 1982), 258-287.

5291.   Lamon, Lester C.   Black Tennesseans, 1900-1930. (Knoxville, University of Tennessee Press, 1977)

5292.   Lapp, Rudolph M.   Blacks in Gold Rush California. (New Haven, Connecticut, Yale University Press, 1977)

5293.   Ligthfoot, Billy Bob.   "The Negro Exodus from Comanche County, Texas." SWHR 56 (January, 1953), 407-416.

5294. Litwack, Leon F.   North of Slavery: the Negro in the Free States, 1790-1860.   (Chicago, University of Chicago Press, 1961)

5295.   Logan, Frenise A.   "The Movement of Negroes from North Carolina, 1876-1894." NCHR 33 (January, 1956), 45-65.

5296.   Madyun, Gail, Larry Malone, and Robert Fikes, Jr. "Black Pioneers in San Diego: 1880-1920." JSDH 27 (Spring, 1981), 91-114.

5297.   Meier, August and Elliott Rudwick.   From Plantation to Ghetto. Rev. ed. (New York, Hill and Wang, 1970)

5298.   Meyer, Douglas K.   "Changing Negro Residential Patterns in Michigan's Capital, 1915-1970." MH 56 (Summer, 1972), 151-167.

5299.   Mullin, Gerald W.   Flight and Rebellion: Slave Resistance in Eighteenth-Century Virginia.   (New York, Oxford University Press, 1972)

5300.   Murphy, James B.   "Slavery and Freedom in Appalachia: Kentucky as a Demographic Case Study." KHSR 80 (Spring, 1982), 151-169.

5301. Nielson, David Gordon. Black Ethos: Northern Urban Negro Life and Thought, 1890-1930. (Westport, Connecticut, Greenwwod Press, 1977)

5302.   Painter, Nell   Irvin.   "Millenarian Aspects of the Exodus to Kansas of 1879." JSH 9 (Spring, 1976), 331-338.

5303.   Peoples, Morgan D.   "'Kansas Fever' in North Louisiana." LH (Spring, 1970), 121-136.

5304.   Prunty, Merle, Jr.   "The Renaissance of the Southern Plantation." GR 45 (1955), 459-491.

5305.   Reid, John D.   "Black Urbanization of the South." Phylon 25 (September, 1974), 259-267.

5306.   Ricards, Sherman L. and George M. Blackburn.   "A Demographic History of Slavery: Georgetown County, South Carolina, 1850." SCHM 76 (October, 1975), 215-224.

5307.   Richter, William L.   "Slavery in Baton Rouge, 1820-1860." LH 10 (Spring, 1969), 125-146.

5308.   Rusco, Elmer R.   "Good Time Coming?" Black Nevadans in the Nineteenth Century. (Westport, Connecticut, Greenwood Press, 1975)

5309.   Savage, W. Sherman.   Blacks in the West. (Westport, Connecticut, Greenwood Press, 1976)

5310.   Scheiner, Seth M.   "The New York City Negro and the Tenement, 1880-1910."   NYH 45, i.e.   New York State Historical Association. Proceedings 62 (1964), 304-315.

5311.   Schwendemann, Glenn.   "Nicodemus: Negro Heaven on the Solomon." KHQ 34 (1968), 10-31.

5312.   Seip, Terry L.   "Slaves and Free Negroes in Alexandria, 1850-1860." LH 10 (Spring, 1969), 147-165.

5313.   Shofner, Jerrell H.   "Florida and the Black Migration." FHQ 57 (January, 1979), 267-288.

5314.   Stroman, Carolyn A.   "The Chicago Defender and the Mass Migration of Blacks, 1916-1918." JPC 15 (Fall, 1981), 62-67.

5315.   Sunseri, Alvin R.   "A Note on Slavery and the Black Man in New Mexico."   Negro History Bulletin 38 (October-November, 1975), 457-459.

5316. Sweig, Donald M. "Reassessing the Human Dimension of the Interstate Slave Trade." Prologue 12 (Spring, 1980), 4-21.

5317. Tadman, Michael. "Slave Trading in the Ante-Bellum South: an Estimate of the Extent of the Inter-Regional Slave Trade." JAS 13 (August, 1979), 195-220.

5318. Tansey, Richard. "Bernard Kendig and the New Orleans Slave Trade." LH 23 (Spring, 1982), 158-178.

5319. Taylor, Joseph H. "The Great Migration from North Carolina in 1879." NCHR 31 (January, 1954), 18-33.

5320. Taylor, Quintard. "The Emergence of Black Communities in the Pacific Northwest: 1865-1910." JNH 64 (Fall, 1979), 342-354.

5321. Taylor, Quintard. "Slaves and Free Men: Blacks in the Oregon County, 1840-1860." OHQ 83 (Summer, 1982), 153-170.

5322. Thomas, Herbert A., Jr. "Victims of Circumstance; Negroes in a Southern Town, 1865-1880." KHSR 71 (July, 1973), 253-271.

5323. Thurman, A. Odell. "The Negro in California before 1890." PacH 20 (Summer, 1976), 177-188.

5324. VanDeusen, John G. "Did Republicans 'Colonize' Indiana in 1879?" IMH 30 (1934), 335-346.

5325. Wade, Richard C. Slavery in the Cities: the South, 1820-1860. (New York, Oxford University Press, 1964)

5326. Walker, Juliet E.K. Free Frank: a Black Pioneer on the Antebellum Frontier. (Lexington, University Press of Kentucky, 1983)

5327. Wheeler, James O. and Stanley D. Brunn. "An Agricultural Ghetto: Negroes in Cass County, Michigan, 1845-1968." GR 59 (July, 1969), 317-329.

5328.   Wheeler, James O. and Stanley D. Brunn.   "Negro Migration into Rural Southwestern Michigan." GR 58 (April, 1968), 214-230.

5329. Wilkie, Jane Riblett.   "The Black Urban Population of the Pre-Civil War South."   Phylon 37 (September, 1976), 250-262.

5330.   Wilkie,   Jane   Riblett.   "Urbanization   and De-Urbanization of the Black Population Before the Civil War." Demography 13 (August, 1976), 311-328.

5331. Williams, Melvin R. "A Statistical Study of Blacks in Washington, D.C., in 1860." Columbia Historical Society of Washington, D.C. Records 50 (1980), 172-179.

5332.   Woodruff, James F.   "Some Characteristics of the Alabama Slave Population in 1850."   GR 52 (July, 1962), 379-388.

5333.   Woods, Randall B.   "After the Exodus: John Lewis Waller and the Black Elite, 1878-1900."   KHQ 43 (Summer, 1977), 172-192.

5334.   Woolfolk, George Ruble.   The Free Negro in Texas, 1800-1860: a Study in Cultural Compromise. (Ann Arbor, Michigan, University Microfilms, 1976)

5335. Woolfolk, George R. "Turner's Saftey Valve and Free Negro Westward Migration." PNQ 56 (July, 1965), 125-130.

Indian migration

By 1800, most of the land north of the Ohio River and east of the Mississippi had come under white control. A few of these works treat Indians in the South, but most are concerned with migration west of the Mississippi. Most also involve migration that was the result of Indian-white contact. Although the broad outline of the story continues to reflect the disastrous results of that contact for Indians, the specifics vary considerably depending on when, where, and between which groups interaction occurred.

5350. Anderson, Gary Clayton. "Early Dakota Migration and Intertribal War: a Revision." WestHQ 11 (January, 1980), 17-36.

5351. Anderson, Gary Clayton. "The Removal of the Mdewakanton Dakota in 1837: a Case for Jacksonian Paternalism." SDH 10 (Fall, 1980), 310-333.

5352. Anson, Bert. "Chief Francis Lafontaine and the Miami Emigration from Indiana." IMH 60 (September, 1964), 241-268.

5353. Baird, W. David. The Quapaw Indians: a History of the Downstream People. (Norman, University of Oklahoma Press, 1980)

5354. Bauman, Robert F. "Kansas, Canada, or Starvation." MH 36 (1952), 287-299.

5355. Bee, Robert L. Crosscurrents along the Colorado: the Impact of Government Policy on the Quechan Indians. (Tucson, University of Arizona Press, 1981)

5356. Berkhofer, Robert F., Jr. The White Man's Indian: Images of the American Indian from Columbus to the Present. (New York, Knopf, 1978)

5357. Blaine, Martha Royce. The Ioway Indians. (Norman, University of Oklahoma Press, 1979)

5358. Blu, Karen I. The Lumbee Problem: the Making of an American Indian People. (Cambridge, England, Cambridge University Press, 1980)

5359. Bowden, Henry Warner. American Indians and Christian Missions: Studies in Cultural Conflict. (Chicago, University of Chicago Press, 1981)

5360. Carter, L. Edward. "The Seminole Nation after Leaving Florida, 1855-1860." CO 55 (Winter, 1977-1978), 433-453.

5361. Colley, Charles C. "The Missionization of the Coast Miwok Indians of California." CHSQ 49 (June, 1970), 143-162.

5362. Cook, Sherburne Friend. The Conflict Between the California Indian and White Civilization. 4 vols. (Berkeley, University of California Press, 1943)

5363. Cook, Sherburne Friend. The Population of the California Indians, 1769-1970. (Berkeley, University of California Press, 1976)

5364. Danziger, Edmund Jefferson, Jr. The Chippewas of Lake Superior. (Norman, University of Oklahoma Press, 1978)

5365. Drinnon, Richard. Facing West: the Metaphysics of Indian-Hating and Empire-Building. (Minneapolis, University of Minnesota Press, 1980)

5366. Fernandez, Ferdinand F. "Except a California Indian: a Study in Legal Discrimination." SCQ 50 (Summer, 1968), 161-175.

5367. Finger, John R. "The Abortive Second Cherokee Removal, 1841-1844." JSouH 47 (May, 1981), 207-226.

5368. Gibson, Charles. "Conquest, Capitulation, and Indian Treaties." AHR 83 (February, 1978), 1-15.

5369. Glassner, Martin Ira. "Population Figures for Mandan Indians." IH 7 (Spring, 1974), 41-46.

5370. Green, Michael D. The Politics of Indian Removal: Creek Government and Society in Crisis. (Lincoln, University of Nebraska Press, 1982)

5371. Guest, Francis F. "An Examination of the Thesis of S.F. Cook on the Forced Conversion of Indians in the California Missions." SCQ 61 (Spring, 1979), 1-77.

5372. Hagan, William T. United States-Comanche Relations: the Reservation Years. (New Haven, Yale University Press, 1976)

5373. Hauptman, Laurence M. "Senecas and Subdividers: Resistance to Allotment of Indian Lands in New York, 1875-1906." Prologue 9 (Summer, 1977), 105-116.

5374. Haviland, William A. and Marjory W. Power. The Orginal Vermonters: Native Inhabitants, Past and Present. (Hanover, New Hampshire, University Press of New England, 1981)

5375. Heizer, Robert Fleming. "The California Indians: Archaeology, Varieties of Culture, Arts of Life." CHSQ 41 (March, 1962), 1-28.

5376. Herzberg, Stephen J. "The Menominee Indians: from Treaty to Termination." WMH 60 (Summer, 1977), 267-329.

5377. Horsman, Reginald. Expansion and American Indian Policy, 1783-1812. (East Lansing, Michigan State Univeristy Press, 1967)

5378. Keller, Robert H. American Protestantism and United States Indian Policy, 1869-1882. (Lincoln, University of Nebraska Press, 1983)

5379. Kelly, Lawrence C. The Assault on Assimilation: John Collier and the Origins of Indian Policy Reform. (Albuquerque, University of New Mexico Press, 1983)

5380. Kersey, Harry A., Jr. "Florida Seminoles and the Census of 1900." FHQ 60 (October, 1981), 145-160.

5381. King, Duane H., ed. The Cherokee Indian Nation: a Troubled Nation. (Knoxville, University of Tennessee Press, 1979)

5382. Layton, Thomas N. "From Pottage to Portage: a Perspective on Aboriginal Horse Use in the Northern Great Basin Prior to 1850." NHSQ 21 (Winter, 1978), 243-257.

5383. Littlefield, Daniel F., Jr. Africans and Seminoles: from Removal to Emancipation. (Westport, Connecticut, Greenwood Press, 1977)

5384. Littlefield, Daniel F., Jr. The Cherokee Freedmen: from Emancipation to American Citizenship. (Westport, Connecticut, Greenwood Press, 1978)

5385. Littlefield, Daniel F., Jr. The Chickasaw Freedmen: a People Without a Country. (Westport, Connecticut, Greenwood Press, 1980)

5386. Lurie, Nancy Oestreich. "Wisconsin: a Natural Laboratory for North American Indian Studies." WMH 53 (Autumn, 1969), 3-20.

5387. McLoughlin, William G. and Walter H. Conser, Jr. "The Cherokees in Transition: a Statistical Analysis of the Federal Cherokee Census of 1835." JAH 64 (1977), 678-703.

5388. Manzo, Joseph T. "Emigrant Indian Objections to Kansas Residence." KH 4 (Winter, 1981), 247-254.

5389. Meyer, Roy W. The Village Indians of the Upper Missouri: the Mandans, Hidatsas, and Arikaras. (Lincoln, University of Nebraska Press, 1977)

5390. Miner, H. Craig, and William E. Unrau. The End of Indian Kansas: a Study of Cultural Revolution, 1854-1871. (Lawrence, Regents Press of Kansas 1978)

5391. Munkres, Robert L. "Indian-White Contact Before 1870: Cultural Factors in Conflict." JW 10 (1971), 439-473.

5392. Ourada, Patricia K. The Menominee Indians: a History. (Norman, University of Oklahoma Press, 1979)

5393. Parsons, Joseph A., Jr. "Civilizing the Indians of the Old Northwest, 1800-1810." IMH 56 (September, 1960), 195-216.

5394. Prucha, Francis Paul. "Indian Removal and the Great American Desert." IMH 59 (December, 1963), 299-322.

5395. Ruby, Robert H. and John A. Brown. The Cayuse Indians: Imperial Tribesmen of Old Oregon. (Norman, University of Oklahoma Press, 1972)

5396. Sheehan, Bernard W. Seeds of Extinction: Jeffersonian Philanthropy and the American Indian. (Chapel Hill, University of North Carolina Press, 1973)

5397. Sievers, Michael A. "Westward by Indian Treaty: the Upper Missouri Example." NH 56 (Spring, 1975), 77-107.

5398. Skelton, William B. "Army Officers' Attitudes Toward Indians, 1830-1860." PNQ 67 (July, 1976), 113-124.

5399. Smaby, Beverly P. "The Mormons and the Indians: Conflicting Ecological Systems in the Great Basin." AS 16 (Spring, 1975), 35-48.

5400. Smyly, John and Carolyn Smyly. "Koona: Life and Death of a Haida Village." AW 13 (January/February,1976), 14-19.

5401. Special issue on Indian colonization in Oklahoma. Chronicles of Oklahoma 53 (Winter, 1975-1976).

5402. Spicer, Edward Holland. "European Expansion and the Enclavement of Southwestern Indians." ArW 1 (Summer, 1959), 132-145.

5403. Thompson, Gerald. The Army and the Navaho. (Tucson, University of Arizona Press, 1976)

5404. Trafzer, Clifford E. The Kit Carson Campaign: the Last Great Navajo War. (Norman, University of Oklahoma Press, 1982)

5405. Trennert, Robert A. "The Business of Indian Removal: Deporting the Potawatomi from Wisconsin, 1851." Old Fort News 43 (No. 3, 1980), 99-113.

5406. Unrau, William E. "Removal, Death, and Legal Reincarnation of the Kaw People." IH 9 (Winter, 1976), 2-9.

5407. Van Every, Dale. Disinherited: the Lost Birthright of the American Indian. (New York, Morrow, 1966)

5408. Weslager, Clinton Alfred. The Delaware Indian Westward Migration: with the Texts of Two Manuscripts (1821-22) Responding to General Lewis Cass's Inquiries about Lenape Culture and Language. (Wallingford, Pennsylvania, Middle Atlantic Press, 1978)

5409. White, Lonnie J. "The Cheyenne Barrier on the Kansas Frontier, 1868-1869." ArW 4 (Spring, 1962), 51-64.

5410. White, Richard. "Indian Land Use and Environmental Change: Island County, Washington: a Case Study." ArW 17 (Winter, 1975), 327-338.

5411. Williams, Walter L., ed. Southeastern Indians since the Removal Era. (Athens, University of Georgia Press, 1979)

5412. Worchester, Donald E. The Apaches: Eagles of the Southwest. (Norman, University of Oklahoma Press, 1979)

5413. Wright, J. Leitch, Jr. The Only Land They Knew: the Tragic Story of the American Indians in the Old South. (New York, Free Press, 1981)

Factors affecting migration

Some scholars have been more interested in why people moved than in who the migrants were. The studies listed here generally lack quantitative, descriptive information on the migrants themselves. Instead, they focus on factors such as promotional literature, assessments of land, technological change, government policies, a search for the ideal environment, the presence or absence of water, previous settlement, and the hope for riches as influences on migration. The studies cited under population turnover often correlate the frequency of migration with social and economic characteristics of individual migrants in an effort to assess motive. In addition, readers should recall that the abundant literature based on letters, diaries, and memoirs, which provides individual examples for many of the general points discussed in these works, has been omitted from this bibliography altogether. State and local historical publications are full of this kind of material, some of which has been published in anthologies.

5450. Allen, R.H. "The Spanish Land Grant System as an Influence in the Agricultural Development of California." AgH 9 (1935), 127-142.

5451. Baur, John E. "California's Nineteenth-Century Futurists." SCQ 53 (Spring, 1971), 1-40.

5452.   Baur, John E.   The Health Seekers of Southern California, 1870-1900. (San Marino, California, Huntington Library, 1959)

5453.   Bennett, J.A.   "Immigration, 'Blackbirding', Labour Recruiting? The Hawaiian Experience, 1877-1887." Journal of Pacific History 11 (1976), 3-27.

5454.   Best, Gary Dean.   "Jacob H. Schiff's Galveston Movement: an   Experiment   in   Immigrant   Deflection, 1907-1914." AJA 30 (April, 1978), 43-79.

5455.   Bieber, Ralph P.   "California Gold Mania." MVHR 35 (June, 1948), 3-28.

5456.   Bieber, Ralph P.   "The Southwestern Trails to California in 1849." MVHR 12 (December, 1925), 342-375.

5457.   Billington, Ray Allen.   Land of Savagery, Land of Promise: the European Image of the American Frontier in the Nineteenth Century. (New York, Norton, 1981)

5458.   Blouet, Brian W. and Frederick C. Luebke, eds.   The Great Plains: Environment and Culture. (Lincoln, University of Nebraska Press, 1979)

5459.   Bogue, Margaret Beattie.   "The Swamp Land Act and Wet Land Utilization in Illinois, 1850-1890."   AgH 25 (October, 1951), 169-180.

5460.   Bowden, Martyn J.   "The Great American Desert and the American Frontier, 1800-1882: Popular Images of the Plains." In Tamara K. Hareven, ed. Anonymous Americans. (Englewood Cliffs, New Jersey, Prentice-Hall, 1971), 48-79.

5461.   Burghart, Andrew Frank.   "The Location of River Towns in the Central Lowland of the United States." AAG 49 (September, 1959), 305-323.

5462.   Campbell, Ballard C.   "The Good Roads Movement in Wisconsin, 1890-1911." WMH 49 (Summer, 1966), 273-293.

5463.   Carlson, Alvar Ward.   "Rural Settlement Patterns in the San Luis Valley: a Comparative Study." CM (Spring, 1967), 111-128.

5464.   Chessman, G. Wallace.   "Town Promotion in the Progressive Era: the Case of Newark, Ohio."   OH 87 (Summer, 1978), 253-275.

5465.   Clevinger, Woodrow R.   "Southern Appalachian Highlanders in Western Washington."   PNQ 33 (1942), 3-25.

5466. Clevinger, Woodrow R. "The Appalachian Mountaineers in the Upper Cowlitz Basin." PNQ 29 (1938), 115-134.

5467.   Coelho, Philip R.P. and Katherine H. Daigle.   "The Effects of Developments in Transportation on the Settlement of the Inland Empire." AgH 56 (January, 1982), 22-36.

5468.   Corbett, William P. "Men, Mud, and Mules: the Good Roads Movement in Oklahoma, 1900-1910." CO 58 (Summer, 1980), 132-149.

5469.   Darroch, A. Gordon.   "Migrants in the Nineteenth Century: Fugitives or Families in Motion."   JFH 6 (Fall, 1981), 257-277.

5470.   Degler, Carl N.   "The West as a Solution to Urban Unemployment."   NYH 36, i.e.   New York Historical Association. Proceedings 53 (1955), 63-84.

5471.   Dorsett, Lyle W.   "Town Promotion in Nineteenth-Century Vermont." NEQ 40 (June, 1967), 275-279.

5472.   Doyle, James.   "American Literary Images of the Canadian Prairies, 1860-1910." GPQ 3 (Winter, 1983), 30-38.

5473.   Eby, Cecil D. "America as 'Asylum': a Dual Image." AQ 14 (Fall, 1962), 483-489.

5474.   Edmunds, R. David.   The Potawatomis: Keepers of the Fire. (Norman, University of Oklahoma Press, 1978)

5475.   Edwards, G. Thomas.   "Irrigation in Eastern Washington, 1906-1911:   the Promotional Photographs of Asahel Curtis." PNQ 72 (July,1981), 112-120.

5476.   Eidem, R.J.   "North Dakota Preaching Points: a Synopsis of Settlement." NDH 45 (Winter, 1978), 10-13.

5477. Forsythe, James L. "Environmental Considerations in the Settlement of Ellis County, Kansas." AgH 51 (January, 1977), 38-50.

5478. Fuller, Justin. "Boom Towns and Blast Furnaces: Town Promotion in Alabama, 1885-1893." AR 29 (January, 1976), 37-48.

5479. Gates, Paul W. "Federal Land Policies in the Southern Public Land States." AgH 53 (January, 1979), 206-227.

5480. Gates, Paul W. "Tenants of the Log Cabin." MVHR 49 (June, 1962), 3-31.

5481. Gilman, Carolyn. "Perceptions of the Prairie: Cultural Contrasts on the Red River Trails." MnH 46 (Fall, 1978), 112-122.

5482. Gilpin, William. Mission of the North American People, Geographical, Social, and Political. (Philadelphia, J.B. Lippincott & Company, 1873)

5483. Glaab, Charles N. "Jesup W. Scott and a West of Cities." OH 73 (Winter, 1964), 3-12.

5484. Glaab, Charles N. "Visions of Metropolis: William Gilpin and Theories of City Growth in the American West." WMH 45 (Autumn, 1961), 21-31.

5485. Gower, Calvin W. "Aids to Prospective Prospectors: Guidebooks and Letters from Kansas Territory, 1858-1860." KHQ 43 (Spring, 1977), 67-77.

5486. Greb, B. Allen. "Opening a New Frontier: San Francisco, Los Angeles, and the Panama Canal, 1900-1914." PHR 47 (August, 1978), 405-424.

5487. Hague, Harlan. The Road to California: the Search for a Southern Overland Route, 1540-1848. (Glendale, California, Clark, 1978)

5488. Hamburg, James F. "Railroads and the Settlement of South Dakota During the Great Dakota Boom, 1878-1887." SDH 5 (Spring, 1975), 165-178.

5489. Hammer, Kenneth M. "Come to God's Country: Promotional Efforts in Dakota Territory, 1861-1889." SDH 10 (Fall, 1980), 291-309.

5490. Handley, Lawrence R. "Settlement Across Northern Arkansas as Influenced by the Missouri and North Arkansas Railroad." AkHQ 33 (Winter, 1974), 273-292.

5491. Hauptman, Laurence M. "Mythologizing Westward Expansion: Schoolbooks and the Image of the American Frontier Before Turner." WestHQ 8 (July, 1977), 269-282.

5492. Hauptman, Laurence M. "Westward the Course of Empire: Geography Schoolbooks and Manifest Destiny, 1783-1893." Historian 40 (May, 1978), 423-440.

5493. Hewes, Leslie. "The Oklahoma Ozarks as the Land of the Cherokees." GR 32 (1942), 269-281.

5494. Hewes, Leslie. "Some Features of Early Woodland and Prairie Settlement in a Central Iowa County." AAG 40 (March, 1950), 40-57.

5495. Hewes, Leslie and Philip E. Frandson. "Occupying the Wet Prairie: the Role of Artificial Drainage in Story County, Iowa." AAG 42 (March, 1952), 24-50.

5496. Holmes, William F. "Labor Agents and the Georgia Exodus, 1899-1900." SAQ 79 (Autumn, 1980), 436-448.

5497. Hoyt, Joseph Bixby. "The Cold Summer of 1816." AAG 48 (June, 1958), 118-131.

5498. Hudson, John. "Towns of the Western Railroads." GPQ 2 (Winter, 1982), 41-54.

5499. Hulbert, Archer Butler. Soil: its Influence on the History of the United States. (New Haven, Connecticut, Yale University Press, 1930)

5500. Interrante, Joseph. "You Can't Go to Town in a Bathtub: Automobile Movement and the Reorganization of Rural American Space, 1900-1930." RHR 21 (Fall, 1979), 151-168.

5501.   Jakle, John A.   Images of the Ohio Valley: a Historical Geography of Travel, 1740 to 1860.   (New York, Oxford University Press, 1977)

5502.   Jakle, John A.   "Salt in the Ohio Valley Frontier, 1770-1820." AAG 59 (December, 1969), 687-709.

5503.   Johansen, Dorothy O.   "A Working Hypothesis for the Study of Migrations." PHR 36 (February, 1967), 1-12.

5504.   Johnson, Hildegard Binder. Order upon the Land: the U.S. Rectangular Land Survey and the Upper Mississippi Country. (New York, Oxford University Press, 1976)

5505.   Jones, Billy Mac.   Health Seekers in the Southwest, 1817-1900. (Norman, University of Oklahoma Press, 1967)

5506.   Jones, Michael Owen.   "Climate and Disease: the Traveler Describes America."   BHM 41 (May-June, 1967), 254-266.

5507.   Jordan, Terry G.   "Between the Forest and the Prairie." AgH 38 (October, 1964), 205-216.

5508.   Jordan, Terry G. "Pioneer Evaluation of Vegetation in Frontier Texas." SWHQ 76 (1973), 233-254.

5509.   Kaatz, Martin Richard.   "The Black Swamp: a Study in Historical Geography." AAG 45 (March, 1955), 1-35.

5510.   Kollmorgan, Walter M.   "The Woodsman's Assaults on the Domain of the Cattleman." AAG 59 (June, 1969), 215-239.

5511.   Larsen, Arthur J.   "Roads and the Settlement of Minnesota." MnH 21 (1940), 225-244.

5512.   Lang, Herbert H.   "The New Mexico Bureau of Immigration, 1800-1912." NMHR 51 (July, 1976), 193-214.

5513.   Lee, Susan Previant.   "Antebellum Land Expansion: Another View." AgH 52 (October, 1978), 488-502.

5514.   Lewis, G. Malcolm. "William Gilpin and the Concept of the Great Plains Region." AAG 56 (March, 1966), 33-51.

5515. Lovin, Hugh T. "'Duty of Water' in Idaho: a 'New West' Irrigation Controversy, 1890-1920." ArW 23 (Spring, 1981), 5-28.

5516. McGregor, Alexander C. "The Economic Impact of the Mullan Road on Walla Walla, 1860-1883." PNQ 65 (July, 1974), 118-129.

5517. Marx, Leo. The Machine in the Garden: Technology and the Pastoral Ideal in America. (New York, Oxford University Press, 1964)

5518. Moehlman, Arthur Henry. "The Red River of the North." GR 25 (January, 1935), 79-91.

5519. Mussey, Barrows. "Yankee Chills, Ohio Fever." NEQ 22 (December, 1949), 435-451.

5520. Noggle, Burl. "Anglo Observers of the Southwest Borderlands, 1825-1890: the Rise of a Concept." ArW 1 (Summer, 1959), 105-131.

5521. Palmer, Edgar Zavitz. "The Correctness of the 1890 Census of Population for Nebraska Cities." NH 32 (December, 1951), 259-267.

5522. Peters, Bernard C. "Early Town-Site Speculation in Kalamazoo County." MH 56 (Fall, 1972), 201-215.

5523. Peters, Bernard C. "Michigan's Oak Openings: Pioneer Perceptions of a Vegetative Landscape." Journal of Forest History 22 (January, 1978), 18-23.

5524. Powell, J.M. Mirrors of the New World: Images and Image-Makers in the Settlement Process. (Hamden, Connecticut, Dawson/Archon, 1977)

5525. Powell, Lawrence N. "The American Land Company and Agency: John A. Andrew and the Northernization of the South." CWH 21 (December, 1974), 293-308.

5526. Preston, Robert M. "The Great Fire of Emmitsburg, Maryland: Does a Catastrophic Event Cause Mobility?" MHM 77 (June, 1982), 172-182.

5527. Rayman, Ronald. "The Black Hawk Purchase: Stimulus to the Settlement of Iowa, 1832-1851." Western Illinois Regional Studies 3 (Fall, 1980), 141-153.

5528. Rister, Carl Coke. "The Oilman's Frontier." MVHR 37 (June, 1950), 3-16.

5529. Rosowski, Susan J. "Willa Cather's A Lost Lady: Art Versus the Closing Frontier." GPQ 2 (Fall, 1982), 239-248.

5530. Ross, Margaret. "The New Madrid Earthquake." AkHQ 27 (Summer, 1968), 83-104.

5531. Savage, James P., Jr. "Do-it-Yourself Books for Illinois Immigrants." ISHSJ 57 (Spring, 1964), 30-48.

5532. Shanabruch, Charles. "The Louisiana Immigration Movement, 1891-1907: an Analysis of Efforts, Attitudes, and Opportinities." LH 18 (Spring, 1977), 203-226.

5533. Shortridge, James R. "The Alaskan Agricultural Empire: an American Agrarian Vision, 1898-1929." PNQ 69 (October, 1978), 145-158.

5534. Shortridge, James R. "The Evaluation of the Agricultural Potential of Alaska." PNQ 68 (April, 1977), 88-98.

5535. Smith, Henry Nash. Virgin Land; the American West as Symbol and Myth. (Cambridge, Massachusetts, Harvard University Press, 1950)

5536. Smith, Henry Nash. "The Western Frontier in Imaginative Literature, 1818-1891." MHVR 36 (December, 1949), 479-490.

5537. Stilgoe, John R. Metropolitan Corridor: Railroads and the American Scene. (New Haven, Connecticut, Yale University Press, 1983)

5538. Sutherland, Daniel E. "Michigan Emigrant Agent: Edward H. Thomson." MH 59 (Spring-Summer, 1975), 3-37.

5539. Thacker, Robert. "The Plains Landscape and Descriptive Technique." GPQ 2 (Summer, 1982), 146-156.

5540. Thompson, Kenneth. "Climatotherapy in California." CHSQ 50 (June, 1971), 111-130.

5541. Thompson, Kenneth. "Insalubrious California: Perception and Reality." AAG 59 (March, 1969), 50-64.

5542. Travis, Paul D. "Changing Climate in Kansas: a Late-Nineteenth-Century Myth." KH 1 (Spring, 1978), 48-58.

5543. Trewartha, Glenn T. "Some Regional Characteristics of American Farmsteads." AAG 38 (1948), 162-225.

5544. Ullman, Edward L. "Rivers as Regional Bonds: the Columbia-Snake Example." GR 41 (April, 1951), 210-225.

5545. Unruh, John D., Jr. The Plains Across: the Overland Emigrants and the Trans-Mississippi West, 1840-1860. (Urbana, University of Illinois Press, 1979)

5546. Wahl, E.W. "A Comparison of the Climate of the Eastern United States During the 1830's with the Current Normals." MWR 96 (1968), 73-82.

5547. Wahl, E.W. and T.L. Lawson. "The Climate of the Mid-nineteenth Century United States Compared to Current Normals." MWR 98 (1970), 259-265.

5548. Wahlquist, Wayne L. "A Review of Mormon Settlement Literature." UHQ 45 (Winter, 1977), 4-21.

5549. Walker, Robert H. "The Poet and the Rise of the City." MVHR 49 (June, 1962), 85-99.

5550. Walker, Robert H. "The Poets Interpret the Western Frontier." MVHR 47 (March, 1961), 619-635.

5551. Warne, Clinton Lee. "Some Effects of the Introduction of the Automobile on Highways and Land Values in Nebraska." NH 38 (March, 1957), 43-59.

5552. Watkins, Beverly. "Efforts to Encourage Immigration to Arkansas, 1865-1874." AkHQ 38 (Spring, 1979), 32-62.

5553. Wells, Ronald A. "Migration and the Image of America in England: a Study of The Times in the Nineteenth Century." ISSQ 28 (Autumn, 1975), 32-62.

5554. Winther, Oscar Osburn. "The Use of Climate as a Means of Promoting Migration to Southern California." MVHR 33 (December, 1946), 411-424.

5555. Wright, Alfred J. "Ohio Town Patterns." GR 27 (October, 1937), 615-624.

Urbanization

During the nineteenth century, Americans, old and new, moved into cities so often that half the people were urban dwellers by 1920. This is the third great theme of migration during this period. Although the processes by which this happened often were linked to immigration and other aspects of internal migration, it is worth giving this topic separate attention, if only because urban history has become an area of professional specialization. The studies which follow have been divided into two groups. General works are those that examine more than one place and often more than one topic. Urban biographies are studies of a particular place, sometimes tracing the history of the community itself, and sometimes using a given town as a setting in which to explore more general issues. Although this is not an exhaustive bibliography in urban history, students who read widely should have a good sense of the field when they are done.

General

This category includes everything that remains when the urban biographies are removed. There are, however, two things that stand out about these works. First, the quality may be consistently higher than for any other group of studies. Second, urban history in general has a more elaborate and fully developed set of theories than any other aspect of demographic history, with the possible exception of the history of fertility control. Readers who enjoy theory should enter this literature via Handlin and Burchard, Schlesinger, Tilly, and Weber. These works are not exclusively American in their focus. Those who prefer texts or surveys will be well served by Chudacoff, Glaab and Brown, Green, and Thernstrom and Sennett. Examples of some of the more interesting possibilities of urban history can be found in the studies by Barth, Bender, Palm, Pred, and Ward.

5600. Abbott, Carl. Boosters and Businessmen: Popular Economic Thought and Urban Growth in the Antebellum Middle West. (Westport, Connecticut, Greenwood Press, 1981)

5601. Abrahamson, Mark and Michael A. DuBick. "Patterns of Urban Dominance: the U.S. in 1890." ASR 42 (October, 1977), 756-768.

5602. Agnew, John A. and Kevin R. Cox. "Urban In-Migration in Historical Perspective: an Approach to Measurement." HM 12 (Fall, 1979), 145-155.

5603. -----. "Artists Draw South Dakota: Panoramic Views of Pioneer Towns." SDH 8 (Summer, 1978), 221-249.

5604. Baker, O.E. "Rural-Urban Migration and the National Welfare." AAG 23 (1933), 59-126.

5605. Barth, Gunther Paul. City People: the Rise of Modern City Culture in Nineteenth-Century America. (New York, Oxford University Press, 1980)

5606. Basset, T.D. Seymour. "A Case Study of Urban Impact on Rural Society: Vermont, 1840-1880." AgH 30 (1956), 28-34.

5607. Bender, Thomas. Community and Social Change in America. (New Brunswick, New Jersey, Rutgers University Press, 1978)

5608. Bender, Thomas. Toward an Urban Vision: Ideas and Institutions in Nineteenth-Century America. (Lexington, University of Kentucky Press, 1975)

5609. Boyer, Paul. Urban Masses and Moral Order in America, 1820-1920. (Cambridge, Massachusetts, Harvard University Press, 1978)

5610. Brown, Richard D. "The Emergence of Urban Society in Rural Massachusetts, 1760-1820." JAH 61 (June, 1974), 29-51.

5611. Brownell, Blaine A. "Introduction: Urban Themes in the American South." JUH 2 (February, 1976), 139-145.

5612. Brownell, Blaine A. and David R. Goldfield, eds. The City in Southern History: the Growth of Urban Civilization in the South. (Port Washington, New York, Kennikat Press, 1977)

5613. Brunger, Eric. "Dairying and Urban Development in New York State, 1850-1900." AgH 29 (October, 1955), 169-174.

5614. Chudacoff, Howard P. The Evolution of American Urban Society. (Englewood Cliffs, New Jersey, Prentice-Hall, 1975)

5615. Cornehls, James V. and Delbert A. Taebel. "The Outsiders and Urban Transportation." SSJ 13 (April, 1976), 61-74.

5616. Crowther, Simeon J. "Urban Growth in the Mid-Atlantic States, 1785-1850." JEH 36 (September, 1976), 624-644.

5617. Cumbler, John T. "The City and Community: the Impact of Urban Forces on Working Class Behavior." JUH 3 (August, 1977), 427-442.

5618. Danbom, David B. The Resisted Revolution: Urban America and the Industrialization of Agriculture, 1900-1930. (Ames, Iowa State University Press, 1979)

5619. Donaldson, Scott. "City and Country: Marriage Proposals." AQ 20 (Fall, 1968), 547-566.

5620. Dykstra, Robert R. "Town-Country Conflict: a Hidden Dimension in American Social History." AgH 38 (October, 1964), 195-204.

5621. Ellsworth, Clayton S. "The Coming of Rural Consolidated Schools to the Ohio Valley, 1892-1912." AgH 30 (July, 1956), 119-128.

5622. Foster, Mark S. From Streetcar to Superhighway: American City Planners and Urban Transportation, 1900-1940. (Philadelphia, Temple University Press, 1981)

5623. Franch, Michael S. "The Congregational Community in the Changing City, 1840-1870." MHM 71 (Fall, 1976), 367-380.

5624. Glaab, Charles N. and A. Theodore Brown. A History of Urban America. (New York, Macmillan, 1967)

5625. Goldfield, David R. "The Urban South: a Regional Framework." AHR 86 (December, 1981), 1009-1034.

5626. Goldfield, David R. and Blaine A. Brownell. Urban America: From Downtown to No Town. (Boston, Houghton Mifflin, 1979)

5627. Goldstein, Sidney. "Migration: Dynamic of the American City." AQ 4 (Winter, 1954), 337-348.

5628. Grant, H. Roger. "The Unbuilt Interurbans of Nevada." NHSQ 23 (Fall, 1980), 148-156.

5629. Green, Constance M. The Rise of Urban America. (New York, Harper and Row, 1965)

5630. Handlin, Oscar and John Burchard, eds. The Historian and the City. (Cambridge, Massachusetts, M.I.T. Press, 1963)

5631. Hart, John Fraser. "Loss and Abandonment of Cleared Farm Land in the Eastern United States." AAG 58 (September, 1968), 417-440.

5632. Hayter, Earl W. The Troubled Farmer, 1850-1900: Rural Adjustment to Industrialism. (DeKalb, Northern Illinois University Press, 1968)

5633. Horton, Loren N. "Through the Eyes of Artists; Iowa Towns in the 19th Century." Palimpsest 59 (September/October, 1978), 133-147.

5634. Larsen, Lawrence H. The Urban West at the End of the Frontier. (Lawrence, Regents Press of Kansas, 1978)

5635. Light, Ivan. "From Vice District to Tourist Attraction: the Moral Career of American Chinatown: 1880-1940." PHR 43 (August, 1974), 367-394.

5636. McDonald, Norbert. "Population Growth and Change in Seattle and Vancouver, 1880-1960." PHR 39 (August, 1970), 297-322.

5637. Machor, James L. "Urbanization and the Western Garden: Synthesizing City and Country in Antebellum America." SAQ 81 (Autumn, 1982), 413-428.

5638. McShane, Clay. "Transforming the Use of Urban Space: a Look at the Revolution in Street Pavements, 1880-1924." JUH 5 (May, 1979), 279-307.

5639. Maldonado, Edwin. "Urban Growth during the Canal Era: the Case of Indiana." ISSQ 31 (Winter, 1978-1979), 20-37.

5640. Miller, Zane L. "Scarcity, Abundance, and American Urban History." JUH 4 (February, 1978), 131-155.

5641. Palm, Risa. The Geography of American Cities. (New York, Oxford University Press, 1981)

5642. Perry, David C. and Alfred J. Watkins, eds. The Rise of the Sunbelt Cities. (Beverly Hills, California, Sage Publications, 1977)

5643. Pessen, Edward. "The Social Configuration of the Antebellum City: an Historical and Theoretical Inquiry." JUH 2 (May, 1976), 267-306.

5644. Peterson, Charles S. "Urban Utah: toward a Fuller Understanding." UHQ 47 (Summer, 1979), 227-235.

5645. Peterson, Jon A. "The City Beautiful Movement: Forgotten Origins and Lost Meanings." JUH 2 (August, 1976), 415-434.

5646. Pred, Allan Richard. "The Intrametropolitan Location of American Manufacturing." AAG 54 (June, 1964), 165-180.

5647. Pred, Allan Richard. The Spatial Dynamics of U.S. Urban-Industrial Growth, 1800-1914:   Interpretive and Theoretical Essays. (Cambridge, Massachusetts, M.I.T. Press, 1966)

5648. Pred, Allan Richard. Urban Growth and the Circulation of Information: the United States System of Cities, 1790-1840. (Cambridge, Massachusetts, Harvard University Press, 1973)

5649. Pred, Allan Richard. Urban Growth and City-Systems in the United States, 1840-1860. (Cambridge, Massachusetts, Harvard University Press, 1980)

5650. Riefler, Roger F. "Nineteenth-Century Urbanization Patterns in the United States." JEH 39 (December, 1979), 961-974.

5651. Robinson, Michael. "The Suburban Ideal: Nineteenth-Century Planned Communities." Historic Preservation 30 (April-June, 1978), 24-29.

5652. Scarpaci, Jean, ed. Immigrant Women and the City. Special issue of Journal of Urban History 4 (May, 1978).

5653. Schlesinger, Arthur M. "The City in American History." MVHR 27 (June, 1940), 43-66.

5654. Schnell, J. Christopher and Patrick E. McLear. "Why the Cities Grew: a Historiographical Essay on Western Urban Growth, 1850-1880." MoHSB 28 (1972), 162-177.

5655. Scott, Roy V. "Railroads and Farmers: Educational Trains in Missouri, 1902-1914." AgH 36 (January, 1962), 3-15.

5656. Siegel, Adrienne. The Image of the American City in Popular Literature, 1820-1870. (Port Washington, New York, Kennikat, 1981)

5657. Siegel, Adrienne. "When Cities Were Fun: the Image of the American City in Popular Books, 1840-1870." JPC 9 (Winter, 1975), 573-582.

5658. Simmons, James W. "Changing Residence in the City: a Review of Intraurban Mobility." GR 58 (October, 1968), 622-651.

5659. Simpson, Michael. "Two Traditions of American Planning: Olmsted and Burnham; a Review Article." Town Planning Review 47 (April, 1976), 174-179.

5660. Sprague, Stuart Seely. "Town Making in the Era of Good Feelings: Kentucky 1814-1820." KHSR 72 (October, 1974), 337-341.

5661. Still, Bayrd. "Patterns of Mid-Nineteenth Century Urbanization in the Middle West." MVHR 28 (September, 1941), 187-206.

5662. Taeuber, Conrad. "Rural-Urban Migration." AgH 15 (1941), 151-160.

5663. Thernstrom, Stephan and Richard Sennett, eds. Nineteenth-Century Cities; Essays in the New Urban History. (Yale Conference on the Nineteenth-Century Industrial City, New Haven, 1968) (New Haven, Connecticut, Yale University Press, 1969)

5664. Tilly, Charles. An Urban World. (Boston, Little, Brown, 1974)

5665. Ward, David. Cities and Immigrants: a Geography of Change in Nineteenth-Century America. (New York, Oxford University Press, 1971)

5666. Ward, David. "A Comparative Historical Geography of Street-car Suburbs in Boston, Massachusetts, and Leeds, England, 1850-1920." AAG 54)December, 1964), 477-489.

5667. Weber, Adna Ferrin. The Growth of Cities in the Nineteenth Century: a Study in Statistics. (Ithaca, New York, Cornell University Press, 1963; repr. of New York, Columbia University, 1899)

5668. Wilkie, Jane Riblett. "The United States Population by Race and Urban-Rural Residence, 1790-1860: Reference Tables." Demography 13 (February, 1976), 139-148.

5669. Winpenny, Thomas R. "The Nefarious Philadelphia Plan and Urban America: a Reconsideration." PMHB 101 (January, 1977), 103-113.

Urban biographies

This section includes works that focus on a single town or city, or in some cases on several cities in order to make comparisons. The places are located all over the country, and general readers should make an effort to choose studies with an eye to distribution. Some authors really are writing the history or "biography" of a chosen community; others have selected places to study as convenient sites to test an hypothesis or examine an issue of historical importance. Not surprisingly, most of these works focus on successful places, but there are some that examine towns that failed in the race to become urban centers. The reasons for decline are as varied as those that spelled success. The books are almost uniformly interesting and informative. The articles vary more in quality and sophistication, but all can be read with profit. No one single work stands out as the classic, or the obvious place to start. The most sensible way to approach these studies is through some of the more important of the general works on urbanization.

5700.   Abbott, Carl.   "'Necessary Adjuncts to its Growth': the Railroad Suburbs of Chicago, 1854-1875." ISHSJ 73 (Summer, 1980), 117-131.

5701.   Allen, James B.   "The Company Town: a Passing Phase of Utah's Industrial Development." UHQ 34 (Spring, 1966), 138-160.

5702.   Arnold, Joseph L.   "Suburban Growth and Municipal Annexation in Baltimore, 1745-1918."   MHM 73 (Summer, 1978), 109-128.

5703.   Ashcroft, Bruce.   "Socorro's Boom Town Decade." El Palacio 87 (Summer, 1981), 3-9.

5704.   Aspin,   Chris.   "The   Fall   of   Troy: a Nineteenth-Century English Mining Venture in Nevada." NHSQ 21 (Summer, 1978), 130-142.

5705. Barth, Gunther Paul. Instant Cities: Urbanization and the Rise of San Francisco and Denver. (New York, Oxford University Press, 1975)

5706. Bate, Kerry William. "Iron City, Mormon Mining Town." UHQ 50 (Winter, 1982), 47-58.

5707. Bauer, Craig A. "From Burnt Canes to Budding City: a History of the City of Kenner, Louisiana." LH 23 (Fall, 1982), 353-382.

5708. Beirue, D. Randall. "Residential Growth and Stability in the Baltimore Industrial Community of Canton During the Late Nineteenth Century." MHM 74 (March, 1979), 39-51.

5709. Bell, Marion L. Crusade in the City: Revivalism in Nineteenth-Century Philadelphia. (Lewisburg, Pennsylvania, Bucknell University Press, 1977)

5710. Bernard, Richard M. "A Portrait of Baltimore in 1800: Economic and Occupational Patterns in an Early American City." MHM 69 (Winter, 1974), 341-360.

5711. Bitton, Davis. "The Making of a Community: Blackfoot, Idaho, 1878-1910." IY 19 (Spring, 1975), 2-15.

5712. Blouin, Francis X., Jr. The Boston Region, 1810-1850: a Study of Urbanization. (Ann Arbor, Michigan, UMI Research, 1980)

5713. Blumin, Stuart M. The Urban Threshold: Growth and Change in a Nineteenth-Century American Community. (Chicago, University of Chicago Press, 1976)

5714. Bolding, Gary. "Change, Continuity, and Commercial Identity in a Southern City, New Orleans, 1850-1950." LS 14 (Summer, 1975), 161-178.

5715. Boman, Martha. "A City of the Old South: Jackson, Mississippi, 1850-1860." JMsH 15 (January, 1953), 1-32.

5716. Bosley, Donald R. "A Montana Town That Is No More." Montana: the Magazine of Western History 25 (October, 1975), 38-51.

5717. Bowers, Paul C., Jr., and Goodwin F. Berquist, Jr. "Worthington, Ohio: James Kolbourn's Episcopal Haven on the Western Frontier." OH 85 (Summer, 1976), 247-262.

5718. Bradshaw, James Stanford. "Grand Rapids, 1870-1880: Furniture City Emerges." MH 55 (Winter, 1971), 321-342.

5719. Brown, Andrew Theodore. Frontier Community: Kansas City to 1870. (Columbia, University of Missouri Press, 1963)

5720. Brown, Andrew Theodore and Lyle W. Dorsett. K.C.: a History of Kansas City, Missouri. (Boulder, Colorado, Prunett, 1978)

5721. Browne, Gary Lawson. Baltimore in the Nation, 1789-1861. (Chapel Hill, University of North Carolina Press, 1980)

5722. Buder, Stanley. Pullman: an Experiment in Industrial Order and Community Planning, 1880-1930. (New York, Oxford University Press, 1967)

5723. Carter, Margaret. "Bennett--Town or Illusion?" Alaska Journal 8 (Winter, 1978), 52-59.

5724. Condit, Carl W. The Railroad and the City: a Technological and Urbanistic History of Cincinnati. (Columbus, Ohio State University Press, 1977)

5725. Conzen, Kathleen Neils. Immigrant Milwaukee, 1836-1860: Accommodation and Continuity in a Frontier City. (Cambridge, Massachusetts, Harvard University Press, 1976)

5726. Combler, John T. Working-Class Community in Industrial America: Work, Leisure, and Struggle in Two Industrial Cities, 1880-1930. (Westport, Connecticut, Greenwood Press, 1979)

5727. Cross, Norman W. "New England City, Dakota Territory: a Narrative History, 1887-1912." NDH 47 (Summer, 1980), 4-10.

5728. Cutler, William W. III and Howard Gillette, Jr. The Divided Metropolis: Social and Spatial Dimensions of

Philadelphia, 1800-1975. (Westport, Connecticut, Greenwood Press, 1980)

5729. Davies, Edward J., II. "Elite Migration and Urban Growth: the Rise of Wilkes-Barre in the Northern Anthracite Region, 1820-1880." PH 45 (October, 1978), 291-314.

5730. Davis, Charles M. "The Cities and Towns of the High Plains of Michigan." GR (October, 1938), 664-673.

5731. Decker, Peter R. Fortunes and Failures: White Collar Mobility in Nineteenth-Century San Francisco. (Cambridge, Massachusetts, Harvard University Press, 1978)

5732. DeMille, Janice F. "Shonesburg: the Town Nobody Knows." UHQ 45 (Winter, 1977), 47-60.

5733. Dixon, E.C. "Newport, its Rise and Fall." WMH 25 (June, 1942), 444-455.

5734. Doherty, Herbert J., Jr. "Jacksonville as a Nineteenth-Century Railroad Center." FHQ 58 (April, 1980), 373-386.

5735. Doyle, Don Harrison. The Social Order of a Frontier Community: Jacksonville, Illinois, 1825-1870. (Urbana, University of Illinois Press, 1978)

5736. Dykstra, Robert R. The Cattle Towns: a Social History of the Kansas Trading Centers. (New York, Knopf, 1968)

5737. Ebner, Michael H. "'In the Suburbes of Toun': Chicago's North Shore to 1871." CH 11 (Summer, 1982), 66-77.

5738. Egerton, John. Visions of Utopia: Nashoba, Rugby, Rushkin, and the "New Communities" in Tennessee's Past. (Knoxville, University of Tennessee Press, 1977)

5739. Esslinger, Dean R. Immigrants and the City: Ethnicity and Mobility in a Nineteenth-Century Midwestern Community. (Port Washington, New York, Kennikat Press, 1975)

5740.   Feil, Lin B.   "Helvetia: Boom Town of the Santa Ritas."   JArH 9 (Summer, 1968), 77-95.

5741.   Feldman, Jacob S.   "The Pioneers of a Community: Regional Diversity among the Jews of Pittsburgh, 1845-1861." AJA 32 (November, 1980), 119-124.

5742.   Fellman, Jerome D.   "Pre-Building Growth Patterns in Chicago."   AAG 47 (March, 1957), 59-82.

5743.   Fine, Gary Alan.   "The Pinkston Settlement: an Historical and Social Psychological Investigation of the Contact Hypothesis."   Phylon 40 (September, 1979), 229-242.

5744.   Fogelson, Robert M.   The Fragmented Metropolis: Los Angeles, 1850-1930.   (Cambridge, Massachusetts, Harvard University Press, 1967)

5745.   Folger, Fred.   "Trilby--an Early History, 1835-1919." NOQ 50 (Spring, 1978), 43-53.

5746.   Folsom, Burton W., Jr.   Urban Capitalists: Entrepreneurs and City Growth in Pennsylvania's Lackawanna and Lehigh Regions, 1800-1920.   (Baltimore, Johns Hopkins University Press, 1981)

5747.   Frisch, Michael H.   Town into City: Springfield, Massachusetts, and the Meaning of Community, 1840-1880. (Cambridge, Massachusetts, Harvard University Press, 1972)

5748.   Garr, Daniel J.   "Los Angeles and the Challenge of Growth, 1835-1849."   SCQ 61 (Summer, 1979), 147-158.

5749.   Gates, Grace Hooten.   "Anniston: Model City and Rival City."   AR 31 (January, 1978), 33-47.

5750.   Gilchrist, David T., ed.   The Growth of the Seaport Cities, 1790-1825.   (Charlottesville, University of Virginia Press, 1967)

5751.   Goldthwaite, James W.   "A Town that Has Gone Down Hill."   GR 17 (October, 1927), 527-542.

5752. Goldman, Mark. High Hopes: the Rise and Decline of Buffalo, New York. (Albany, State University of New York Press, 1983)

5753. Grant, H. Roger. "Portrait of a Workers' Utopia: the Labor Exchange and the Freedom, Kansas, Colony." KHQ 43 (Spring, 1977), 56-66.

5754. Griffen, Clyde and Sally Griffen. Natives and Newcomers: the Ordering of Opportunity in Mid-Nineteenth Century Poughkeepsie. (Cambridge, Massachusetts, Harvard University Press, 1978)

5755. Griffin, Richard W. "Poor White Laborers in Southern Cotton Factories, 1789-1865." SCHM 61 (January, 1960), 26-40.

5756. Griswold del Castillo, Richard. The Los Angeles Barrio, 1850-1890: a Social History. (Berkeley, University of California Press, 1979)

5757. Hamilton, Kenneth Marvin. "Townsite Speculation and the Origin of Boley, Oklahoma." CO 55 (Summer, 1977), 180-189.

5758. Hatch, Elvin. Biography of Small Town. (New York, Columbia University Press, 1979)

5759. Haywood, C. Robert. "Pearlett: a Mutual Aid Colony." KHQ 42 (Autumn, 1976), 263-276.

5760. Hershberg, Theodore, ed. Philadelphia: Work, Space, Family, and Group Experience in the Nineteenth Century: Essays Toward an Interdisciplinary History of the City. (New York, Oxford University Press, 1981)

5761. Hill, Rita and Janaloo Hill. "Alias Shakespeare: the Town Nobody Knew." NMHR 42 (July, 1967), 211-227.

5762. Holli, Melvin G. "Before the Car: Nineteenth-Century Detroit's Transformation from a Commercial to an Industrial City." MH 64 (March/April, 1980), 33-39.

5763. Hollingsworth, J. Rogers and Ellen Jane Hollingsworth. Dimensions in Urban History: Historical and Social Science

Perspectives on Middle-Sized American Cities. (Madison, University of Wisconsin Press, 1979)

5764. Horton, Loren N. "River Town: Davenport's Early Years." Palimpsest 60 (January/February, 1979), 16-27.

5765. Hosack, Robert E. "Chanute--the Birth of a Town." KHQ 41 (Winter, 1975), 468-487.

5766. Huggins, Kay Haire. "City Planning in North Carolina, 1900-1929." NCHR 46 (October, 1969), 377-397.

5767. James, Preston E. "Vicksburg: a Study in Urban Geography." GR 21 (April, 1931), 234-243.

5768. Jarzombek, Michelle. "The Memphis-South Memphis Conflict, 1826-1850." THQ 41 (Spring, 1982), 23-36.

5769. Johnson, Paul E. A Shopkeeper's Millenium: Society and Revivals in Rochester, New York, 1815-1837. (New York, Hill and Wang, 1978)

5770. Jucha, Robert J. "The Anatomy of a Streetcar Suburb: a Development History of Shadyside, 1852-1916." WPHM 62 (October, 1979), 301-319.

5771. Kershner, Frederick D., Jr. "From Country Town to Industrial City: the Urban Pattern in Indianapolis." IMH 45 (December, 1949), 327-338.

5772. Kirk, Gordon W., Jr. The Promise of American Life: Social Mobility in a Nineteenth-Century Immigrant Community, Holland, Michigan, 1847-1894. (Philadelphia, American Philosophical Society, 1978)

5773. Knights, Peter R. The Plain People of Boston, 1830-1860; a Study in City Growth. (New York, Oxford University Press, 1971)

5774. Lauer, Jeanette C. and Robert H. Lauer. "St. Louis and the 1880 Census: the Shock of Collective Failure." MoHR 76 (January, 1982), 151-163.

5775.   Lawther,   Dennis   E.   "Mount   Washington: a Demographic Study of the Influence of Changing Technology, 1870-1910." WPHM 64 (January, 1981), 47-72

5776. Lewis, David Rich. "La Plata, 1891-1893: Boom, Bust, and Controversy." UHQ 50 (Winter, 1982), 5-21.

5777.   Littlefield, Daniel F., Jr., and Lonnie E. Underhill. "Kildare, Oklahoma Territory: Story of an Agricultural Boom Town." Great Plains Journal 15 (Fall, 1975), 29-54.

5778. Long, Durward. "The Historical Beginnings of Ybor City and Modern Tampa." FHQ 45 (July, 1966), 31-44.

5779. Long, Durward.   "The Making of Modern Tampa: a City of the New South, 1885-1911." FHQ 49 (April, 1971), 333-345.

5780.   McDonald,   Michael   J.   Knoxville,   Tennessee: Continuity and Change in an Appalachian City. (Knoxville, University of Tennessee Press, 1983)

5781. McLear, Patrick E. "Economic Growth and the Panic of 1857 in Kansas City." MoHSB 26 (1970), 144-156.

5782.   Marsh, Margaret Sammartino.   "Suburbanization and the Search for Community: Residential Decentralization in Philadelphia, 1880-1900." PH 44 (April, 1977), 99-116.

5783.   Martin, Michael Crowel.   Chinatown's Angry Angel: the Story of Donaldina Cameron.   (Palo Alto, California, Pacific Books, 1977)

5784. Martinez, Oscar J. Border Boom Town: Ciudad Juarez since 1848. (Austin, University of Texas Press, 1978)

5785.   Mawn, Geoffrey P.   "Promoters, Speculators, and the Selection of the Phoenix Townsite." ArW 19 (Autumn, 1977), 207-224.

5786.   Mayer, Harold M.   "The Launching of Chicago: the Situation and the Site." CH 9 (Summer, 1980), 68-79.

5787. Meredith, Howard L. and George H. Shirk. "Oklahoma City: Growth and Reconstruction, 1889-1939." CO 55 (Fall, 1977), 293-308.

5788. Miller, Roberta Balstad. City and Hinterland: a Case Study of Urban Growth and Regional Development. (Westport, Connecticut, Greenwood Press, 1979)

5789. Miller, Roger and Joseph Siry. "The Emerging Suburb: West Philadelphia, 1850-1880." PH 46 (April, 1980), 99-144.

5790. Miller, Zane L. Boss Cox's Cincinnati: Urban Politics in the Progressive Era. (New York, Oxford University Press, 1968)

5791. Millet, Donald J. "Town Development in Southwest Louisiana: 1865-1900." LH 13 (Spring, 1972), 139-168.

5792. Mitchell, Robert J. "Tradition and Change in Rural New England: a Case Study of Brooksville, Maine, 1850-1870."   Maine Historical Society Quarterly 18 (Fall, 1978), 87-106.

5793. Moehring, Eugene P. Public Works and the Patterns of Urban Real Estate Growth in Manhattan, 1835-1894. (New York, Arno, 1981)

5794. Moore, John Hammond. "Appomattox: Profile of a Mid-Nineteenth-Century Community." VMHB 88 (October, 1980), 478-491.

5795. Morrow, Lynn. "New Madrid and its Hinterland: 1783-1826." MoHSB 36 (July, 1980), 241-250.

5796. Muller, Edward K. "Selective Urban Growth in the Middle Ohio Valley, 1800-1860." GR 66 (April, 1976), 178-199.

5797. Nadeau, Josephine, E. "Ripon: Ethnic and General Development."   PacH 20 (1976), 52-66 (Part 1); PacH 20 (1976), 189-201 (Part 2); PacH 20 (1976), 305-315 (Part 3).

5798. Napier, Rita. "Economic Democracy in Kansas: Speculation and Townsite Preemption in Kickapoo." KHQ 40 (Autumn, 1974), 349-369.

5799. Nichols, Cheryl Griffith. "Pulaski Heights: Early Suburban Development in Little Rock, Arkansas." AkHQ 41 (Summer, 1982), 129-145.

5800. Niemeyer, Glenn A. "'Oldsmaar for Health, Wealth, Happiness.'" FHQ 46 (July, 1967), 18-28.

5801. Olmsted, Roger. "The City That Was." CHQ 55 (Summer, 1976), 121-136.

5802. Olson, Sherry H. Baltimore: the Building of an American City. (Baltimore, Johns Hopkins University Press, 1980)

5803. Parker, Watson. Deadwood: the Golden Years. (Lincoln, University of Nebraska Press, 1981)

5804. Pearson, Jim B. "Life in LaBelle: a New Mexico Mining Town." NMHR 45 (April, 1970), 147-158.

5805. Pendergast, Beth. "Smithton, Missouri." MoHR 70 (January, 1976), 134-141.

5806. Preston, Howard L. Automobile Age Atlanta: the Making of a Southern Metropolis, 1900-1935. (Athens, University of Georgia Press, 1979)

5807. Quastler, I.E. The Railroads of Lawrence, Kansas, 1854-1900: a Case Study in the Causes and Consequences of an Unsuccessful American Urban Railroad Program. (Lawrence, Kansas, Coronado, 1979)

5808. Ratzlaff, Robert K. "Le Hunt Kansas: the Making of a Cement Ghost Town." KHQ 43 (Summer, 1977), 203-216.

5809. Reichard, Maximilian. "Black and White on the Urban Frontier: the St. Louis Community in Transition, 1800-1830." MoHSB 33 (October, 1976), 3-17.

5810. Rengstorf, Susan Redman. "A Neighborhood in Transition: Sedamsville, 1880-1950." CHSB 39 (Summer, 1981), 175-194.

5811. Rhoda, Richard. "Urban Transport and the Expansion of Cincinnati, 1858 to 1920." CHSB 35 (Summer, 1977) 131-143.

5812. Rice, Bradley R. "Mountain View Georgia: the Rough and Not so Ready Suburb." Atlanta Historical Journal 24 (Winter, 1980), 26-40.

5813. Riley, Mark B. "Edgefield: a Study of an Early Nashville Suburb." THQ 37 (Summer, 1978), 133-154.

5814. Rowe, Janet C. "The Lock Mill, Loose Creek, Missouri: the Center of a Self-Sufficient Community, 1848-1900." MoHR 75 (April, 1981), 285-293.

5815. Salter, John R., Jr. Jackson, Mississippi: an American Chronicle of Struggle and Schism. (Hicksville, New York, Exposition, 1979)

5816. Scheiber, Harry N. "Urban Rivalry and Internal Improvements in the Old Northwest, 1820-1860." OH 7 (October, 1962), 227-239.

5817. Schnell, J. Christopher. "Chicago Versus St. Louis: a Reassessment of the Great Rivalry." MoHR 71 (April, 1977), 245-265.

5818. Schwartz, Joel and Daniel Prosser, eds. Cities of the Garden State: Essays in the Urban and Suburban History of New Jersey. (Dubuqne, Iowa, Kendall/Hunt, 1977)

5819. Sears, Joan N. "Town Planning in White and Habersham Counties, Georgia." GHQ 54 (Spring, 1970), 20-40.

5820. Sehr, Timothy J. "Three Gilded Age Suburbs of Indianapolis: Irvington, Brightwood, and Woodruff Place." IMH 77 (December, 1981), 305-332.

5821. Shankman, Arnold. "Happyville, the Forgotten Colony." AJA 30 (April, 1978), 3-19.

5822. Share, Allan J. Cities in the Commonwealth: Two Centuries of Urban Life in Kentucky. (Lexington, University Press of Kentucky, 1982)

5823. Silag, William. "Sioux City: an Iowa Boom Town." AI 44 (Spring, 1979), 587-601.

5824. Simon, Roger D. "The City-Building Process: Housing and Services in New Milwaukee Neighborhoods." American Philosophical Society. Transactions 68 (July, 1978), 5-64.

5825. Simon, Roger D. "Housing and Services in an Immigrant Neighborhood: Milwaukee's Ward 14." JUH 2 (August, 1976), 435-458.

5826. Sisk, Glenn N. "Towns of the Alabama Black Belt." MA 39 (April, 1957), 85-95.

5827. Spann, Edward K. The New Metropolis: New York City, 1840-1857. (New York, Columbia University Press, 1981)

5828. Stewart, Peter C. "Railroads and Urban Rivalries in Antebellum Eastern Virginia." VMHB 81 (January, 1973), 3-22.

5829. Still, Bayrd. "The Development of Milwaukee in the Early Metropolitan Period." WMH 25 (March, 1942), 297-307.

5830. Still, Bayrd. "Milwaukee, 1870-1900: the Emergence of a Metropolis." WMH 23 (1939), 138-162.

5831. Sullivan, Margaret Lo Piccolo. "St. Louis Ethnic Neighborhoods, 1850-1930: an Introduction." MoHSB 33 (January, 1977), 64-76.

5832. Summerville, James. "The City and the Slum: 'Black Bottom' in the Development of South Nashville." THQ 40 (Summer, 1981), 182-192.

5833. Tarr, Joel Arthur. Transportation Innovation and Changing Spatial Patterns in Pittsburgh, 1850-1934. (Chicago, Public Works Historical Society, 1978)

5834. Taylor, David G. "Boom Town Leavenworth: the Failure of a Dream." KHQ 38 (1972), 389-415.

5835. Taylor, Morris F. "The Town Boom in Las Animas and Baca Counties." CM 55 (Spring/Summer, 1978), 111-132.

5836. Taylor, Rosser H. "Hamburg: an Experiment in Town Promotion." NCHR 11 (1934), 20-38.

5837. Telling, Irving. "Coolidge and Thoreau: Forgotten Frontier Towns." NMHR 29 (July, 1954), 210-233.

5838. Timmons, W.H. "The El Paso Area in the Mexican Period, 1821-1848." SWHQ 84 (July, 1980), 1-28.

5839. Torbert, Edward N. "The Evolution of Land Utilization in Lebanon, New Hampshire." GR 25 (April, 1935), 209-230.

5840. Tucey, Mary and David Hornbeck. "Anglo Immigration and the Hispanic Town: a Study of Urban Change in Monterey, California, 1835-1850." SSJ 13 (April, 1976), 1-7.

5841. Viehe, Fred W. "Black Gold Suburbs: the Influence of the Extractive Industry on the Suburbanization of Los Angeles, 1890-1930." JUH 8 (November, 1981), 3-26.

5842. Voss, Stuart F. "Town Growth in Central Missouri, 1815-1860: an Urban Chaparral." MoHR 64 (October, 1969), 64-80 (Part I); 64 (January, 1970), 197-217 (Part II); 64 (April, 1970), 322-335 (Part III).

5843. Wade, Richard C. The Urban Frontier: Pioneer Life in Early Pittsburgh, Cincinnati, Lexington, Louisville and St. Louis. (Chicago, University of Chicago Press, 1964)

5844. Walkowitz, Daniel J. Worker City, Company Town: Iron and Cotton-Worker Protest in Troy and Cohoes, New York, 1855-84. (Urbana, University of Illinois Press, 1978).

5845. Wallace, Anthony F.C. Rockdale: the Growth of an American Village in the Early Industrial Revolution. (New York, Knopf, 1978)

5846. Warner, Sam Bass, Jr. The Private City: Philadelphia in Three Periods of its Growth. (Philadelphia, University of Pennsylvania Press, 1968)

5847. Warner, Sam Bass, Jr. Streetcar Suburbs: the Process of Growth in Boston, 1870-1900. (Cambridge, Massachusetts, Harvard Univeristy Press, 1962)

5848. Weatherford, John W. "The Short Life of Manhattan, Ohio." OhHQ 65 (October, 1956), 376-398.

5849. Weaver, Blanche Henry Clark. "Shifting Residential Patterns of Nashville." THQ 18 (March, 1959), 20-34.

5850. Webb, Bernice Larson. "Company Town in Louisiana Style." LH 9 (Fall, 1968), 325-340.

5851. Weber, Michael P. "Residential and Occupational Patterns of Ethnic Minorities in Nineteenth-Century Pittsburgh." PH 44 (October, 1977), 317-334.

5852. Wells, Eugene Tate. "The Growth of Independence, Missouri, 1827-1850." MoHSB 16 (October, 1959), 33-46.

5853. West, Elliott. "Five Idaho Mining Towns: a Computer Profile." PNQ 73 (July, 1982), 108-120.

5854. Weygand, James Lamar. "Locke, Indiana: the Making of a Ghost Village." IMH 73 (March, 1977), 32-51.

5855. Wheeler, Kenneth W. To Wear a City's Crown: the Beginnings of Urban Growth in Texas, 1836-1865. (Cambridge, Massachusetts, Harvard University Press, 1968)

5856. Wilson, Harold Fisher. "The Roads of Windsor." GR 21 (July, 1931), 379-397.

5857. Winn, Karl. "The Seattle Jewish Community: a Photographic Essay." PNQ 70 (April, 1979), 69-74.

5858. Wyman, Walker D. "Council Bluffs and the Westward Movement." IJH 47 (April, 1949), 99-118.

5859. Yelton, Susan. "Newnansville: a Lost Florida Settlement." FHQ 53 (January, 1975), 319-331.

5860. Zunz, Olivier. "The Organization of the American City in the Late Nineteenth-Century: Ethnic Structure and Spatial Arrangement in Detroit." JUH 3 (August, 1977), 443-466.

5861. Zunz, Olivier, William A. Ericson, and Daniel J. Fox. "Sampling for a Study of the Population and Land Use of Detroit in 1880-1885." SSH 1 (Spring, 1977), 307-332.

Recent

Migration patterns after 1920 are a curious blend of old themes and new trends. It would, however, be almost impossible to understand the significance of most of these works without some familiarity with nineteenth-century history. This is especially true when new destinations and new migrants join or replace the old.

International Migration

Major changes in the laws affecting immigration between 1917 and 1924, and in 1965 combined with two world wars and several economic swings (one rather pronounced) to alter how many people came to this country in any given year and who those people were. There are numerous government-sponsored studies and works in sociological journals that can be used to supplement these historically-oriented materials.

5900. Bayor, Ronald H. Neighbors in Conflict: the Irish, Germans, Jews, and Italians of New York City, 1929-1941. (Baltimore, Johns Hopkins University Press, 1978)

5901. Betten, Neil and Raymond A. Mohl. "From Discrimination to Repatriation: Mexican Life in Gary, Indiana, During the Great Depression." PHR 42 (August, 1973), 370-388.

5902. Bodnar, John E. "Immigration, Kinship, and the Rise of Working-Class Realism in Industrial America." JSH 14 (Fall, 1980), 45-65.

5903. Bodnar, John E., Roger Simon, and Michael P. Weber. Lives of their Own: Blacks, Italians and Poles in Pittsburgh, 1900-1960. (Urbana, University of Illinois Press, 1982)

5904. Boyd, Monica. "The Changing Nature of Central and Southeast Asian Immigration to the United States, 1961-1972." IMR 8 (Winter, 1974), 507-519.

5905. Boyd, Monica. "Immigration Policies and Trends: a Comparison of Canada and the United States." Demography 13 (February, 1976), 83-104.

5906.   Daniels, Roger.   The Politics of Prejudice: the Anti-Japanese Movement in California, and the Struggle for Japanese Exclusion. (Berkeley, University of California Press, 1962)

5907.   DeRose, Christine A.   "Inside 'Little Italy':   Italian Immigrants in Denver." CM 54 (Summer, 1977), 277-293.

5908.   Dinnerstein, Leonard and David M. Reimers.   Ethnic Americans: a History of Immigration and Assimilation.   (New York, Harper and Row, 1975)

5909.   Fleming, Donald Harnish and Bernard Bailyn, eds.   The Intellectual Migration: Europe and America, 1930-1960. (Cambridge,   Massachusetts,   Belknap   Press   of   Harvard Univrsity Press, 1969)

5910.   Fortney, Judith.   "Immigrant Professionals: a Brief Historical Survey." IMR 6 (Spring, 1972), 50-62.

5911.   Fortney,   Judith.   "International   Migration   of Professionals." PS 24 (July, 1970), 217-232.

5912.   Frisbie, Parker.   "Illegal Migration from Mexico to the United States: a Longitudinal Analysis."   IMR 9 (Spring, 1975), 3-13.

5913.   Gamboa, Erasmo.   "Mexican Migration into Washington State: a History, 1940-1950." PNQ 72 (July, 1981), 121-131.

5914.   Garcia, Juan Ramon.   Operation Wetback: the Mass Deportation of Mexican Undocumented Workers in 1954. (Westport, Connecticut, Greenwood, Press, 1980)

5915.   Hawley, Ellis W.   "The Politics of the Mexican Labor Issue, 1950-1965." AgH 40 (July, 1966), 157-176.

5916.   Hess, Gary R.   "The 'Hindu' in America: Immigration and Naturalization Policies and India, 1917-1946." PHR 38 (February, 1969), 59-79.

5917.   Hoffman, Abraham.   Unwanted Mexican Americans in the Great Depression: Repatriation Pressures, 1929-1939. (Tucson, University of Arizona Press, 1974)

5918. Jackman, Jarrell C. "Exiles in Paradise: German Emigres in Southern California, 1933-1950." SCQ 61 (Summer, 1979), 183-205.

5919. Jenkins, Craig. "Push/Pull in Illegal Mexican Migration to the U.S." IMR 11 (Summer, 1977), 178-179.

5920. Keely, Charles B. "The Development of U.S. Immigration Policy since 1965." Journal of International Affairs 33 (Fall/Winter, 1979), 249-263.

5921. Keely, Charles B. "Effects of the Immigration Act of 1965 on Selected Population Characteristics of Immigrants to the United States." Demography 8 (May, 1971), 157-169.

5922. Keely, Charles B. "Effects of U.S. Immigration Law on Manpower Characteristics of Immigrants." Demography 12 (May, 1975), 179-191.

5923. Kessner, Thomas and Betty Boyd Caroli. Today's Immigrants, Their Stories: a New Look at the Newest Americans. (New York, Oxford University Press, 1981)

5924. Kim, Hyung-chan. The Korean Diaspora: Historical and Sociological Studies of Korean Immigration and Assimilation in North America. (Santa Barbara, California, ABC-Clio, 1977)

5925. Kurti, Laszlo. "Hungarian Settlement and Building Practices in Pennsylvania and Hungary: a Brief Comparison." PA 12 (February, 1980), 34-53.

5926. Lieberson, Stanley. A Piece of the Pie: Blacks and White Immigrants since 1880. (Berkeley, University of California Press, 1980)

5927. Maldonado, Edwin. "Contract Labor and the Origins of Puerto Rican Communities in the United States." IMR 13 (Spring, 1979), 103-121.

5928. Martinez, Oscar J. "Chicanos and the Border Cities: an Interpretive Essay." PHR 46 (February, 1977), 85-106.

5929. North, David S. "The Immigration of Non-Professional Workers to the United States." IMR 6 (Spring, 1972), 64-73.

5930. Pacyga, Dominic A. "Polish Immigrant to the United States before World War II: an Overview." PAS 39 (Spring, 1982), 28-37.

5931. Reisler, Mark. "Always the Laborer, Never the Citizen: Anglo Perceptions of the Mexican Immigrant During the 1920's." PHR 45 (May, 1976), 231-254.

5932. Rock, Kenneth W. "'Unsere Leute': the Germans from Russia in Colorado." CM 54 (Spring, 1977), 155-183.

5933. Romo, Ricardo. "Work and Restlessness: Occupational and Spatial Mobility among Mexicanos in Los Angeles, 1918-1928." PHR 46 (May, 1977), 157-180.

5934. Rosales, Francisco Arturo and Daniel T. Simon. "Mexican Immigrant Experience in the Urban Midwest: East Chicago, Indiana, 1919-1945." IMH 77 (December, 1981), 333-357.

5935. Simon, Daniel T. "Mexican Repatriation in East Chicago, Indiana." JES 2 (Summer, 1974), 11-23.

5936. Szajkowski, Zosa. "Deportation of Jewish Immigrants and Returnees after World War I." AJHQ 67 (June, 1978), 291-306.

5937. Tsai, Shih-shan Henry. "The Chinese in Arkansas." AJ 8 (Spring/Summer, 1981), 1-18.

5938. Woolfson, Peter. "The Rural Franco-American in Vermont." VH 50 (Summer, 1982), 151-162.

5939. Wren, Benjamin. "The Rising Sun on the Mississippi, 1900-1975." LH 17 (Summer, 1976), 321-333.

5940. Yu, Eui-Young. "Koreans in America: an Emerging Ethnic Minority." AJ 4 (1977), 117-131.

Internal Migration

The materials here are divided into works on local and regional patterns and studies of urbanization, both general and particular. Smaller numbers, different issues, and different methods make the subdivisions of the nineteenth-century materials either irrelevant or unnecessary.   In addition to the categories of twentieth-century materials already mentioned as excluded from this bibliography, readers should keep in mind that many communities have reports from planning commissions, zoning boards, and other agencies that a serious researcher might want to examine.   The standards of selection have worked to exclude almost everything on the most recent trend in internal migration--to the sunbelt.   This phenomenon has not yet been studied historically.

Local and regional

Every important aspect of local and regional migration, except the move to the sunbelt is represented here, by titles that are self-explanatory.   The studies of black migration out of the South by Farley, Fligstein, Henri, and Johnson and Campbell, cited in the nineteenth-century section, should be consulted by readers interested in that topic.

5950.   Abbey, Sue Wilson.   "The Ku Klux Klan in Arizona, 1921-1925." JArH 14 (Spring, 1973), 10-30.

5951.   Appleton, John B.   "Migration and Economic Opportunity in the Pacific Northwest."   GR 31 (January, 1941), 46-62.

5952.   Baker, O.E.   "Land Utilization in the United States: Geographical Aspects of the Problem."   GR 13 (January, 1923), 1-26.

5953.   Barton, Thomas Frank.   "Another Look at Nonfarm Dwellers in Indiana." IASSP 11 (October, 1976), 65-80.

5954.   Bayor, Ronald H.   "Italians, Jews, and Ethnic Conflict." IMR 6 (1972), 377-391.

5955.   Bremer, Richard B.   "Patterns of Spatial Mobility: a Case Study of Nebraska Farmers 1890-1970."   AgH 48 (October, 1974), 529-542.

5956.   Brilliant, Ashley E.   "Some Aspects of Mass Motorization in Southern California, 1919-1929." SCQ 47 (June, 1965), 191-208.

5957.   Byrne, Daniel and Stuart Plattner.   "Ethnicity at Soulard Farmers Market since 1930." MoHSB 36 (April, 1980), 174-181.

5958.   Cahill, Edward E.   "Migration and Decline of the Black Population in Rural and Non-Metropolitan Areas." Phylon 25 (September, 1974), 284-292.

5959.   Caruso, Samuel T.   "After Pearl Harbor: Arizona's Response to the Gila River Relocation Center."   JArH 14 (Winter, 1973), 335-346.

5960.   Clayton, James L.   "The Impact of the Cold War on the Economics of California and Utah, 1946-1965." PHR 36 (November, 1967), 449-473.

5961.   Clayton, James L.   "An Unhallowed Gathering: the Impact of Defense Spending on Utah's Population Growth, 1940-1964." UHQ 34 (Summer, 1966), 227-242.

5962.   Cohn, John M.   "Demographic Studies of Jewish Communities in the United States: a Bibliographic Introduction and Survey." AJA 32 (April, 1980), 35-51.

5963.   Coleman, A. Lee and Larry D. Hall.   "Black Farm Operators and Farm Population, 1900-1970:   Alabama and Kentucky." Phylon 40 (December, 1979), 387-402.

5964.   Conner, Ruth.   "Charlie Sam and the Sojourners." JArH 14 (Winter, 1973), 303-316.

5965.   Daniel, Pete. "The Transformation of the Rural South: 1930 to the Present." AgH 55 (July, 1981), 231-248.

5966.   Davis, Kenneth S.   "Portrait of a Changing Kansas." KHQ 42 (Spring, 1976), 24-47.

5967.   Downes, Randolph C.   "Ohio Population Trends, 1920-1940." OAHQ 51 (July-September, 1942), 219-232.

5968.   Dubrovsky, Gertrude.   "Farmingdale, New Jersey: a Jewish Farm Community." AJHQ 66 (June, 1977), 485-497.

5969. Durr, W. Theodore. "People of the Peninsula." MHM 77 (March, 1982), 27-53.

5970.   Everett, George A., Jr.   "The History of the German-American Community of Gluckstadt, Mississippi: a Study in Persistence." JMsH 38 (November, 1976), 361-369.

5971.   Finley, Robert and E.M. Scott.   "A Great Lakes-to-Gulf Profile of Dispersed Dwelling Types." GR 30 (July, 1940), 412-419.

5972. Grubbs, Donald H. "The Story of Florida's Migrant Farm Workers." FHQ 40 (October, 1961), 103-122.

5973. Guest, Avery M. "Ecological Succession in the Puget Sound Region." JUH 3 (February, 1977), 181-210.

5974.   Hecht, Irene W.D.   "Kinship and Migration: the Making of an Oregon Isolate Community." JIH 8 (Summer, 1977), 45-67.

5975. Higgs, Robert. "The Boll Weevil, the Cotton Economy, and Black Migration, 1910-1930."   AgH 50 (April, 1976), 335-350.

5976. Hofsommer, Donovan L. "Town Building on a Texas Short Line: the Quanah, Acme and Pacific Railway, 1909-1929." ArW 21 (Winter, 1979), 355-368.

5977. Howard-Filler, Saralee R. "Michigan's 'Plain People'." MH 66 (May/June, 1982), 24-33.

5978. Johnson, Rayburn W. "Population Trends in Tennessee from 1940 to 1950." THQ 11 (September, 1952), 254-262.

5979.   Jones, David C.   "The Strategy of Railway Abandonment: the Great Northern in Washington and British Columbia, 1917-1935." WestHQ 11 (April, 1980), 140-158.

5980. Kale, Steven. "Small-Town Population Change in the Central Great Plains: an Investigation of Recent Trends." Rocky Mountain Social Science Journal 12 (January, 1975), 29-43.

5981. Kirker, Harold. "California Architecture and its Relation to Contemporary Trends in Europe and America." CHSQ 51 (Winter, 1972), 289-304.

5982. Kitano, Harry H.L. "Japanese Americans: the Development of a Middleman Minority." PHR 43 (November, 1974), 500-519.

5983. Landing, James E. "Geographical Change among Eastern Christians in the Chicago Area." Illinois Geograpical Society. Bulletin 17 (June, 1975), 40-46.

5984. Latta, Maurice C. "The Economic Effects of Drouth and Depression upon Custer County, 1929-1942." NH 33 (December, 1952), 221-236.

5985. Mather, Eugene Cotton and John F. Hart. "Fences and Farms." GR 44 (1954), 201-223.

5986. Mirkowich, Nicholas. "Recent Trends in Population Distribution in California." GR 31 (April, 1941), 300-307.

5987. Murphy, Don R. "One Hundred Years of Utah Climate." UHQ 46 (Fall, 1978), 396-375.

5988. Nash, Gerald D. The American West in the Twentieth Century: a Short History of an Urban Oasis. (Englewood Cliffs, New Jersey, Prentice-Hall, 1973)

5989. O'Brien, Robert William. "Reaction of the College Nisei to Japan and Japanese Foreign Policy from the Invasion of Manchuria to Pearl Harbor." PNQ 36 (1945), 19-28.

5990. Rowland, Mary. "Kansas and the Highways, 1917-1930." KH 5 (Spring, 1982), 33-51.

5991. Ruxin, Robert H. "The Jewish Farmer and the Small-Town Jewish Community: Schoharie County, New York." AJA 29 (April, 1977), 3-21.

5992.   Sato, Susie.   "Before Pearl Harbor: Early Japanese Settlers in Arizona." JArH 14 (Winter, 1973), 317-334.

5993.   Schmidt, William T.   "The Impact of Camp Shelby in World War II on Hattiesburg, Mississippi." JMsH 39 (February, 1977), 41-50.

5994.   Sherman, William C.   "Ethnic Distribution in Western North Dakota." NDH 46 (Winter, 1979), 4-12.

5995.   Siemankowski, Francis.   "The Making of the Polish-American Community: Sloan, New York, as a Case Study." PAS 34 (Autumn, 1977), 56-67.

5996.   Slatta, Richard W.   "Chicanos in the Pacific Northwest: a Demographic and Socioeconomic Portrait." PNQ 70 (October, 1979), 155-162.

5997.   Sorkin, Alan L.   "The Economic and Social Status of the American Indian, 1940-1970." Journal of Negro Education 45 (Fall, 1976), 432-447.

5998.   Speare, Alden, Jr.   "Home Ownership, Life Cycle Stage, and Residential Mobility." Demography 7 (November, 1970), 449-458.

5999.   Stein, Walter J.   California and the Dust Bowl Migration. (Westport, Connecticut, Greenwood Press, 1973)

6000.   Thornbrough, Emma Lou.   "Segregation in Indiana During the Klan Era of the 1920's." MVHR 47 (March, 1961), 594-618.

6001.   Uhlenberg, Peter R.   "Demographic Correlates of Group Achievement: Contrasting Patterns of Mexican-Americans and Japanese-Americans." Demography 9 (February, 1972), 119-128.

6002.   Vickers, Ruth Petway.   "Japanese-American Relocation." AkHQ 10 (Summer, 1951), 168-176.

6003.   Wilhelm, Gene, Jr.   "Shenandoah Resettlements." PA 14 (March, 1982), 15-40.

6004. Wilson, Benjamin C. "Idlewild: a Black Eden in Michigan." MH 65 (September/October, 1981), 33-37.

6005. Worster, Donald. Dust Bowl: the Southern Plains in the 1930's. (New York, Oxford University Press, 1979)

Urbanization

The basic texts and surveys cited earlier are good places to begin a study of how urbanization proceeded after 1920. There are a few general works here, sprinkled in amongst the urban biographies. Jackson's study of suburbs has been included, in spite of its very recent publication, because it is virtually unique in emphasis, and offers a major historical analysis of one of the emergent themes of twentieth-century demographic history.

6050. Abbott, Carl. The New Urban America: Growth and Politics in Sunbelt Cities. (Chapel Hill, University of North Carolina Press, 1981)

6051. Abbott, Carl. "Suburb and City: Changing Patterns of Socioeconomic Status in Metropolitan Denver since 1940." SSH 2 (Fall, 1977), 53-71.

6052. Adams, Charles L. "Las Vegas as Border Town: an Interpretive Essay." NHSQ 21 (Spring, 1978), 51-55.

6053. Agoes, Carol. "Ethnic Groups in the Ecology of North American Cities." Canadian Ethnic Studies 11 (1979), 1-18.

6054. Alexander, Thomas G. "Ogden, a Federal Colony in Utah." UHQ 47 (Summer, 1979), 290-309.

6055. Barrows, Robert G. "Hurryin' Hoosiers and the American 'Pattern': Geographical Mobility in Indianapolis and Urban North America." SSH 5 (Spring, 1981), 197-222.

6056. Bauman, John F. "Downtown Versus Neighborhood: Focusing on Philadelphia in the Metropolitan Era, 1920-1980." PH 48 (January, 1981), 3-20.

6057. Bennion, Lowell C. and Merrill K. Ridd. "Utah's Dynamic Dixie: Satellite of Salt Lake, Las Vegas, or Los Angeles?" UHQ 47 (Summer, 1979), 310-327.

6058. Blejwas, Stanislaus. "A Polish Community in Transition: the Evolution of Holy Cross Parish, New Britain, Connecticut." PAS 35 (Spring-Autumn, 1978), 23-53.

6059. Blejwas, Stanislaus. "A Polish Community in Transition: the Origins of Holy Cross Parish, New Britain, Connecticut." PAS 34 (Spring, 1977), 26-69.

6060. Bufkin, Don. "From Mud Village to Modern Metropolis: the Urbanization of Tucson." JArH 22 (Spring, 1981), 63-98.

6061. Castillo, Adelaida. "Filipino Migrants in San Diego, 1900-1946." JSDH 22 (Summer, 1976), 26-35.

6062. Connolly, Harold X. A Ghetto Grows in Brooklyn. (New York, New York University Press, 1977)

6063. Corzine, Jay and Irene Dabrowski. "The Ethnic Factor and Neighborhood Stability: the Czechs in Soulard and South St. Louis." MoHSB 33 (January, 1977), 87-93.

6064. Cuba, Stanley L. "A Polish Community in the Urban West: St. Joseph's Parish in Denver, Colorado." PAS 36 (Spring, 1979), 33-74.

6065. Davis, Allison and John Dollard. Children of Bondage: the Personality Development of Negro Youth in the Urban South. (Washington, D.C., American Council on Education, 1940)

6066. Donaldson, Alice. "Rhetoric of a Small Midwestern Town." MoHR 75 (July, 1981), 448-463.

6067. Downs, Anthony. Opening up the Suburbs: an Urban Strategy for America. (New Haven, Connecticut, Yale University Press, 1973)

6068. Ericksen, Eugene P. and William L. Yancey. "Work and Residence in Industrial Philadelphia." JUH 5 (February, 1979), 147-182.

6069.   Farley,   Reynolds.   "Residential   Segregation   in
Urbanized Areas of the United States in 1970:   an Analysis
of Social Class and Racial Differences."   Demography 14
(November, 1977), 497-518.

6070.   Flowerdew,   Robin.   "Spatial   Patterns   of   Residential
Segregation   in   a   Southern   City."   JAS 13 (April, 1979),
93-107.

6071.   Foster,   Mark   S.   "The   Automobile   in   the   Urban
Environment: Planning for an Energy-Short Future."   Public
Historian 3 (Fall, 1981), 23-31.

6072.   Foster, Mark S.   "The Model-T, the Hard Sell, and Los
Angeles's Urban Growth: the Decentralization of Los Angeles
during the 1920's."   PHR 44 (November, 1975), 459-484.

6073.   Franklin,   Vincent   P.   The   Education   of   Black
Philadelphia: the   Social   and   Educational   History   of   a
Minority Community, 1900-1950.   (Philadelphia, University of
Pennsylvania Press, 1979)

6074.   Gans, Herbert J.   The Levittowners: Ways of Life and
Politics in a New Suburban Community.   (New York, Vintage
Books, 1967)

6075.   Guest, Avery M, Barrett A. Lee, and Lynn Staeheli.
"Changing Locality Identification in the Metropolis: Seattle,
1920-1978."   ASR 47 (August, 1982), 543-549.

6076.   Handlin, Oscar.   The Newcomers: Negroes and Puerto
Ricans in a Changing Metropolis.   (Cambridge, Massachusetts,
Harvard University Press, 1959)

6077.   Hirsch,   Arnold   Richard.   Making the Second Ghetto:
Race   and   Housing   in   Chicago,   1940-1960.   (New   York,
Cambridge University Press, 1983)

6078.   Jackson,   Kenneth   T.   The Crabgrass Frontier: The
Suburbanization of the United States.   (New York, Oxford
University Press, 1985)

6079.   Kersten,   Earl   W.,   Jr.   and   D.   Reid   Ross.   "Clayton: a
New Metropolitan Focus in the St. Louis Area."   AAG 58
(December, 1968), 637-649.

6080. Kiser, Clyde Vernon. <u>Sea Island to City: a Study of St. Helena Islanders in Harlem and Other Urban Centers</u>. (New York, Columbia University Press, 1932)

6081. Konig, Michael. "Phoenix in the 1950's: Urban Growth in the 'Sunbelt'." <u>ArW</u> 24 (Spring, 1982), 19-38.

6082. Krause, Corinne Azen. "Urbanization Without Breakdown: Italian, Jewish, and Slavic Immigrant Women in Pittsburgh, 1900 to 1945." <u>JUH</u> 4 (May, 1978), 291-306.

6083. Larsen, Lawrence H. and Roger T. Johnson. "A Story That Never Was: North Dakota's Urban Development." <u>NDH</u> 47 (Fall, 1980), 4-10.

6084. Lonsdale, Richard E. and Clyde E. Browning. "Rural-Urban Locational Preferences of Southern Manufacturers." <u>AAG</u> 61 (1971), 255-268.

6085. Luckingham, Bradford. "Urban Development in Arizona: the Rise of Phoenix." <u>JArH</u> 22 (Summer, 1981), 197-234.

6086. McGovern, James R. "Pensacola, Florida: a Military City in the New South." <u>FHQ</u> 59 (July, 1980), 24-41.

6087. McLear, Patrick E. "Land Speculators and Urban and Regional Development: Chicago in the 1930's." <u>Old Northwest</u> 6 (Summer, 1980), 137-151.

6088. Margon, Arthur. "Indians and Immigrants: a Comparison of Groups New to the City." <u>JES</u> 4 (Winter, 1977), 17-28.

6089. Masotti, Louis H. and Jeffery K. Hadden, eds. <u>Suburbia in Transition</u>. (New York, New Viewpoint, 1974)

6090. Melzer, Richard. "A Death in Dawson: the Demise of a Southwestern Company Town." <u>NMHR</u> 55 (October, 1980), 309-330.

6091. Miller, Zane L. <u>Suburb: Neighborhood and Community in Forest Park, Ohio, 1935-1976</u>. (Knoxville, University of Tennessee Press, 1981)

6092.   Mohl, Raymond A. and Neil Betten.   "Ethnic Adjustment in the Industrial City: the International Institute of Gary. 1919-1940." IMR 6 (Winter, 1972), 361-376.

6093.   Monkkonen, Eric H.   "Toward an Understanding of Urbanization: Drunk Arrests in Los Angeles." PHR 50 (May, 1981), 234-244.

6094.   Moynihan, Daniel Patrick.   "Patterns of Ethnic Succession: Blacks and Hispanics in New York City." PSQ 94 (Spring, 1979), 1-14.

6095.   Nelson, Howard J.   "The Vernon Area, California--a Study of the Political Factor in Urban Geography." AAG 42 (1952), 177-191.

6096.   Olien, Roger M. and Diana Davids Olien. Oil Booms: Social Change in Five Texas Towns. (Lincoln, University of Nebraska Press, 1982)

6097.   Parker, Russell D.   "The Black Community in a Company Town: Alcoa, Tennessee, 1919-1939." THQ 37 (Summer, 1978), 203-221.

6098.   Randall, Duncan P. "Wilmington, North Carolina: the Historical Development of a Port City." AAG 58 (September, 1968), 441-451.

6099.   Roberts, Shirley J.   "Minority-Group Poverty in Phoenix: a Socio-Economic Survey." JArH 14 (Winter, 1973), 347-362.

6100.   Russell, Emily W.B.   "Mt. Tabor, New Jersey: an Environmental History." NJH 95 (Autumn, 1977), 157-169.

6101.   St.Clair, David J.   "The Motorization and Decline of Urban Public Transit, 1935-1950." JEH 41 (September, 1981), 579-600.

6102.   Sorrelle, James M.   "'An de Po Cullud Man is in de Wuss Fix uv Awl': Black Occupational Status in Houston, Texas, 1920-1940." Houston Review 1 (Spring, 1979), 14-26.

6103.   Shumway, Gary L.   "Blanding: the Making of a Community." UHQ 48 (Fall, 1980), 390-405.

6104.   Taylor, Quintard.   "The Great Migration: the Afro-American Communities of Seattle and Portland During the 1940's." ArW 23 (Summer, 1981), 109-126.

6105.   Teaford, Jon C.   City and Suburb: the Political Fragmentation   of   Metropolitan   America,   1850-1970. (Baltimore, Johns Hopkins University Press, 1979)

6106.   VanArsdol, Maurice D., Jr., and Leo A. Schuerman. "Redistribution and Assimilation of Ethnic Populations: the Los Angeles Case." Demography 8 (November, 1971), 459-480.

6107.   Vance, James E., Jr.   "Geography and the Study of Cities."   American   Behavioral   Scientist   22 (September/October, 1978), 131-149.

6108.   Varady, David P.   "Migration and Mobility Patterns of the Jewish Population of Cincinnati." AJA 32 (April, 1980), 78-88.

6109.   Warner, Sam Bass, Jr.   The Way We Really Live: Social Change in Metropolitan Boston since 1920.   (Boston, Trustees of the Public Library of the City of Boston, 1977)

6110.   Warner, Sam Bass, Jr., and Sylvia Fleisch.   "The Past of Today's Present: a Social History of America's Metropolises, 1960-1980." JUH 3 (November, 1976), 3-118.

6111.   Weber, Michael, John Bodnar, and Roger Simon. "Seven Neighborhoods: Stability and Change in Pittsburgh's Ethnic Community, 1930-1960."   WPHM 64 (April, 1981), 121-150.

6112.   Williams, Lee.   "Newcomers to the City: a Study of Black Population Growth in Toledo, Ohio, 1910-1930." OH 89 (Winter, 1980), 5-24.

5
Family and Demographic History

The connections between family and demographic history range from obvious links, such as the forming of families through marriage, to subtle ties involving the interaction of the nineteenth-century demographic revolutions and the concurrent debates over the desireability of new roles for family members. Not all family historians are interested in or aware of demographic issues. Thus, much of the material in this chapter does not explicitly refer to matters of population. It can, however, be read with profit by demographic historians. After an opening section of works with broad theoretical or chronological orientations, the bibliography is divided into periods along the lines of the earlier chapters. Family historians might prefer different divisions. There is sufficient material for Early America and the Nineteenth Century to permit additional categories. In both periods, the first set of citations refer to studies on the internal working of families ranging from household structures to roles within the family. The second category includes studies of how families actually fit into society, as well as debates over what the ideal relationships should be.

Theory and General Histories

Students unfamiliar with family history will find some of the following works useful places to start. Gordon and Seward provide general accounts of the history of American families. Both authors are sociologists by training; Gordon, however, writes more like an historian. The collection of essays edited by Demos and Boocock is also valuable. Calhoun is a classic older study with distinct interpretations and a perspective that goes beyond American families. Books by Goode, Shorter, and Stone say little about American families, but can be read with profit for comparative purposes. There are numerous theories about the family. One that has been influential in historical writing has been the idea of the life cycle, later modified to the life course. Start with Glick, and Spanier and Glick and then look at Elder, Hareven, and Vinovskis for this perspective. Rapp, Ross, and Bridenthal, Vogel, and Wells offer several possible alternatives. For changing roles of women and children in the family over long periods, Degler, Kett, and Modell, Furstenberg, and Hershberg are good places to start. The documentary collections by Breckenridge and Bremner (cited in the second part of the nineteenth-century material) are excellent, but are probably best read after some of the works just mentioned.

7000. Antler, Joyce. "'After College, What?': New Graduates and the Family Claim." AQ 32 (Fall, 1980), 409-434.

7001. Aptheker, Bettina. Woman's Legacy: Essays on Race, Sex, and Class in American History. (Amherst, University of Massachusetts Press, 1982)

7002. Berch, Bettina. "Scientific Management in the Home: the Empress's New Clothes." JAC 3 (Fall, 1980), 440-445.

7003. Boocock, Sarane Spence. "Historical and Sociological Research on the Family and the Life Cycle: Methodological Alternatives." In John Demos and Sarane Spence Boocock, eds. Turning Points: Historical and Sociological Essays on the Family. (Chicago, University of Chicago Press, 1978; supplement to AJS 84), 336-394.

7004. Brandenstein, Sherilyn. "The Colorado Cottage Home." CM 53 (Summer, 1977), 229-242.

7005. Breckinridge, Sophonisba Preston. The Family and the State: Select Documents. (New York, Arno Press, 1972; reprint of Chicago, University of Chicago Press, 1934)

7006. Brobeck, Stephen. "Images of the Family: Portrait Paintings as Indices of American Family Culture, Structure, and Behavior, 1730-1860." Journal of Psychohistory 5 (Summer, 1977), 81-106.

7007. Brown, Steven E. "Sexuality and the Slave Community." Phylon 42 (Spring, 1981), 1-10.

7008. Burnham, Dorothy. "The Life of the Afro-American Woman in Slavery." IJWS 1 (July/August, 1978), 363-377.

7009. Bushman, Richard L. "Family Security in the Transition from Farm to City, 1750-1850." JFH 6 (Fall, 1981), 238-256.

7010. Butler, Anne M. "Military Myopia: Prostitution on the Frontier." Prologue 13 (Winter, 1981), 232-250.

7011. Calhoun, Arthur Wallace. A Social History of the American Family from Colonial Times to the Present. 3 volumes. (Cleveland, Arthur H. Clark Co., 1917-1919)

7012. Carrell, Kimberley W. "The Industrial Revolution Comes to the Home: Kitchen Design Reform and Middle-Class Women." JAC 2 (Fall, 1979), 488-499.

7013. Chafe, William H. "Sex and Race: the Analogy of Social Control." Massachusetts Review 18 (Spring, 1977), 146-176.

7014. Christensen, Harold T. "Mormon Sexuality in Cross-Cultural Perspective." DJMT 10 (Autumn, 1976), 62-75.

7015. Cohen, Lizabeth A. "Embellishing a Life of Labor: an Interpretation of the Material Culture of American Working-Class Homes, 1885-1915." JAC 3 (Winter, 1980), 752-775.

7016. Contosta, David R. "Origins of Early Domestic Architecture in Lancaster, Ohio." Old Northwest 7 (Fall, 1981), 201-216.

7017. Cook, Sherburne Friend. "The Stability of Indian Custom Marriage." IH 7 (Summer, 1974), 33-34.

7018.   Cooper, Patricia Irvin.   "A Quaker-Plan House in Georgia." PA 10 (June, 1978), 15-34.

7019.   Davis, Angela Y.   Women, Race and Class.   (New York, Random House, 1981)

7020.   Davis, Glenn.   Childhood and History in America. (New York, Psychohistory, 1976)

7021.   Demos, John, and Sarane Spence Boocock, eds. Turning Points; Historical and Sociological Essays on the Family.   (Chicago, University of Chicago Press, 1978; supplement to AJS 84)

7022.   Degler, Carl N.   At Odds: Women and the Family in America from the Revolution to the Present.   (New York, Oxford University Press, 1980)

7023.   Dublin, Thomas.   "Women Workers and the Study of Social Mobility." JIH 9 (Spring, 1979), 647-665.

7024.   Elder, Glen H., Jr.   "Family History and the Life Course." JFH 2 (Winter, 1977), 279-304.

7025.   Faragher, John Mack.   "History from the Inside-Out: Writing the History of Women in Rural America."   AQ 33 (Winter, 1981), 537-557.

7026.   Filler, Louis.   Vanguards and Followers: Youth in the American Tradition.   (Chicago, Nelson-Hall, 1978)

7027.   Foner, Anne.   "Age Stratification and the Changing Family."   In John Demos and Sarane Spence Boocock, eds. Turning Points; Historical and Sociological Essays on the Family.   (Chicago, University of Chicago Press, 1978; supplement to AJS 84); 340-365.

7028.   Fridkis, Arl Lloyd.   "Desertion in the American Jewish Immigrant Family: the Work of the National Desertion Bureau in Cooperation with the Industrial Removal Office." AJH 71 (December, 1981), 285-299.

7029.   Gagnon, John H.   "Sex Research and Social Change." Archives of Sexual Behavior 4 (March, 1975), 111-142.

7030. Garcia, Mario T. "The Chicana in American History: the Mexican Women of El Paso, 1880-1920--a Case Study." PHR 49 (May, 1980), 315-337.

7031.   Geelhoed, E. Bruce.   "Business and the American Family: a Local View." ISSQ 33 (Autumn, 1980), 58-67.

7032. Gibson, Geoffrey. "Kin Family Network: Overheralded Structure in Past Conceptualizations of Family Functioning." JMF 34 (February, 1972), 13-23.

7033.   Glick, Paul C.   "The Life Cycle of the Family." Marriage and Family Living 17 (February, 1955), 3-9.

7034.   Goode, William Josiah.   "Force and Violence in the Family." JMF 33 (November, 1971), 624-636.

7035. Goode, William Josiah. "Violence Between Intimates." In William Josiah Goode. Explorations in Social Theory. (New York, Oxford University Press, 1973), 145-197.

7036. Goode, William Josiah. World Revolution and Family Patterns. (New York, Free Press of Glenco, 1963)

7037. Gordon, Linda. "Domestic Revolution: History of a Good Idea." Radical America 15 (November-December, 1981), 63-68.

7038. Gordon, Linda. "The Long Struggle for Reproductive Rights." Radical America 15 (Spring, 1981), 75-88.

7039.   Gordon, Michael, comp. The American Family in Social-Historical Perspective.   2nd ed.   (New York, St. Martin's Press, 1978)

7040. Gordon, Michael. The American Family: Past, Present and Future. (New York, Random House, 1978)

7041. Graham, Patricia Albjerg. "Expansion and Exclusion: a History of Women in American Higher Education." Signs 4 (Summer, 1978), 759-773.

7042. Halla, Frank L. "Childhood, Culture, and Society in Psychoanalysis and History."   Historian 39 (May, 1977), 423-438.

7043. Hansen, Klaus J. "Mormon Sexuality and American Culture." DJMT 10 (Autumn, 1976), 45-56.

7044. Hareven, Tamara K. "Family Time and Historical Time." Daedalus 106 (Spring, 1977), 57-70.

7045. Hareven, Tamara K. "Introduction: the Historical Study of the Family in Urban Society." JUH 1 (May, 1975), 259-267.

7046. Hareven, Tamara K. "The Last Stage: Historical Adulthood and Old Age." Daedalus 105 (Fall, 1976), 13-27.

7047. Harris, Barbara J. Beyond her Sphere: Women and the Professions in American History. (Westport, Connecticut, Greenwood Press, 1978)

7048. Harris, William G. "Research on the Black Family: Mainstream and Dissenting Perspectives." JES 6 (Winter, 1979), 45-64.

7049. Hensley, J. Clark. "Trends in Baptist Family Life." Baptist History and Heritage 17 (January, 1982), 3-12,62.

7050. Hoover, Dwight W. "'Home and Family.'" ISSQ 33 (Autumn, 1980), 7-18.

7051. Jordan, Winthrop D. "Searching for Adulthood in America." Daedulus 105 (Fall, 1976), 1-11.

7052. Kanter, Rosabeth Moss. "Families, Family Processes, and Ecomonic Life: Toward Systematic Analysis of Social Historical Research." In John Demos and Sarane Spence Boocock, eds. Turning Points: Historical and Sociological Essays on the Family. (Chicago, University of Chicago Press, 1978, supplement to AJS 84), 316-339.

7053. Kessler-Harris, Alice. Out to Work: a History of Wage-Earning Women in the United States. (New York, Oxford University Press, 1982)

7054. Kett, Joseph F. Rites of Passage: Adolesence in America, 1790 to the Present. (New York, Basic Books, 1977)

7055. Kidwell, Clara Sue. "The Power of Women in Three American Indian Societies." JES 6 (Fall, 1978), 113-121.

7056. Landes, Joan B. "Women, Labor and Family Life: a Theoretical Perspective." Science and Society 41 (Winter, 1977-1978), 386-409.

7057. Laslett, Barbara. "The Family as a Public and Private Institution: an Historical Perspective." JMF 35 (August, 1973), 480-492.

7058. Lieberman, Richard K. "A Measure for the Quality of Life: Housing." HM 11 (Summer, 1978), 129-134.

7059. Marcus, Jacob R. The American Jewish Woman: a Documentary History. (New York, KTAV, 1981)

7060. Marcus, Jacob R. The American Jewish Woman, 1654-1980. (New York, KTAV, 1981)

7061. Mergen, Bernard. "The Discovery of Children's Play." AQ 27 (October, 1975), 399-420.

7062. Mishler, Elliot G. and Nancy E. Waxler. "Family Interaction Processes and Schizophrenia: a Review of Current Theories." Merrill-Palmer Quarterly of Behavior and Development 11 (1965), 269-315.

7063. Modell, John, Frank F. Furstenberg, Jr., and Theodore Hershberg. "Social Change and Transitions to Adulthood in Historical Perspective." JFH 1 (Autumn, 1976), 7-32.

7064. Myres, Sandra L. "Mexican Americans and Westering Anglos: a Feminine Perspective." NMHR 57 (October, 1982), 319-333.

7065. Neuman, R.P. "Masturbation, Madness, and the Modern Concepts of Childhood and Adolescence." JSH 8 (Spring, 1975), 1-27.

7066. Pleck, Elizabeth H. "Two Worlds in One: Work and Family." JHS 10 (Winter, 1976), 178-195.

7067. Pollard, Leslie J. "Aging and Slavery: a Gerontological Approach." JNH 66 (Fall, 1981), 228-234.

7068. Rapp, Rayna, Ellen Ross, and Renate Bridenthal. "Examining Family History." FS 5 (Spring, 1979), 174-200.

7069. Riley, Glenda. "Women in the West." JAC 3 (Summer, 1980), 311-329.

7070. Riley, Glenda, et.al. "Women in the West." JW 21 (April, 1982), 2-88.

7071. Rivers, Theodore John. "Widows' Rights in Anglo-Saxon Law." AJLH 19 (July, 1975), 208-215.

7072. Rogers, Gayle J. "The Changing Image of the Southern Woman: a Performer on a Pedestal." JPC 16 (Winter, 1982), 60-67.

7073. Rosenzweig, Mark R. "The Demand for Children in Farm Households." Journal of Political Economy 85 (February, 1977), 123-146.

7074. Roth, Darlene. "Feminine Marks on the Landscape: an Atlanta Inventory." JAC 3 (Winter, 1980), 673-685.

7075. Russell-Wood, A.J.R. "The Black Family in the Americas." Societas 8 (Winter, 1978), 1-38.

7076. Schlenker, Jon A. "An Historical Analysis of the Family Life of the Choctaw Indians." Southern Quarterly 13 (July, 1975), 323-324.

7077. Schramm, Sarah Slavin. Plow Women Rather than Reapers: an Intellectual History of Feminism in the United States. (Metuchen, New Jersey, Scarecrow, 1979)

7078. Scott, Anne Firor. "What, Then, Is the American: This New Woman?" JAH 65 (December, 1978), 679-703.

7079. Scura, Dorthy McInnis. "The Southern Lady in the Early Novels of Ellen Glasgow." MQ 31 (Winter, 1977-1978), 17-31.

7080.   Seward, Rudy Ray.   The American Family: a Demographic History.   (Beverly   Hills, California, Sage Publications, 1978)

7081.   Shorter, Edward.   The Making of the Modern Family. (New York, Basic Books, 1975)

7082.   Smelser, Neil J. and Sydney Halpern.   "The Historical Triangulation of Family, Economy, and Education."   In John Demos and Sarane Spence Boocock, eds.   Turning Points: Historical and Sociological Essays on the Family.   (Chicago, University of Chicago Press, 1978; supplement to AJS 84), 288-315.

7083.   Smith, Daniel Blake.   "The Study of the Family in Early America: Trends, Problems, and Prospects."   WMQ 39 (January, 1982), 3-28.

7084.   Spanier, Graham B. and Paul C. Glick.   "The Life Cycle of American Families: an Expanded Analysis."   JFH 5 (Spring, 1980), 97-111.

7085.   Stone, Lawrence.   The Family, Sex and Marriage in England, 1500-1800.   (New York, Harper and Row, 1977)

7086.   Uhlenberg, Peter.   "Death and the Family."   JFH 5 (Fall, 1980), 313-320.

7087.   Vinovskis, Maris A.   "From Household Size to the Life Course: Some Observations on Recent Trends in Family History."   American   Behavioral   Scientist   21 (November/December, 1977), 263-287.

7088.   Vogel, Lise.   "The Contested Domain: a Note on the Family in the Transition to Capitalism."   Marxist Perspectives 1 (Spring, 1978), 50-73.

7089.   Wall, Rita Turner.   "The Vanishing Tenant Houses of Rural Georgia."   GHQ 65 (Fall, 1981), 251-262.

7090.   Walters, R.G.   "Sexual Matters as Historical Problems: a   Framework   of   Analysis."   Societas 6 (Summer, 1976), 157-175.

7091. Weissbach, Lee Shai. "The Townes of Massachusetts: a Pilot Study in Genealogy and Family History." EICH 118 (July, 1982), 200-220.

7092. Wells, Robert V. "Demographic Change and the Life Cycle of American Families." JIH 2 (Autumn, 1971), 273-282.

7093. West, Elliott. "Scarlet West: the Oldest Profession in the Trans-Mississippi West." Montana 31 (April, 1981), 16-27.

7094. Williams, Harvey. "Social Isolation and the Elderly Immigrant Woman." PacH 26 (Summer, 1982), 15-23.

7095. Wolfe, Margaret Ripley. "The Southern Lady: Long Suffering Counterpart of the Good Ole' Boy." JPC 11 (Summer, 1977), 18-27.

7096. Yanagisako, Sylvia Junko. "Women-Centered Kin Networks in Urban Bilateral Kinship." American Ethnologist 4 (May, 1977), 207-226.

7097. Zunz, Olivier. "Neighborhoods, Homes, and the Dual Housing Market." MH 66 (November/December, 1982), 33-41.

Early America

Families in the 1980s are clearly different from those that existed before 1800. Less certain, however, is when the change began and what it means. In the absence of a widely accepted chronology of family history, the divisions used earlier in the bibliography will be applied here. Note also that many family historians have used what is essentially political periodization, even though the reasons for doing so are not necessarily strong. The quality of these works is extraordinarily high. Studies given specific mention are the best places to start, but not stop.

Family Structures and Domestic Relations

The studies included here focus on the internal workings of the family. This means anything from the size and composition of households to relationships between husbands and wives, parents and children, or masters and servants.

Morgan's book on Puritan families is the place to start because of its comprehensiveness and later influence. Books by Demos and Frost reflect this influence in important contributions. For household structures and family size, see the studies by Greven and Wells, and materials on childbearing in early America in Chapter Two. Scholars interested in the roles of women should also consult Carr and Walsh, and Ulrich for the seventeenth century, and Benson, Cott, Kerber, Norton, and Wilson for the eighteenth, as starters. Children receive special notice from Cremin, Fleming, Greven, Homan, and Wishy. Demos, Faragher, Fischer, and Waters have begun the study of old age. Gutman and Kulikoff make helpful remarks on black families in the early years of slavery.

7100.   Alsop, James D.   "Sir Samuel Argall's Family, 1560-1620." VMHB 90 (October, 1982), 472-484.

7101. Auwers, Linda. "Fathers, Sons, and Wealth in Colonial Windsor, Connecticut." JFH 3 (Summer, 1978), 136-149.

7102.   Beales, Ross W., Jr.   "In Search of the Historical Child: Miniature Adulthood and Youth in Colonial New England." AQ 27 (October, 1975), 379-398.

7103. Benson, Mary Sumner. Women in Eighteenth-Century America: a Study of Opinion and Social Usage. (New York, Columbia University Press, 1935)

7104.   Bloch, Ruth H.   "American Feminine Ideals in Transition: the Rise of the Moral Mother, 1785-1815." FS 4 (June, 1978), 100-126.

7105. Boatwright, Elanor M. "The Political and Civil Status of Women in Georgia, 1783-1860." GHQ 25 (December, 1941), 301-324.

7106. Boyett, Gene W. "Aging in Seventeenth-Century New England." NEHGR 134 (July, 1980), 181-193.

7107. Buel, Joy Day and Richard Buel, Jr. The Way of Duty: a Woman and her Family in Revolutionary America. (New York, W.W. Norton, 1984)

7108.   Calvert,   Karin.   "Children   in   American   Family Portraiture, 1670-1810." WMQ 39 (January, 1982), 87-113.

7109. Carr, Lois Green and Lorena S. Walsh. "The Planter's Wife: the   Experience   of   White   Women   in Seventeenth-Century Maryland."   WMQ 34 (October, 1977), 542-571.

7110.   Chipman, Donald.   "The Onate-Mochtezuma-Zaldivar Families of Northern New Spain." NMHR 52 (October, 1977), 297-310.

7111. Clinton, Catherine. "Equally their Due: the Education of the Planter Daughter in the Early Republic." Journal of the Early Republic 2 (Spring, 1982), 39-60.

7112. Cott, Nancy F. The Bonds of Womanhood: "Woman's Sphere" in New England, 1780-1835.   (New Haven, Yale University Press, 1977)

7113.   Cott, Nancy F. "Eighteenth-Century Family and Social Life Revealed in Massachusetts Divorce Records."   JSH 10 (Fall, 1976), 20-43.

7114.   Cremin,   Lawrence   A.   American   Education: The Colonial Experience, 1607-1783. (New York, Harper and Row, 1970).

7115.   Cremin, Lawrence A.   "The Family as Educator: Some Comments on the Recent Historiography"   Teachers College Record 76 (1974), 250-265.

7116. Demos, John. A Little Commonwealth: Family Life in Plymouth Colony. (New York, Oxford University Press, 1970)

7117.   Demos, John. "Old Age in Early New England."   In John Demos and Sarane Spence Boocock, eds.   Turning Points; Historical and Sociological Essays on the Family. (Chicago, University of Chicago Press, 1978; supplement to AJS 84), 248-287.

7118.   Downsbrough, Bruce.   "Household Size and Composition in French Louisiana, 1721-1732."   (Schenectady, New York, unpublished seminar paper, Union College, 1974)

7119. Earle, Alice Morse. Child Life in Colonial Days.
(New York, Macmillan Company, 1904)

7120. Earle, Alice Morse. Colonial Dames and Good Wives.
(Boston, Houghton Mifflin and Co., 1895)

7121. Faragher, John Mack. "Old Women and Old Men in
Seventeenth-Century Wethersfield, Connecticut." Women's
Studies 4 (1976), 11-31.

7122. Farber, Bernard. Guardians of Virtue: Salem Families
in 1800. (New York, Basic Books, 1972)

7123. Fischer, David Hackett. Growing Old in America.
(New York, Oxford University Press, 1977)

7124. Flaherty, David H. Privacy in Colonial New England.
(Charlottesville, University Press of Virginia, 1972)

7125. Fleming, Sandford. Children and Puritanism; the Place
of Children in the Life and Thought of the New England
Churches, 1620-1847. (New Haven, Connecticut, Yale
University Press, 1933)

7126. Frost, Jerry William. "As the Twig is Bent: Quaker
Ideas of Childhood." Quaker History 60 (Autumn, 1971),
67-87.

7127. Frost, Jerry William. The Quaker Family in Colonial
America: a Portrait of the Society of Friends. (New York,
St. Martin's Press, 1973)

7128. Furstenberg, Frank F., Jr. "Industrialization and the
American Family: a Look Backward." ASR 31 (June, 1966),
326-327,

7129. Gelles, Edith B. "Abigail Adams: Domesticity and the
American Revolution." NEQ 52 (December, 1979), 500-521.

7130. Greven, Philip J., Jr. "The Average Size of Families
and Households in the Province of Massachusetts in 1764 and
in the United States in 1790: an Overview." In Peter
Laslett, ed. Household and Family in Past Time. (Cambridge,
England, Cambridge University Press, 1972), 545-560.

7131. Greven, Philip J., Jr. The Protestant Temperament: Patterns of Child-Rearing, Religious Experience, and the Self in Early America. (New York, Knopf, 1977)

7132. Gutman, Herbert George. The Black Family in Slavery and Freedom, 1750-1925. (New York, Pantheon Books, 1976)

7133. Henretta, James A. "Families and Farms: Mentalite in Pre-Industrial America." WMQ 35 (January, 1978), 3-32.

7134. Hiner, N. Ray. "Adolescence in Eighteenth-Century America." History of Childhood Quarterly 3 (Fall, 1975), 253-280.

7135. Hoffer, Peter C. and N.E.H. Hull. Murdering Mothers: Infanticide in England and New England, 1558-1803. (New York, New York University Press, 1981)

7136. Homan, Walter Joseph. Children and Quakerism; a Study of the Place of Children in the Theory and Practice of the Society of Friends, Commonly Called Quakers. (New York, Arno Press, 1972; Repr. of Berkeley, California, Printed at the Gillick Press, 1939)

7137. Illick, Joseph E.   "Child-Rearing in Seventeenth-Century England and America."   In Lloyd DeMause, ed. The History of Childhood. (New York, Psychohistory Press, 1974), 303-350.

7138. Jacob, Kathryn A. "The Woman's Lot in Baltimore Town: 1729-1797." MHM 71 (Fall, 1976), 283-295.

7139. Jedrey, Christopher M. The World of John Cleaveland: Family and Community in Eighteenth-Century New England. (New York, Norton, 1979)

7140. Kerber, Linda K. "Daughters of Columbia: Educating Women for the Republic, 1787-1805." In Stanley Elkins and Eric McKittrick, eds. The Hofstadter Aegis. (New York, Alfred A. Knopf, 1974), 36-59.

7141. Kerber, Linda K. "The Republican Mother: Women and the Enlightenment--an American Perspective." AQ 28 (Summer, 1976), 187-205.

7142. Kerber, Linda K. Women of the Republic: Intellect and Ideology in Revolutionary America. (Chapel Hill, Institute of Early American History and Culture, 1980)

7143. Kiefer, Monica Mary. American Children through their Books, 1700-1835. (Philadelphia, University of Pennsylvania Press, 1948)

7144. Kiefer, Monica Mary. "Early American Childhood in the Middle Atlantic Area." PMHB 68 (January, 1944), 3-37.

7145. Koehler, Lyle. A Search for Power: the "Weaker Sex" in Seventeenth-Century New England. (Urbana, University of Illinois Press, 1980)

7146. Kulikoff, Allan. "The Beginnings of the Afro-American Family in Maryland." In Aubrey C. Land, et. al., eds. Law, Society, and Politics in Early Maryland; Proceedings of the First Conference on Maryland History, June 14-15, 1974. (Baltimore, Johns Hopkins University Press, 1976), 171-196.

7147. Lantz, Herman R., et.al. "Preindustrial Patterns in the Colonial Family in America: a Content Analysis of Colonial Magazines." ASR 33 (June, 1968), 413-426.

7148. Lantz, Herman R., Jane Keys, and Martin Schultz. "The American Family in the Preindustrial Period: from Base Lines in History to Change." ASR 40 (February, 1975), 21-36.

7149. Lantz, Herman R., Raymond L. Schmitt and Richard Herman. "The Pre-Industrial Family in America: a Further Examination of Early Magazines." AJS 79 (November, 1973), 566-588.

7150. Lantz, Herman R., Martin Schultz, and Mary O'Hara. "The Changing American Family from the Preindustrial to the Industrial Period: a Final Report." ASR 42 (June, 1977), 406-421.

7151. Levy, Barry. "'Tender Plants': Quaker Farmers and Children in the Delaware Valley, 1681-1735." JFH 3 (Summer, 1978), 116-135.

7152.   Lewis,   Jan.   "Domestic   Tranquillity   and   the
Management   of   Emotion   among   the   Gentry   of
Pre-Revolutionary   Virginia."   WMQ   39   (January,   1982),
135-149.

7153.   Lewis, Ronald L.   "Slave Families at Early Chesapeake
Ironworks."   VMHB 86 (April, 1978), 169-179.

7154.   Masson, Margaret W.   "The Typology of the Female as
a Model for the Regenerate: Puritan Preaching, 1690-1730."
Signs 2 (Winter, 1976), 304-315.

7155.   Morgan, Edmund S.   The Puritan Family: Religion and
Domestic Relations in Seventeenth-Century New England.
(New York, Harper & Row, 1966)

7156.   Morgan, Edmund S.   Virginians at Home: Family Life
in the Eighteenth Century.   (Williamsburg, Virginia, Colonial
Williamsburg, 1952)

7157.   Morris, Richard Brandon.   "Women's Rights in Early
American Law."   In his Studies in the History of American
Law, with Special Reference to the Seventeenth and
Eighteenth Centuries.   (New York, Columbia University Press,
1930)

7158.   Norton, Mary Beth.   "Eighteenth-Century American
Women in Peace and War: the Case of the Loyalists."   WMQ
33 (July, 1976), 386-409.

7159.   Norton,   Mary Beth.   Liberty's Daughters: the
Revolutionary Experience of American Women, 1750-1800.
(Boston, Little, Brown, 1980)

7160.   Reinier, Jacqueline S.   "Rearing the Republican Child:
Attitudes and Practices in Post-Revolutionary Philadelphia."
WMQ 39 (January, 1982), 150-163.

7161.   Shammas, Carole.   "The Domestic Environment in Early
Modern England and America."   JSH 14 (Fall, 1980), 3-24.

7162.   Smith,   Daniel Blake.   "Autonomy and Affection:
Parents and Children in Eighteenth-Century Chesapeake
Families."   Psychohistory Review 6 (Fall/Winter, 1977-1978),
32-51.

7163. Smith, Daniel Blake. Inside the Great House: Planter Family Life in Eighteenth-Century Chesapeake Society. (Ithaca, New York, Cornell University Press, 1980)

7164. Smith, Dorothy H. "Orphans in Anne Arundel County, Maryland, 1704-1709." Maryland Magazine of Genealogy 3 (Spring, 1980), 34-42.

7165. Somerville, James K. "The Salem (Mass.) Woman in the Home, 1660-1770." Eighteenth-Century Life 1 (September, 1974), 11-14.

7166. Spruill, Julia Cherry. Women's Life and Work in the Southern Colonies. (New York, Russell and Russell, 1969; repr. of Chapel Hill, University of North Carolina Press, 1938)

7167. Steffen, Charles G. "The Sewall Children in Colonial New England." NEHGR 131 (July, 1977), 163-172.

7168. Thompson, Roger. Women in Stuart England and America: a Comparative Study. (London, Routledge and Kegan Paul, 1974)

7169. Ulrich, Laurel Thatcher. Good Wives: Image and Reality in Northern New England, 1650-1750. (New York, Knopf, 1982)

7170. Van Kirk, Sylvia. Many Tender Ties: Women in Fur-Trade Society, 1670-1870. (Norman, University of Oklahoma Press, 1983)

7171. Walsh, Andrew S. and Robert V. Wells. "Population Dynamics in the Eighteenth-Century Mississippi River Valley: Acadians in Louisiana." JSH 11 (Summer, 1978), 521-545.

7172. Waters, John J. "Family, Inheritance, and Migration in Colonial New England: the Evidence from Guilford, Connecticut." WMQ 39 (January, 1982), 64-86.

7173. Watson, Alan D. "Household Size and Composition in Pre-Revolutionary North Carolina." MQ 31 (Fall, 1978), 551-569.

7174. Watson, Alan D. "Women in Colonial North Carolina: Overlooked and Underestimated." <u>NCHR</u> 58 (Winter, 1981), 1-22.

7175. Wells, Robert V. "Household Size and Composition in the British Colonies in America, 1675-1775." <u>JIH</u> 4 (Spring, 1974), 543-570.

7176. Wilson, Joan Hoff. "The Illusion of Change: Women and the American Revolution." In Alfred Young, ed. <u>The American Revolution: Explorations in the History of American Radicalism</u>. (DeKalb, Illinois, Northern Illinois University Press, 1976), 383-445.

7177. Wishy, Bernhard W. <u>The Child and the Republic: the Dawn of Modern American Child Nurture</u>. (Philadelphia, University of Pennsylvania Press, 1968)

7178. Withey, Lynne E. "Household Structure in Urban and Rural Areas: the Case of Rhode Island, 1774-1800." <u>JFH</u> 3 (1978), 37-50.

7179. Zuckerman, Michael. "William Byrd's Family." <u>PAH</u> 12 (1979), 255-311.

Family, Society, and Values

The works cited here offer insights about how families functioned as parts of society in terms of a variety of specific issues ranging from crime, economics, and inheritance to morality, politics, and religion. Bailyn's two books are almost required reading because of their direct influence and through the efforts of some of his students such as Demos, Greven, Norton, Vinoskis, and Zuckerman. Rothman's note on colonial families comments on Bailyn's study of education.

7200. Adams, Charles F. "Some Phases of Sexual Morality and Church Discipline in Colonial New England." <u>MHSP</u>, 2nd ser., 6 (1891), 477-516.

7201. Bailyn, Bernard. <u>Education in the Forming of American Society</u>. (Chapel Hill, University of North Carolina Press, 1960)

7202. Bailyn, Bernard. The New England Merchants in the Seventeenth Century. (Cambridge, Massachusetts, Harvard University Press, 1955)

7203. Biemer, Linda Briggs. Women and Property in Colonial New York: the Transition from Dutch to English Law, 1643-1727. (Ann Arbor, Michigan, UMI Research Press, 1983)

7204. Brown, Richard D. "The Founding Fathers of 1776 and 1787: a Collective View." WMQ 33 (July, 1976), 465-480.

7205. Burrows, Edwin G. and Michael Wallace. "The American Revolution: the Ideology and Psychology of National Liberation." PAH 6 (1972), 167-306.

7206. Cott, Nancy F. "Young Women in the Second Great Awakening in New England." FS 3 (Fall, 1975), 15-29.

7207. Cowing, Cedric B. "Sex and Preaching in the Great Awakening." AQ 20 (Fall, 1968), 624-644.

7208. Demos, John. "Underlying Themes in the Witchcraft of Seventeenth-Century New England." AHR 75 (June, 1970), 1311-1326.

7209. DeMotte, Charles M. "Family and Social Structure in Colonial New Haven." Connecticut Review 9 (November, 1975), 82-95.

7210. Eller, Ronald D. "Land and Family: an Historical View of Preindustrial Appalachia." Appalachian Journal 6 (Winter, 1979), 82-109.

7211. Erikson, Kai T. Wayward Puritans; a Study in the Sociology of Deviance. (New York, Wiley, 1966)

7212. Fitzroy, Herbert William Keith. "The Punishment of Crime in Provincial Pennsylvania." PMHB 60 (July, 1936), 242-269.

7213. Flaherty, David H. "Law and the Enforcement of Morals in Early America." PAH 5 (1971), 201-253.

7214. Gladwin, Lee A. "Tobacco and Sex: Some Factors Affecting Non-marital Sexual Behavior in Colonial Virginia." JSH 12 (Fall, 1978), 57-75.

7215. Goebel, Julius, Jr., and T. Raymond Naughton. Law Enforcement in Colonial New York; a Study in Criminal Procedure (1664-1776). (Montclair, New Jersey, Patterson Smith, 1970; repr. of New York, Commonwealth Fund, 1944)

7216. Goldin, Claudia and Kenneth Sokoloff. "Women, Children, and Industrialization in the Early Republic: Evidence from the Manufacturing Censuses." JEH 42 (December, 1982), 741-774.

7217. Greenberg, Douglas. Crime and Law Enforcement in the Colony of New York, 1691-1776. (Ithaca, New York, Cornell University Press, 1976)

7218. Gunderson, Joan R. "The Non-institutional Church: the Religious Role of Women in Eighteenth-Century Virginia." Historical Magazine of the Protestant Episcopal Church 51 (December, 1982), 347-357.

7219. Gunderson, Joan R. and Gwen Victor Gampel. "Married Women's Legal Status in Eighteenth-Century New York and Virginia." WMQ 39 (January, 1982), 114-134.

7220. Hall, Peter Dobkin. "Family Structure and Economic Organization: Massachusetts Merchants, 1700-1850." In Tamara K. Hareven, ed. Family and Kin in Urban Communities, 1700-1930. (New York, New Viewpoints, 1977), 38-61.

7221. Harris, P.M.G. "The Social Origins of American Leaders: the Demographic Foundations." PAH 3 (1969), 157-344.

7222. Hedges, James Blaine. The Browns of Providence Plantations. vol. 1. (Cambridge, Massachusetts, Harvard University Press, 1952)

7223. Hemphill, C. Dallett. "Women in Court: Sex-Role Differentiation in Salem, Massachusetts, 1636 to 1683." WMQ 39 (January, 1982), 164-175.

7224. Jedrey, Christopher M. The World of John Cleaveland: Family and Community in Eighteenth-Century New England. (New York, W.W. Norton, 1979)

7225. Johnson, Paul E. "The Modernization of Mayo Greenleaf Patch: Land, Family, and Marginality in New England, 1766-1818." NEQ 55 (December, 1982), 488-516.

7226. Labaree, Leonard Woods. Conservatism in Early American History. (New York, New York University Press, 1948)

7227. Lounsbury, Carl. "The Development of Domestic Architecture in the Albemarle Region." NCHR 54 (Winter, 1977), 17-48.

7228. Marcuse, Peter. "Housing in Early City Planning." JUH 6 (February, 1980), 153-176.

7229. Marietta, Jack Donald. Ecclesiastical Discipline in the Society of Friends, 1682-1776. (Unpublished Ph.D. Dissertation, Stanford University, 1968)

7230. Moran, Gerald F. "Conditions of Religous Conversion in the First Society of Norwich, Connecticut, 1718-1744." JSH 5 (Spring, 1972), 331-343.

7231. Moran, Gerald F. "Religious Renewal, Puritan Tribalism, and the Family in Seventeenth-Century Milford, Connecticut." WMQ 36 (April, 1979), 236-254.

7232. Moran, Gerald F., and Maris A. Vinovskis. "The Puritan Family and Religion: a Critical Reappraisal." WMQ 38 (January, 1982), 29-63.

7233. Morgan, Edmund S. "The Puritans and Sex." NEQ 15 (December, 1942), 591-607.

7234. Oberholzer, Emil. Delinquent Saints; Disciplinary Action in the Early Congregational Churches of Massachusetts. (New York, Columbia University Press, 1956)

7235. Parkes, Henry B. "Morals and Law Enforcement in Colonial New England." NEQ 5 (July, 1932), 431-452.

7236. Parkes, Henry B. "Sexual Morals and the Great Awakening." NEQ 3 (January, 1930), 133-135.

7237. Pope, Robert G. The Half-Way Covenant: Church Membership in Puritan New England. (Princeton, New Jersey, Princeton University Press, 1969)

7238. Rothman, David J. "A Note on the Study of the Colonial Family." WMQ 23 (October, 1966), 627-634.

7239. Salmon, Marylynn. "Women and Property in South Carolina: the Evidence from Marriage Settlements, 1730 to 1830." WMQ 39 (October, 1982), 655-685.

7240. Scott, Arthur Pearson. Criminal Law in Colonial Virginia. (Chicago, University of Chicago Press, 1930)

7241. Semmes, Raphael. Crime and Punishment in Early Maryland. (Baltimore, Johns Hopkins Press, 1938)

7242. Semonche, John E. "Common-Law Marriage in North Carolina: a Study in Legal History." AJLH 9 (October, 1965), 320-349.

7243. Smith, Daniel Blake. "Morality and Family in the Colonial Chesapeake." JIH 8 (Winter, 1978), 403-427.

7244. Soltow, Lee. "Housing Characteristics on the Pennsylvania Frontier: Mifflin County Dwelling Values in 1798." PH 47 (January, 1980), 57-70.

7245. Speth, Linda E. and Alison Duncan Hirsch. Women, Family, and Community in Colonial America: Two Perspectives. (New York, Haworth, 1983)

7246. Stiles, Henry Reed. Bundling: its Origin, Progress, and Decline in America. (Albany, New York, Knickerbocker Publishing Company, 1871)

7247. Swann, Lee Ann Caldwell. "Landgrants to Georgia Women, 1755-1775." GHQ 61 (Spring, 1977), 23-34.

7248. Sydnor, Charles Sockett. Gentlemen Freeholders: Political Practices in Washington's Virginia. (Chapel Hill, University of North Carolina Press, 1952)

7249.   Watson, Alan D.   "Orphanage in Colonial North Carolina: Edgecombe County as a Case Study."   NCHR 52 (April, 1975), 105-119.

7250.   Weiss, Harry Bischoff and Grace M. Weiss.   An Introduction to Crime and Punishment in Colonial New Jersey. (Trenton, New Jersey, Past Times Press, 1960)

7251.   White, Philip L.   The Beekmans of New York in Politics and Commerce, 1647-1877.   (New York, New York Historical Society, 1956)

The Nineteenth Century

The extraordinary demographic changes that occurred during the nineteenth century were paralleled by altered family patterns.   Surprisingly, some of the underlying structures were less affected than more culturally-defined roles.   In addition to actual changes, which are discussed in many of the works in the first section to follow, nineteenth-century Americans debated the desirability of past and future shifts at length and with passion.   Many works in the second part are concerned with this debate.   Additional material on family structures and the debate on the family can be found in studies on fertility, mortality, and migration.

Family Structures and Domestic Relations

The literature cited in this section is rich and varied.   There are no general studies of family structures for the nineteenth century.   Books by Ryan and Sennett, however, provide in-depth probes of the workings of families in specific settings. There are also a number of studies that merit comment as places to start on specific topics.   Kobrin and Laslett offer excellent information on household size and composition. Achenbaum has written perceptively on old age and can be read with value along with Fischer's book mentioned in the analygous section under Early America.   Faragher and Jeffrey have studied what happened to families (especially women) in the west.   Gutman's book, also cited under Early America, is the place to start reading about black families, but students will want to follow that work with Blassingame, Genovese, Owens, and Pleck.   Degler's book cited in the first section in the chapter has much to offer about women in the nineteenth century. Servants, often women, have been studied by Katzman and Sutherland. Byington provides an older, but still useful, analysis of how families earned and spent their money in a steel-mill town.

7300. Achenbaum, W. Andrew. Old Age in the New Land: the American Experience since 1790. (Baltimore, Johns Hopkins University Press, 1978)

7301. Achenbaum, W. Andrew. "The Obsolence of Old Age in America, 1865-1914." JSH 8 (Fall, 1974), 48-62.

7302. Amos, Harriet E. "'City Belles': Images and Realities of White Women in Antebellum Mobile." AR 34 (January, 1981), 3-19.

7303. Atkins, Annette. "Women on the Farming Frontier: the View from Fiction." Midwest Review 3 (Spring, 1981), 1-10.

7304. Basch, Norma. "Invisible Women: the Legal Fiction of Marital Unity in Nineteenth-Century America." FS 5 (Summer, 1979), 346-366.

7305. Beecher, Maureen Ursenbach. "Women's Work on the Mormon Frontier." UHQ 49 (Summer, 1981), 276-290.

7306. Bigham, Darrel E. "The Black Family in Evansville and Vanderburgh County, Indiana, in 1880." IMH 75 (June, 1979), 117-146.

7307. Bigham, Darrel E. "The Black Family in Evansville and Vanderburgh County, Indiana: a 1900 Postscript." IMH 78 (June, 1982), 154-169.

7308. Bigham, Darrel E. "Family Structure of Germans and Blacks in Evansville and Vanderburgh County, Indiana, in 1880: a Comparative Study." Old Northwest 7 (Fall, 1981), 255-275.

7309. Blackburn, George and Sherman L. Ricards. "The Mother-Headed Family among Free Negroes in Charleston, South Carolina, 1850-1860." Phylon 42 (Spring, 1981), 11-25.

7310.   Blassingame, John W.   The Slave Community: Plantation Life in the Ante-Bellum South. Revised and Enlarged Edition. (New York, Oxford University Press, 1979)

7311. Bledstein, Burton J. The Culture of Professionalism: the Middle Class and the Development of Higher Education in America. (New York, W.W. Norton, 1976)

7312. Blumin, Stuart M. "Rip Van Winkle's Grandchildren: Family and Household in the Hudson Valley, 1800-1860." JUH 1 (May, 1975), 293-315.

7313.   Bodnar, John E.   "Socialization and Adaptation: Immigrant Families in Scranton, 1880-1890." PH 43 (April, 1976), 147-162.

7314. Bridges, William E. "Family Patterns and Social Values in America, 1825-1875." AQ 17 (Spring, 1965), 3-11.

7315.   Bushman, Claudia L.   "A Good Poor Man's Wife": Being a Chronicle of Harriet Hanson Robinson and her Family in New England. (Hanover, New Hampshire, University Press of New England, 1981)

7316. Bushman, Claudia L., ed. Mormon Sisters: Women in Early Utah. (Cambridge, Massachusetts, Emmeline Press, 1976)

7317.   Bushman, Richard L.   "Family Security in the Transition from Farm to City, 1750-1850." JFH. 6 (Fall, 1981), 238-256.

7318.   Byington, Margaret Frances.   Homestead: the Households of a Mill Town. (Pittsburgh, Center for International Studies, 1974; repr. of New York, Charities Publication Committee, 1910)

7319. Chudacoff, Howard P. "The Life Course of Women: Age and Age Consciousness, 1865-1915." JFH 5 (Fall, 1980), 274-292.

7320. Chudacoff, Howard P. "New Branches on the Tree: Household Structure in Early Stages of the Family Cycle in Worcester, Massachusetts, 1860-1880." AASP 86 (1976), 303-320.

7321. Clark, Clifford E., Jr. "Domestic Architecture as an Index to Social History: the Romantic Revival and the Cult of Domesticity in America, 1840-1870." JIH 7 (Summer, 1976), 33-56.

7322. Cody, Cheryll Ann. "Naming, Kinship, and Estate Dispersal: Notes on Slave Family Life on a South Carolina Plantation, 1786 to 1833." WMQ 39 (January, 1982), 192-211.

7323. Connelly, Mark Thomas. The Response to Prostitution in the Progressive Era. (Chapel Hill, University of North Carolina, 1980)

7324. Cooke, Edward S., Jr. "Domestic Space in the Federal-Period Inventories of Salem Merchants." EICH 116 (October, 1980), 248-264.

7325. Cott, Nancy F. "Notes toward an Interpretation of Antebellum Childrearing." Psychohistory Review 6 (Spring, 1978), 4-20.

7326. Creighton, Margaret S. "The Captain's Children: Life in the Adult World of Whaling, 1852-1907." American Neptune 38 (July, 1978), 203-216.

7327. DeGraaf, Lawrence B. "Race, Sex, and Region: Black Women in the American West, 1850-1920." PHR 49 (May, 1980), 285-313.

7328. Drago, Edmund L. "Sources at the National Archives for Genealogical and Local History Research: the Black Household in Dougherty County, Georgia, 1870-1900." Prologue 14 (Summer, 1982), 81-88.

7329. Dubovik, Paul N. "Housing in Holyoke and its Effects on Family Life, 1860-1910." HJWM 4 (Spring, 1975), 40-50.

7330. Elder, Glen H., Jr. and Richard C. Rockwell. "Marital Timing in Women's Life Patterns." JFH 1 (Autumn, 1976), 34-53.

7331. Epstein, Barbara Leslie. The Politics of Domesticity: Women, Evangelism, and Temperance in Nineteenth-Century America. (Middletown, Connecticut, Wesleyan University Press, 1981)

7332.   Faragher, John Mack.   Women and Men on the Overland Trail. (New Haven, Yale University Press, 1979)

7333. Fischer, Christiane. "Women in California in the Early 1850's." SCQ 60 (Fall, 1978), 231-253.

7334.   Fox-Genovese, Elizabeth.   "Scarlett O'Hara: the Southern Lady as New Woman." AQ 33 (Fall, 1981), 391-411.

7335.   Frankfurt, Roberta.   Collegiate Women: Domesticity and Career in Turn-of-the-Century America. (New York, New York University Press, 1977)

7336.   Fry, Mildred Covey.   "Women on the Ohio Frontier: the Marietta Area." OH 90 (Winter, 1981), 55-73.

7337.   Genovese, Eugene D.   Roll, Jordan, Roll: the World the Slaves Made. (New York, Panthenon Books, 1974)

7338.   Gilmore, Al-Tony, ed.   Revisiting Blassingame's The Slave Community: the Scholars Respond.   (Westport, Connecticut, Greenwood Press, 1978)

7339.   Glasco, Laurence A.   "The Life Cycles and Household Structure of American Ethnic Groups: Irish, Germans, and Native-Born Whites in Buffalo, New York, 1855." JUH 1 (May, 1975), 339-364.

7340.   Goldin, Claudia Dale.   "Female Labor Force Participation: the Origin of Black and White Differences, 1870 and 1880." JEH 37 (March, 1977), 87-108.

7341.   Good, Susan Thompson.   "Interior Life: an Iowa Farmhouse in the Late-1800's." Palimpsest 60 (March/April, 1979), 35-46.

7342.   Griffen, Clyde and Sally Griffen. "Family and Business in a Small City: Poughkeepsie, New York, 1850-1880." JUH 1 (May, 1975), 316-338.

7343.   Griswold, Robert L.   "Apart but not Adrift: Wives, Divorce, and Independence in California, 1850-1890." PHR 49 (May, 1980), 265-283.

7344. Griswold del Castillo, Richard. "La Familia Chicana: Social Changes in the Chicano Family of Los Angeles, 1850-1880." JES 3 (Spring, 1975), 41-58.

7345. Groneman, Carol. "Working-Class Immigrant Women in Mid-Nineteenth-Century New York: the Irish Woman's Experience." JUH 4 (May, 1978), 255-273.

7346. Gutman, Herbert George. "Persistent Myths about the Afro-American Family." JIH 6 (Autumn, 1975), 181-210.

7347. Hagler, D. Harland. "The Ideal Woman in the Antebellum South: Lady or Farmwife?" JSouH 46 (August, 1980), 405-418.

7348. Hampsten, Elizabeth. Read this Only to Yourself: the Private Writings of Midwestern Women, 1880-1910. (Bloomington, Indiana University Press, 1982)

7349. Hareven, Tamara K. "Family Time and Historical Time." Daedlus 106 (Spring, 1977), 57-70.

7350. Hareven, Tamara K. "The Laborers of Manchester, New Hampshire, 1912-1922: the Role of Family and Ethnicity in Adjustment to Industrial Life." LbH 16 (Spring, 1975), 249-265.

7351. Hargreaves, Mary W.M. "Women in the Agricultural Settlement of the Northern Plains." AgH 50 (January, 1976), 179-189.

7352. Harper, C.W. "House Servants and Field Hands: Fragmentation in the Antebellum Slave Community." NCHR 55 (January, 1978), 42-59.

7353. Harper, Jared V. "Marriage as an Adaptive Strategy among Irish Travelers in South Carolina." SouS 20 (Summer, 1981), 174-184.

7354. Harris, William. "Work and the Family in Black Atlanta, 1880." JSH 9 (Spring, 1976), 319-330.

7355. Hewitt, Nancy A. Women's Activism and Social Change: Rochester, N.Y., 1822-1872. (Ithaca, New York, Cornell University Press, 1984)

7356. Hogeland, Ronald W. "Charles Hodge, the Association of Gentlemen and Ornamental Womanhood: 1825-1855." Journal of Presbyterian History 53 (Fall, 1975), 239-255.

7357. Horton, James Oliver and Lois E. Horton. Black Bostonians: Family Life and Community Struggle in the Antebellum North. (New York, Holmes and Meier, 1979)

7358. Horwitz, Richard P. "Architecture and Culture: the Meaning of the Lowell Boarding House." AQ 25 (March, 1973), 64-82.

7359. Jeffrey, Julie Roy. Frontier Women: the Trans-Mississippi West, 1840-1880. (New York, Hill and Wang, 1979)

7360. Jones, Jacqueline. "'My Mother Was Much of a Woman': Black Women, Work, and the Family under Slavery." FS 8 (Summer, 1982), 235-269.

7361. Jones, James P. "The Illinois Negro Law of 1853--Racism in a Free State." Illinois Quarterly 40 (Winter, 1977), 5-22.

7362. Katzman, David M. Seven Days a Week: Women and Domestic Service in Industrializing America. (New York, Oxford University Press, 1978)

7363. Kelley, Mary. "At War with Herself: Harriet Beecher Stowe as Woman in Conflict within the Home." AS 19 (Fall, 1978), 23-40.

7364. Kelley, Mary. "A Woman Alone: Catharine Maria Sedgwick's Spinsterhood in Nineteenth-Century America." NEQ 51 (June, 1978), 209-225.

7365. Kennedy, Susan Estabrook. If All We Did Was to Weep at Home: a History of White Working-Class Women in America. (Bloomington, Indiana University Press, 1979)

7366. Klaczynska, Barbara. "Why Women Work: a Comparison of Various Groups--Philadelphia, 1910-1930." LbH 17 (Winter, 1976), 73-87.

7367. Kleinberg, Susan J. "Technology and Women's Work: the Lives of Working Class Women in Pittsburgh, 1870-1900." LbH 17 (Winter, 1976), 58-72.

7368. Kobrin, Frances E. "The Fall of Household Size and the Rise of the Primary Individual in the United States." Demography 13 (February, 1976), 127-138.

7369. Labinjoh, Justin. "The Sexual Life of the Oppressed: an Examination of the Family Life of Ante-Bellum Slaves." Phylon 35 (December, 1974), 375-387.

7370. Lammermeier, Paul J. "The Urban Black Family of the Nineteenth Century: a Study of Black Family Structure in the Ohio Valley, 1850-1880." JMF 35 (August, 1973), 440-456.

7371. Laslett, Barbara. "Household Structure on an American Frontier: Los Angeles, California, in 1850." AJS 81 (July, 1975), 109-128.

7372. Laslett, Barbara. "Social Change and the Family: Los Angeles, California, 1850-1870." ASR 42 (April, 1977), 268-291.

7373. Lebsock, Suzanne. "Free Black Women and the Question of Matriarchy: Petersburg, Virginia, 1784-1820." FS 8 (Summer, 1982), 271-292.

7374. Lebsock, Suzanne. The Free Women of Petersburg: Status and Culture in a Southern Town, 1784-1860. (New York, W. W. Norton, 1984)

7375. Luria, Daniel D. "Wealth, Capital, and Power: the Social Meaning of Home Ownership." JIH 7 (Autumn, 1976), 261-282.

7376. McGettigan, James William, Jr. "Boone County Slaves: Sales, Estate Divisions, and Families, 1820-1865, Part I." MoHR 72 (January, 1978), 176-197.

7377. McGettigan, James William, Jr. "Boone County Slaves: Sales, Estate Devisions, and Families, 1820-1865, Part II." MoHR 72 (April, 1978), 271-295.

7378. McGovern, James R. Yankee Family. (New Orleans, Polyanthos, 1975)

7379. Modell, John. "The Japanese American Family: a Perspective for Future Investigations." PHR 37 (February, 1968), 67-82.

7380. Modell, John, Frank F. Furstenberg, Jr., and Theodore Hershberg. "Social Change and Transitions to Adulthood in Historical Perspective." JFH 1 (Autumn, 1976), 7-32.

7381. Modell, John and Tamara K. Hareven. "Urbanization and the Malleable Household: an Examination of Boarding and Lodging in American Families." JMF 35 (August, 1973), 467-479.

7382. Morgan, Myfanwy and Hilda H. Golden. "Immigrant Families in an Industrial City: a Study of the Households in Holyoke, 1880." JFH 4 (Spring, 1979), 59-68.

7383. Moynihan, Ruth Barnes. "Children and Young People on the Overland Trail." WestHQ 6 (July, 1975), 279-294.

7384. Owens, Leslie Howard. This Species of Property: Slave Life and Culture in the Old South. (New York, Oxford University Press, 1976)

7385. Pleck, Elizabeth H. "The Two-Parent Household: Black Family Structure in Late Nineteenth-Century Boston." JSH 6 (Fall, 1972), 3-31.

7386. Rabkin, Peggy A. Fathers to Daughters: the Legal Foundations of Female Emancipation. (Westport, Connecticut, Greenwood Press, 1980)

7387. Range, Jane and Maris A. Vinovskis. "Images of Elderly in Popular Magazines: a Content Analysis of Littell's Living Age, 1845-1882." SSH 5 (Spring, 1981), 123-170.

7388. Riley, Glenda. Frontierswomen: the Iowa Experience. (Ames, Iowa State University Press, 1981)

7389. Riley, Glenda. "Images of the Frontierswoman: Iowa as a Case Study." WestHQ 8 (April, 1977), 189-202.

7390. Riley, Glenda. "'Not Gainfully Employed': Women on the Iowa Frontier, 1833-1870." PHR 49 (May, 1980), 237-264.

7391. Riley, Glenda. "Women Pioneers in Iowa." Palimpsest 57 (March/April, 1976), 34-53.

7392. Ripley, C. Peter. "The Black Family in Transition: Louisiana, 1860-1865." JSouH 41 (August, 1975), 369-380.

7393. Rodgers, Daniel T. "Socializing Middle-Class Children: Institutions, Fables, and Work Values in Nineteenth-Century America." JSH 13 (Spring, 1980), 354-367.

7394. Rugoff, Milton. The Beechers: an American Family in the Nineteenth Century. (New York, Harper and Row, 1981)

7395. Ryan, Mary P. Cradle of the Middle Class: the Family in Oneida County, New York, 1790-1865. (Cambridge, England, Cambridge University Press, 1981)

7396. Schwartz, Hillel. "Adolescence and Revivals in Ante-Bellum Boston." Journal of Religious History 8 (December, 1974), 144-158.

7397. Sennett, Richard. Families against the City; Middle Class Homes of Industrial Chicago, 1872-1890. (Cambridge, Massachusetts, Harvard University Press, 1970)

7398. Sennett, Richard. "Middle-Class Families and Urban Violence: the Experience of a Chicago Community in the Nineteenth Century." In Tamara K. Hareven, ed. Anonymous Americans. (Englewood Cliffs, New Jersey, Prentice Hall, 1971), 280-305.

7399. Shiflett, Crandall A. "The Household Composition of Rural Black Families: Louisa County, Virginia, 1880." JIH 6 (Autumn, 1975), 235-260.

7400. Slater, Peter Gregg. Children in the New England Mind: in Death and in Life. (Hamden, Connecticut, Archon, 1977)

7401. Smallwood, James. "Emancipation and the Black Family: a Case Study in Texas." SSQ 57 (March, 1977), 849-857.

7402. Smith, Daniel Scott. "Life Course, Norms, and the Family System of Older Americans in 1900." JFH 4 (Fall, 1979), 285-298.

7403. Steckel, Richard H. "Slave Marriage and the Family." JFH 5 (Winter, 1980), 406-421.

7404. Stratton, Joanna L. Pioneer Women: Voices from the Kansas Frontier. (New York, Simon and Schuster, 1981)

7405. Suitor, J. Jill. "Husbands' Participation in Childbirth: a Nineteenth-Century Phenomenon." JFH 6 (Fall, 1981), 278-293.

7406. Sunoo, Sonia S. "Korean Women Pioneers of the Pacific Northwest." OHQ 79 (Spring, 1978), 51-63.

7407. Sutherland, Daniel E. Americans and their Servants: Domestic Service in the United States from 1800 to 1920. (Baton Rouge, Louisiana State University Press, 1981)

7408. Tentler, Leslie Woodcock. Wage-Earning Women: Industrial Work and Family Life in the United States, 1900-1930. (New York, Oxford University Press, 1979)

7409. Thomas, Samuel J. "Catholic Journalists and the Ideal Woman in Late Victorian America." IJWS 4 (January/February, 1981), 89-100.

7410. Twombly, Robert C. "Saving the Family: Middle Class Attraction to Wright's Prairie House, 1901-1909." AQ 27 (March, 1975), 57-72.

7411. Walkowitz, Daniel J. "Statistics and the Writing of Working Class Culture: a Statistical Portrait of the Iron Workers in Troy, New York, 1860-1880." LbH 15 (Summer, 1974), 416-460.

7412. Wetherell, Charles. "Slave Kinship: a Case Study of the South Carolina Good Hope Plantation, 1835-1856." JFH 6 (Fall, 1981), 294-308.

7413. White, John. "Whatever Happened to the Slave Family in the Old South?" JAS 8 (December, 1974), 383-390.

7414. Wiener, Jonathan M. "Female Planters and Planters' Wives in Civil War and Reconstruction: Alabama, 1850-1870." AR 30 (April, 1977), 135-149.

7415. Wiley, Bell Irvin. Confederate Women. (Westport, Connecticut, Greenwood Press, 1975)

7416. Williams, Blaine T. "The Frontier Family: Demographic Fact and Historical Myth." In Harold M. Hollingsworth and Sandra L. Myers, eds. Essays on the American West. (Austin, University of Texas Press, 1969), 40-65.

7417. Wyatt-Brown, Bertram. "Three Generations of Yankee Parenthood: the Tappan Family, a Case Study of Antebellum Nurture." Illinois Quarterly 38 (Fall, 1975), 12-28.

Family, Society, and Values

The debate on the family that emerged in response to the demographic revolutions of the nineteenth century produced a huge literature that has been subject to extensive analysis. There is, however, no synthesis of this material. In fact, many scholars seem unaware of studies of this debate outside those of their own immediate interest. To get a sense of what the actual debaters said, refer to Abbot, Addams, Alcott, and Sanger. The most impressive historical writing has, in one way or another, focused most often on women. Lerner, Ryan, and Page Smith offer different ways of synthesizing the evidence. Barker-Benfield, Bullough and Bullough, and Walters discuss attitudes regarding sex and sexuality in western culture and nineteenth-century America. Studying the process by which women's roles were defined, and what those roles were should begin with Chafe, Douglas, Filene, Lerner, Smith-Rosenberg, and Welter. For women in the work place, start with Dublin and Hareven; for women in politics, Flexner, Kraditor, and Scott are excellent. Prostitution was a major concern of the period, as is evident from Connelly, Pivar, and Sanger. Sklar's study of Catherine Beecher offers an in-depth look at one moderate reformer; Kern and Munch examine a variety of utopian critics of the family. Efforts to improve family life by improving housing have been studied by Cohn, Hayden, and Wright. There are a number of short essays on childhood, but in general the material on this topic is not as rich for the nineteenth century as it is for pre-1800. Kett, Tiffin, and Schlossman offer interesting, if limited, studies. Although not directly concerned with children's roles, much can be gleaned from Daniel Calhoun on intelligence in America, Cremin and Kaesteel and Vinovskis on education, and David Rothman on asylums.

7500.   Abbott, John Stevens Cabot.   The Mother at Home: or, the Principles of Maternal Duty.   (Boston, Crocker and Brewster, 1833).

7501.   Adams, Donald R., Jr.   "Residential Construction Industry in the Early Nineteenth Century."   JEH 35 (December, 1975), 794-816.

7502. Addams, Jane. A New Conscience and an Ancient Evil. (New York, Macmillan, 1912)

7503.   Alaya, Flavia.   "Victorian Science and the 'Genius' of Woman."   Journal of the History of Ideas 38 (April-June, 1977), 261-280.

7504.   Alcott, William Andrus.   The Young Husband: or, Duties of Man in the Marriage Relation. (Boston, G.W. Light, 1839)

7505.   Alcott, William Andrus.   The Young Wife: or, Duties of Woman in the Marriage Relation.   (Boston, G.W. Light, 1837)

7506.   Alexander, Robert L.   "Baltimore Row Houses of the Early Nineteenth Century."   AS 16 (Fall, 1975), 65-76.

7507.   Allen, Lee Norcross.   "The Woman Suffrage Movement in Alabama, 1910-1920."   AR 11 (April, 1958), 83-99.

7508.   Allmendinger, David F., Jr.   "Mount Holyoke Students Encounter the Need for Life-Planning, 1837-1850."   HEQ 19 (Spring, 1979), 27-46.

7509.   Ashby, LeRoy.   "'Recreate this Boy': Allendale Farm, the Child, and Progressivism."   MA 58 (January, 1976), 31-53.

7510. Barker-Benfield, Graham J. The Horrors of the Half-Known Life: Male Attitudes Toward Women and Sexuality in Nineteenth Century America. (New York, Harper and Row, 1976)

7511. Barlow, William and David O. Powell. "Homeopathy and Sexual Equality: the Controversy over Coeducation at Cincinnati's Pulte Medical College, 1873-1879." OH 90 (Spring, 1981), 101-113.

7512. Belding, Robert E. "The Dubuque Female Seminary: Catharine Beecher's Blueprint for Nineteenth Century Women's Education." Palimpsest 63 (March/April, 1982), 34-41.

7513. Birch, Eugenie Ladner and Deborah S. Gardner. "The Seven-Percent Solution: a Review of Philanthropic Housing, 1870-1910." JUH 7 (August, 1981), 403-438.

7514. Blackburn, George M. and Sherman L. Ricards. "The Prostitutes and Gamblers of Virginia City, Nevada: 1870." PHR 48 (May, 1979), 239-258.

7515. Blackmar, Betsy. "Re-walking the 'Walking City': Housing and Property Relations in New York City, 1780-1840." RHR 21 (Fall, 1979), 131-148.

7516. Blair, Karen J. The Clubwoman as Feminist: True Womanhood Redefined, 1868-1914. (New York, Holmes and Meier, 1980)

7517. Borchert, James. Alley Life in Washington: Family, Community, Religion, and Folklife in the City, 1850-1970. (Urbana, University of Illinois Press, 1980)

7518. Bordin, Ruth. Woman and Temperance: the Quest for Power and Liberty, 1873-1900. (Philadelphia, Temple University Press, 1981)

7519. Bremner, Robert Hamlett, comp. Children and Youth in America: a Documentary History. 3 volumes. (Cambridge, Massachusetts, Harvard University Press, 1970-1974)

7520. Bullough, Vern L. and Bonnie Bullough. Sin, Sickness, and Sanity: a History of Sexual Attitudes. (New York, Garland, 1977)

7521. Burnham, John C. "Medical Inspection of Prostitutes in America in the Nineteenth Century: the St. Louis Experiment and its Sequel." BHM 45 (May-June, 1971), 203-218.

7522. Calhoun, Daniel Hovey. The Intelligence of a People. (Princeton, New Jersey, Princeton University Press, 1973)

7523. Calverton, Victor Francis. The Bankruptcy of Marriage. (New York, Arno Press, 1972; repr. of New York, Macaulay Company, 1928)

7524. Campbell, D'Ann. "Women's Life in Utopia: the Shaker Experiment in Sexual Equality Reappraised--1810 to 1860." NEQ 51 (March, 1978), 23-38.

7525. Cannon, Charles A. "The Awesome Power of Sex: the Polemical Campaign Against Mormon Polygamy." PHR 43 (February, 1974), 61-82.

7526. Chafe, William Henry. Women and Equality: Changing Patterns in American Culture. (New York, Oxford University Press, 1977)

7527. Child, Lydia Maria (Francis). The Mother's Book. (New York, Arno Press, 1972; repr. of Boston, Carter, Hendee and Babcock, 1831)

7528. Clark, Dennis. "Babes in Bondage: Indentured Irish Children in Philadelphia in the Nineteenth Century." PMHB 101 (October, 1977), 475-486.

7529. Clayton, James L. "The Supreme Court, Polygamy, and the Enforcement of Morals in Nineteenth-Century America: an Analysis of Reynolds v. United States." DJMT 12 (Winter, 1979), 46-61.

7530. Cohn, Jan. The Palace or the Poorhouse: the American House as a Cultural Symbol. (East Lansing, Michigan State University Press, 1979)

7531. Connelly, Mark Thomas. The Response to Prostitution in the Progressive Era. (Chapel Hill, University of North Carolina Press, 1980)

7532. Cowan, Ruth S. "A Case Study of Technological and Social Change: the Washing Machine and the Working Wife." In Mary Hartman and Lois Banner, eds. Clio's Consciousness Raised. (New York, Harper Colophon Books, 1974), 245-253.

7533. Cremin, Lawrence A. American Education: the National Experience, 1783-1876. (New York, Harper & Row, 1980)

7534. Curtis, Bruce. "Victorians Abed: William Graham Sumner on the Family, Women, and Sex." AS 18 (Spring, 1977), 101-122.

7535. Degler, Carl N. "What Ought to Be and What Was: Women's Sexuality in the Nineteenth Century." AHR 79 (December, 1974), 1467-1490.

7536. Dick, Everett. "Sunbonnet and Calico, the Homesteader's Consort." NH 47 (March, 1966), 3-13.

7537. Ditzion, Sidney. Marriage, Morals and Sex in America: a History of Ideas. (New York, Bookman Associates, 1953)

7538. Douglas, Ann. The Feminization of American Culture. (New York, Knopf, 1977)

7539. Drachman, Virginia G. "Female Solidarity and Professional Success: the Dilemma of Women Doctors in Late Nineteenth-Century America." JSH 15 (Summer, 1982), 607-619.

7540. Dublin, Thomas. Women at Work: the Transformation of Work and Community in Lowell, Massachusetts, 1826-1860. (New York, Columbia University Press, 1979)

7541. Dublin, Thomas. "Women, Work, and the Family: Female Operatives in the Lowell Mills, 1830-1860." FS 3 (Fall, 1975), 30-39.

7542.   Dublin, Thomas.   "Women, Work, and Protest in the Early Lowell Mills: 'The Oppressing Hand of Avarice Would Enslave Us.'" LbH (April, 1975), 99-116.

7543.   DuBois, Ellen Carol.   Feminism and Suffrage: the Emergence of an Independent Women's Movement in America, 1848-1869.   (Ithaca, New York, Cornell University Press, 1978)

7544.   Early, Frances H.   "The French-Canadian Family Economy and Standard-of-Living in Lowell, Massachusetts, 1870." JFH 7 (Summer, 1982), 180-199.

7545.   Epstein, Amy Kallamn.   "Multifamily Dwellings and the Search for Respectability: Origins of the New York Apartment House."   Urbanism Past and Present 5 (Summer, 1980), 29-39.

7546.   Feldman, Egal.   "Prostitution, the Alien Woman, and the Progressive Imagination, 1910-1915."   AQ 19 (Summer, 1967), 192-206.

7547.   Filene, Peter Gabriel.   Him/Her/Self: Sex Roles in Modern America.   (New York, Harcourt, Brace, Jovanovich, 1975)

7548.   Fink, Arthur E.   "Changing Philosophies and Practices in North Carolina Orphanages."   NCHR 48 (October, 1971), 333-358.

7549.   Fishbein, Leslie.   "Harlot or Heroine? Changing Views of Prostitution, 1870-1920."   Historian 43 (November, 1980), 23-35.

7550.   Fisher, Marcelia C.   "The Orphan's Friend: Charles Collins Townsend and the Orphan's Home of Industry." Palimpsest 60 (November-December, 1979), 184-196.

7551.   Flexner, Eleanor.   Century of Struggle: the Woman's Rights Movement in the United States.   Rev. ed. (New York, Belknap Press of Harvard University Press, 1975)

7552.   Fogarty, Robert S. and H. Roger Grant.   "Free Love in Ohio: Jacob Beilhart and the Spirit Fruit Colony."   OH 89 (Spring, 1980), 206-221.

7553. Foster, Lawrence. "Free Love and Feminism: John Humphrey Noyes and the Oneida Community." Journal of the Early Republic 1 (Summer, 1981), 165-183.

7554. Foster, Lawrence. Religion and Sexuality: Three American Communal Experiments of the Nineteenth Century. (New York, Oxford University Press, 1981)

7555. Fowler, William Worthington. Woman on the American Frontier. (Hartford, Connecticut, S.S. Scranton, 1876)

7556. Frey, Cecile P. "The House of Refuge for Colored Children." JNH 66 (Spring, 1981), 10-25.

7557. Furer, Howard B. "The American City: a Catalyst for the Women's Rights Movement." WMH (Summer, 1969), 285-305.

7558. Garrison, Dee. "The Tender Technicians: the Feminization of Public Librarianship, 1876-1905." In Mary S. Hartman and Lois Banner, eds. Clio's Consciousness Raised. (New York, Harper & Row, 1974), 158-178.

7559. Glassberg, David. "Restoring a 'Forgotten Childhood': American Play and the Progressive Era's Elizabethan Past." AQ 32 (Fall, 1980), 351-368.

7560. Greenwald, Maurine Weiner. Women, War, and Work: the Impact of World War I on Women Workers in the United States. (Westport, Connecticut, Greenwood Press, 1980)

7561. Goldin, Claudia Dale. "Female Labor Force Participation: the Origin of Black and White Differences, 1870 and 1880." JEH 37 (March, 1977), 87-108.

7562. Goldin, Claudia Dale. "The Work and Wages of Single Women, 1870 to 1920." JEH 40 (March, 1980), 81-88.

7563. Goldman, Marion. "Sexual Commerce on the Comstock Lode." NHSQ 21 (Summer, 1978), 99-129.

7564. Goldwater, Michel. "Poverty and Relief in San Francisco at the End of the Nineteenth Century." WSJHQ 13 (January, 1981), 160-167.

7565.   Gordon, Michael. "From an Unfortunate Necessity to a Cult of Mutual Orgasm: Sex in American Marital Education Literature, 1830-1940."   In James M. Henslin, ed., Studies in the Sociology of Sex.   (New York, Appleton-Century-Crofts, 1971), 53-77.

7566.   Grant, H. Roger. "The New Communitarianism: the Case of Three Intentional Colonies, 1890-1905."   ISSQ 30 (Spring, 1977), 59-71.

7567.   Green, Nancy.   "Female Education and School Competition, 1820-1850." HEQ 18 (Summer, 1978), 129-142.

7568.   Haller, Mark Hughlin.   Eugenics: Hereditarian Attitudes in American Thought. (New Brunswick, New Jersey, Rutgers University Press, 1963)

7569. Hareven, Tamara K. Family Time and Industrial Time: the Relationship between the Family and Work in a New England Industrial Community.   (Cambridge, England, Cambridge University Press, 1982)

7570. Hargis, Donald E. "Women's Rights: California 1849." HSSCQ 37 (December, 1955), 320-334.

7571. Hass, Paul H. "Sin in Wisconsin: the Teasdale Vice Committee of 1913." WMH 49 (Winter, 1965-6), 138-151.

7572. Hayden, Dolores. The Grand Domestic Revolution: a History of Feminist Designs for American Homes, Neighborhoods, and Cities. (Cambridge, Massachusetts, MIT Press, 1981)

7573. Heisner, Beverly. "Harriet Morrison Irwin's Hexagonal House: an Invention to Improve Domestic Dwellings." NCHR 58 (Spring, 1981), 105-124.

7574. Herman, Sondra R. "Loving Courtship or the Marriage Market? The Ideal and its Critics, 1871-1911." AQ 25 (May, 1973), 235-252.

7575.   Hersh, Blanche Glassman.   The Slavery of Sex: Feminist-Abolitionists in America. (Urbana, University of Illinois Press, 1978)

7576. Hirata, Lucie Cheng. "Free, Indentured, Enslaved: Chinese Prostitutes in Nineteenth-Century America." Signs 5 (Autumn, 1979), 3-29.

7577. Horton, James Oliver. "Generations of Protest: Black Families and Social Reform in Ante-Bellum Boston." NEQ 49 (June, 1976), 242-256.

7578. Howard, Ronald L. A Social History of American Family Sociology, 1865-1940. (Westport, Connecticut, Greenwood Press, 1981)

7579. Hudson, John. "Frontier Housing in North Dakota." NDH 42 (Fall, 1975), 4-15.

7580. Hudson, Winthrop S. "Early Nineteenth-Century Evangelical Religion and Women's Liberation." Foundations 23 (April-June, 1980), 181-185.

7581. Ichioka, Yuji. "Ameyuki-San: Japanese Prostitutes in Nineteenth-Century America." AJ 4 (1977), 1-21.

7582. Jable, J. Thomas. "Aspects of Moral Reform in Early Nineteenth-Century Pennsylvania." PMHB 102 (July, 1978), 344-363.

7583. Jensen, Richard. "Family, Career, and Reform: Women Readers of the Progressive Era." In Michael Gordon, ed. The American Family in Social-Historical Perspective. (New York, St. Martin's Press, 1973), 267-280.

7584. Johnson, Kenneth R. "Florida Women Get the Vote." FHQ 48 (January, 1970), 299-312.

7585. Jones, Arnita Ament. "Free Love and Communal Households: Robert Dale Owen and Fanny Wright on Women's Rights." IASSP 9 (1974), 93-102.

7586. Jones, Jacqueline. "Women Who Were More than Men: Sex and Status in Freedmen's Teaching." HEQ 19 (Spring, 1979), 47-59.

7587. Kadzielski, Mark A. "'As a Flower Needs Sunshine': the Origins of Organized Children's Recreation in Philadelphia, 1886-1911." JSpH 4 (Summer, 1977), 169-207.

7588. Kaestel, Carl F. and Maris A. Vinovskis. "From Apron Strings to ABC's: Parents, Children, and Schooling in Nineteenth-Century Massachusetts."   In John Demos and Sarane Spence Boocock, eds. Turning Points: Historical and Sociological Essays on the Family. (Chicago, University of Chicago Press, 1978; supplement to AJS 84), 39-80.

7589. Kern, Louis J. "Ideoogy and Reality: Sexuality and Women's Status in the Oneida Community." RHR 20 (Spring/Summer, 1979), 180-205.

7590. Kern, Louis J. An Ordered Love: Sex Roles and Sexuality in Victorian Utopias-the Shakers, the Mormons, and the Oneida Community. (Chapel Hill, University of North Carolina Press, 1981)

7591. Kett, Joseph F. "Adolescence and Youth in Nineteenth-Century America." JIH 2 (Autumn, 1971), 283-298.

7592. Kett, Joseph F. "Growing up in Rural New England." In Tamara K. Hareven, ed. Anonymous Americans (Englewood Cliffs, New Jersey, Prentice-Hall, 1971), 1-16.

7593. Kirschner, Don S. "The Perils of Pleasure: Commercial Recreation, Social Disorder, and Moral Reform in the Progressive Era." AS 21 (Fall, 1980), 27-42.

7594. Klaczynska, Barbara. "Why Women Work: a Comparison of Various Groups--Philadelphia, 1910-1930." LbH 17 (Winter, 1976), 73-87.

7595. Kleinberg, Susan J. "Technology and Women's Work: the Lives of Working Class Women in Pittsburgh, 1870-1900." LbH 17 (Winter, 1976), 57-72.

7596. Klotter, James C. "Sex, Scandal, and Suffrage in the Gilded Age." Historian 42 (February, 1980), 225-243.

7597. Kraditor, Aileen S. The Ideas of the Woman Suffrage Movement, 1890-1920. (New York, Columbia University Press, 1965)

7598. Kushner, Howard I. "Nineteenth-Century Sexuality and the 'Sexual Revolution' of the Progressive Era." Canadian Review of American Studies 9 (Spring, 1978), 34-49.

7599. Lacy, James M. "New Mexican Women in Early American Writings." NMHR 34 (January, 1959), 41-51.

7600. Langum, David J. "Californio Women and the Image of Virtue." SCQ 59 (Fall, 1977), 245-250.

7601. Larson, T.A. "Woman Suffrage in Western America." UHQ 38 (Winter, 1970), 7-19.

7602. Lasser, Carol S. "A 'Pleasingly Oppressive' Burden: the Transformation of Domestic Service and Female Charity in Salem, 1800-1840." EICH 116 (July, 1980), 156-175.

7603. Leach, William. True Love and Perfect Union: the Feminist Reform of Sex and Society. (New York, Basic Books, 1980)

7604. Leonard, Carol and Isidor Wallimann. "Prostitution and Changing Morality in the Fronter Cattle Towns of Kansas." KH 2 (Spring, 1979), 34-53.

7605. Lerner, Gerda. The Female Experience: an American Documentary. (Indianapolis, Bobbs-Merrill, 1977)

7606. Lerner, Gerda. "The Lady and the Mill Girl: Changes in the Status of Women in the Age of Jackson." AS 10 (Spring, 1969), 5-15.

7607. Lerner, Gerda. The Woman in American History. (Menlo Park, California, Addison-Wesley, 1971)

7608. Ludmerer, Kenneth M. Genetics and American Society: a Historical Apprasial. (Baltimore, Johns Hopkins University Press, 1972)

7609. McDowell, John Patrick. The Social Gospel in the South: the Woman's Home Mission Movement in the Methodist Episcopal Church, South, 1886-1939. (Baton Rouge, Louisiana State University Press, 1982)

7610. McElroy, James L. "Social Control and Romantic Reform in Antebellum America: the Case of Rochester, New York." NYH 58, i.e., New York State Historical Assocation. Proceedings 75 (1977), 17-46.

7611.   McGovern, James R.   "'Sporting Life on the Line':
Prostitution in Progressive-Era Pensacola." FHQ 54 (October,
1975), 131-144.

7612.   McIntosh, Maria Jane. Woman in America: her Work
and her Reward. (New York, D. Appleton and Co., 1850)

7613.   McLoughlin, William G.   "Evangelical Childrearing in
the Age of Jackson: Francis Wayland's Views on When and
How to Subdue the Willfulness of Children." JSH 9 (Fall,
1975), 20-34.

7614.   MacNeill, Norman.   "Infant Welfare as Taught in
Philadelphia One Hundred Years Ago." AMH n.s. 8 (1936),
36-43.

7615.   Mandelker, Ira L.   "Religion, Sex, and Utopia in
Nineteenth-Century America." Social Research 49 (Autumn,
1982), 730-751.

7616.   Martin, Michael J. and Glenn H. Smith.   "Vice and
Violence in Ward County, North Dakota, 1905-1920." NDH 47
(Spring, 1980), 10-21.

7617.   Massa, Ann. "Black Women in the 'White City'." JAS
8 (December, 1974), 319-337.

7618.   Matthews, Jean V.   "'Woman's Place' and the Search
for Identity in Ante-Bellum America." Canadian Review of
American Studies 10 (Winter, 1979), 289-304.

7619.   Morris, Ann N.   "The History of the St. Louis
Protestant Orphan Asylum" MoHSB 36 (January, 1980), 80-91.

7620.   Mulligan, Raymond A.   "New York Foundlings at
Clifton-Morenci: Social   Justice   in   Arizona   Territory,
1904-1905." ArW 6 (Summer, 1964), 104-118.

7621.   Muncy, Raymond Lee. Sex and Marriage in Utopian
Communities; Nineteenth Century America.   (Bloomington,
Indiana University Press, 1973)

7622.   Patterson, R.S. and Patricia Rooke.   "The Delicate
Duty of Child Saving: Coldwater, Michigan, 1871-1896." MH
61 (Fall, 1967), 195-219.

7623. Perry, Lewis. Childhood, Marriage, and Reform: Henry Clarke Wright, 1797-1870. (Chicago, University of Chicago Press, 1980)

7624. Perry, Lewis. "'Progress, not Pleasure, is our Aim': the Sexual Advice of an Antebellum Radical." JSH 12 (Spring, 1979), 354-366.

7625. Pessen, Edward. "The Marital Theory and Practice of the Antebellum Urban Elite." NYH 53, i.e. New York State Historical Association. Proceedings 70 (1972), 389-410.

7626. Petrick, Paula. "Capitalists with Rooms: Prostitution in Helena, Montana, 1865-1900." Montana 31 (April, 1981), 28-41.

7627. Pivar, David J. "Cleansing the Nation: the War on Prostitution, 1917-1921." Prologue 12 (Spring, 1980), 28-40.

7628. Pivar, David J. Purity Crusade: Sexual Morality and Social Control, 1868-1900. (Westport, Connecticut, Greenwood Press, 1973)

7629. Pohl, Frances K. "Historical Reality or Utopian Ideal? the Woman's Building at the World's Columbian Exposition, Chicago, 1893." IJWS 5 (September/October, 1982), 289-311.

7630. Pollard, Leslie J. "Black Beneficial Societies and the Home for Aged and Infirm Colored Persons: a Research Note." Phylon 41 (September, 1980), 230-234.

7631. Porterfield, Amanda. Feminine Spirituality in America: from Sarah Edwards to Martha Graham. (Philadelphia, Temple University Press, 1980)

7632. Potter, David Morris. "American Women and the American Character." In his History and American Society: Essays of David M. Potter. (New York, Oxford University Press, 1973), 277-303.

7633. Pride, Nancy. "Incidents Preceding the Louisiana Child Labor Law of 1912." LH 19 (Fall, 1978), 437-445.

7634. Rapson, Richard L. "The American Child as Seen by British Travelers, 1845-1935." AQ 17 (Fall, 1965), 520-534.

7635. Reynolds, David S. "The Feminization Controversy: Sexual Stereotypes and the Paradoxes of Piety in Nineteenth-Century America." NEQ 53 (March, 1980), 96-106.

7636. Romanofsky, Peter. "Saving the Lives of the City's Foundlings: the Joint Committee and New York City Child Care Methods, 1860-1907." New York Historical Society. Quarterly 61 (January/April, 1977), 49-68.

7637. Rosenberg, Charles E. "Sexuality, Class, and Role in Nineteenth-Century America." AQ 25 (May, 1973), 131-153.

7638. Rosenberg, Rosalind. "In Search of Woman's Nature, 1850-1920." FS 3 (Fall, 1975), 141-154.

7639. Rosenblum, Naomi L. "The Housing of Lynn's Shoe Workers in 1915" EICH 115 (October, 1979), 221-231.

7640. Rotella, Elyce K. From Home to Office: U.S. Women at Work, 1870-1930. (Ann Arbor, Michigan, UMI Research, 1981)

7641. Rothman, David J. The Discovery of the Asylum: Social Order and Disorder in the New Republic. (Boston, Little, Brown, 1971)

7642. Rothman, Ellen K. "Sex and Self-Control: Middle-Class Courtship in America, 1770-1870." JSH 15 (Spring, 1982), 409-425.

7643. Rothman, Sheila M. Woman's Proper Place: a History of Changing Ideals and Practices, 1870 to the Present. (New York, Basic Books, 1978)

7644. Ryan, Mary P. Womanhood in America, from Colonial Times to the Present. (New York, New Viewpoints, 1975)

7645. Ryan, Mary P. "A Woman's Awakening: Evangelical Religion and the Families of Utica, New York, 1800-1840." AQ 30 (Winter, 1978), 602-623.

7646. Ryan, Thomas G. "Supporters and Opponents of Prohibition: Iowa in 1917." AI 46 (Winter, 1983), 510-522.

7647. Sanger, William W. The History of Prostitution: its Extent, Causes, and Effects throughout the World. (New York, Harper and Brothers, 1869)

7648. Schlossman, Steven L. Love and the American Delinquent: the Theory and Practice of "Progressive" Juvenile Justice, 1825-1920. (Chicago, University of Chicago Press, 1977)

7649. Schwantes, Carlos A. "Free Love and Free Speech on the Pacific Northwest Frontier: Proper Victorians vs. Portland's 'Filthy Firebrand'." OHQ 82 (Fall, 1981), 271-293.

7650. Scott, Anne Firor. The Southern Lady: from Pedestal to Politics, 1830-1930. (Chicago, University of Chicago Press, 1970)

7651. Scott, Anne Firor. "Women's Perspective on the Patriarchy in the 1850's." JAH 61 (June, 1974), 52-64.

7652. Sears, Hal D. The Sex Radicals: Free Love in High Victorian America. (Lawrence, Regents Press of Kansas, 1977)

7653. Seller, Maxine S. "Beyond the Stereotype: a New Look at the Immigrant Woman, 1880-1924." JES 3 (Spring, 1975), 59-70.

7654. Simmons, Olivette. The Case of America's Dependent Children. (Schenectady, New York, Unpublished Senior Thesis, Union College, 1976)

7655. Sklar, Kathryn Kish. Catherine Beecher: a Study in American Domesticity. (New Haven, Connecticut, Yale University Press, 1973)

7656. Smith, Daniel Scott. "The Dating of the American Sexual Revolution: Evidence and Interpretation." In Michael Gordon, ed. The American Family in Social-Historical Perspective. (New York, St. Martin's Press, 1978), 321-335.

7657. Smith, Page. Daughters of the Promised Land: Women in American History. (Boston, Little, Brown, 1970)

7658.   Smith, Wilda M.   "A Half Century of Struggle: Gaining Woman Suffrage in Kansas." KH 4 (Summer, 1981), 74-95.

7659.   Smith-Rosenberg, Carroll.   "Beauty, the Beast, and the Militant Woman; a Case Study in Sex Roles and Social Stress in Jacksonian America." AQ 23 (October, 1971), 562-584.

7660.   Smith-Rosenberg, Carroll.   "Davey Crockett as Trickster: Pornography, Liminality, and Symbolic Inversion in Victorian America." Journal of Contemporary History 17 (April, 1982), 325-350.

7661.   Smith-Rosenberg, Carroll.   "The Female World of Love and Ritual: Relations Between Women in Nineteenth-Century America." Signs 1 (Autumn, 1975), 1-29.

7662.   Smith-Rosenberg, Carroll.   "The Hysterical Woman: Sex Roles and Role Conflict in Nineteenth-Century America." Social Research 39 (Winter, 1972), 652-678.

7663.   Smith-Rosenberg, Carroll.   "Sex as Symbol in Victorian-Purity: an Ethnohistorical Analysis of Jacksonian America." In John Demos and Sarane Spence Boocock, eds. Turning Points; Historical and Sociological Essays on the Family.   (Chicago, University of Chicago Press, 1978; supplement to AJS 84), 212-247.

7664.   Stansell, Christine.   "Women, Children, and the Uses of the Streets: Class and Gender Conflict in New York City, 1850-1860." FS 8 (Summer, 1982), 309-335.

7665.   Steen, Ivan D.   "Cleansing the Puritan City: the Reverend Henry Morgan's Antivice Crusade in Boston." NEQ 54 (September, 1981), 385-411.

7666.   Stewart, Janet Ann.   "The Mansions of Main Street." JArH 20 (Summer, 1979), 193-222.

7667.   Strickland, Charles.   "A Transcendentalist Father: the Child-Rearing Practices of Bronson Alcott." PAH 3 (1969), 3-73.

7668. Strong, Bryan. "Toward a History of the Experiential Family: Sex and Incest in the Nineteenth-Century Family." JMF 35 (August, 1973), 457-466.

7669. Sugar, Hermina. "The Role of Women in the Settlement of the Western Reserve, 1796-1815." OAHQ 46 (1937), 51-67.

7670. Suitor, J. Jill. "Husband's Participation in Childbirth: a Nineteenth-Century Phenomenon." JFH 6 (Fall, 1981), 278-293.

7671. Tansey, Richard. "Prostitution and Politics in Antebellum New Orleans." SouS 18 (Winter, 1979), 449-479.

7672. Taylor, Antoinette Elizabeth. "The Last Phase of the Woman Suffrage Movement in Georgia." GHQ 43 (1959), 11-28.

7673. Taylor, Antoinette Elizabeth. "The Origins of the Woman Suffrage Movement in Georgia." GHQ 28 (June, 1944), 63-79.

7674. Taylor, Antoinette Elizabeth. "Revival and Development of the Woman Suffrage Movement in Georgia." GHQ 42 (1958), 339-354.

7675. Taylor, Antoinette Elizabeth. "The Woman Suffrage Movement in Arkansas." AkHQ 15 (Spring, 1956), 17-52.

7676. Taylor, Antoinette Elizabeth. "The Woman Suffrage Movement in Florida." FHQ 36 (1957), 42-60.

7677. Taylor, Antoinette Elizabeth. "The Woman Suffrage Movement in Mississippi, 1890-1920." JMsH 30 (1968), 1-34.

7678. Taylor, Antoinette Elizabeth. "The Woman Suffrage Movement in North Carolina." NCHR 38 (January, 1961), 46-42; (April, 1961), 173-189.

7679. Taylor, Sandra C. "Abby M. Colby: the Christian Response to a Sexist Society." NEQ 52 (March, 1979), 68-79.

7680.   Terrell, Karen A.   "Exposure of Prostitution in Western   Massachusetts: 1911."   Historical   Journal   of Massachusetts 8 (June, 1980), 3-11.

7681. Thomas, Robert David. "John Humphrey Noyes and the Oneida Community: a 19th-Century American Father and his Family." Psychohistory Review 6 (Fall/Winter, 1977-1978), 68-87.

7682.   Thomas, Robert David.   The Man Who Would Be Perfect: John Humphrey Noyes and the Utopian Impulse. (Philadelphia, University of Pennsylvania Press, 1977)

7683. Tiffin, Susan. In Whose Best Interest? Child Welfare Reform in the Progressive Era.   (Westport, Connecticut, Greenwood Press, 1982)

7684.   Travis, Anthony R.   "The Origin of Mothers' Pensions in Illinois." ISHSJ 68 (November, 1975), 421-428.

7685.   Tressman, Ruth.   "Home on the Range."   NMHR 26 (January, 1951), 1-17.

7686.   Tucker, Barbara M.   "The Family and Industrial Discipline in   Ante-Bellum New England."   LbH 21 (Winter, 1979-1980), 55-74.

7687.   Tygiel, Jules.   "Housing in Late Nineteenth-Century American Cities: Suggestions for Research."   HM 12 (Spring, 1979), 84-97.

7688.   Tylor, Peter.   '"Denied the Power to Choose the Good': Sexuality and Mental Defect in   American Medical Practice 1850-1920." JSH 10 (June, 1977), 472-489.

7689.   Tyrrell, Ian R.   "Drink and Temperance in the Antebellum South: an Overview and Interpretation."   JSouH 48 (November, 1982), 485-510.

7690. Tyrrell, Ian R. "Women and Temperance in Antebellum America, 1830-1860." CWH 28 (June, 1982), 128-152.

7691.   Walters, Ronald G.   "The Erotic South: Civilization and Sexuality in American Abolitionism."   AQ 25 (May, 1973), 177-201.

7692. Walters, Ronald G., ed. <u>Primers for Prudery: Sexual Advice to Victorian America</u>. (Englewood Cliffs, New Jersey: Prentice-Hall, 1973)

7693. Webster, Janice Reiff. "Domestication and Americanization: Scandinavian Women in Seattle, 1888 to 1900." <u>JUH</u> 4 (May, 1978), 275-290.

7694. Weiner, Nella Fermi. "On Feminism and Birth Control Propaganda (1790-1840)." <u>IJWS</u> 3 (September/October, 1980), 411-430.

7695. Welsch, Roger L. "Nebraska Log Construction: Momentum in Tradition." <u>NH</u> 61 (Fall, 1980), 310-335.

7696. Welter, Barbara. "Anti-Intellectualism and the American Woman: 1800-1860." <u>MA</u> 48 (October, 1966), 258-270.

7697. Welter, Barbara. "The Cult of True Womanhood: 1820-1860." <u>AQ</u> 18 (Summer, 1966), 151-174.

7698. Welter, Barbara. "The Feminization of American Religion: 1800-1860." In Mary S. Hartman and Lois Banner, eds. <u>Clio's Conscoiusness Raised: New Perspectives on the History of Women</u>. (New York, Harper and Row, 1974), 137-157.

7699. Wilke, Phyllis Kay. "Physical Education for Women at Nebraska University, 1879-1923." <u>NH</u> 56 (Summer, 1975), 192-220.

7700. Williamson, Joel. <u>New People: Miscegenation and Mulattoes in the United States</u>. (New York, Free Press, 1980)

7701. Wilson, Margaret Gibbons. <u>The American Woman in Transition: the Urban Influence, 1870-1920</u>. (Westport, Connecticut, Greenwood Press, 1979

7702. Wohl, R. Richard. "The 'Country Boy' Myth and its Place in American Urban Culture: the Nineteenth-Century Contribution." <u>PAH</u> 3 (1969), 75-156.

7703. Wolfe, Allis Rosenberg. "Women, Consumerism and the National Consumers' League in the Progressive Era, 1900-1923." LbH 16 (Summer, 1975), 378-392.

7704.   Wortman,   Marlene   Stein.   "Domesticating   the Nineteenth-Century American City." Prospects 3 (1977), 531-572.

7705. Wright, Gwendolyn. Building the Dream: a Social History of Housing in America. (New York, Pantheon, 1981)

7706. Wright, Gwendolyn. Moralism and the Model Home: Domestic Architecture and Cultural Conflict in Chicago, 1873-1913. (Chicago, University of Chicago Press, 1980)

7707. Wrobel, Arthur. "Mark Twin Baits the Masters: 'Some Thoughts on the Science of Onanism'." JPC 15 (Spring, 1982), 53-59.

7708. Wyman, Margaret. "The Rise of the Fallen Woman." AQ 3 (Summer, 1951), 167-177.

Recent America

Every decent public and academic library in the country has numerous books on contemporary families. Sociological journals, both general and specialized, devote ample space to the same topic. Thus, the works cited here are no more than the tip of the iceberg. Much of the available material continues to study themes that emerged in the nineteenth century. In some ways, this whole chapter can be seen as a manifestation of the professional study of the family, in which amateurs like those who carried on the nineteenth-century debate were shoved into the background. There are, however, a few works that open up new areas of interest, or put new twists on old ideas. Mead and Parsons and Bales are important figures in this process, and demonstrate quite different approaches to the family. Friedan and Morgan are not family-studies professionals, but do mark out major alternatives regarding post-World War II feminism. Advice literature in the twentieth century has a different tone, even if the topics are similar. For example, see Neill and Spock regarding child-rearing. Comfort, Hite, Kinsey, and Masters and Johnson write about human sexuality in ways never seen before in America. Intellectual historians such as Lasch and Robinson have begun to explore the significance of this writing. The concept of the life cycle, applied to family life by Glick (see first section), has been popularized by Sheehy, and subjected to major criticism and reworking by Elder. Graebner on retirement and Lubove on social security offer important historical studies of two major aspects of the increasing number and proportion of elderly Americans since 1920.   Davis presents some theoretical approaches to the study of illegitimacy, a topic that may be of major interest to future historians writing on the 1970s and 1980s.

7800.   Ackerman, Nathan W., ed.   Family Process.   (New York, Basic Books, 1970).

7801.   Anderson, Karen.   Wartime Women: Sex Roles, Family Relations, and the Status of Women During World War II. (Westport, Connecticut, Greenwood, Press, 1981)

7802.   Bailey, Jennifer.   "The Dangers of Femininity in Willa Cather's Fiction."   JAS 16 (December, 1982), 391-406.

7803.   Banner, Lois W.   Women in Modern America: a Brief History.   (New York, Harcourt, Brace, Jovanovich, 1975)

7804.   Bauman, John F.   "Safe and Sanitary Without the Costly Frills: the Evolution of Public Housing in Philadelphia, 1929-1941."   PMHB 101 (January, 1977), 114-128.

7805.   Bennett, Sheila Kishler and Glen H. Elder, Jr. "Women's Work in the Family Economy: a Study of Depression Hardship in Women's Lives."   JFH 4 (Summer, 1979), 153-176.

7806.   Blackwelder, Julia Kirk.   "Quiet Suffering: Atlanta Women in the 1930's."   GHQ 61 (Summer, 1977), 112-124.

7807.   Blackwelder, Juila Kirk.   "Women in the Work Force: Atlanta, New Orleans, and San Antonio, 1930 to 1940."   JUH 4 (May, 1978), 331-358.

7808.   Calhoun, Richard B.   In Search of the New Old: Redefining Old Age in America: 1945-1970.   (New York, Elsevier, 1978)

7809. Cantor, Milton and Bruce Laurie. Class, Sex, and the Woman Worker. (Westport, Connecticut, Greenwood Press, 1977)

7810. Chafe, William Henry. The American Woman: her Changing Social, Economic, and Political Roles, 1920-1970. (New York, Oxford, University Press, 1972)

7811. Chafe, William H. Women and Equality: Changing Patterns in American Culture. (New York, Oxford University Press, 1977)

7812. Clive, Alan. "Women Workers in World War II: Michigan as a Test Case." LbH 20 (Winter, 1979), 44-72.

7813. Comfort, Alex, ed. The Joy of Sex: a Cordon Bleu Guide to Lovemaking. (New York, Crown, 1972)

7814. Comfort, Alex, ed. More Joy; a Lovemaking Companion to The Joy of Sex. (New York, Crown, 1974)

7815. Conk, Margo A. "Accuracy, Efficiency, and Bias: the Interpretation of Women's Work in the U.S. Census of Occupations, 1890-1940." HM 14 (Spring, 1981), 65-72.

7816. Cutright, Phillips. "Components of Change in the Number of Female Family Heads Aged 15-44: United States, 1940-1970." JMF 36 (November, 1974), 714-721.

7817. Davis, Kingsley. "Illegitimacy and the Social Structure." AJS 45 (September, 1939), 215-233.

7818. Davis, Kingsley. "Sexual Behavior." In Robert King Merton and Robert A. Nisbet, eds. Contemporary Social Problems, 4th ed. (New York, Harcourt, Brace, Jovanovich, 1976), 281-261.

7819. Demos, John and Virginia Demos. "Adolesence in Historical Perspective." JMF 31 (November, 1969), 632-638.

7820. Downs, Anthony. "The Impact of Housing Policies on Family Life in the United States since World War II." Daedalus 106 (Spring, 1977), 163-180.

7821. Dubbert, Joe L. A Man's Place: Masculinity in Transition. (Englewood Cliffs, New Jersey, Prentice-Hall, 1979)

7822. Elder, Glen H., Jr. Children of the Great Depression: Social Change in Life Experience. (University of Chicago Press, Chicago, 1974)

7823. Elder, Glen H., Jr., and Jeffrey K. Liker. "Hard Times in Women's Lives: Historical Influences Across Forty Years." AJS 88 (September, 1982), 241-269.

7824. Erikson, Erik Homburger. Childhood and Society. 2nd ed. (New York, W.W. Norton, 1964)

7825. Erikson, Erik Homburger. Insight and Responsibility; Lectures on the Ethical Implications of Psychoanalytic Thought. (New York, W.W. Norton, 1964)

7826. Espenshade, Thomas J. "The Value and Cost of Children." Population Bulletin 32 (April, 1977), 1-47.

7827. Evans, Sara. Personal Politics: the Roots of Women's Liberation in the Civil Rights Movement and the New Left. (New York, Knopf, 1979)

7828. Fairbanks, Robert B. "Housing the City: the Better Housing League and Cincinnati, 1916-1939." OH 89 (Spring, 1980), 157-180.

7829. Filene, Peter Gabriel. Him/Her/Self: Sex Roles in Modern America. (New York, Harcourt Brace Jovanovich, 1975)

7830. Freedman, Estelle B. "The New Woman: Changing Views of Women in the 1920's." JAH 61 (September, 1974), 372-393.

7831. Friedan, Betty. The Feminine Mystique. (New York, Norton, 1963)

7832. Gardner, Hugh. The Children of Prosperity: Thirteen Modern American Communes. (New York, St. Martin's Press, 1978)

7833.   Garvey, Timothy J.   "The Duluth Homesteads: a Successful Experiment in Community Housing."   MnH 46 (Spring, 1978), 2-16.

7834.   Glenn, Ellen Nakano.   "The Dialetics of Wage Work: Japanese-American Women and Domestic Service, 1905-1940." FS 6 (Fall, 1980), 432-471.

7835.   Graebner, William.   A History of Retirement: the Meaning and Function of an American Institution, 1885-1978. (New Haven, Yale University Press, 1980)

7836.   Graebner, William.   "The Unstable World of Benjamin Spock: Social Engineering in a Democratic Culture, 1917-1950."   JAH 67 (December, 1980),   612-629.

7837.   Haley, Jay, comp.   Changing Families: a Family Therapy Reader. (New York, Grune and Stratton, 1971)

7838.   Hareven, Tamara K.   "The Dynamics of Kin in an Industrial Community."   In John Demos and Sarane Spence Boocock, eds.   Turning Points: Historical and Sociological Essays on the Family. (Chicago, University of Chicago Press, 1978; supplement to AJS 84), 151-182.

7839.   Harley, Sharon and Rosalyn Terborg-Penn, eds.   The Afro-American Woman: Struggles and Images.   (Port Washington, New York, Kennikat, 1978)

7840.   Hite, Shere.   The Hite Report: a Nationwide Study on Female Sexuality. (New York, Macmillan, 1976)

7841.   Hurst, Marsha and Ruth E. Zambrana.   "The Health Careers of Urban Women: a Study in East Harlem."   Signs 5, Supplement (Spring, 1980), 112-126.

7842.   Jackson, Anthony.   A Place Called Home: a History of Low-Cost Housing in Manhattan. (Cambridge, Massachusetts, MIT Press, 1976)

7843.   Jencks, Christopher, et. al.   Inequality: a Reassessment of the Effect of Family and Schooling in America. (New York, Harper and Row, 1972)

7844. Journal of Social Issues 22 (April, 1966), "The Sexual Renaissance in America." Special issue on sex in contemporary America.

7845. Keniston, Kenneth. Youth and Dissent: the Rise of a New Opposition. (New York, Harcourt Brace Jovanovich, 1971)

7846. Kihlstedt, Folke T. "The Automobile and the Transformation of the American House, 1910-1935." Michigan Quarterly Review 19/20 (Fall, 1980/Winter, 1981), 555-570.

7847. Kingston, Maxine Hong. Woman Warrior: Memoirs of a Girlhood among Ghosts. (New York, Knopf, 1976)

7848. Kinsey, Alfred Charles, et. al. Sexual Behavior in the Human Female. (Philadelphia, Saunders, 1953)

7849. Kinsey, Alfred Charles, et. al. Sexual Behavior in the Human Male. (Philadelphia, Saunders, 1948)

7850. Kyvig, David E. "Women Against Prohibition." AQ 28 (Fall, 1976), 465-482.

7851. Lasch, Christopher. Haven in a Heartless World: the Family Beseiged. (New York, Basic Books, 1977)

7852. Leotta, Louis. "Abraham Epstein and the Movement for Old Age Security." LbH 16 (Summer, 1975), 359-377.

7853. Levering, Patricia W. and Ralph B. Levering. "Women in Relief: the Carroll County Children's Aid Society in the Great Depression." MHM 72 (Winter, 1977), 534-546.

7854. Lewis, David L. "Sex and the Automobile: from Rumble Seats to Rockin' Vans." Michigan Quarterly Review 19/20 (Fall, 1980/Winter, 1981), 518-528.

7855. Light, Ivan. "The Ethnic Vice Industry, 1880-1944." ASR 42 (June, 1977), 464-479.

7856. Lopata, Helena Znaniecki. "The Chicago Woman: a Study of Patterns of Mobility and Transportation." Signs 5, Supplement (Spring, 1980), 161-169.

7857.   Lubove, Roy.   The Struggle for Social Security, 1900-1935.   (Cambridge, Massachusetts, Harvard University Press, 1968)

7858.   Macfarlane, Jean W.   "Perspectives on Personality Consistency and Change from the Guidance Study."   Vita Humana 7 (1964), 115-126.

7859.   Markusen, Ann R.   "City Spatial Structure, Woman's Household Work, and National Urban Policy."   Signs 5, Supplement (Spring, 1980), 22-44.

7860.   Marsden, Michael T.   "The Concept of the Family in the Fiction of Louis L'Amour."   NDQ 46 (Summer, 1978), 12-21.

7861.   Masters, William H. and Virginia E. Johnson.   Human Sexual Inadequacy.   (Boston, Little, Brown, 1970)

7862.   Masters, William H. and Virginia E. Johnson.   Human Sexual Response.   (Boston, Little, Brown, 1966)

7863.   Masters, William H., et.al.   The Pleasure Bond: a New Look at Sexuality and Commitment.   (Boston, Little, Brown, 1974)

7864.   Mead, Margaret.   Coming of Age in Samoa: a Psychological Study of Primitive Youth for Western Civilization.   (New York, W. Morrow, 1961)

7865.   Mead, Margaret.   "Cultural Determinants of Sexual Behavior."   In William Caldwell Young, ed.   Sex and Internal Secretions, 3rd ed.   2 vols.   (Baltimore, Williams and Wilkins, 1961), v.2, 1433-1479.

7866.   Mead, Margaret.   From the South Seas: Studies of Adolescence and Sex in Primitive Society.   (New York, W. Morrow, 1939)

7867.   Mead, Margaret.   Male and Female: a Study of the Sexes in a Changing World.   (New York, W. Morrow, 1949)

7868.   Milkman, Ruth.   "Redefining 'Women's Work': the Sexual Division of Labor in the Auto Industry During World War II."   FS 8 (September, 1982), 336-372.

7869. Miller, Zane L. and Geoffrey Giglierano. "Downtown Housing: Changing Plans and Perspectives, 1948-1980." CHSB 40 (Fall, 1982), 167-190.

7870. Mindel, Charles H. and Robert W. Habenstein. Ethnic Families in America: Patterns and Variations. (New York, Elsevier, 1976)

7871. Modell, John. "Suburbanization and Change in the American Family." JIH 9 (Spring, 1979), 621-646.

7872. Morantz, Regina Markell. "The Scientist as Sex Crusader: Alfred C. Kinsey and American Culture." AQ 29 (Winter, 1977), 563-589.

7873. Morgan, Marabel. The Total Woman. (Old Tappan, New Jersey, F.H. Revell, 1973)

7874. Mulder, John M. "The Heavenly City and Human Cities: Washington Gladden and Urban Reform." OH 87 (Spring, 1978), 151-174.

7875. Neill, Alexander Sutherland. Summerhill: a Radical Approach to Child Rearing. (New York, Hart Publishing Company, 1962)

7876. Newsweek, "Saving the Family" 91 (May 15, 1978), 63-90.

7877. Oppenheimer, Valerie Kincade. "The Life Cycle Squeeze: the Interaction of Men's Occupational and Family Life Cycles." Demography 11 (May, 1974), 227-245.

7878. Parker, Jacqueline K. and Edward M. Carpenter. "Julia Lathrop and the Children's Bureau: the Emergence of an Institution." Social Service Review 55 (March, 1981), 60-77.

7879. Parsons, Talcott and Robert F. Bales. Family, Socialization, and Interaction Process. (Glencoe, Illinois, Free Press, 1955)

7880. Philips, Peter. "Gender-Based Wage Differentials in Pennsylvania and New Jersey Manufacturing, 1900-1950." JEH 42 (March, 1982), 181-186.

7881. Pommer, Richard. "The Architecture of Urban Housing in the United States during the Early 1930's." Society of Architectural Historians. Journal 37 (December, 1978), 235-264.

7882. Reiss, Ira L. The Social Context of Pre-marital Sexual Permissiveness. (New York, Holt, Rinehart and Winston, 1967)

7883. Ridley, Jeanne Claire. "On the Consequences of Demographic Change for the Roles and Status of Women." In U. S. Commission on Population Growth and the American Future. Demographic and Social Aspects of Population Growth. Edited by Charles F. Westoff and Robert Parke, Jr. (Washington, Government Printing Office, 1972), 289-304.

7884. Robinson, Paul. The Modernization of Sex: Havelock Ellis, Alfred Kinsey, William Masters and Virginia Johnson. (New York, Harper and Row, 1976)

7885. Rosenberg, Rosalind. Beyond Separate Spheres: Intellectual Roots of Modern Feminism. (New Haven, Connecticut, Yale University Press, 1982)

7886. Rothschild, Mary Aickin. "To Scout or to Guide? the Girl Scout-Boy Scout Controversy, 1912-1941." Frontiers 6 (Fall, 1981), 115-121.

7887. Saegert, Susan. "Masculine Cities and Feminine Suburbs: Polarized Ideas, Contradictory Realities." Signs 5, Supplement (Spring, 1980), 96-111.

7888. Sandell, Steven H. "Women and the Economics of Family Migration." Review of Economics and Statistics 59 (November, 1977), 406-414.

7889. Scharf, Lois. To Work and to Wed: Female Employment, Feminism, and the Great Depression. (Westport, Connecticut, Greenwood Press, 1980)

7890. Schneider, David Murray. American Kinship: a Cultural Account. 2nd ed. (Chicago, University of Chicago Press, 1980)

7891. Seller, Maxine. "The Education of the Immigrant Woman, 1900-1935." JUH 4 (May, 1978), 307-330.

7892. Sheehy, Gail. Passages: Predictable Crises of Adult Life. (New York, Dutton, 1976)

7893. Smith, C. Calvin. "Diluting an Institution: the Social Impact of Warld War II on the Arkansas Family." AkHQ 39 (Spring, 1980), 21-34.

7894. Smith, Judith E. "Our Own Kind: Family and Community Networks." RHR 17 (Spring, 1978), 99-120.

7895. Smith, Raymond T. "The Nuclear Family in Afro-American Kinship." Journal of Comparative Family Studies 1 (1970), 55-70.

7896. Smith, Wilford E. "Mormon Sex Standards on College Campuses, or Deal Us Out of the Sexual Revolution!" DJMT 10 (Autumn, 1976), 76-81.

7897. Spock, Benjamin McLane. Baby and Child Care, numerous editions. Originally published as The Common Sense Book of Baby and Child Care. (New York, Duell, Sloan and Pearce, 1946)

7898. Stack, Carol B. All Our Kin: Strategies for Survival in a Black Community. (New York, Harper & Row, 1974)

7899. Stevens, Kenneth R. "United States v. 31 Photographs: Dr. Alfred C. Kinsey and Obscenity Law." IMH 71 (December, 1975), 299-318.

7900. Taylor, Anne Robinson. "The Virginal Male as Hero in American Films." Southwest Review 63 (Autumn, 1978), 317-329.

7901. Travis, Anthony R. "Sophonisba Breckinridge, Militant Feminist." MA 58 (April-July, 1976), 111-118.

7902. Vanek, Joann. "Work, Leisure, and Family Roles: Farm Households in the United States, 1920-1955." JFH 5 (Winter, 1980), 422-431.

7903.   Voigt, David.   "Sex in Baseball: Reflections of Changing Taboos." JPC 12 (Winter, 1978), 389-403.

7904. Waite, Linda J. "Working Wives: 1940-1960." ASR 41 (February, 1976), 65-80.

7905.   Walker, Roger W.   "The A.F.L. and Child-Labor Legislation: an Exercise in Frustration." LbH 11 (Summer, 1970), 323-340.

7906. Wall, Helena M. "Feminism and the New England Hospital, 1949-1961." AQ 32 (Fall, 1980), 435-452.

7907. Wandersee, Winifred D. Women's Work and Family Values: 1920-1940.   (Cambridge, Massachusetts, Harvard Univeristy Press, 1981)

7908.   Weiner, Lynn.   "'Our Sister's Keepers':   the Minneapolis Woman's Christian Association and Housing for Working Women." MnH 46 (Spring, 1979), 189-200.

7909. Weiss, Nancy Rottishman. "Mother, the Invention of Necessity: Dr. Benjamin Spock's Baby and Child Care." AQ 29 (Winter, 1977), 519-546.

7910.   Wells, Robert V.   "Women's Lives Transformed: Demographic and Family Patterns in America, 1600-1970." In Carol Berkin and Mary Beth Norton, eds. The Women of America: A History. (Boston, Houghton Mifflin, 1979), 16-33.

7911.   Wertheimer, Barbara Mayer.   We Were There: the Story of Working Women in America. (New York, Pantheon, 1977)

7912. Wojniusz, Helen K. "Ethnicity and other Variables in the Analysis of Polish American Women." PAS 34 (Autumn, 1977), 26-37.

7913. Ziegler, Suzanne. "The Family Unit and International Migration: the Perception of Italian Immigrant Children." IMR 11 (Fall, 1977), 326-333.

6
Population, Economics, Politics, and Society

The inclusion of this chapter in this bibliography is what makes this a work on demographic history instead of historical demography. The latter takes a more limited approach to the study of demography, asking about the size and growth of past populations, and the processes that gave rise to those characteristics. The former seeks to understand the consequences of those patterns, and the non-demographic causes that shaped various demographic processes. Some historical demographers might have no interest in this part of the bibliography. At the other extreme, it is possible to argue that demography is so central to the shaping of the past that almost everything historians write about should interest demographic historians. To include everything written on American history would be as absurd as to deny the importance of demography to history and so include nothing. Hence this chapter tries to present readers with a comprehensive but comprehensible selection of materials which demonstrate the complex links among population, economics, politics, and society. Many of these studies explicitly touch on one or more of the demographic patterns discussed elsewhere in the bibliography. Some, however, do not make direct mention of population, though the links are obvious and would presumably be recognized by the authors.

This chapter is organized in a very simple fashion. The three general periods used throughout the study provide the primary divisions. Materials on economics are listed first, largely because economists tend to be more explicitly aware of the links between their concerns and demography. Politics comes next, in part because of the tremendous importance migration (in all its forms) has had in shaping American political forms and issues. The works listed under society are studies that deserve mention, but which do not clearly belong under economics or politics. Some of them might have been included in the values-oriented sections of earlier chapters; similarly, other scholars might have placed works cited earlier, especially those on regionalism and cultural pluralism here. Decisions on where to place a particular work reflect matters of emphasis and orientation, with less explicitly demographic studies being placed here.

Early America

Although this division is, to some degree, arbitrary, in that many of the themes encountered in works cited here carry over at least into the nineteenth century, colonial historians have been leaders in their awareness of the importance of demographic issues. They have also been unusually sensitive to the complex interactions among demographic, economic, political, and social patterns. This awareness is evident not only in the citations that follow, but also in many of the works on particular groups or communities listed above in the chapters on fertility, migration, and families.

Economics

This section is deceptively short because many of the works cited under migration and settlement in the English colonies and those treating early American families have significant discussions on the inter-relationships of demographic and economic structures. Major themes to look for in these works, and those cited earlier include sources of labor, distribution of wealth and opportunities for upward mobility, trade networks, standards of living, and the economic consequences of cultural pluralism.

8000. Anderson, Terry L. "Economic Growth in Colonial New England: 'Statistical Renaissance'." JEH 39 (March, 1979), 243-257.

8001. Anderson, Terry L. and Robert Paul Thomas. "White Population, Labor Force and Extensive Growth of the New England Economy in the Seventeenth Century." JEH 33 (September, 1973), 634-667.

8002. Ball, Duane E. "Dynamics of Population and Wealth in Eighteenth-Century Chester County, Pennsylvania." JIH 6 (Spring, 1976), 621-644.

8003. Galenson, David W. "White Servitude and the Growth of Black Slavery in Colonial America." JEH 41 (March, 1981), 39-47.

8004. Gallman, Robert E. "Influences on the Distribution of Landholdings in Early Colonial North Carolina." JEH 42 (September, 1982), 549-575.

8005. Herndon, G. Melvin. "Indian Agriculture in the Southern Colonies." NCHR 44 (July, 1967), 283-297.

8006. Jones, E.L. "Creative Disruptions in American Agriculture, 1620-1820." AgH 48 (October, 1974), 510-528.

8007. Kulikoff, Allan. "Black Society and the Economics of Slavery." MHM 70 (Summer, 1975), 203-210.

8008. Kulikoff, Allan. "The Economic Growth of the Eighteenth-Century Chesapeake Colonies." JEH 39 (March, 1979), 275-288.

8009. Levine, Gaynell S. "Colonial Long Island Grave Stones: Trade Network Indicators, 1670-1799." In Peter Benes, ed. Puritan Gravestone Art II: the Dublin Seminar for New England Folklife: Annual Proceedings 1978 (Boston, Boston University, 1978), 46-57.

8010. Lydon, James G. "New York and the Slave Trade, 1700 to 1774." WMQ 35 (April, 1978), 375-394.

8011. Maar, Charles. "The High Dutch and the Low Dutch in New York, 1624-1924." NYH 5, i.e. New York State Historical Association. Proceedings 22 (1924), 317-329.

8012.   Menard, Russell R.   "From Servants to Slaves: the Transformation of the Chesapeake Labor System."   SouS 16 (Winter, 1977), 355-390.

8013.   Morris, Francis Grave and Phyllis Mary Morris. "Economic Conditions in North Carolina about 1780."   NCHR 16 (1939), 107-133; 296-327.

8014.   Puckrein, Gary.   "Climate, Health, and Black Labor in the English Americas."   JAS 13 (August, 1979), 179-193.

8015.   Ray, Arthur J.   Indians in the Fur Trade: Their Role as Trappers, Hunters, and Middlemen in the Lands Southwest of Hudson Bay, 1660-1870.   (Toronto, University of Toronto, Press, 1974)

8016.   Sainsbury, John A.   "Indian Labor in Early Rhode Island."   NEQ 48 (September, 1975), 378-393.

8017.   Salinger, Sharon V.   "Colonial Labor in Transition: the Decline of Indentured Servitude in Late Eighteenth-Century Philadelphia."   LbH 22 (Spring, 1981), 165-191.

8018.   Shammas, Carole.   "The Determinants of Personal Wealth in Seventeenth-Century England and America."   JEH 37 (September, 1977), 675-689.

8019.   Smith, Billy G.   "The Material Lives of Laboring Philadelphians, 1750 to 1800."   WMQ 38 (April, 1981), 163-202.

Politics

Many of the community studies cited earlier in the bibliography comment on politics as well as economics.   Of the works listed here, Bonomi, Ireland, and Leiby are important because of their discussion of the ethnic dimension in politics, a theme that is common in writing on the nineteenth century.   Nash analyzes the importance of the nascent cities in pre-Revolutionary America, and Cook looks at the nature of politics in many of New England's small towns.

8050. Balckie, William R. "Indians of New York City and Vicinity." NYH 4, i.e. New York State Historical Association. Proceedings (January, 1923), 41-48.

8051. Blackwelder, Ruth. "The Attitude of the North Carolina Moravians Toward the American Revolution." NCHR 9 (1932), 1-21.

8052. Bonomi, Patricia U. A Factious People: Politics and Society in Colonial New York. (New York, Columbia University Press, 1971)

8053. Buffinton, Arthur H. "The Policy of Albany and English Westward Expansion." MVHR 8 (March, 1922), 327-366.

8054. Cook, Edward M., Jr. The Fathers of the Towns: Leadership and Community Structure in Eighteenth-Century New England. (Baltimore, Johns Hopkins University Press, 1976)

8055. Crandall, Ralph J. and Ralph J. Coffman. "From Emmigrants to Rulers: the Charlestown Oligarchy in the Great Migration." NEHGR 131 (January, 1977), 3-27.

8056. Curtis, George B. "The Colonial County Court, Social Forum, and Legislative Precedent: Accomack County, Virginia, 1633-1639." VMHB 85 (July, 1977), 274-288.

8057. Daniels, Bruce C. "Connecticut's Villages Become Mature Towns: the Complexity of Local Institutions, 1676 to 1776." WMQ 34 (January, 1977), 83-103.

8058. Davis, Joseph L. Sectionalism in American Politics, 1774-1787. (Madison, University of Wisconsin Press, 1977)

8059. Dill, Alonzo Thomas. "Sectional Conflict in Colonial Virginia." VMHB 87 (July, 1979), 300-315.

8060. Dorpalen, Andreas. "The Political Influence of the German Element in Colonial America." PH 6 (1939), 147-158, 221-239.

8061.   Ekirch, A. Roger.   "Poor Carolina": Politics and Society in Colonial North Carolina, 1729-1776. (Chapel Hill, University of North Carolina Press, 1981)

8062.   Evans, Emory G.   "The Colonial View of the West." ISHSJ 69 (May, 1976), 84-90.

8063.   Ganyard, Robert L.   "Threat from the West: North Carolina and the Cherokee, 1776-1778."   NCHR 45 (January, 1968), 47-66.

8064.   Giraud, Marcel.   "France and Louisiana in the Early Eighteenth Century."   MVHR 36 (March, 1950), 657-674.

8065.   Henretta, James A.   "Southern Social Structure and the American War for Independence."   West Georgia College Studies in the Social Sciences 15 (June, 1976), 1-14.

8066.   Ireland, Owen.   "The Ethnic-Religious Dimensions of Pennsylvania Politics, 1778-1779."   WMQ 30 (July, 1973), 423-448.

8067.   Jillson, Calvin and Thornton Anderson.   "Realignments in the Convention of 1787:   the Slave Trade Compromise." Journal of Politics 39 (August, 1977), 712-729.

8068.   Johnson, Hildegard Binder.   "The Germantown Protest of 1688 Against Negro Slavery."   PMHB 65 (April, 1941), 145-156.

8069.   Jordan, David W.   "Elections and Voting in Early Colonial Maryland."   MHM 77 (Fall, 1982), 238-265.

8070.   Kawashima, Yasu.   "Jurisdiction of the Colonial Courts over the Indians in Massachusetts, 1689-1763."   NEQ 42 (December, 1969), 532-550.

8071.   Leiby, Adrian Coulter.   The Revolutionary War in the Hackensack Valley; the Jersey Dutch and the Neutral Ground, 1775-1783.   (New Brunswick, New Jersey, Rutgers University Press, 1962)

8072.   Leyburn, James G.   "Presbyterian Immigrants and the American Revolution."   Journal of Presbyterian History 54 (Spring, 1976), 9-32.

8073. Nash, Gary B. The Urban Crucible: Social Change, Political Consciousness, and the Origins of the American Revolution. (Cambridge, Massachusetts, Harvard University Press, 1979)

8074. Nelson, William H. The American Tory. (Oxford, Clarendon Press, 1961)

8075. Purvis, Thomas L. "'High-Born, Long Recorded Families': Social Origins of New Jersey Assemblymen, 1703 to 1776." WMQ 37 (October, 1980), 529-615.

8076. Rhonda, James P. "'We Are Well as We Are': an Indian Critique of Seventeenth-Century Christian Missions." WMQ 34 (January, 1977), 66-82.

8077. Ryerson, Richard Allen. "Political Mobilization and the American Revolution: the Resistance Movement in Philadelphia, 1765-1776." WMQ 31 (October, 1972), 565-588.

8078. Ryerson, Richard Allen. The Revolution Is Now Begun: the Radical Committees of Philadelphia, 1765-1776. (Philadelphia, University of Pennsylvania Press, 1978)

8079. Shepard, E. Lee. "'The Ease and Convenience of the People': Courthouse Locations in Spotsylvania County, 1720-1840." VMHB 87 (July, 1979), 279-299.

8080. Stoudt, John Joseph. "The German Press in Pennsylvania and the American Revolution." PMHB 59 (1935), 74-90.

8081. Whittenberg, James P. "Planters, Merchants, and Lawyers: Social Change and the Origins of the North Carolina Regulation." WMQ 34 (April, 1977), 215-238.

8082. Young, Alfred Fabian, ed. The American Revolution: Explorations in the History of American Radicalism. (DeKalb, Illinois, Northern Illinois University Press, 1976)

8083. Young, Chester Raymond. "The Stress of War upon the Civilian Population of Virginia, 1739-1760." WVH 27 (July, 1966), 251-277.

8084.   Young, Mary E.   "Creek Frauds: a Study in
Conscience and Corruption." MVHR 42 (1955), 411-437.

Society

Several major themes emerge from the literature listed below.
One of the most important is the development of regional
and sectional differences, often accompanied by various
degrees of conflict, with roots in racial, religious, and
cultural antagonisms. Bridenbaugh, Klein, and Kulikoff are
helpful on these matters, as are the essays in the two
readers edited by Land, Carr, and Papenfuse and by Tate and
Ammerman. Many of these works focus on the Middle and
Southern Colonies because the corresponding studies of New
England are located in the section on Migration and
Settlement in the English Colonies in Chapter Four. The
emergence of economic classes based on unequal distribution
of wealth can be studied in works by Henretta, Kulikoff,
Land, and Lemon and Nash. Warden critiques this literature.
Henretta's book on the evolution of American society is a
wide-ranging   commentary   that   is   very   conscious   of
demographic change. Goveia's study of slave society in the
Leeward Islands in the eighteenth century is included here
both to provide a comparison to mainland societies based on
slavery and to set an example of how those societies might
be studied.

8100.   Alexander, John K.   Render Them Submissive:
Responses to Poverty in Philadelphia, 1760-1800. (Amherst,
University of Massachusetts Press, 1980)

8101. Beeman, Richard R. "The New Social History and the
Search for 'Community' in Colonial America." AQ 29 (Fall,
1977), 422-443.

8102.   Beeman, Richard R.   "Social Change and Cultural
Conflict in Virginia: Lunenburg County, 1746 to 1774."
WMQ 35 (July, 1978), 455-476.

8103. Beeman, Richard R. and Rhys Isaac. "Cultural Conflict
and Social Change in the Revolutionary South: Lunenburg
County, Virginia." JSouH 46 (November, 1980), 525-550.

8104. Berlin, Ira. "The Slave Trade and the Development of Afro-American Society in English Mainland North America, 1619-1755." SouS 20 (Summer, 1981), 122-136.

8105. Bonomi, Patricia U. and Peter R. Eisenstadt. "Church Adherence in the Eighteenth-Century British American Colonies." WMQ 39 (April, 1982), 245-286.

8106. Breen, Timothy Hall. "Looking out for Number One: Conflicting Cultural Values in Early Seventeenth-Century Virginia." SAQ 78 (Summer, 1979), 342-360.

8107. Bridenbaugh, Carl. Myths and Realities: Societies of the Colonial South. (Baton Rouge, Louisiana State University Press, 1958)

8108. Chappell, Edward A. "Acculturation in the Shenandoah Valley: Rhenish Houses of the Massanutten Settlement." APSP 124 (February 29, 1980), 55-89.

8109. Cohen, Lester H. "Eden's Constitution: the Paradisiacal Dream and Enlightenment Values in Late Eighteenth-Century Literature of the American Frontier." Prospects 3 (1977), 83-109.

8110. Craven, Wesley Frank. The Southern Colonies in the Seventeenth Century, 1607-1689. (Baton Rouge, Louisiana State University Press, 1949)

8111. Crevecoeur, Michel-Guillaume St. Jean de. Letters from an American Farmer. (London, Printed for T. Davies, etc., 1782)

8112. Faber, Eli. "Puritan Criminals: the Economic, Social, and Intellectual Background to Crime in Seventeenth-Century Massachusetts." PAH 11 (1977-1978), 81-144.

8113. Fliegelman, Jay. Prodigals and Pilgrims: the American Revolution Against Patriarchal Authority, 1750-1800. (Cambridge, England, Cambridge University Press, 1982)

8114. Foner, Philip Sheldon. History of Black Americans: from Africa to the Emergence of the Cotton Kingdom. (Westport, Connecticut, Greenwood Press, 1975)

8115. Gagliardo, John G. "Germans and Agriculture in Colonial Pennsylvania." PMHB 83 (April, 1959), 192-218.

8116. Galenson, David W. "'Middling People' or 'Common Sort'?" the Social Origins of some Early Americans Reexamined." WMQ 35 (July, 1978), 499-524.

8117. Galenson, David W. "The Social Origins of some Early Americans: Rejoinder." (with a reply by Mildred Campbell) WMQ 36 (April, 1979), 264-286.

8118. Goveia, Elsa V. Slave Society in the British Leeward Islands at the End of the Eighteenth Century. (New Haven, Connecticut, Yale University Press, 1965)

8119. Halliburton, R., Jr. Red over Black: Black Slavery among the Cherokee Indians. (Westport, Connecticut, Greenwood Press, 1977)

8120. Henretta, James A. "Economic Development and Social Structure in Colonial Boston." WMQ 22 (1965), 75-92.

8121. Henretta, James A. The Evolution of American Society, 1700-1815: an Interdisciplinary Analysis. (Lexington, Massachusetts, Heath, 1973)

8122. Heyrman, Christine Leigh. "The Fashion among More Superior People: Charity and Social Change in Provincial New England, 1700-1740." AQ 34 (Summer, 1982), 107-124.

8123. Hornick, Nancy Slocum. "Anthony Benezet and the Africans' School: Toward a Theory of Full Equality." PMHB 99 (October, 1975), 399-421.

8124. Innes, Stephen. "Land Tenancy and Social Order in Springfield, Massachusetts, 1652 to 1702." WMQ 35 (January, 1978), 33-56.

8125. Jones, Douglas Lamar. "The Strolling Poor: Transiency in Eighteenth-Century Massachusetts." JSH 8 (Spring, 1975), 28-54.

8126.   Kenney, Alice P.   "Private Worlds in the Middle Colonies: an Introduction to Human Tradition in American History." NYH 51, i.e. New York State Historical Association. Proceedings 68 (1970), 5-32.

8127.   Klein, Milton M.   "Shaping the American Tradition: the Microcosm of Colonial New York." NYH 59, i.e. New York State Historical Association.   Proceedings 76 (1978), 173-197.

8128.   Klingberg, Frank J.   "The   Anglican Minority in Colonial Pennsylvania with Particular Reference to the Indian." PMHB 65 (July, 1941), 276-299.

8129.   Kulikoff, Allan. "The Colonial Chesapeake: Seedbed of Antebellum Southern Culture?"   JSouH 45 (November, 1979), 513-540.

8130.   Kulikoff, Allan.   "The Origins   of Afro-American Society in Tidewater Maryland and Virginia, 1700 to 1790." WMQ 35 (April, 1978), 226-259.

8131.   Kulikoff, Allan.   "The Progress of Inequality in Revolutionary Boston." WMQ 28 (July, 1971), 375-412.

8132.   Lachance, Paul. "Intermarriage and French Cultural Persistence in Late Spanish and Early American New Orleans."   Histoire Social-Social History 15 (May, 1982), 47-81.

8133.   Land, Aubrey C.   Colonial Maryland: a History. (Millwood, New York, KTO, 1981)

8134. Land, Aubrey C. "Economic Base and Social Structure: the Northern Chesapeake in the Eighteenth Century." JEH 25 (December, 1965), 639-654.

8135.   Land, Aubrey C., Lois Green Carr, and Edward C. Papenfuse, eds. Law, Society, and Politics in Early Maryland. (Baltimore, Johns Hopkins University Press, 1977)

8136.   LeFevre, Ralph.   "The Hugenots--the First Settlers in the Province of New York." NYH 2, i.e. New York State Historical Association. Preoceedings 19 (1921), 177-185.

8137. Lemon, James T. and Gary B. Nash. "The Distribution of Wealth in Eighteenth-Century America: a Century of Change in Chester County, Pennsylvania, 1693-1802." JSH 2 (Fall, 1968), 1-24.

8138. Lower, A.R.M. "New France in New England." NEQ (April, 1929), 278-295.

8139. McCoy, Drew R. "Jefferson and Madison on Malthus: Population Growth in Jeffersonian Political Economy." VMHB 88 (July, 1980), 259-276.

8140. Marraro, Howard A. "Italo-Americans in Eighteenth-Century New York." NYH 21, i.e. New York Historical Association. Proceedings 38 (1940), 316-323.

8141. Meyer, Larry L. "A State of Less than Enchantment; New Mexico in 1776: the Forces and Nations that Shaped the Early American West." AW 12 (September, 1975), 4-9.

8142. Miller, Richard G. "Gentry and Entrepreneurs: a Socioeconomic Analysis of Philadelphia in the 1790's." Rocky Mountain Social Science Journal 12 (January, 1975), 71-84.

8143. Nash, Gary B. "Urban Wealth and Poverty in Pre-Revolutionary America." JIH 6 (Spring, 1976), 545-584.

8144. Nybakken, Elizabeth I. "New Light on the Old Side: Irish Influences on Colonial Presbyterialism." JAH 68 (March, 1982), 813-832.

8145. Overton, Jacqueline. "The Quakers on Long Island." NYH 21, i.e. New York State Historical Association. Proceedings 38 (1940), 151-161.

8146. Peyer, Jean. "Jamaica, New York, 1656-1776: Class Structure and Social Mobility." Journal of Long Island History 14 (Fall, 1977), 34-47.

8147. Rasmussen, William M.S. "Designers, Builders, and Architectural Traditions in Colonial Virginia." VMHB 90 (April, 1982), 198-212.

8148. Rutman, Darrett B., Charles Wetherell, and Anita H. Rutman. "Rhythms of Life: Black and White Seasonality in the Early Chesapeake." JIH 11 (Summer, 1980), 29-53.

8149. Schwarz, Philip J. "Gabriel's Challenge: Slaves and Crime in Late Eighteenth-Century Virginia." VMHB 90 (July, 1982), 283-309.

8150. Shryock, Richard H. "British vs. German Traditions in Colonial Agriculture." MVHR 26 (June, 1939), 39-54.

8151. Slaughter, Thomas Paul. "'Every Man Here is Upon an Equallity': Robert Stratford Byrne, Customs Collection, and Intercultural Conflict in the Colonial Chesapeake." MdH 10 (Spring, 1979), 29-41.

8152. Smith, Raoul N. "The Interest in Language and Languages in Colonial and Federal America." APSP 123 (February, 1979), 29-46.

8153. Soderlund, Jean R., et.al., eds. William Penn and the Founding of Pennsylvania, 1680-1684: a Documentary History. (Philadelphia, University of Pennsylvania Press, 1983)

8154. Sutherland, Daniel E. "The Servant Problem: an Index of Antebellum Americanism." SouS 18 (Winter, 1979), 488-503.

8155. Tate, Thaddeus W. and David L. Ammerman, eds. The Chesapeake in the Seventeenth Century: Essays on Anglo-American Society. (Chapel Hill, University of North Carolina Press, 1979)

8156. Thomas, G.E. "Puritans, Indians, and the Concept of Race." NEQ 48 (March, 1975), 3-27.

8157. Thompson, R. "Seventeenth-Century English and Colonial Sex Ratios: a Postscript." PS 28 (March, 1974), 153-165.

8158. Tolles, Frederick B. "The Culture of Early Pennsylvania." PMHB 81 (April, 1957), 119-137.

8159.   Ulrich, Laurel Thatcher.   "'A Friendly Neighbor':
Social Dimensions of Daily Work in Northern Colonial New
England." FS 6 (Summer, 1980), 392-405.

8160.   Ulrich, Laurel Thatcher.   "Psalm-tunes, Periwigs, and
Bastards: Ministerial Authority in Early Eighteenth-Century
Durham."   Historical New Hampshire 36 (Winter, 1981),
255-279.

8161.   Warden,   G.B.   "Inequality   and   Instability   in
Eighteenth-Century Boston: a Reapprasial."   JIH 6 (Spring,
1976), 585-620.

8162.   Willingham, William F.   "Religious Conversion in the
Second Society of Windham, Connecticut, 1723-1743:   a Case
Study." Societas 6 (Spring, 1976), 109-119.

8163.   Zuckerman, Michael, ed.   Friends and Neighbors:
Group Life in America's First Plural Society. (Philadelphia,
Temple University Press, 1982)

The Nineteenth Century

The demographic revolutions of the nineteenth century were
accompanied by equally profound changes in economic,
political, and social structures.   Cause and effect are not
easily distinguished in the complex interactions of the time.
Readers of these materials should keep in mind that some of
them describe actual changes while others discuss what
nineteenth-century Americans thought ought to happen.
Chapters Two to Five all contain additional works that can
be read in conjunction with these articles and books.   If
nothing else, these works demonstrate the extraordinary
productivity and insight of students of the American past.
Without them, scholars who aimed to become demographic
historians would have to be content to remain historical
demographers.

Economics

Most students of the interaction of population and the
economy focus on one of several important topics.   There
are, however, three more general texts that provide beginners

with good places to start.   Easterlin is the first choice because he is an economist who emphasizes demographic patterns.   Bruchey and North are also helpful.   It is difficult to single out other works, but readers should have little trouble in selecting works on slaves and free blacks, immigrants, urbanization and urban places, agriculture and rural America, family life (especially with regard to the roles of women and children), and the development of industry (as distinct from urbanization).   Erickson, Kelley, and Thomas are useful as means to place the American experience in an international perspective.

8200. Adams, Donald R., Jr. "The Standard of Living During American Industrialization: Evidence from the Brandywine Region, 1800-1860." <u>JEH</u> 42 (December, 1982), 903-917.

8201. Africa, Philip. "Slaveholding in the Salem Community, 1771-1851." <u>NCHR</u> 54 (July, 1977), 271-307.

8202. Aldrich, Mark. "Progressive Economists and Scientific Racism: Walter Willcox and Black Americans, 1895-1910." <u>Phylon</u> 40 (March, 1979), 1-14.

8203.   Archibald, Robert.   "The Economy of the Alta California Mission, 1803-1821."   <u>SCQ</u> 58 (Summer, 1976), 227-240.

8204. Asher, Robert. "Union Nativism and the Immigrant Response." <u>LbH</u> 23 (Summer, 1982), 325-348.

8205. Barron, Hal Seth. "The Impact of Rural Depopulation on the Local Economy: Chelsea, Vermont, 1840-1900." <u>AgH</u> 54 (April, 1980), 318-335.

8206.   Blocker, Jack S., Jr.   "Market Integration, Urban Growth, and Economic Change in an Ohio County, 1850-1880." <u>OH</u> 90 (Autumn, 1981), 298-316.

8207. Bodnar, John E. "Immigration and Modernization: the Case of Slavic Peasants in Industrial America." <u>JSH</u> 10 (Fall, 1976), 44-71.

8208.   Bodnar, John E.   "The Impact of the 'New Immigration' on the Black Worker: Steelton, Pennsylvania, 1880-1920." <u>LbH</u> 17 (Spring, 1976), 214-229.

8209. Brandfon, Robert L. "The End of Immigration to the Cotton Fields." MVHR 50 (March, 1964), 591-611.

8210. Brownlee, W. Elliot. "Household Values, Women's Work, and Economic Growth, 1800-1930." JEH 39 (March, 1979), 199-209.

8211. Bruchey, Stuart Weems. Growth of the Modern American Economy. (New York, Dodd, Mead, 1975)

8212. Buettinger, Craig. "Economic Inequality in Early Chicago, 1849-1850." JSH 11 (Spring, 1978), 413-418.

8213. Cayton, Andrew R.L. "The Fragmentation of 'A Great Family': the Panic of 1819 and the Rise of a Middling Interest in Boston, 1818-1822." Journal of the Early Republic 2 (Summer, 1982), 143-168.

8214. Clark, Christopher. "The Household Economy, Market Exchange, and the Rise of Capitalism in the Connecticut Valley, 1800-1860." JSH 13 (Winter, 1979), 169-189.

8215. Clifton, James M. "Twilight Comes to the Rice Kingdom: Postbellum Rice Culture on the South Atlantic Coast." GHQ 62 (Summer, 1978), 146-154.

8216. Cochran, Thomas C. Frontiers of Change: Early Industrialism in America. (New York, Oxford University Press, 1981)

8217. Cochrane, Willard W. The Development of American Agriculture: a Historical Analysis. (Minneapolis, University of Minnesota Press, 1979)

8218. Coelho, Philip R.P. and James F. Shepherd. "The Impact of Regional Differences in Prices and Wages on Economic Growth: the United States in 1890." JEH 39 (March, 1979), 69-85.

8219. Cohen, William. "Negro Involuntary Servitude in the South, 1865-1940: a Preliminary Analysis." JSouH 42 (February, 1976), 31-60.

8220.   Curtis, James R.   "'New Chicago of the Far West':
Land Speculation in Alviso, California, 1890-1891." California
History 61 (Spring, 1982), 36-45.

8221.   Droze, W.H.   "Changing the Plains Environment: the
Afforestation of the Trans-Mississippi West."   AgH 51
(January, 1977), 6-22.

8222.   Easterlin, Richard Ainley.   "Population Issues in
American Economic History: a Survey and Critique."   In
Robert E. Gallman, ed.   Recent Developments in the Study of
Business and Economic History: Essays in Honor of Herman
E. Krooss.   (Greenwich, Connecticut, JAI Press, 1977),
131-158.

8223.   Easterlin, Richard Ainley.   Population, Labor Force,
and Long Swings in Economic Growth: the American
Experience.   (New York, National Bureau of Economic
Research; distributed by Columbia University Press, 1968)

8224.   Edwards, G. Thomas.   "'The Early Morning of Yakima's
Day of Greatness':   the Yakima County Agricultural Boom of
1905-1911." PNQ 73 (April, 1982), 78-89.

8225.   Erickson, C.J.   "Who Were the English and Scots
Immigrants to the United States in the Late Nineteenth
Century?"   In   David Victor Glass and Roger Revelle, eds.
Population and Social Change.   (New York, Crane, Russak,
1972), 347-381.

8226.   Feller, Irwin.   "The Urban Location of United States
Invention, 1860-1910." EEH 8 (Spring, 1971), 285-303.

8227.   Fleisig, Heywood.   "Slavery, the Supply of Agricultural
Labor, and the Industrialization of the South."   JEH 36
(September, 1976), 572-597.

8228.   Folsom, Burton W., Jr.   "Like Fathers, Unlike Sons:
the Fall of the Business Elite in Scranton, Pennsylvania,
1880-1920." PH 46 (October, 1980), 291-309.

8229.   Gallaway, Lowell E. and Richard K. Vedder.   "The
Increasing Urbanization Thesis-Did 'New Immigrants' to the
United States Have a Particular Fondness for Urban Life?"
EEH 8 (Spring, 1971), 305-320.

8230.   Ghent, Joselyn Maynard and Frederic Cople Jaher. "The Chicago Business Elite: 1830-1930.   A Collective Biography." Business History Review 50 (Autumn, 1976), 288-328.

8231.   Glassberg, Eudice.   "Work, Wages, and the Cost of Living,   Ethnic   Differences,   and   the   Poverty   Line, Philadelphia, 1880." PH 46 (January, 1979), 17-58.

8232.   Gold, David M.   "Jewish Agriculture in the Catskills, 1900-1920." AgH 55 (January, 1981), 31-49.

8233. Haber, Carole. "Mandatory Retirement in 19th-Century America: the Conceptual Basis for a New Work Cycle." JSH 12 (Fall, 1978), 77-96.

8234.   Harley, C. Knick.   "Western Settlement and the Price of Wheat, 1872-1913." JEH 38 (December, 1978), 865-878.

8235.   Harrison, William B. and Jang H. Yoo.   "Labor Immigration   in   1890-1914:   Wage   Retardation   vs. Growth-Conducive Hypothesis." SSJ 18 (April, 1981), 1-12.

8236.   Hanlan, James P.   The Working Population of Manchester, New Hampshire, 1840-1886. (Ann Arbor, UMI Research Press, 1981)

8237. Hellwig, David J. "Black Attitudes Toward Immigrant Labor in the South, 1865-1910."   FCHQ 54 (April, 1980), 151-168.

8238. Hewes, Leslie. "Early Fencing on the Western Margin of the Prairie." AAG 71 (December, 1981), 499-526.

8239. Higgs, Robert. "Race, Skills, and Earnings: American Immigrants in 1909." JEH 31 (June, 1971), 420-428.

8240.   Higgs, Robert.   "Racial Wage Differentials in Agriculture: Evidence from North Carolina in 1887." AgH 52 (April, 1978), 308-311.

8241.   Higgs, Robert.   "The Wealth of Japanese Tenant Farmers in California, 1909." AgH 53 (April, 1979), 488-493.

8242. Ichioka, Yuji. "Asian Immigrant Coal Miners and the United Mine Workers of America: Race and Class at Rock Springs, Wyoming, 1907." AJ 6 (Fall, 1979), 1-23.

8243. Ingham, John N. "Rags to Riches Revisited: the Effect of City Size and Related Factors on the Recruitment of Business Leaders." JAH 63 (December, 1976), 615-637.

8244. Jacobs, Wilbur R. "The Great Despoliation: Environmental Themes in American Frontier History." PHR 47 (February, 1978), 1-26.

8245. Jensen, Joan M. "Canning Comes to New Mexico: Women and the Agriculture Extension Service, 1914-1919." NMHR 57 (October, 1982), 361-386.

8246. Jeremy, David J. Transatlantic Industrial Revolution: the Diffusion of Textile Technologies Between Britain and America, 1790-1830's. (Cambridge, Massachusetts, MIT Press, 1981)

8247. Kartman, Lauraine Levy. "Jewish Occupational Roots in Baltimore at the Turn of the Century." MHM 74 (March, 1979), 52-61.

8248. Katz, Michael B., Michael J. Doucet and Mark J. Stern. The Social Organization of Early Industrial Capitalism. (Cambridge, Massachusetts, Harvard University Press, 1982)

8249. Katz, Michael B., and Mark J. Stern. "Fertility, Class, and Industrial Capitalism: Erie County, New York, 1855-1915." AQ 33 (Spring, 1981), 63-92.

8250. Kearl, J.R., Clayne L. Pope, and Larry T. Wimmer. "Household Wealth in a Settlement Economy: Utah, 1850-1870." JEH 40 (September, 1980), 477-496.

8251. Kelley, Allen C. "Demographic Change and Economic Growth: Australia, 1861-1911." EEH 5 (1968), 207-277.

8252. Kelley, Allen C. "Demographic Cycles and Economic Growth: the Long Swing Reconsidered." JEH 29 (December, 1969), 633-656.

8253.   Kelley, Allen C.   "International Migration and Economic Growth: Australia, 1865-1935." JEH 25 (September, 1965), 333-354.

8254.   Kessner, Thomas.   "Jobs, Ghettoes, and the Urban Economy, 1880-1935." AJH 71 (December, 1981), 218-238.

8255.   Keuchel, Edward F.   "The Polish American Migrant Worker: the New York Canning Industry, 1900-1935." PAS 33 (Autumn, 1976), 43-51.

8256.   King, J. Crawford, Jr.   "The Closing of the Southern Range: an Exploratory Study." JSouH 48 (February, 1982), 53-70.

8257.   Kinsey, Winston Lee.   "The Immigrant in Texas Agriculture During Reconstruction." AgH 53 (January, 1979), 125-141.

8258.   Kirk, Gordon W. and Carolyn T. Kirk.   "The Immigrant, Economic Opportunity, and Type of Settlement in Nineteenth-Century America." JEH 38 (March, 1978), 226-234.

8259.   Klingaman, David C. and Richard K. Vedder, eds. Essays in Nineteenth-Century Economic History: the Old Northwest. (Athens, Ohio University Press, 1975)

8260.   Kotlikoff, Laurence J. and Sebastian E. Pinera.   "The Old South's Stake in the Inter-Regional Movement of Slaves, 1850-1860." JEH 37 (June, 1977), 434-450.

8261.   Lane, A.T.   "American Labour and European Immigrants in the Late Nineteenth Century." JAS 11 (August, 1977), 241-260.

8262.   Lewis, Carolyn Baker.   "Cultural Conservatism and Pioneer Florida Viticulture." AgH 53 (July, 1979), 622-636.

8263.   Loehr, Rodney C.   "Self-Sufficiency on the Farm." AgH 26 (April, 1952), 37-41.

8264.   McGouldrick, Paul F. and Michael B. Tannen.   "Did American Manufacturers Discriminate Against Immigrants Before 1914?" JEH 37 (September, 1977), 723-746.

8265.   McWhiney,   Grady.   "The   Revolution   in
Nineteenth-Century Alabama Agriculture." AR 31 (January,
1978), 3-32.

8266.   Mandle, Jay R.   The Roots of Black Poverty: the
Southern Plantation Economy after the Civil War. (Durham,
North Carolina, Duke University Press, 1978)

8267.   Manring, Randall C.   "Population and Agriculture in
Nodaway County, Missouri, 1850 to 1860." MoHR 72 (July,
1978), 388-411.

8268. Matthaei, Julie A. An Economic History of Women in
America: Women's Work, the Sexual Division of Labor, and
the Development of Capitalism. (New York, Schocken, 1982)

8269. Matthies, Susan A. "Families at Work: an Analysis by
Sex of Child Workers in the Cotton Textile Industry." JEH
42 (March, 1982), 173-180.

8270.   Mennel, Robert M.   "'The Family System of Common
Farmers':   the   Early   Years   of   Ohio's   Reform   Farm,
1858-1884." OH 89 (Summer, 1980), 279-322.

8271.   Mennel, Robert M.   "'The Family System of Common
Farmers':   the Origins of Ohio's Reform Farm, 1840-1858."
OH 89 (Spring, 1980), 125-156.

8272. Mercer, Lloyd J. Railroads and Land Grant Policy: a
Study in Government Intervention. (New York, Academic
Press, 1982)

8273. Muller, Edward K. and Paul A. Groves. "The Changing
Location of the Clothing Industry: a Link to the Social
Geography of Baltimore in the Nineteenth Century." MHM 71
(Fall, 1976), 403-420.

8274. North, Douglass Cecil. The Economic Growth of the
United States, 1790-1860. (Englewood Cliffs, New Jersey,
Prentice-Hall, 1961)

8275. Ong, Paul M. "Chinese Labor in Early San Francisco:
Racial   Segmentation   and   Industrial   Expansion."   AJ   8
(Spring-Summer, 1981), 69-92.

8276.   Ong, Paul M.   "An Ethnic Trade: the Chinese Laundries in Early California." JES 8 (Winter, 1981), 95-113

8277. Parmet, Robert D. Labor and Immigration in Industrial America. (Boston, Twayne, 1981)

8278. Peterson, Charles S. "The 'Americanization' of Utah's Agriculture." UHQ 42 (Spring, 1974), 108-125.

8279. Poulson, Barry W. and James Holyfield, Jr. "A Note on European Migration to the United States: a Cross Spectral Analysis." EEH 11 (Spring, 1974), 299-310.

8280.   Rodgers, Daniel T.   The Work Ethic in Industrial America, 1850-1920. (Chicago, University of Chicago Press, 1978)

8281.   Schachter, Joseph.   "Net Immigration of Gainful Workers into the United States, 1870-1930." Demography 9 (February, 1972), 87-105.

8282.   Schafer, Joseph.   "Was the West a Saftey Valve for Labor?" MVHR 24 (December, 1937), 299-314.

8283. Scranton, Philip. "An Immigrant Family and Industrial Enterprise: Sevill Schofield and the Philadelphia Textile Manufacture, 1845-1900." PMHB 106 (July, 1982), 365-392.

8284. Shepperson, Wilbur Stanley. "Industrial Emigration in Early Victorian Britain." JEH 13 (Spring, 1953), 179-192.

8285.   Shlomowitz, Ralph.   "The Origins of Southern Sharecropping." AgH 53 (July, 1979), 557-575.

8286. Soltow, Lee. "Land Inequality on the Frontier: the Distribution of Land in East Tennessee at the Beginning of the Nineteenth Century." SSH 5 (Summer, 1981), 275-291.

8287. Spivey, Donald. Schooling for the New Slavery: Black Industrial Education, 1868-1915.   (Westport, Connecticut, Greenwood Press, 1978)

8288. Thomas, Brinley. Migration and Economic Growth; a Study of Great Britain and the Atlantic Economy. 2nd ed. (Cambridge, England, Cambridge University Press, 1973)

8289.   Townes, A. Jane.   "The Effect of Emancipation on Large Landholdings, Nelson and Goochland Counties, Virginia." JSouH 45 (August, 1979), 403-412.

8290.   Uselding, Paul.   "Conjectural Estimates of Gross Human Capital Inflows to the American Economy: 1790-1860." EEH 9 (Fall, 1971), 49-61.

8291.   Weber, Michael P. and Anthony E. Boardman. "Economic Growth and Occupational Mobility in 19th-Century Urban America: a Reappraisal." JSH 11 (Fall, 1977), 52-74.

8292.   Wilkinson, Maurice.   "Evidences of Long Swings in the Growth of Swedish Population and Related Economic Variables." JEH 27 (March, 1967), 17-38.

8293.   Williamson, Jeffrey G.   "Migrations to the New World: Long Term Influences and Impact." EEH 11 (Summer, 1974), 357-389.

8294.   Wilms, Douglas C.   "Cherokee Acculturation and Changing Land Use Practices." CO 56 (Fall, 1978), 331-343.

8295.   Yellowitz, Irwin.   "Jewish Immigrants and the American Labor Movement, 1900-1920." AJH 71 (December, 1981), 188-217.

Politics

Population and politics interacted in a variety of complex patterns that differed noticeably according to time and place. Perhaps the most common element in these studies is the role of immigrants in particular and migration in general in determining both the structures and issues of politics. Of the works on the ethnic impact on parties and voting, those by Benson, Formisano, Jensen, and Kleppner offer good places to start. Alcorn's essay is a short, but important, study of how stable politics could evolve in a mobile society. Robinson is the one required item here on slavery and politics; writing on slavery and the sectional crisis obviously goes far beyond the scope of this bibliography.   Other political themes include the role of women (see also discussions of women's roles in Chapter Five) and the westward expansion of the United States (Billington is the place to start).   The impact of population on diplomacy, important in westward expansion, broadened to other concerns at the end of the century.   Leavitt's study of Milwaukee is a fascinating account of how matters of health and death became entangled in local politics on very specific issues.

8300.   Abramowitz, Jack.   "The Negro in the Agrarian Revolt." AgH 24 (April, 1950), 89-95.

8301.   Akin, Edward N.   "When a Minority Becomes the Majority: Blacks in Jacksonville Politics, 1887-1907." FHQ 53 (October, 1974), 123-145.

8302.   Albright, Robert E.   "Politics and Public Opinion in the Western Statehood Movement of the 1880's."   PHR 3 (1934), 296-306.

8303.   Alcorn, Richard S.   "Leadership and Stability in Mid-Nineteenth Century America: a Case Study of an Illinois Town." JAH 61 (December, 1974), 685-702.

8304.   Alexander, Thomas B., et.al.   "The Basis of Alabama's Ante-Bellum Two-Party System."   AR 19, no. 4 (1966), 243-276.

8305.   Allen, Leola.   "Anti-German Sentiment in Iowa during World War I." AI 42 (Fall, 1974), 418-429.

8306.   Allswang, John M.   Bosses, Medicines, and Urban Voters: an American Symbiosis.   (Port Washington, New York, Kennikat, 1977)

8307.   Ander, O. Fritiof.   "The Swedish-American Press and the Election of 1892." MVHR 23 (1937), 533-554.

8308.   Anderson, Eric.   Race and Politics in North Carolina, 1872-1902: the Black Second.   (Baton Rouge, Louisiana State University Press, 1981)

8309.   Anderson, Stuart.   Race and Rapprochement: Anglo-Saxonism and Anglo-American Relations, 1895-1904. (Rutherford, New Jersey, Fairleigh Dickinson University Press, 1981)

8310.   Bailey, Thomas A.   "California, Japan, and the Alien Land Legislation of 1913." PHR 1 (1932), 36-59.

8311.   Baker, Jean H.   Ambivalent Americans: the Know-Nothing Party in Maryland. (Baltimore, Johns Hopkins University Press, 1977)

8312.   Banner, James M.   To the Hartford Convention: the Federalists   and   the   Origins   of   Party   Politics   in Massachusetts, 1789-1815. (New York, Knopf, 1970)

8313.   Baum, Dale.   "The 'Irish Vote' and Party Politics in Massachusetts, 1860-1876." CWH 26 (June, 1980), 117-141.

8314.   Bean, William G.   "Puritan Versus Celt, 1850-1860." NEQ 7 (1934), 70-89.

8315.   Benson, Lee.   The Concept of Jacksonian Democracy: New York as a Test Case. (Princeton, New Jersey, Princeton University Press, 1961)

8316.   Best, Gary Dean.   To Free a People: American Jewish Leaders and the Jewish Problem in Eastern Europe, 1890-1914. (Westport, Connecticut, Greenwood Press, 1982)

8317.   Betten, Neil.   "The Origins of Ethnic Radicalism in Northern Minnesota, 1900-1920." IMR 4 (Spring, 1970), 44-56.

8318.   Billington, Ray Allen.   The Protestant Crusade, 1800-1860:   a   Study of the Origins of American Nativism. (New York, Macmillan, 1938)

8319.   Bitzes, John G.   "The Anti-Greek Riot of 1909--South Omaha." NH 51 (Summer, 1970), 199-224.

8320.   Blackett, R.J.M.   Building an Antislavery Wall: Black Americans in the Atlantic Abolitionist Movement, 1830-1860. (Baton Rouge, Louisiana State University Press, 1983)

8321.   Blodgett, Geoffrey.   "Yankee Leadership in a Divided City: Boston, 1860-1910." JUH 8 (August, 1982), 371-396.

8322.   Boeck, George A.   "A Historical Note on the Uses of Census Returns." MA 44 (January, 1962), 46-50.

8323. Boyett, Gene W. "Quantitative Differences Between the Arkansas Whig and Democratic Parties, 1836-1850." AkHQ 34 (Autumn, 1975), 214-226.

8324. Broadbent, T.L. "The German-Language Press in California: a Record of German Immigration." JW 10 (October, 1971), 637-661.

8325. Broussard, James H. "The North Carolina Federalists, 1800-1816." NCHR 55 (January, 1978), 18-41.

8326. Broussard, James H. "Some Determinants of Know-Nothing Electoral Strength in the South, 1856." LH 7 (Winter, 1966), 5-20.

8327. Brown, Elizabeth Gaspar. "Poor Relief in a Wisconsin County, 1846-1866: Administration and Recipients." AJLH 20 (April, 1976), 79-117.

8328. Buhle, Mary Jo. Women and American Socialism, 1870-1920. (Urbana, University of Illinois Press, 1981)

8329. Bukowczyk, John J. "The Immigrant 'Community' Re-examined: Political and Economic Tensions in a Brooklyn Polish Settlement, 1888-1894." PAS 37 (Autumn, 1980), 5-16.

8330. Buroker, Robert L. "From Voluntary Association to Welfare State: the Illinois Immigrant's Protective League, 1908-1926." JAH 58 (December, 1971), 643-660.

8331. Burton, David H. "The Influence of the American West on the Imperialist Philosophy of Theodore Roosevelt." ArW 4 (Spring, 1962), 5-26.

8332. Campbell, Ballard C. "Ethnicity and the 1893 Wisconsin Assembly." JAH 62 (June, 1975), 74-94.

8333. Campbell, Ballard C. Representative Democracy: Public Policy and Midwestern Legislatures in the Late Nineteenth Century. (Cambridge, Massachusetts, Harvard University Press, 1980)

8334. Campbell, Randolph B. and Richard G. Lowe. Wealth and Power in Antebellum Texas. (College Station, Texas A&M University Press, 1977)

8335. Carranco, Lynwood. "Chinese Expulsion from Humboldt County." PHR 30 (November, 1961), 329-340.

8336. Carranco, Lynwood and Estle Beard. Genocide and Vendetta: the Round Valley Wars of Northern California. (Norman, University of Oklahoma Press, 1981)

8337. Carter, Edward C. II. "A 'Wild Irishman' under Every Federalist's Bed: Naturalization in Philadelphia, 1789-1806." PMHB 94 (July, 1970), 331-346.

8338. Cary, Lorin Lee. "The Wisconsin Loyalty Legion, 1917-1918." WMH 53 (Autumn, 1969), 33-50.

8339. Chern, Kenneth S. "The Politics of Patriotism: War, Ethnicity, and the New York Mayoral Campaign, 1917." New York State Historical Society Quarterly 63 (October, 1979), 290-313.

8340. Child, Clifton J. "German-American Attempts to Prevent the Exportation of Munitions of War, 1914-1915." MVHR 25 (1938), 351-368.

8341. Chrislock, Carl H. Ethnicity Challenged: the Upper Midwest Norwegian-American Experience in World War I. (Northfield, Minnesota, Norwegian-American Historical Association, 1981)

8342. Clark, Dan E. "Manifest Destiny and the Pacific." PHR 1 (1932), 1-17.

8343. Clark, John Garretson. New Orleans, 1718-1812: an Economic History. (Baton Rouge, Louisiana State University, 1970)

8344. Cohen, Lucy M. "Entry of Chinese to the Lower South from 1865 to 1870: Policy Dilemmas." SouS 17 (Spring, 1978), 5-38.

8345. Colgrove, Kenneth W. "The Attitude of Congress Toward the Pioneers of the West from 1789 to 1820." IJHP 8 (January, 1910), 3-129.

8346. Colgrove, Kenneth W. "The Attitude of Congress Toward the Pioneers of the West, 1820-1850." IJHP 9 (April, 1911), 196-302.

8347. Cooper, William James Jr. Liberty and Slavery: Southern Politics to 1860. (New York, Knopf, 1983)

8348. Cooper, William James Jr. The South and the Politics of Slavery, 1828-1856. (Baton Rouge, Louisiana State University Press, 1978)

8349. Coser, Lewis A. The Functions of Social Conflict. (Glencoe, Illinois, Free Press, 1956)

8350. Cuddy, Edward. "Irish-Americans and the 1916 Election: an Episode in Immigrant Adjustment." AQ 21 (Summer, 1969), 228-243.

8351. Curran, Thomas J. Xenophobia and Immigration, 1820-1930. (Boston, Twayne, 1975)

8352. Daniel, Pete. "Up from Slavery and Down to Peonage: the Alonzo Bailey Case." JAH 57 (December, 1970), 654-670.

8353. Daniels, George H. "Immigrant Vote in the 1860 Election: the Case of Iowa." MA 44 (July, 1962), 146-162.

8354. Dennen, R. Taylor. "Some Efficiency Effects of Nineteenth-Century Federal Land Policy: a Dynamic Analysis." AgH 51 (October, 1977), 718-736.

8355. Dennison, George M. "An Empire of Liberty: Congressional Attitudes Toward Popular Sovereignty in the Territories, 1787-1867." MdH 6 (Spring, 1975), 19-40.

8356. Deusner, Charles E. "The Know Nothing Riots in Louisville." KHSR 61 (April, 1963), 122-147.

8357. Deutsch, Albert. "The First U.S. Census of the Insane (1840) and its Use as Pro-Slavery Propaganda." BHM 15 (1944), 469-482.

8358. Dorpalen, Andreas. "The German Element and the Issues of the Civil War." MVHR 29 (June, 1942), 55-76.

8359.   Drake, Richard B.   "Freedmen's Aid Societies and Sectional Compromise." JSouH 29 (May, 1963), 175-186.

8360.   Duff, John B.   "The Versailles Treaty and the Irish-Americans." JAH 55 (December, 1968), 582-598.

8361.   Eisinger, Peter K.   "Ethnic Political Transition in Boston, 1884-1933:   Some Lessons for Contemporary Cities." PSQ 93 (Summer, 1978), 217-239.

8362.   Elazar, Daniel J.   "Political Culture on the Plains." WestHQ 11 (July, 1980), 261-283.

8363.   Erie, Steven P.   "Politics, the Public Sector, and Irish Social Mobility: San Francisco, 1870-1900." Western Political Quarterly 31 (June, 1978), 274-289.

8364.   Ernst, Robert.   "Economic Nativism in New York City During the 1840's." NYH 29, i.e. New York State Historical Association. Proceedings 46 (1948), 170-186.

8365.   Ewers, John C.   "Intertribal Warfare as the Precursor of Indian-White Warfare on the Northern Great Plains." WestHQ 6 (October, 1975), 397-410.

8366.   Fee, Walter Ray.   The Transition from Aristocracy to Democracy in New Jersey, 1789-1829.   (Sommerville, New Jersey, Somerset Press, 1933)

8367.   Field, Alexander James.   "Economic and Demographic Determinants of Educational Commitment: Massachusetts, 1855." JEH 39 (June, 1979), 439-457

8368.   Field, Phyllis F.   The Politics of Race in New York: the Struggle for Black Suffrage in the Civil War Era. (Ithaca, New York, Cornell University Press, 1982)

8369.   Fischer, David Hackett.   The Revolution of American Conservatism: the Federalist Party in the Era of Jeffersonian Democracy. (New York, Harper and Row, 1965)

8370.   Flanagan, Maureen A.   "The Ethnic Entry into Chicago Politics: the United Societies for Local Self-Government and the Reform Charter of 1907." ISHSJ 75 (Spring, 1982), 2-14.

8371.   Folsom, Burton W., Jr.   "Immigrant Voters and the Non-Partisan League in Nebraska, 1917-1920."   GPQ 1 (Summer, 1981), 159-168.

8372.   Folsom, Burton W.   "Tinkerers, Tipplers, and Traitors: Ethnicity and Democratic Reform in Nebraska During the Progressive Era."   PHR 50 (February, 1981), 53-75.

8373.   Fordyce, Wellington G.   "Nationality Groups in Cleveland Politics."   OAHQ 46 (1937), 109-127.

8374.   Formisano, Ronald P.   The Birth of Mass Political Parties, Michigan, 1827-1861.   (Princeton, New Jersey, Princeton University Press, 1971)

8375.   Formisano, Ronald P.   "The Edge of Caste: Colored Suffrage in Michigan, 1827-1861."   MH 56 (Spring, 1972), 19-41.

8376.   Fox, Stephen C.   "Politicians, Issues, and Voter Preference in Jacksonian Ohio: a Critique of an Interpretation."   OH 86 (Summer, 1977), 155-170.

8377.   Franklin, John Hope.   "The Southern Expansionists of 1846."   JSouH 25 (August, 1959), 323-338.

8378.   Garver, Frank Harmon.   "The Attitude of the Constitutional Convention of 1787 Toward the West."   PHR 5 (1936), 349-358.

8379.   Gavins, Raymond.   "Urbanization and Segregation: Black Leadership Patterns in Richmond, Virginia, 1900-1920."   SAQ 79 (Summer, 1980), 257-273.

8380.   Glass, Mary Ellen.   "The Silver Governors: Immigrants in Nevada Politics. Part I."   NHSQ 21 (Fall, 1978), 170-188.

8381.   Glass, Mary Ellen.   "The Silver Governors: Immigrants in Nevada Politics.   Part II."   NHSQ 21 (Winter, 1978), 263-278.

8382.   Goldstein, Judith.   "Ethnic Politics: the American Jewish Committee as Lobbyist, 1915-1917."   AJHQ 65 (September, 1975), 36-58.

8383.   Goodman, Paul.   The Democratic-Republicans of Massachusetts: Politics in a Young Republic.   (Cambridge, Massachusetts, Harvard University Press, 1964)

8384.   Graymont, Barbara.   "New York State Indian Policy after the Revolution."   NYH 57, i.e.   New York State Historical Association.   Proceedings 74 (1976), 438-474.

8385.   Grob, Gerald N.   "The Political System and Social Policy in the Nineteenth Century: Legacy of the Revolution." MA 58 (January, 1976), 5-19.

8386.   Gudelunas, William, Jr.   "Nativism and the Demise of Schuylkill   County   Whiggery: Anti-Slavery   or Anti-Catholicism."   PH 45 (July, 1978), 222-236.

8387.   Gutman, Herbert George.   "The Buena Vista Affair, 1874-1875."   PMHB 88 (July, 1964), 251-293.

8388.   Hackett, D.L.A.   "Slavery, Ethnicity, and Sugar: an Analysis of Voting Behavior in Louisiana, 1828-1844."   LS 13 (Summer, 1974), 73-118.

8389.   Hahn, Steven.   The Roots of Southern Populism: Yeoman Farmers and the Transformation of the Georgia Upcountry, 1850-1890.   (New York, Oxford University Press, 1983)

8390.   Hall, Kermit L.   "Social Backgrounds and Judicial Recruitment: a Nineteenth-Century Perspective on the Lower Federal Judiciary."   Western Political Quarterly 29 (June, 1976), 243-257.

8391.   Hammarberg, Melvyn.   The Indiana Voter: the Historical Dynamics of Party Allegiance During the 1870's. (Chicago, University of Chicago Press, 1977)

8392.   Harding, Vincent.   There Is a River: the Black Struggle for Freedom in America.   (New York, Harcourt, Brace, Jovanovich, 1981)

8393.   Haury, David A.   "German-Russian Immigrants to Kansas and American Politics."   KH 3 (Winter, 1980), 226-237.

8394.   Henderson, H. James.   "Quantitative Approaches to Party Formation in the United States Congress: a Comment." WMQ 30 (April, 1973), 307-324.

8395.   Hennessey, Gregg R.   "The Politics of Water in San Diego, 1895-1897." JSDH 24 (Summer, 1978), 367-383.

8396.   Hennessey, Melinda Meek.   "Political Terrorism in the Black Belt: the Eutaw Riot." AR 33 (January, 1980), 35-48.

8397.   Hennessey, Melinda Meek.   "Race and Violence in Reconstruction New Orleans: the 1868 Riot." LH 20 (Winter, 1979), 77-91.

8398.   Hickey, Donald R.   "The Darker Side of Democracy: the Baltimore Riots of 1812." MdH 7 (Fall, 1976), 1-19.

8399.   Higgs,   Robert.   "Landless by Law: Japanese Immigrants in California Agriculture to 1941."   JEH 38 (March, 1978), 205-225.

8400.   Hill, Esther V. "The Iroquois Indians and Their Lands since   1783."   NYH   11, i.e. New York State Historical Association. Proceedings 28 (1930), 335-353.

8401.   Hill, Leslie G.   "A Moral Crusade: the Influence of Protestantism on Frontier Society in Missouri."   MoHR 45 (October, 1950), 16-34.

8402.   Hilldrup, Robert Leroy.   "Cold War Against the Yankees in the Ante-Bellum Literature of Southern Women." NCHR 31 (July, 1954), 370-384.

8403.   Hinckley, Ted C.   "The Presbyterian Leadership in Pioneer Alaska." JAH 52 (March, 1966), 742-756.

8404.   Holmes, Jack David Lazarus.   "The Underlying Causes of the Memphis Race Riot of 1866." THQ 17 (September, 1958), 195-221.

8405.   Hunt, Thomas C.   "The Bennett Law of 1890: Focus of Conflict   Between Church and State in Education." Journal of Church and State 23 (Winter, 1981), 69-93.

8406.   Hurt, Peyton.   "The Rise and Fall of the 'Know Nothings' in California."   CHSQ 9 (March-June, 1930), 16-49, 99-128.

8407.   Ichioka, Yuji.   "The Early Japanese Immigrant Quest for Citizenship: the Background of the 1922 Ozawa Case." AJ 4 (1977), 1-22.

8408.   Ilisevich, Robert D.   "Class Structure and Politics in Crawford County, 1800-1840."   WPHM 63 (April, 1980), 95-119.

8409.   Issel, William.   "Class and Ethnic Conflict in San Francisco Political History: the Reform Charter of 1898." LbH 18 (Summer, 1977), 341-359.

8410.   Jacobs, Sylvia M.   The African Nexus: Black American Perspectives on the European Partitioning of Africa, 1880-1920.   (Westport, Connecticut, Greenwood Press, 1981)

8411.   Jensen, Richard J.   The Winning of the Midwest: Social and Political Conflict, 1888-1896.   (Chicago, University of Chicago Press, 1971)

8412.   Johnson, David A.   "Industry and the Individual on the Far Western Frontier: a Case Study of Politics and Social Change in Early Nevada."   PHR 51 (August, 1982), 243-264.

8413.   Johnson, Niel M.   "The Missouri Synod Lutherans and the War Against the German Language, 1917-1923."   NH 56 (Spring, 1975), 136-144.

8414.   Juhnke, James C.   "Mob Violence and Kansas Mennonites in 1918."   KHQ 43 (Autumn, 1977), 334-350.

8415.   Kahrl, William L.   "The Politics of California Water: Owens Valley and the Los Angeles Aqueduct, 1900-1927." CHQ 55 (Spring, 1976), 2-25.

8416.   Kamphoefner, Walter D.   "St. Louis Germans and the Republican Party, 1848-1860."   MA 57 (April, 1975), 69-88.

8417.   Kane, Murray.   "Some Considerations on the Safety Valve Doctrine."   MVHR 23 (September, 1936), 169-188.

8418.   Karlin, Jules Alexander.   "New Orleans Lynchings of 1891 and the American Press." LHQ 24 (1941), 187-204.

8419.   Kelleher, Daniel T.   "St. Louis' 1916 Residential Segregation Ordinance." MoHSB 26 (1970), 239-248.

8420.   Kelley, Bruce Gunn.   "Ethnocultural Voting Trends in Rural Iowa, 1890-1898." AI 44 (Fall, 1978), 441-461.

8421.   Kennedy, Philip W.   "The Racial Overtones of Imperialism as a Campaign Issue, 1900." MA 48 (July, 1966), 196-205.

8422.   Kinzer, Donald Louis.   "The Poltical Uses of Anti-Catholicism: Michigan and Wisconsin, 1890-1894." MH 39 (September, 1955), 312-326.

8423.   Kipp, Samuel M., III.   "Old Notables and Newcomers: the Economic and Political Elite of Greensboro North Carolina, 1880-1920." JSouH 43 (August, 1977), 373-394.

8424.   Kleppner, Paul.   Cross of Culture: a Social Analysis of Midwestern Politics, 1850-1900.   (New York, Free Press, 1970)

8425.   Kleppner, Paul et al.   The Evolution of American Electoral Systems.   (Westport, Connecticut, Greenwood Press, 1981)

8426.   Knapp, Ronald G. and Laurence M. Hauptman. "'Civilization over Savagery':   the Japanese, the Formosan Frontier, and United States Indian Policy, 1895-1915." PHR 49 (November, 1980), 647-652.

8427.   Knobel, Dale T.   "'Native Soil':   Nativists, Colonizationists, and the Rhetoric of Nationality." CWH 27 (December, 1981), 314-337.

8428.   Kostiainen, Auvo.   The Forging of Finnish-American Communism, 1917-1924:   a Study in Ethnic Radicalism. (Turku, Finland, Migration Institute, 1978)

8429.   Kremm, Thomas W.   "Cleveland and the First Lincoln Election: the Ethnic Response to Nativism." JIH 8 (Summer, 1977), 69-86.

8430. Lea, Arden J. "Cotton Textiles and the Federal Child Labor Act of 1916." LbH 16 (Fall, 1975), 485-494.

8431. Leavitt, Judith W. The Healthiest City: Milwaukee and the Politics of Health Reform. (Princeton, Princeton University Press, 1982)

8432. Leinenweber, Charles. "The Class and Ethnic Bases of New York City Socialism, 1904-1915." LbH 22 (Winter, 1981), 31-56.

8433. Lemons, J. Stanley. "The Cuban Crisis of 1895-1898: Newspapers and Nativism." MoHR 60 (October, 1965), 63-74.

8434. Leslie, William R. "The Pennsylvania Fugitive Slave Act of 1826." JSouH 4 (November, 1952), 429-445.

8435. Lindberg, Duane R. "Pastors, Prohibition, and Politics: the Role of Norwegian Clergy in the North Dakota Abstinence Movement, 1880-1920." NDQ 49 (Autumn, 1981), 21-38.

8436. Lorence, James J. "Business and Reform: the American Asiatic Association and the Exclusion Laws, 1905-1907." PHR 39 (November, 1970), 421-438.

8437. Lovett, Bobby L. "Memphis Riots: White Reaction to Blacks in Memphis, May 1865-July 1866." THQ 38 (Spring, 1979), 9-33.

8438. Lucas, Henry S. "The Political Activities of the Dutch Immigrants from 1847 to the Civil War." IJHP 26 (April, 1928), 171-203.

8439. Luebke, Frederick C. Bonds of Loyalty: German-Americans and World War I. (DeKalb, Northern Illinois University Press, 1974)

8440. Luebke, Frederick C. "Main Street and the Countryside: Patterns of Voting in Nebraska During the Populist Era." NH 50 (Fall, 1969), 257-275.

8441. Lyman, Edward Leo. "Elimination of the Mormon Issue from Arizona Politics, 1889-1894." ArW 24 (Autumn, 1982), 205-228.

8442. Mabee, Carleton. "Control by Blacks over Schools in New York State, 1830-1930." Phylon 40 (March, 1979), 29-40.

8443. McClymer, John F. "The Federal Government and the Americanization Movement, 1915-1924." Prologue 10 (Spring, 1978), 22-41.

8444. Madison, James. Notes of Debates in the Federal Convention of 1787. With an Introduction by Adrienne Koch. (Athens, Ohio University Press, 1966)

8445. Malin, James C. "At What Age Did Men Become Reformers?" KHQ 29 (Autumn, 1963), 250-266.

8446. Mann, Arthur. "British Social Thought and American Reformers of the Progressive Era." MHVR 42 (1956), 672-692.

8447. Mannard, Joseph G. "The 1839 Baltimore Nunnery Riot: an Episode in Jacksonian Nativism and Social Violence." MdH 11 (Spring, 1980), 13-27.

8448. Marcus, Alan I. "Professional Revolution and Reform in the Progressive Era: Cincinnati Physicians and the City Elections of 1897 and 1900." JUH 5 (February, 1979), 183-207.

8449. Marsh, Margaret S. Anarchist Women, 1870-1920. (Philadelphia, Temple University Press, 1981)

8450. Marraro, Howard A. "Lincoln's Italian Volunteers from New York." NYH 24, i.e. New York States Historical Association. Proceedings 41 (1943), 56-67.

8451. Matthews, Fred H. "White Community and 'Yellow Peril'." MVHR 50 (March, 1964), 612-633.

8452. Melder, Keith E. Beginnings of Sisterhood: the American Woman's Rights Movement, 1800-1850. (New York, Schoken, 1977)

8453. Monaghan, Jay. "Did Abraham Lincoln Receive the Illinois German Vote?" ISHSJ 35 (1942), 133-139.

8454. Moody, Eric N. "Nevada's Anti-Mormon Legislation of 1887 and Southern Idaho Annexation." NHSQ 22 (Spring, 1979), 21-32.

8455. Moore, William Haas. "Prisioners in the Promised Land: the Molokans in World War I." ArH 14 (1973), 281-302.

8456. Morrison, Howard Alexander. "Gentlemen of Proper Understanding: a Closer Look at Utica's Anti-Abolitionist Mob." NYH 62, i.e. New York State Historical Association. Proceedings 79 (1981), 61-82.

8457. Mulkern, John. "Western Massachusetts in the Know-Nothing Years: an Analysis of Voting Patterns." HJWM 8 (January, 1980), 14-25.

8458. Nelli, Humbert S. "John Powers and the Italians: Politics in a Chicago Ward, 1896-1921." JAH 67 (June, 1970), 67-84.

8459. Nelson, Douglas W. "The Alien Land Law Movement of the Late Nineteenth Century." JW 9 (January, 1970), 46-59.

8460. Nieman, Donald G. To Set the Law in Motion: the Freedmen's Bureau and the Legal Rights of Blacks, 1865-1868. (Millwood, New York, KTO, 1979)

8461. Olin, Spencer C., Jr. "European Immigrant and Oriental Alien: Acceptance and Rejection by the California Legislature of 1913." PHR 35 (August, 1966), 303-316.

8462. Osofsky, Gilbert. "Progressivism and the Negro: New York, 1900-1915." AQ 16 (Summer, 1964), 153-168.

8463. Parish, John Carl. "The Emergence of the Idea of Manifest Destiny." In his Persistence of the Western Movement and other Essays. (Berkeley, University of California Press, 1943), 47-77.

8464. Paul, Rodman W. "The Origin of the Chinese Issue in California." MVHR 25 (September, 1938), 181-196.

8465.   Pessen, Edward.   "Social Structure and Politics in American History." AHR 87 (December, 1982), 1290-1341.

8466.   Petersen, Peter L.   "Language and Loyalty: Governor Harding and Iowa's Danish-Americans During World War I." AI 42 (Fall, 1974), 405-417.

8467.   Peterson, Richard H.   "Anti-Mexican Nativism in California, 1848-1853: a Study of Cultural Conflict." SCQ 62 (Winter, 1980), 309-327.

8468.   Piccarello, Louis J.   "Social Structure and Public Welfare Policy in Danvers, Massachusetts: 1750-1850." EICH 118 (October, 1982), 248-263.

8469.   Pienkos, Donald.   "Politics, Religion, and Change in Polish Milwaukee, 1900-1930." WMH 61 (Spring, 1978), 179-209.

8470.   Pisani, Donald J.   "Water Law Reform in California, 1900-1913." AgH 54 (April, 1980), 295-317.

8471.   Pitt, Leonard.   "The Beginnings of Nativism in California." PHR 30 (February, 1961), 23-38.

8472.   Poll, Richard D.   "The Mormon Question Enters National Politics, 1850-1856." UHQ 25 (April, 1957), 117-131.

8473.   Preston, William, Jr.   Aliens and Dissenters: Federal Suppression of Radicals, 1903-1933.   (Cambridge, Massachusetts, Harvard University Press, 1963)

8474.   Price, Edward.   "The Black Voting Rights Issue in Pennsylvania, 1780-1900." PMHB 100 (July, 1976), 356-373.

8475.   Rackleff, Robert V.   "Anti-Catholicism and the Florida Legislature, 1911-1919." FHQ 50 (April, 1972), 352-365.

8476.   Ratcliffe, Donald J.   "Politics in Jacksonian Ohio: Reflections on the Ethnocultural Interpretation." OH 88 (Winter, 1979), 5-36.

8477.   Redard, Thomas E.   "The Election of 1844 in Louisiana: a New Look at the Ethno-cultural Approach." LH 22 (Fall, 1981), 419-433.

8478. Reuter, William C. "The Anatomy of Political Anglophobia in the United States, 1865-1900." MA 61 (April-July, 1979), 117-132.

8479. Richmond, Douglas W. "Mexican Immigration and Border Strategy During the Revolution, 1910-1920." NMHR 57 (July, 1982), 269-288.

8480. Ridgway, Whitman H. Community Leadership in Maryland, 1790-1840: a Comparative Analysis of Power in Society. (Chapel Hill, University of North Carolina Press, 1979)

8481. Risjord, Norman K. "Virginians and the Constitution: a Multivariant Analysis." WMQ 31 (October, 1974), 613-632.

8482. Robinson, Donald L. Slavery in the Structure of American Politics, 1765-1820. (New York, Harcourt Brace Jovanovich, 1971)

8483. Rodgers, Jack Warner. "The Foreign Language Issue in Nebraska, 1918-1923." NH 39 (March, 1958), 1-22.

8484. Rogers, O.A., Jr. "The Elaine Race Riots of 1919." AkHQ 19 (Summer, 1960), 142-150.

8485. Rorabaugh, W.J. "Rising Democratic Spirits: Immigrants, Temperance, and Tammany Hall, 1854-1860." CWH 22 (June, 1976), 138-157.

8486. Rosenbaum, Robert J. Mexicano Resistance in the Southwest: "The Sacred Right of Self-Preservation." (Austin, University of Texas Press, 1981)

8487. Roucek, Joseph S. and Bernard Eisenberg, eds. America's Ethnic Politics. (Westport, Connecticut, Greenwood Press, 1982)

8488. Rowley, William E. "The Irish Aristocracy of Albany, 1789-1878." NYH 52, i.e. New York State Historical Association. Proceedings 69 (1971), 275-304.

8489. Russell, James M. "Politics, Municipal Services, and the Working Class in Atlanta, 1865-1890." GHQ 66 (Winter, 1982), 467-491.

8490. Ryan, Mary P. "Party Formation in the United States Congress, 1789 to 1796: a Quantitative Analysis." WMQ 28 (October, 1971), 523-542.

8491. Sandmeyer, Elmer C. "California Anti-Chinese Legislation and the Federal Courts: a Study in Federal Relations." PHR 5 (1936), 189-211.

8492. Sandos, James A. "International Water Control in the Lower Rio Grande Basin, 1900-1920." AgH 54 (October, 1980), 490-501.

8493. Schneider, John C. "Public Order and the Geography of the City: Crime, Violence, and the Police in Detroit, 1845-1875." JUH 4 (February, 1978), 183-208.

8494. Schneider, John C. "Urbanization and the Maintenance of Order: Detroit, 1824-1847." MH 60 (Fall, 1976), 260-281.

8495. Shepard, E. Lee. "Courts in Conflict: Town-County Relations in Post-Revolutionary Virginia." VMHB 85 (April, 1977), 184-199.

8496. Shields, James and Leonard Weinberg. "Reactive Violence and the American Frontier: a Contemporary Evaluation." Western Political Quarterly 29 (Marcy, 1976), 86-101.

8497. Shortridge, Ray Myles. "An Assessment of the Frontier's Influence on Voter Turnout." AgH 50 (July, 1976), 445-459.

8498. Shull, Charles W. and Louis J. McGuiness. "The Changing Pattern of Personel in the Michigan Legislature: 1887-1947." MH 35 (December, 1951), 467-478.

8499. Silcox, Harry C. "Delay and Neglect: Negro Public Education in Antebellum Philadelphia, 1800-1860." PMHB 97 (October, 1973), 444-464.

8500. Smith, Donnal V. "The Influence of the Foreign-Born of the Northwest in the Election of 1860." MVHR 19 (September, 1932), 192-204.

8501.   Smith, George Winston.   "Ante-Bellum Attempts of Northern Business Interests to 'Redeem' the Upper South." JSouH 11 (May, 1945), 177-213.

8502.   Smith, George Winston.   "Some Northern Wartime Attitudes Toward the Post-Civil War South."   JSouH 10 (August, 1944), 253-274.

8503.   Smith, Karen L.   "The Campaign for Water in Central Arizona, 1890-1903." ArW 23 (Summer, 1981), 127-148.

8504.   Smith, Timothy L.   "Protestant Schooling and American Nationality, 1800-1850." JAH 53 (March, 1967), 679-695.

8505.   Solomon, Barbara Miller.   "The Intellectual Background of the Immigration Restriction Movement in New England." NEQ 25 (March, 1952), 47-59.

8506.   Sosna, Morton.   "The South in the Saddle: Racial Politics   During the Wilson Years."   WMH 54 (Autumn, 1970), 30-49.

8507.   Stanley, Gerald.   "Racism and the Early Republican Party: the 1856 Presidential Election in California."   PHR 43 (May, 1974), 171-187.

8508.   Stanley, Gerald.   "Slavery and the Origins of the Republican Party in California." SCQ 60 (Spring, 1978), 1-16.

8509.   Sullivan, Margaret L.   "Conflict on the Frontier: the Case   of   Harney   County,   Oregon,   1870-1900."   PNQ 66 (October, 1975), 174-181.

8510.   Sunseri, Alvin R.   Seeds of Discord: New Mexico in the   Aftermath   of   the   American   Conquest,   1846-1861. (Chicago, Nelson-Hall, 1979)

8511.   Sutton, Robert P.   "Sectionalism and Social Structure: a   Case   Study   of   Jeffersonian   Democracy."   VMHB 80 (January, 1972), 70-84.

8512.   Sweeney, Kevin.   "Run, Romanism, Representation, and Reform: Coalition   Politics   in   Massachusetts,   1847-1853." CWH 22 (June, 1976), 116-137.

8513.   Thelen, David P. and Leslie H. Fishel, Jr. "Reconstruction in the North: the World Looks at New York's Negroes, March 16, 1867." NYH 49, i.e., New York State Historical Association. Proceedings 66 (1968), 405-440.

8514. Thompson, Alan S. "Southern Rights and Nativism as Issues in Mobile Politics, 1850-1861." AR 35 (April, 1982), 127-141.

8515.   Urban, C. Stanley. "The Ideology of Southern Imperialism: New Orleans and the Caribbean, 1845-1860." LHQ 39 (January, 1956), 48-73.

8516. Vandal, Gilles. "The Origins of the New Orleans Riot of 1866, Revisited." LH 22 (Spring, 1981), 135-165.

8517. Van Meeter, Sondra. "Black Resistance to Segregation in the Wichita Public Schools, 1870-1912." Midwest Quarterly 20 (October, 1978), 64-77.

8518. Violette, E.M. "Early Settlements in Missouri." MoHR 1 (October, 1906), 38-52.

8519.   Visher, Stephen S.   "The Geography of Indiana's Governors." IMH 35 (1939), 58-65.

8520.   Waldenrath, Alexander.   "The German Language Newspress in Pennsylvania During World War I." PH 42 (January, 1975), 25-41.

8521.   Watne, Joel Andrew.   "Public Opinion Toward Non-Conformists and Aliens During 1917, as Shown by the Fargo Forum." NDH 34 (Winter, 1967), 5-29.

8522. Watson, Harry L. Jacksonian Politics and Community Conflict: the Emergence of the Second American Party System in Cumberland County, North Carolina. (Baton Rouge, Louisiana State University Press, 1981)

8523. Watts, Eugene J. "Property and Politics in Atlanta, 1865-1903." JUH 3 (May, 1977), 295-322.

8524. Watts, Eugene J. The Social Bases of City Politics: Atlanta, 1865-1903. (Westport, Connecticut, Greenwood Press, 1978)

8525. Weber, David J. "American Westward Expansion and the Breakdown of Relations Between Pobladores and 'Indios Barbaros' on Mexico's Far Northern Frontier, 1821-1846." NMHR 56 (July, 1981), 221-238.

8526. Weinberg, Albert Katz. Manifest Destiny; a Study of Nationalist Expansionism in American History. (Baltimore, John Hopkins Press, 1935)

8527. Weisz, Howard. "Irish-American Attitudes and the Americanization of the English-Language Parochial School." NYH 51, i.e. New York State Historical Association. Proceedings 70 (1972), 157-176.

8528. Williams, Marilyn Thornton. "New York City's Public Baths: a Case Study in Urban Progressive Reform." JUH 7 (November, 1980), 49-81.

8529. Wiltz, John E. "APA-Ism in Kentucky and Elsewhere." KHSR 56 (April, 1958), 143-155.

8530. Wingfield, Marshall. "Tennessee's Mormon Massacre." THQ 17 (March, 1958), 19-36.

8531. Woody, Robert H. "The Labor and Immigration Problem of South Carolina During Reconstruction." MVHR 18 (September, 1931), 195-212.

8532. Wooster, Ralph A. "An Analysis of the Membership of the Texas Succession Convention." SWHQ 62 (January, 1959), 322-335.

8533. Wooster, Ralph A. "An Analysis of the Texas Know-Nothings." SWHQ 70 (January, 1967), 414-423.

Society

An eclectic sampling of the studies cited in this section should convince most readers that the nineteenth-century demographic revolutions had profound social consequences. That should be apparent to anyone who has explored a significant amount of the material cited in previous chapters, especially the ones on migration and the family. One might argue that many of these works could have been listed elsewhere. The reason most of these studies are here is that they often focus on images and ideas, and on culture in a very general sense, whereas the works listed elsewhere often had a more demographic or sociological orientation. Nevertheless, the line is not distinct. New students of what may be referred to as American character, if such a thing exists, should start with recent books on the subject by Gorer, Kammen, Potter, Riesman, and Wiebe. Tocqueville is, of course, an all-time classic. Two works that deserve special mention are Goffman's book on non-verbal communication, which is especially difficult in a pluralistic society, and Zelinsky's extraordinary study of how to study geographic differences in culture in the United States.

Many of the more narrowly focused works consider images of or attitudes held by Blacks, Indians, Mexicans, and European immigrants. Related subjects include ideas of and about work and laborers (especially in cities) and criminals. Education, and its role in assimilation, is another important topic.

8600. Achenbaum, W. Andrew. Old Age in the New Land: the American Experience since 1790. (Baltimore, Johns Hopkins University Press, 1978)

8601. Alvarez, Eugene. "Southern Hospitality as Seen by Travelers, 1820-1860." Studies in Popular Culture 2 (Spring, 1979), 24-32.

8602. Andrews, Horace. "Kansas Crusade: Eli Thayer and the New England Emigrant Aid Company." NEQ 35 (December, 1962), 497-514.

8603. Angelo, Richard. "The Students at the University of Pennsylvania and the Temple College of Philadelphia, 1873-1906: Some Notes on Schooling, Class and Social Mobility in the Late Nineteenth Century." HEQ 19 (Summer, 1979), 179-205.

8604. Appel, John J. "Jews in American Caricature: 1820-1914." AJH 71 (September, 1981), 103-133.

8605. Arensberg, Conrad. "Culture as Behavior: Structure and Emergence." Annual Review of Anthropology 1 (1972), 1-26.

8606. Ash, Stephen V. "Middle Tennessee Society in Transition, 1860-1870." MdH 13 (Spring/Summer, 1982), 18-38.

8607. Atack, Jeremy and Fred Bateman. "Egalitarianism, Inequality, and Age: the Rural North in 1860." JEH 41 (March, 1981), 85-93.

8608. Bailey, David T. and Bruce E. Haulman. "Patterns of Landholding in Santa Fe in 1860 and 1870." SSJ 13 (October, 1976), 9-19.

8609. Bannister, Turpin C. "Early Town Planning in New York State." NYH 24, i.e., New York State Historical Association. Proceedings 41 (1943), 185-195.

8610. Bardaglio, Peter W. "Italian Immigrants and the Catholic Church in Providence, 1890-1930." RIH 34 (May, 1975), 46-57.

8611. Barton, H. Arnold. "Swedish Immigrants and the Churches." SPHQ 27 (April, 1976), 83-85.

8612. Barton, Michael. Goodmen: the Character of Civil War Soldiers. (University Park, Pennsylvania State University Press, 1981)

8613. Belding, Robert E. "Academies and Iowa's Frontier Life." AI 44 (Summer, 1978), 335-358.

8614. Berger, Michael L. The Devil Wagon in God's Country: the Automobile and Social Change in Rural America, 1893-1929. (Hamden, Connecticut, Archon, 1979)

8615. Berkman, Brenda. "The Vanishing Race: Conflicting Images of the American Indian in Children's Literature, 1880-1930." NDQ 44 (Spring, 1976), 31-40.

8616. Berrol, Selma C. "Education and Economic Mobility: the Jewish Experience in New York City, 1880-1920." AJHQ 65 (March, 1976), 257-271.

8617. Berrol, Selma C. "In their Image: German Jews and the Americanization of the Ost Juden in New York City."

NYH 63, i.e. New York State Historical Association. Proceedings 80 (1982), 417-433.

8618. Berrol, Selma C. "School Days on the Old East Side: the Italian and Jewish Experience." NYH 57, i.e. New York State Historical Association. Proceedings 74 (1976), 200-213.

8619. Berrol, Selma C. "Turning Little Aliens into Little Citizens: Italians and Jews in New York City Public Schools, 1900-1914." American Italian Historical Association. Proceedings of the Seventh Annual Conference. (November, 1974), 32-41.

8620. Betts, Raymond F. "Immense Dimensions: the Impact of the American West on Late Nineteenth-Century European Thought about Expansion." WestHQ 10 (April, 1979), 149-166.

8621. Bicha, Karel D. "Hunkies: Stereotyping the Slavic Immigrants, 1890-1920." JAEH 2 (Autumn, 1982), 16-38.

8622. Biebel, Charles D. "Cultural Change on the Southwest Frontier: Albuquerque Schooling, 1870-1895." NMHR 55 (July, 1980), 209-230.

8623. Bieder, Robert E. "Scientific Attitudes Toward Indian Mixed-Bloods in Early Nineteenth-Century America." JES 8 (Summer, 1980), 17-30.

8624. Billman, Carol. "McGuffey's Readers and Alger's Fiction: the Gospel of Virtue According to Popular Children's Literature." JPC 11 (Winter, 1977), 614-619.

8625. Bledstein, Burton. The Culture of Professionalism: the Middle Class and the Development of Higher Education in America. (New York, Norton, 1976)

8626. Blegen, Theodore C. "Cleng Peerson and the Norwegian Immigration." MVHR 7 (March, 1921), 303-331.

8627. Bloomfield, Anne. "The Real Estate Associates: a Land and Housing Developer of the 1870's in San Francisco." Society of Architectural Historican. Journal 37 (March, 1978), 13-33.

8628. Blumin, Stuart M. "Age and Inequality in Antebellum America: the Case of Kingston, New York." <u>SSH</u> 6 (Summer, 1982), 369-380.

8629. Bodenhamer, David J. "Law and Disorder on the Early Frontier: Marion County, Indiana, 1823-1850." <u>WestHQ</u> 10 (July, 1979), 323-336.

8630. Bodnar, John E. "Materialism and Morality: Slavic-American Immigrants and Education, 1890-1940." <u>JES</u> 3 (Winter, 1976), 1-19.

8631. Bogue, Allan G. "The Iowa Claim Clubs: Symbol and Substance." <u>MVHR</u> 45 (September, 1958), 231-253.

8632. Bogue, Allan G. "Pioneer Farmers and Innovation." <u>IJH</u> 56 (January, 1958), 1-36.

8633. Bolin, Winifred Wandersee. "Heating up the Melting Pot: Settlement Work and Americanization in Northeast Minneapolis." <u>MnH</u> 45 (Summer, 1976), 58-69.

8634. Boston. City Council. Committee on Census of 1850. <u>Report of the Committee Appointed by the City Council; and also a Comparative View of the Population of Boston in 1850, with the Births, Marriages,and Deaths in 1849 and 1850</u>, by Jesse Chickering, M.D. (Boston, J.H. Eastburn, City Printer, 1851)

8635. Botein, Barbara. "The Hennessey Case; an Episode in Anti-Italian Nativism." <u>LH</u> 20 (Summer, 1979), 261-279.

8636. Bracken, Alexander E. "Middletown Before the Lynds: Geographical and Social Mobility in Muncie, 1850-1880." <u>ISSQ</u> 31 (Winter, 1978-1979), 38-45.

8637. Bruce, Dickson, D., Jr. <u>Violence and Culture in the Antebellum South</u>. (Austin, University of Texas Press, 1979)

8638. Burton, William L. "Indiana's Ethnic Regiments." <u>JPC</u> 14 (Fall, 1980), 229-241.

8639. Burton, William L. "'Title Deed to America': Union Ethnic Regiments in the Civil War." <u>APSP</u> 124 (December, 1980), 455-463.

8640. Butterfield, Roy L. "On the American Migrations."
NYH 38, i.e. New York State Historical Association.
Proceedings 55 (1957), 368-386.

8641. Campbell, Randolph B. "Population Persistence and
Social Change in Nineteenth-Century Texas: Harrison
County, 1850-1880." JSouH 48 (May, 1982), 185-204.

8642. Carper, James C. "The Popular Ideology of Segregated
Schooling: Attitudes Toward the Education of Blacks in
Kansas, 1854-1900." KH 1 (Winter, 1978), 254-265.

8643.   Chase, Hal S. "Struggle for Equality: Fort Des
Moines Traning Camp for Colored Officers, 1917." Phylon 39
(December, 1978), 297-310.

8644.   Christy, Howard A. "Open Hand and Mailed Fist:
Mormon-Indian Relations in Utah, 1847-1852." UHQ 46
(Summer, 1978), 216-235.

8645.   Clifford, Geraldine Joncich.   "Home and School in
19th-Century America: Some Personal-History Reports from
the United States." HEQ 18 (Spring, 1978), 3-34.

8646.   Cohen, Patricia Cline.   "Statistics and the State:
Changing Social Thought and the Emergence of a Quantitative
Mentality in America, 1790 to 1820." WMQ 38 (January,
1981), 35-55.

8647.   Coray, Michael S. "'Democracy' on the Frontier: a
Case Study of Nevada Editorial Attitudes on the Issue of
Non-White Equality." NHSQ 21 (Fall, 1978), 189-204.

8648.   Cowles, Karen. "The Industrialization of Duquesne and
the Circulation of Elites, 1891-1933." WPHM 62 (January,
1979), 1-18.

8649.   Danbom, David B. "Rural Education Reform and the
Country Life Movement, 1900-1920." AgH 53 (April, 1979),
462-474.

8650.   Dancis, Bruce.   "Social Mobility and Class
Consciousness: San Francisco's International Workmen's
Association in the 1880's." JSH 11 (Fall, 1977), 75-98.

8651. Dannenbaum, Jed. "Immigrants and Temperance: Ethnocultural Conflict in Cincinnati, 1845-1860." OH 87 (Spring, 1978), 125-139.

8652. Dannenbaum, Jed. "The Origins of Temperance Activism and Militancy among American Women." JSH 15 (Winter, 1981), 235-252.

8653. David, John R. "Joseph K. Emmet as Fritz, our German Cousin: the Stage Immigrant and the American Dream." MoHR 73 (January, 1979), 198-217.

8654. David, Paul A., et.al. Reckoning with Slavery: a Critical Study in the Quantitative History of American Negro Slavery. (New York, Oxford University Press, 1976)

8655. Davies, Edward J., II. "Regional Networks and Social Change: the Evolution of Urban Leadership in the Northern Anthracite Coal Region, 1840-1880." JSH 16 (Fall, 1982), 47-73.

8656. Davis, Ronald L.F. "Community and Conflict in Pioneer Saint Louis, Missouri." WestHQ 10 (July, 1979), 337-356.

8657. Dawson, Jan C. "The Puritan and the Cavalier: the South's Perception of Contrasting Traditions." JSouH 44 (November, 1978), 597-614.

8658. Decker, Peter R. "Jewish Merchants in San Francisco: Social Mobility on the Urban Frontier." AJH 68 (June, 1979), 396-407.

8659. Diggins, John P. "Slavery, Race, and Equality: Jefferson and the Pathos of the Enlightenment." AQ 28 (Summer, 1976), 206-228.

8660. Dittmer, John. Black Georgia in the Progressive Era, 1900-1920. (Urbana, University of Illinois Press, 1977)

8661. Dodd, Jill Siegel. "The Working Classes and the Temperance Movement in Ante-Bellum Boston." LbH 19 (Fall, 1978), 510-531.

8662.   Downey, Dennis B.   "Tradition and Acceptance: American Catholics and the Columbian Exposition."   MA 63 (April-July, 1981), 79-92.

8663.   Doyle, Don Harrison.   "The Social Functions of Voluntary Associations in a Nineteenth-Century American Town."   SSH 1 (Spring, 1977), 333-355.

8664.   Doyle, Don Harrison.   "Social Theory and New Communities in Nineteenth-Century America."   WestHQ 8 (April, 1977), 151-165.

8665.   Dyer, Thomas G.   "An Early Black Textbook: Floyd's Flowers or Duty and Beauty for Colored Children."   Phylon 37 (December, 1976), 359-361.

8666.   Dysart, Jane E.   "Another Road to Disappearance: Assimilation of Creek Indians in Pensacola, Florida, During the Nineteenth Century."   FHQ 61 (July, 1982), 37-48.

8667.   Dysart, Jane E.   "Mexican Women in San Antonio, 1830-1860:   the Assimilation Process."   WestHQ 7 (October, 1976), 365-375.

8668.   Edwards, Malcolm.   "'The War of Complexional Distinction':   Blacks in Gold Rush California and British Columbia."   CHQ 56 (Spring, 1977), 34-45.

8669.   Escott, Paul D.   Slavery Remembered: a Record of Twentieth-Century Slave Narratives.   (Chapel Hill, University of North Carolina Press, 1979)

8670.   Etulain, Richard W.   "Frontier, Region and Myth: Changing Interpretations of Western American Culture."   JAC 3 (Summer, 1980), 268-284.

8671.   Faler, Paul.   "Cultural Aspects of the Industrial Revolution: Lynn, Massachusetts, Shoemakers and Industrial Morality, 1826-1860."   LbH 15 (Summer, 1974), 367-394.

8672.   Farnam, Anne.   "A Society of Societies: Associations and Voluntarism in Early Nineteenth-Century Salem."   EICH 113 (July, 1977), 181-190.

8673. Farrell, Jane A. "Clothing for Adults in Iowa, 1850-1899." AI 46 (Fall, 1981), 100-120.

8674. Faust, Drew Gilpin. "Culture, Conflict, and Community: the Meaning of Power on an Antebellum Plantation." JSH 14 (Fall, 1980), 83-97.

8675. Feldberg, Michael. The Turbulent Era: Riot and Disorder in Jacksonian America. (New York, Oxford University Press, 1980)

8676. Fish, Carl Russell. "The Pilgrim and the Melting Pot." MVHR 7 (December, 1920), 187-205.

8677. Flynt, Wayne. "Religion in the Urban South: the Divided Religious Mind of Birmingham, 1900-1930." AR 30 (April, 1977), 108-134.

8678. Fogarty, Robert S. "American Communes, 1865-1914." JAS 9 (August, 1975), 145-162.

8679. Foner, Philip Sheldon. History of Black Americans: from the Compromise of 1850 to the End of the Civil War. (Westport, Connecticut, Greenwood Press, 1983)

8680. Foner, Philip Sheldon. History of Black Americans: from the Emergence of the Cotton Kingdom to the Eve of the Compromise of 1850. (Westport, Connecticut, Greenwood Press, 1983)

8681. Forbes, Bruce David. "Presbyterian Beginnings in South Dakota, 1840-1900." SDH 7 (Spring, 1977), 115-153.

8682. Frederickson, George M. White Supremacy: a Comparative Study in American and South African History. (New York, Oxford University Press, 1981)

8683. Freedman, Estelle B. Their Sister's Keepers: Women's Prison Reform in America, 1830-1930. (Ann Arbor, University of Michigan Press, 1981)

8684. Fried, Lewis. "Jacob Riis and the Jews: the Ambivalent Quest for Community." AS 20 (Spring, 1979), 5-24.

8685.   Friedman, Lawrence J.   "Racism and Sexism in Ante-Bellum America: the Prudence Crandall Episode Reconsidered." Societas 4 (Summer, 1974), 211-227.

8686.   Friedmann, Karen J.   "Urban Food Marketing in Los Angeles, 1850-1885." AgH 54 (July, 1980), 433-445.

8687.   Garcia, Mario T.   "Americanization and the Mexican Immigrant, 1880-1930." JES 6 (Summer, 1978), 19-34.

8688.   Gerber, David A.   Black Ohio and the Color Line, 1860-1915. (Urbana, University of Illinois Press, 1976)

8689.   Gerber, David A.   "Modernity in the Service of Tradition: Catholic Lay Trustees at Buffalo's St. Louis Church and the Transformation of European Communal Traditions, 1829-1955." JSH 15 (Summer, 1982), 655-684.

8690.   Gettleman, Marvin E.   "Philanthropy as Social Control in Late Nineteenth-Century America: Some Hypotheses and Data on the Rise of Social Work." Societas 5 (Winter, 1975), 49-59.

8691.   Gilje, Paul A.   "The Baltimore Riots of 1812 and the Breakdown of the Anglo-American Mob Tradition." JSH 13 (Summer, 1980), 547-564.

8692.   Goffman, Erving.   The Presentation of Self in Everyday Life. (Garden City, New York, Doubleday, 1959)

8693.   Goldberg, Gordon J.   "Meyer London and the National Social Insurance Movement, 1914-1922." AJHQ 65 (September, 1975), 59-73.

8694.   Gorer, Geoffrey.   The American People; a Study in National Character. Revised edition. (New York, Norton, 1964)

8695.   Gosselman, Carl A.   "A Swedish View in 1826 of American Character." Translated by Ernst Ekman. AQ 14 (Fall, 1962), 495-499.

8696.   Graff, Harvey J.   "Crime and Punishment in the Nineteenth-Century: a New Look at the Criminal." JIH 7 (Winter, 1977), 477-491.

8697. Greenberg, Brian. "Worker and Community: Fraternal Orders in Albany, New York, 1845-1885." MdH 8 (Fall, 1977), 38-53.

8698. Haebler, Peter. "Holyoke's French-Canadian Community in Turmoil: the Role of the Church in Assimilation 1869-1887." HJWM 7 (January, 1979), 5-21.

8699. Hague, Harlan. "Eden Ravished: Pioneer Attitudes Toward Conservation and the Land." AW 14 (May/June, 1977), 30-33; 65-69.

8700. Hale, Frederick. "Baptists and the Norwegian-American Immigrant Milieu." Foundations 24 (April-June, 1981), 122-136.

8701. Haley, Charles. "The Klan in Their Midst: the Ku Klux Klan in Upstate New York Communities." Afro-Americans in New York Life and History 7 (January, 1983), 41-53.

8702. Haller, John S., Jr. Outcasts from Evolution: Scientific Attitudes of Racial Inferiority, 1859-1900. (Urbana, University of Illinois Press, 1971)

8703. Hampel, Robert L. Temperance and Prohibition in Massachusetts, 1813-1852. (Ann Arbor, Michigan, UMI Research, 1982)

8704. Hamre, James S. "Norwegian Immigrants Respond to the Common School: a Case Study of American Values and the Lutheran Tradition." Church History 50 (September, 1981), 302-315.

8705. Hatcher, Mattie Austin. "The Louisiana Background of the Colonization of Texas, 1763-1803." SWHQ 24 (January, 1921), 169-194.

8706. Hedges, James Blaine. "The Colonization Work of the Northern Pacific Railroad." MVHR 13 (December, 1926), 311-342.

8707. Heinerman, Joseph. "Early Utah Pioneer Cultural Societies." UHQ 47 (Winter, 1979), 70-89.

8708. Hellwig, David J. "Afro-American Reactions to the Japanese and the Anti-Japanese Movement, 1906-1924." Phylon 38 (March, 1977), 93-104.

8709. Hellwig, David J. "Black Attitudes Toward Irish Immigrants." MA 59 (January, 1977), 39-49.

8710. Hellwig, David J. "Black Images of Jews: from Reconstruction to Depression." Societas 8 (Summer, 1978), 205-223.

8711. Hellwig, David J. "Black Reactions to Chinese Immigration and the Anti-Chinese Movement: 1850-1910." AJ 6 (Fall, 1979), 25-44.

8712. Hellwig, David J. "Building a Black Nation: the Role of Immigrants in the Thought and Rhetoric of Booker T. Washington." MQ 31 (Fall, 1978), 529-550.

8713. Hesse-Biber, Sharlene. "The Ethnic Ghetto as Private Welfare: a Case Study of Southern Italian Immigration to the United States, 1880-1914." Urban and Social Change Review 12 (Summer, 1979), 9-15.

8714. Higham, John, ed. Ethnic Leadership in America. (Baltimore, Johns Hopkins University Press, 1978)

8715. Higham, John. "Hanging Together: Divergent Unities in American History." JAH 61 (1974), 5-28.

8716. Higham, John. "Integrating America: the Problem of Assimilation in the Nineteenth Century." JAEH 1 (Fall, 1981), 7-25.

8717. Hindus, Michael Stephen. "The Contours of Crime and Justice in Massachusetts and South Carolina, 1767-1878." AJLH 21 (July, 1977), 212-237.

8718. Hindus, Michael Stephen. Prison and Plantation: Crime, Justice, and Authority in Massachusetts and South Carolina, 1767-1878. (Chapel Hill, University of North Carolina Press, 1980)

8719. Holmes, Oliver Wendell and Peter T. Rohrbach. Stagecoach East: Stagecoach Days in the East from the

Colonial Period to the Civil War. (Washington, D.C., Smithsonian Institution Press, 1983)

8720. Horowitz, Murray M. "Ethnicity and Command: the Civil War Experience." Military Affairs 42 (December, 1978), 182-189.

8721. Horsman, Reginald. "Scientific Racism and the American Indian in the Mid-Nineteenth Century." AQ 27 (May, 1975), 152-168.

8722. Howard, Victor B. Black Liberation in Kentucky: Emancipation and Freedom, 1862-1884. (Lexington, University Press of Kentucky, 1983)

8723. Huffman, Frank J., Jr. "Town and Country in the South, 1850-1880: a Comparison of Urban and Rural Social Structures." SAQ 76 (Summer, 1977), 366-381.

8724. Hurst, Marsha. "Integration, Freedom of Choice, and Community Control in Nineteenth-Century Brooklyn." JES 3 (Fall, 1975), 33-55.

8725. Hutslar, Donald A. "The Ohio Farmstead: Farm Buildings as Cultural Artifacts." OH 90 (Summer, 1981), 221-287.

8726. Jaher, Frederick Cople. The Urban Establishment: Upper Strata in Boston, New York, and Charleston, Chicago, and Los Angeles. (Urbana, University of Illinois Press, 1982)

8727. Ibson, John. "Virgin Land or Virgin Mary? Studying the Ethnicity of White Americans." AQ 33 (1981), 284-308.

8728. Issel, William. "Americanization, Acculturation, and Social Control: School Reform Ideology in Industrial Pennsylvania, 1880-1910." JSH 12 (Summer, 1979), 569-590.

8729. Janis, Ralph. "Ethnic Mixture and the Persistence of Cultural Pluralism in the Church Communities of Detroit, 1880-1940." MA 61 (April-July, 1979), 99-114.

8730. Janis, Ralph. "Flirtation and Flight: Alternatives to Ethnic Confrontation in White Anglo-American Protestant Detroit, 1880-1940." JES 6 (Summer, 1978), 1-17.

8731. Jensen, Oliver Omerod. American Album (New York, American Heritage Publishing Company, 1985)

8732. Johnsen, Leigh Dana. "Equal Rights and the 'Heathen "Chinee'": Black Activism in San Francisco, 1865-1875." WestHQ 11 (January, 1980), 57-68.

8733.   Johnson, Michael P.   "Planters and Patriarchy: Charleston, 1800-1860." JSouH 46 (February, 1980), 45-72.

8734. Kaestle, Carl F. and Maris A. Vinovskis. Education and Social Change in Nineteenth-Century Massachusetts. (Cambridge, England, Cambridge University Press, 1980)

8735. Kammen, Michael G. People of Paradox: an Inquiry Concerning the Origins of American Civilization. (New York, Knopf, 1972)

8736. Karcher, Carolyn L. Shadow over the Promised Land: Slavery, Race and Violence in Melville's America. (Baton Rouge, Louisiana State University Press, 1980)

8737. Katz, Michael B., Michael J. Doucet and Mark J. Stern. "Migration and the Social Order in Erie County, New York: 1855." JIH 8 (Spring, 1978), 669-701.

8738.   Kay, Donald.   "British Influence on Mississippi Municipal Place Names." JMsH 36 (August, 1974), 269-272.

8739.   Keller,   Phyllis.   Status   of   Belonging: German-American Intellectuals and the First World War. (Cambridge, Massachusetts, Harvard University Press, 1979)

8740. Kiger, Joseph C. "Social Thought as Voiced in Rural Middle Tennessee Newspapers, 1878-1898." THQ 9 (June, 1950), 131-154.

8741. Kirk, Carolyn Tyirin and Gordon W. Kirk, Jr. "The Impact of the City on Home Ownership: a Comparison of Immigrants and Native Whites at the Turn of the Century." JUH 7 (August, 1981), 471-498.

8742. Kraut, Alan M. "Ethnic Foodways: the Significance of Food in the Designation of Cultural Boundaries Between

Immigrant Groups in the U.S., 1840-1921." JAC 2 (Fall, 1979), 409-420.

8743. Lamar, Howard R. "Public Values and Private Dreams: South Dakota's Search for Identity, 1850-1900." SDH 8 (Spring, 1978), 117-142.

8744. Lapsansky, Emma Jones. "'Since They Got Those Separate Churches': Afro-Americans and Recism in Jacksonian Philadelphia." AQ 32 (Spring, 1980), 54-78.

8745. Larkin, Jack. "The View from New England: Notes on Everyday Life in Rural America to 1850." AQ 34 (no.3, 1982), 244-261.

8746. Laurie, Bruce. "'Nothing on Compulsion': Life Styles of Philadelphia Artisans, 1820-1850." LbH 15 (Summer, 1974), 337-366.

8747. Laurie, Bruce. Working People of Philadelphia, 1800-1850. (Philadelphia, Temple University Press, 1980)

8748. Leach, Richard H. "The Impact of Immigration upon New York." NYH 31, i.e. New York State Historical Association. Proceedings 48 (1950), 15-30.

8749. Lemons, J. Stanley. "Black Stereotypes as Reflected in Popular Culture, 1880-1920." AQ 29 (Spring, 1977), 102-116.

8750. Leonard, Henry B. "Ethnic Conflict and Episcopal Power: the Diocese of Cleveland, 1847-1870." CHR 62 (July, 1976), 388-407.

8751. Levine, Lawrence W. Black Culture and Black Consciousness: Afro-American Folk Thought from Slavery to Freedom. (New York, Oxford University Press, 1977)

8752. Linneman, William R. "Immigrant Stereotypes: 1880-1900." Studies in American Humor 1 (April, 1974), 28-39.

8753. Lovoll, Odd Sverre. A Folk Epic: the Bydclag in America. (Boston, Twayne Norwegian-American Historical Association, 1975)

8754.   Luraghi,   Raimondo.   The   Rise   and   Fall   of   the Plantation South. (New York, New Viewpoints, 1978)

8755. Mabee, Carleton. Black Education in New York State: from   Colonial   to   Modern   Times.   (Syracuse,   Syracuse University Press, 1979)

8756. McCarthy, Kathleen D. Noblesse Oblige: Charity and Cultural   Philanthropy   in   Chicago,   1849-1929.   (Chicago, University of Chicago Press, 1982)

8757.   McClymer,   John   F.   War   and   Welfare: Social Engineering in America, 1890-1925. (Westport, Connecticut, Greenwood Press, 1980)

8758. McDaniel, George W. Hearth and Home: Preserving a People's Culture.   (Philadelphia, Temple University Press, 1982)

8759. McDonald, Forrest and Ellen Shapiro McDonald. "The Ethnic Origins of the American People, 1790." WMQ 37 (April, 1980), 179-199.

8760.   McGaw,   Judith   A.   "'A   Good   Place   to   Work.' Industrial Workers and Occupational Choice: the Case of Berkshire Women." JIH 10 (Autumn, 1979), 227-248.

8761.   Magnuson,   Norris.   Salvation   in   the   Slums: Evangelical Social Work, 1865-1920. (Metuchen, New Jersey, Scarecrow/American Theological Library Association, 1977)

8762.   Mann,   Ralph.   "The   Americanization   of   Arcadia: Images of Hispanic and Gold Rush California." AS 19 (Spring, 1978), 5-19.

8763. Marraro, Howard A. "Italians in New York During the First Half of the Nineteenth Century." NYH 26, i.e. New York State Historical Assocation. Proceedings 43 (1945), 278-306.

8764. Marraro, Howard A. "Italians in New York in the Eighteen Fifties." NYH 30, i.e. New York State Historical Assocation. Proceedings 47 (1949), 181-203; 276-303.

8765. Megehee, Mark K. "Creek Nativism since 1865." CO 56 (Fall, 1978), 282-297.

8766. Merriam, Paul G. "Urban Elite in the Far West: Portland, Oregon, 1870-1890." ArW 18 (Spring, 1976), 41-52.

8767. Meyer, Stephen. "Adapting the Immigrant to the Line: Americanization in the Ford Factory, 1914-1921." JSH 14 (Fall, 1980), 67-82.

8768. Miller, Char. "Puritan, Yankee, and Father: an Intellectual Portrait of Elizur Wright, Esq. (1762-1845)." Connecticut Historical Society Bulletin 44 (October, 1979), 117-128.

8769. Milner, Clyde A., II. "Off the White Road: Seven Nebraska Indian Societies in the 1870's--a Statistical Analysis of Assimilation, Population, and Prosperity." WestHQ 12 (January, 1981), 37-52.

8770. Mohl, Raymond A. Poverty in New York, 1783-1825. (New York, Oxford University Press, 1971)

8771. Monkkonen, Eric H. The Dangerous Class: Crime and Poverty in Columbus Ohio, 1860-1885. (Cambridge, Massachusetts, Harvard University Press, 1975)

8772. Monkkonen, Eric H. "A Disorderly People? Urban Order in the Nineteenth and Twentieth Centuries." JAH 68 (December, 1981), 539-559.

8773. Monkkonen, Eric H. Police in Urban America, 1860-1920. (Cambridge, England, Cambridge University Press, 1981)

8774. Monkkonen, Eric H. "Socializing the New Urbanites: Horatio Alger, Jr.'s Guidebook." JPC 11 (Summer, 1977), 77-87.

8775. Moranian, Suzanne Elizabeth. "Ethnocide in the Schoolhouse: Missionary Efforts to Educate Indian Youth in Pre-Reservation Wisconsin." WMH 64 (Summer, 1981), 242-260.

8776. Morawska, Ewa. "The Internal Status Hierarchy in the East European Immigrant Communities of Johnstown, Pennsylvania, 1890-1930's." JSH 16 (Fall, 1982), 75-107.

8777. Moynihan, Ruth Barnes. Rebel of Rights: Abigail Scott Duniway. (New Haven, Connecticut, Yale University Press, 1983)

8778. Neil, J. Meredith. "'Plain and Simple Principles' for an American Art, 1810." PMHB 93 (July, 1969), 410-416.

8779. Nelson, Frank C. "Norwegian-American Attitudes Toward Assimilation During Four Periods of their History in America, 1825-1930." JES 9 (Spring, 1981), 59-68.

8780. Newman, Harvey K. "Piety and Segregation--White Protestant Attitudes Toward Blacks in Atlanta, 1865-1906." GHQ 63 (Summer, 1979), 238-257.

8781. Olneck, Michael R. and Marvin Lazerson. "The School Achievement of Immigrant Children: 1900-1930." HEQ 14 (Winter, 1974), 453-482.

8782. Osofsky, Gilbert. "Abolitionists, Irish Immigrants, and the Dilemmas of Romantic Nationalism." AHR 80 (October, 1975), 889-912.

8783. Osofsky, Gilbert. "The Enduring Ghetto." JAH 55 (September, 1968), 243-255.

8784. Ostergren, Robert C. "The Immigrant Church as a Symbol of Community and Place in the Upper Midwest." GPQ 1 (Fall, 1981), 225-238.

8785. Oubre, Claude F. Forty Acres and a Mule: the Freedman's Bureau and Black Land Ownership. (Baton Rouge, Louisiana State University Press, 1978)

8786. Owens, Leslie Howard. This Species of Property: Slave Life and Culture in the Old South. (New York, Oxford University Press, 1976)

8787. Paredes, Raymund A. "The Mexican Image in American Travel Literature, 1831-1869." NMHR 52 (January, 1977), 5-29.

8788. Park, Joseph F. "The 1903 'Mexican Affair' at Clifton." JArH 18 (Summer, 1977), 119-148.

8789. Pease, Jane H. and William H. Pease. "Social Structure and the Potential for Urban Change: Boston and Charleston in the 1830's." JUH 8 (February, 1982), 117-195.

8790. Pease, William H. and Jane H. Pease. "Paternal Dilemmas: Education, Property and Patrician Persistence in Jacksonian Boston." NEQ 53 (June, 1980), 147-167.

8791. Pessen, Edward. "How Different from Each Other Were the Antebellum North and South?" AHR 85 (December, 1980), 1119-1149.

8792. Pessen, Edward. "Social Mobility in American History: Some Brief Reflections." JSouH 45 (May, 1979), 165-184.

8793. Peterson, Charles S. "Life in a Village Society, 1877-1920." UHQ 49 (Winter, 1981), 78-96.

8794. Peterson, Richard H. Manifest Destiny in the Mines: a Cultural Interpretation of Anti-Mexican Nativism in California, 1848-1853. (San Francisco, R and E Research, 1975)

8795. Phillips, George Harwood. "Indians in Los Angeles, 1781-1875: Economic Integration, Social Disintegration." PHR 49 (August, 1980), 427-451.

8796. Philpott, Thomas Lee. The Slum and the Ghetto: Neighborhood Deterioration and Middle-Class Reform, Chicago, 1880-1930. (New York, Oxford University Press, 1978)

8797. Piott, Steven L. "The Lesson of the Immigrant: Views of Immigrants in Muckraking Magazines, 1900-1909." AS 19 (Spring, 1978), 21-33.

8798. Porter, Kenneth Wiggins. "'The Boys' War': a Study in Frontier Racial Conflict, Journalism, and Folk History." PNQ 68 (October, 1977), 175-190.

8799. Potter, David Morris. History and American Society: Essays of David M. Potter. Edited by Don E. Fehrenbacher. (New York, Oxford University Press, 1973)

8800. Potter, David Morris. People of Plenty: Economic Abundance and the American Character. (Chicago, University of Chicago Press, 1954)

8801. Prucha, Francis Paul. American Indian Policy in Crisis: Christian Reformers and the Indian, 1865-1900. (Norman, University of Oklahoma Press, 1976)

8802. Quandt, Jean B. "Community in Urban America, 1890-1917:   Reformers, City Planners, and Greenwich Villagers." Societas 6 (Autumn, 1976), 255-273.

8803. Quinlivan, Mary E. "Race Relations in the Antebellum Children's Literature of Jacob Abbott." JPC 16 (Summer, 1982), 27-36.

8804. Rabinowitz, Howard N. Race Relations in the Urban South, 1865-1890. (New York, Oxford University Press, 1978)

8805. Radford, John. "The Charleston Planters in 1860." SCHM 77 (October, 1976), 227-235.

8806. Ralph, Raymond M. "The City and the Church: Catholic Beginnings in Newark, 1840-1870." NJH 96 (Autumn-Winter, 1978), 105-118.

8807. Reidy, Joseph P. "'Negro Election Day' and Black Community Life in New England, 1750-1860." Marxist Perspectives 1 (Fall, 1978), 102-117.

8808.   Reutlinger, Andrew S.   "Reflections on the Anglo-American Jewish Experience: Immigrants, Workers and Entrepreneurs in New York and London, 1870-1914." AJHQ 66 (June, 1977), 473-484.

8809. Rice, C. Duncan. The Rise and Fall of Black Slavery. (New York, Harper and Row, 1975)

8810. Riesman, David. The Lonely Crowd: a Study of the Changing American Character. (New Haven, Yale University Press, 1950)

8811. Ringer, Benjamin B. "We the People" and Others: Duality and America's Treatment of its Racial Minorities. (New York, Tavistock Publications, 1983)

8812. Rockaway, Robert A. "Anti-Semitism in an American City: Detroit, 1850-1914." AJHQ 64 (September, 1974), 42-54.

8813. Rose, Willie Lee. Slavery and Freedom. (New York, Oxford University Press, 1982)

8814. Rossman, Kenneth R. "The Irish in American Drama in the Mid-Nineteenth Century." NYH 21, i.e. New York State Historical Association. Proceedings 38 (1940), 39-53.

8815. Rubenstein, Bruce. "To Destroy a Culture: Indian Education in Michigan, 1855-1900." MH 60 (Summer, 1976), 137-160.

8816. Rubin, Jay. "Black Nativism: the European Immigrant in Negro Thought, 1830-1860." Phylon 39 (September, 1978), 193-202.

8817. Saunders, Robert M. "Crime and Punishment in Early National America: Richmond, Virginia, 1784-1820." VMHB 86 (January, 1978), 33-44.

8818. Schneider, John C. Detroit and the Problem of Order, 1830-1880: a Geography of Crime, Riot and Policing. (Lincoln, University of Nebraska Press, 1980)

8819. Schroeder, Walter A. "Panther Hollow and Dead Elm School: Plant and Animal Place Names in Missouri." MoHR 73 (April, 1979), 321-347.

8820. Seller, Maxine. "The Education of Immigrant Children in Buffalo, New York, 1890-1916." NYH 57, i.e. New York State Historical Association. Proceedings 74 (1976), 183-199.

8821. Sessions, Gene A. and Stephen W. Stathis. "The Mormon Invasion of Russian America: Dynamics of a Potent Myth." UHQ 45 (Winter, 1977), 22-35.

8822. Shafer, Boyd C. "The American Heritage of Hope, 1865-1940." MVHR 37 (December, 1950), 427-450.

8823.   Shankman,   Arnold.   Ambivalent   Friends:
Afro-Americans View the Immigrant. (Westport, Connecticut,
Greenwood Press, 1982)

8824.   Shankman, Arnold.   "'Asiatic Ogre' or 'Desirable
Citizen'?   The Image of Japanese Americans in the
Afro-American Press, 1867-1933." PHR 46 (November, 1977),
567-587.

8825. Shankman, Arnold. "Black on Yellow: Afro-Americans
View Chinese-Americans, 1850-1935."   Phylon 39 (March,
1978), 1-17.

8826.   Shankman,   Arnold.   "This   Menacing   Influx:
Afro-Americans on Italian Immigration to the South,
1880-1915." MQ 31 (Winter, 1977-1978), 67-88.

8827. Sheldon, Marianne Buroff. "Black-White Relations in
Richmond, Virginia, 1782-1820." JSouH 45 (February, 1979),
26-44.

8828. Shergold, Peter R. Working-Class Life: the "American
Standard" in Comparative Perspective, 1899-1913. (Pittsburgh,
University of Pittsburgh Press, 1982)

8829. Sizer, Sandra S. "Politics and Apolitical Religion: the
Great Urban Revivals of the Late Nineteenth Century."
Church History 48 (March, 1979), 81-98.

8830.   Soltow, Lee and Edward Stevens. The Rise of
Literacy and the Common School in the United States: a
Socioeconomic Analysis to 1870. (Chicago, University of
Chicago Press, 1981)

8831. Strombeck, Rita. "Success and the Swedish-American
Ideology." SPHQ 28 (July, 1977), 182-191.

8832. Stroupe, Henry S. "'Cite Them Both to Attend the
Next Church Conference': Social Control by North Carolina
Baptist Churches, 1772-1908."   NCHR 52 (April, 1975),
156-170.

8833. Surratt, Jerry L. "The Role of Dissent in Community
Evolution among Moravians in Salem, 1772-1860." NCHR 52
(July, 1975), 235-255.

8834. Swierenga, Robert P. "Local Cosmopolitan Theory and Immigrant Religion: the Social Basis of the Antebellum Dutch Reformed Schism." JSH 14 (Fall, 1980), 113-135.

8835. Szuberla, Guy. "Three Chicago Settlements: Their Architectural Form and Social Meaning." ISHSJ 70 (May, 1977), 114-129.

8836. Tachibana, Judy M. "Outwitting the Whites: One Image of the Chinese in California Fiction and Poetry, 1849-1924." SCQ 61 (Winter, 1979), 379-389.

8837. Takaki, Ronald T. Iron Cages: Race and Culture in Nineteenth-Century America. (New York, Knopf, 1979)

8838. Tarr, Joel A. "From City to Farm: Urban Wastes and the American Farmer." AgH 49 (October, 1975), 598-612.

8839. Taylor, Arnold H. Travail and Triumph: Black Life and Culture in the South since the Civil War. (Westport, Connecticut, Greenwood Press, 1976)

8840. Thornton, Russell. "Demographic Antecedents of a Revitalization Movement: Population Change, Population Size, and the 1890 Ghost Dance." ASR 46 (February, 1981), 88-96.

8841. Tocqueville, Alexis Charles Henri Maurice Clerel de. Democracy in America. (London, Saunders and Otley, 1835)

8842. Toplin, Robert Brent. "Between Black and White: Attitudes Toward Southern Mulattoes, 1830-1861." JSouH 45 (May, 1979), 185-200.

8843. Trachtenberg, Alan. The Incorporation of America: Culture and Society in the Gilded Age. (New York, Hill and Wang, 1982)

8844. Van Deburg, William L. Slavery and Race in American Popular Culture. (Madison, University of Wisconsin Press, 1984)

8845. Vlach, John Michael. "The Shotgun House: an African Architectural Legacy." PA 8 (1976), 47-56 (Part 1); PA 8 (1976), 57-70 (Part 2).

8846. Wacker, R. Fred. "Assimilation and Cultural Pluralism in American Social Thought." Phylon 40 (December, 1979), 325-333.

8847. Walaskay, Paul William. "The Entertainment of Angels: American Baptists and Americanization, 1890-1925." Foundations 19 (October-December, 1976), 346-360.

8848. Walch, Timothy. "Catholic Social Institutions and Urban Development: the View from Nineteenth-Century Chicago and Milwaukee." CHR 64 (January, 1978), 16-32.

8849. Weinberg, Daniel E. "Ethnic Identity in Industrial Cleveland: the Hungarians 1900-1920." OH 86 (Summer, 1977), 171-186.

8850. Weiss, Michael. "Education, Literacy and the Community of Los Angeles in 1850." SCQ 60 (Summer, 1978), 117-142.

8851. Welter, Rush. "The Frontier West as Image of American Society: Conservative Attitudes Before the Civil War." MVHR 46 (March, 1960), 593-614.

8852. Wiebe, Robert H. The Segmented Society: an Introduction to the Meaning of America. (New York, Oxford University Press, 1975)

8853. Wiener, Jonathan M. Social Origins of the New South: Alabama, 1860-1885. (Baton Rouge, Louisiana State University Press, 1978)

8854. Wilkie, Jane Riblett. "Social Status, Acculturation, and School Attendance in 1850 Boston." JSH 11 (Winter, 1977), 179-192.

8855. Williams, James C. "Cultural Tension: the Origins of American Santa Barbara." SCQ 60 (Winter, 1978), 349-377.

8856. Wilson, Charles R. "Racial Reservations: Indians and Blacks in American Magazines, 1865-1900." JPC 10 (Summer, 1976), 70-79.

8857.   Wittke, Carl Frederick.   "The America Theme in Continental European Literatures."   MVHR 28 (June, 1941), 3-26.

8858.   Wittke, Carl Frederick.   "The Immigrant Theme on the American Stage."   MVHR 39 (September, 1952), 211-232.

8859.   Wood, Raymond F.   "Anglo Influence on Spanish Place Names in California."   SCQ 63 (Winter, 1981), 392-413.

8860.   Woolsey, Ronald C.   "Crime and Punishment: Los Angeles County, 1850-1856."   SCQ 61 (Spring, 1979), 79-98.

8861.   Wrede, Steven.   "The Americanization of Scott County, 1914-1918."   AI 44 (Spring, 1979), 627-638.

8862.   Wu, William F.   The Yellow Peril: Chinese Americans in American Fiction, 1850-1940.   (Hamden, Connecticut, Archon, 1982)

8863.   Zarbin, Earl.   "'The Whole Thing Was Done so Quietly': the Phoenix Lynchings of 1879."   JArH 21 (Winter, 1980), 353-362.

8864.   Zelinsky, Wilbur.   The Cultural Geography of the United States. (Englewood Cliffs, New Jersey, Prentice-Hall, 1972)

Recent

Libraries are full of studies of twentieth-century America that can be used to supplement these selections. One could, quite easily, spend a life time reading in this body of literature alone.   Since neither of the authors of this bibliography have done that, we have probably omitted numerous works that could be mentioned here.   For beginners, however, these studies should provide some places to start.   One important observation is that there are few new themes in the demographic history of the twentieth century.   The emphases may change, and old ideas take on new twists, but there is a remarkable continuity between many of these studies and those entered under earlier periods.   Once again, the twentieth-century sections of earlier chapters merit consultation.

Economics

In addition to these studies, readers should refer to new patterns of immigration and internal mobility after 1920, and to new roles of women and children in families, and of families in society. Gains in health and longevity and changes in childbearing have also had economic consequences.

8900. Bonacich, Edna and John Modell. The Economic Basis of Ethnic Solidarity: Small Business in the Japanese American Community. (Berkeley, University of California Press, 1980)

8901. Bonilla, Frank and Ricardo Campos. "A Wealth of Poor: Puerto Ricans in the New Economic Order." Daedalus 110 (Spring, 1981), 133-176.

8902. Clough, Shepard B. and Lorna Quimby. "Peacham, Vermont: Fifty Years of Economic and Social Change 1929-1979." VH 51 (Winter, 1983), 5-28.

8903. Cramer, M. Richard. "Race and Southern White Workers' Support for Unions." Phylon 39 (December, 1978), 311-321.

8904. Easterlin, Richard A., Michael L. Wachter, and Susan M. Wachter. "The Changing Impact of Population Swings on the American Economy." APSP 122 (June, 1978), 119-130.

8905. Frey, William H. "Black In-Migration, White Flight, and the Changing Economic Base of the Central City." AJS 85 (May, 1980), 1396-1417.

8906. Gottlieb, Peter. "Migration and Jobs: the New Black Workers in Pittsburgh, 1916-1930." WPHM 61 (January, 1978), 1-15.

8907. Janowitz, Barbara. "The Effects of Demographic Factors on Age Composition and the Implications for Per Capita Income." Demography 10 (November, 1973), 507-515.

8908. Lotchin, Roger W. "The City and the Sword: San Francisco and the Rise of the Metropolitan-Military Complex, 1919-1941." JAH 65 (March, 1979), 996-1020.

8909. May, Martha. "The Historical Problem of the Family Wage: the Ford Motor Company and the Five Dollar Day." FS 8 (Summer, 1982), 399-424.

8910. Mayer, Harold M. "The Changing Role of Metropolitan Chicago in the Midwest and the Nation." Illinois Geographical Society. Bulletin 17 (June, 1975), 3-13.

8911. Metzgar, Joseph V. "Guns and Butter: Albuquerque Hispanics, 1940-1975." NMHR 56 (April, 1981), 117-139.

8912. Miller, Ann R. "Changing Work Life Patterns: a Twenty-Five Year Review." AAAPSS No. 435 (January, 1978), 83-101.

8913. Musselman, Barbara L. "Working Class Unity and Ethnic Division: Cincinnati Trade Unionists and Cultural Pluralism." CHSB 34 (Summer, 1976), 121-143.

8914. Radzialowski, Thaddeus. "The Competition for Jobs and Racial Stereotypes: Poles and Blacks in Chicago." PAS 33 (Autumn, 1976), 5-18.

8915. Reinecke, John E. Feigned Necessity: Hawaii's Attempt to Obtain Chinese Contract Labor, 1921-23. (San Francisco, Chinese Materials Center, 1979)

8916. Reisler, Mark. By the Sweat of Their Brow: Mexican Immigrant Labor in the United States, 1900-1940. (Westport, Connecticut, Greenwood Press, 1976)

8917. Sassen-Koob, Saskia. "Immigrant and Minority Workers in the Organization of the Labor Process." JES 8 (Spring, 1980), 1-34.

8918. Wadley, Janet K. and Everett S. Lee. "The Disappearance of the Black Farmer." Phylon 25 (September, 1974), 276-283.

8919. Wang, Peter H. "Farmers and the Immigration Act of 1924." AgH 49 (October, 1975), 647-652.

Politics

Race and ethnicity continue to play important roles in American politics. One political issue that first emerged in the nineteenth century, but which has become increasingly important with movement into the Sunbelt has been the allocation of water rights. The building of highways, and other transportation and communications systems, is also important, but with the exception of Rose, has received little attention.

8950.   Abramson, Paul R.   "Generational Change and the Decline of Party Identification in America: 1952-1974." American Political Science Review 70 (June, 1976), 469-478.

8951.   Alexander, James R.   "The Impact of Environmental Forces on   Municipal Policies: a Reassessment."   Rocky Mountain Social Science Journal 12 (January, 1975), 85-91.

8952.   Allswang, John M.   "The Chicago Negro Voter and the Demographic   Consensus: a Case Study, 1918-1936."   ISHSJ 60 (Summer, 1967), 145-175.

8953.   Barrett, Paul.   "Public Policy and Private Choice: Mass Transit and the Automobile in Chicago Between the Wars." Business History Review 49 (Winter, 1975), 473-497.

8954.   Beeler, Dorothy.   "Race Riot in Columbia, Tennessee: February 25-27, 1946." THQ 39 (Spring, 1980), 49-61.

8955.   Bird, John.   "A History of Water Rights in Nevada: Part II." NHSQ 19 (Spring, 1976), 27-33.

8956.   Blake, Nelson Manfred.   Land into Water--Water into Land: a History of Water Management in Florida. (Talahassee, University Presses of Florida, 1980)

8957.   Brown, Thomas Elton.   "Patriotism or Religion: Compulsory Public Education and Michigan's Roman Catholic Church, 1920-1924." MH 64 (July/August, 1980), 36-42.

8958.   Brye, David L.   Wisconsin Voting Patterns in the Twentieth Century, 1900 to 1950. (New York, Garland, 1979)

8959.   Capeci, Dominic J., Jr.   The Harlem Riot of 1943. (Philadelphia, Temple University Press, 1977)

8960.   Chafe, William H.   Civilities and Civil Rights: Greensboro, North Carolina, and the Black Struggle for Freedom. (New York, Oxford University Press, 1980)

8961.   Cherny, Robert W.   "Isolationist Voting in 1940:   a Statistical Analysis." NH 52 (Fall, 1971), 293-310.

8962.   Colburn, David R. and Richard K. Scher.   Florida's Gubernatorial Politics in the Twentieth Century. (Tallahassee, University Presses of Florida, 1980)

8963.   Dales, David G.   "North Platte Racial Incident: Black-White Confrontation, 1929."   NH 60 (Fall, 1979), 424-446.

8964.   Daniels, Roger.   "Japanese Relocation and Redress in North America: a Comparative View." PacH 26 (Spring, 1982), 2-13.

8965.   Dawes, Kenneth J.   "The North Dakota Children's Code Commission of 1922:   Protecting the Youth."   NDH 48 (Spring, 1981), 12-23.

8966.   DeWitt, Howard A.   "The Watsonville Anti-Filipino Riot of 1930:   a Case Study of the Great Depression and Ethnic Conflict in California." SCQ 61 (Fall, 1979), 291-302.

8967.   Dinnerstein, Leonard.   "Anti-Semitism in the Eightieth Congress: the Displaced Person Act of 1948."   Capitol Studies 6 (Fall, 1978), 11-26.

8968.   Dinwoodie, D.H.   "Deportation: the Immigration Service and the Chicano Labor Movement in the 1930's." NMHR 52 (July, 1977), 193-206.

8969.   Dorsett, Lyle W.   "Kansas City Politics: A Study of Boss Pendergast's Machine." ArW 8 (Summer, 1966), 107-118.

8970.   Downes, Randolph C.   "Negro Rights and White Backlash in the Campaign of 1920." OH 75 (Spring-Summer, 1966), 85-107.

8971.   Dunbar, Robert G.   "Pioneering Groundwater Legislation in the United States: Mortgages, Land Banks, and Institution-Building in New Mexico." PHR 47 (November, 1978), 565-584.

8972.   Fuchs, Lawrence H.   "Presidential Politics in Boston: the Irish Response to Stevenson." NEQ 30 (December, 1957), 435-447.

8973.   Garcia, George F.   "Herbert Hoover and the Issue of Race." AI 44 (Winter, 1979), 507-515.

8974.   Garrett, Stephen A.   "Eastern European Ethnic Groups and American Foreign Policy." PSQ 93 (Summer, 1978), 301-323.

8975.   Gelfand, Mark I.   A Nation of Cities: the Federal Government and Urban America, 1933-1965.   (New York, Oxford University Press, 1975)

8976.   Gerson, Louis L.   "Ethnics in American Politics." Journal of Politics 38 (August, 1976), 336-346.

8977.   Grant, Philip A., Jr.   "Iowa Congressional Leaders, 1921-1932." AI 42 (Fall, 1974), 430-442.

8978.   Grody, Harvey P.   "From North to South: the Feather River Project and Other Legislative Water Struggles in the 1950's." SCQ 60 (Fall, 1978), 287-326.

8979.   Hall, Raymond L.   Black Separatism in the United States.   (Hanover, New Hampshire, University Press of New England, 1978)

8980.   Hellwig, David J.   "Black Leaders and United States Immigration Policy, 1917-1929." JNH 66 (Summer, 1981), 110-127.

8981.   Hellwig, David J.   "Black Leaders and United States Immigration Policy, 1917-1929." Negro History Bulletin 45 (July/August/September, 1982), 65-end.

8982. Henry, Keith S. "Caribbean Migrants in New York: the Passage from Political Quiescence to Radicalism." Afro-Americans in New York Life and History 2 (July, 1978), 29-46.

8983. Hoffman, Abraham. Vision or Villany: Origins of the Owens Valley-Los Angeles Water Controversy. (College Station, Texas A&M University Press, 1981)

8984. Holsinger, M. Paul. "The Oregon School Bill Controversy, 1922-1925." PHR 37 (August, 1968), 327-342.

8985. Hundley, Norris. Dividing the Waters; a Century of Controversy Between the U.S. and Mexico. (Berkeley, University of California Press, 1966)

8986. Hundley, Norris. "The Politics of Water and Geography: California and the Mexican-American Treaty of 1944." PHR 36 (May, 1967), 209-226.

8987. Jackson, Kenneth T. "Race, Ethnicity, and Real Estate Appraisal: the Home Owners Loan Corporation and the Federal Housing Administration." JUH 6 (August, 1980), 419-452.

8988. Jensen, Joan M. "'Disenfranchisement is a Disgrace': Women and Politics in New Mexico, 1900-1940." NMHR 56 (January, 1981), 5-35.

8989. Jorgensen, Joseph G. "A Century of Political Economic Effects on American Indian Society, 1880-1980." JES 6 (Fall, 1978), 1-82.

8990. Kelley, Donald Brooks. "Deep South Dilemma: the Mississippi Press in the Presidential Campaign of 1928." JMsH 25 (April, 1963), 63-92.

8991. Knoke, David and Richard B. Felson. "Ethnic Stratification and Political Cleavage in the United States, 1952-1968." AJS 80 (November, 1974), 630-642.

8992. Knoke, David and Michael Hout. "Social and Demographic Factors in American Political Party Affiliations, 1952-1972." ASR 39 (October, 1974), 700-713.

8993.   Kuehl, Warren F.   "Midwestern Newspapers and Isolationist Sentiment." Diplomatic History 3 (Summer, 1979), 283-306

8994.   LaGumina, Salvatore J.   "Ethnic Groups in the New York Elections of 1970."   NYH 53, i.e. New York State Historical Association. Proceedings 70 (1972), 54-71.

8995.   Lee, Lawrence B.   "California Water Politics: Opposition to the CVP, 1944-1980." AgH 54 (July, 1980), 402-423.

8996.   Levy, Mark R. and Michael S. Kramer.   The Ethnic Factor: how America's Minorities Decide Elections. (New York, Simon and Schuster, 1973)

8997.   Lewis, Peirce F. "Impact of Negro Migration on the Electoral Geography of Flint, Michigan, 1932-1962:   a Cartographic Analysis." AAG 55 (March, 1965), 1-25.

8998.   Lichtman, Allan J.   Prejudice and the Old Politics: the Presidential Election of 1928. (Chapel Hill, University of North Carolina Press, 1979)

8999.   Lyons, Paul.   Philadelphia Communists, 1936-1956. (Philadelphia, Temple University Press, 1982)

9000.   Malone, Michael P. and Dianne G. Dougherty. "Montana's Political Culture: a Century of Evolution." Montana 31 (January, 1981), 44-58.

9001. Miscamble, Wilson D. "Catholics and American Foreign Policy from McKinley to McCarthy: a Historiographical Survey." Diplomatic History 4 (Summer, 1980), 223-240.

9002. Mitchell, Kell F., Jr. "Diplomacy and Prejudice: the Morris-Shidehara Negotiations, 1920-1921."   PHR 39 (February, 1970), 85-104.

9003. Moore, Deobrah Dash. B'nai B'rith and the Challenge of Ethnic Leadership. (Albany, State University of New York Press, 1981)

9004. Nelson, Douglas W. Heart Mountain: the History of an American Concentration Camp. (Madison, State Historical

Society of Wisconsin for the Department of History, University of Wisconsin, 1976)

9005. Newman, Dorthy K., et.al. Protest, Politics and Prosperity: Black Americans and White Institutions. (New York, Pantheon, 1978)

9006. Ng, Wing-cheung. "An Evaluation of the Labor Market Status of Chinese Americans." AJ 4 (1977), 101-122.

9007. O'Brien, Kenneth B., Jr. "Education, Americanization, and the Supreme Court: the 1920's." AQ 13 (Summer, 1961), 161-171.

9008. Ortiz, Roxanne Dunbar. Roots of Resistance: Land Tenure in New Mexico, 1680-1980. (Los Angeles, Chicano Studies Research Center Publications and American Indian Studies Center, 1980)

9009. Pisani, Donald J. "The Strange Death of the California-Nevada Compact: a Study in Interstate Water Negotiations." PHR 47 (November, 1978), 637-658.

9010. Pisani, Donald J. "Western Nevada's Water Crisis, 1915-1935." NHSQ 22 (Spring, 1979), 3-20.

9011. Pratt, Henry J. The Gray Lobby. (Chicago, University of Chicago Press, 1976)

9012. Ralph, John H. and Richard Rubinson. "Immigration and the Expansion of Schooling in the United States, 1890-1970." ASR 45 (December, 1980), 943-954.

9013. Reagan, Hugh D. "Race as a Factor in the Presidential Election of 1928 in Alabama." AR 19 (January, 1966), 5-19.

9014. Reuss, Martin. "The Army Corps of Engineers and Flood-Control Politics on the Lower Mississippi." LH 23 (Spring, 1982), 131-148.

9015. Ridker, Ronald G. "Future Water Needs and Supplies, with a Note on Land Use." In U.S. Commission on Population Growth and the American Future. Population Resources and the Environment. (Edited by Ronald G.

Ridker.   (Washington, D.C., Government Printing Office, 1972), 213-228.

9016. Robbins, William G. "The Willamette Valley Project of Oregon: a Study in the Political Economy of Water Resource Development." PHR 47 (November, 1978), 585-605.

9017. Rose, Mark H. Interstate: Express Highway Politics, 1941-1956. (Lawrence, Regents Press of Kansas, 1979)

9018. Ryan, Thomas G. "Ethnicity in the 1940 Presidential Election in Iowa: a Quantitative Approach." AI 43 (Spring, 1977), 615-635.

9019. Schneider, Mark. "Migration, Ethnicity, and Politics: a Comparative State Analysis." Journal of Politics 38 (November, 1976), 938-962.

9020. Shover, John L. "Ethnicity and Religion in Philadelphia Politics, 1924-1940." AQ 25 (December, 1973), 499-515.

9021. Shradar, Victor L. "Ethnicity, Religion, and Class: Progressive School Reform in San Francisco." HEQ 20 (Winter, 1980), 385-401.

9022. Sitkoff, Harvard. "The Detroit Race Riot of 1943." MH 53 (Summer, 1969), 183-206.

9023. United States. National Advisory Commission on Civil Disorders. Report. (Washington, D.C., Government Printing Office, 1968)

9024. Walker, Forrest A. "Compulsory Health Insurance: the Next Step in Social Legislation." JAH 56 (September, 1969), 290-304.

9025. Weaver, John C. "Lawyers, Lodges, and Kinfolk: the Workings of a South Carolina Political Organization, 1920-1936." SCHM 78 (October, 1977), 272-285.

9026. Weglyn, Nichi. Years of Infamy: the Untold Story of America's Concentration Camps. (New York, Morrow, 1976)

9027. Weiss, Richard. "Ethnicity and Reform: Minorities and the Ambience of the Depression Years." JAH 66 (December, 1979), 566-585.

9028. Welch, Susan. "Women as Political Animals? A Test of some Explanations for Male-Female Political Participation Differences." American Journal of Political Science 21 (November, 1977), 711-730.

9029. Wollenberg, Charles. "Race and Class in Rural California: the El Monte Berry Strike of 1933." CHSQ 51 (Summer, 1972), 155-164.

9030. Zelman, Patricia G. Women, Work, and National Policy: the Kennedy-Johnson Years. (Ann Arbor, Michigan, UMI Research, 1982)

9031. Zink, Steven D. "Cultural Conflict and the 1928 Presidential Campaign in Louisiana." SouS 17 (Summer, 1978), 175-197.

Society

The most important single source on population and American society in this century are the volumes of the 1972 President's Commission on Population and the American Future cited in Chapter One under American Demographic History. Gastil's book is an important effort to define the regions of the United States. Herberg offers an intriguing look at the future of pluralism; Vogt and Albert look at its present in a study that can serve as a model of method. The Calhoun essay on population density examines behavior among rats, but it was much discussed regarding its applicability to humans when first published. Thus, it is a part of America's demographic history, as well as a possible model for understanding our past. Choldin and McGinty list works expanding on and critiquing Calhoun.

9050. Abbott, Carl. "Plural Society in Colorado: Ethnic Relations in the Twentieth Century." Phylon 39 (September, 1978), 250-260.

9051. Alba, Richard D. "Social Assimilation among American Catholic National-Origin Groups." ASR 41 (December, 1976), 1030-1046.

9052. Arce, Carlos H. "A Reconstruction of Chicano Culture and Identity." Daedalus 110 (Spring, 1981), 117-191.

9053. August, Jack. "The Anti-Japanese Crusade in Arizona's Salt River Valley, 1934-1935." ArW 21 (Summer, 1979), 113-126.

9054. Baskin, John. New Burlington: the Life and Death of an American Village. (New York, Norton, 1976)

9055. Bearden, Russell. "The False Rumor of Tuesday: Arkansas's Internment of Japanese-Americans." AkHQ 41 (Winter, 1982), 327-339.

9056. Berthold, Marti. The Interrelationship of History and Demography as Reflected in Periodical Literature from 1920-1970. (Unpublished paper, Union College, 1971)

9057. Betten, Neil. "Polish American Steelworkers: Americanization Through Industry and Labor." PAS 33 (Autumn, 1976), 31-42.

9058. Blau, Joseph P. "A Philosophic View of the City." AQ 9 (Winter, 1957), 454-458.

9059. Boldt, Edward D. "The Death of Hutterite Culture: an Alternative Interpretation." Phylon 41 (December, 1980), 390-395.

9060. Broussard, Albert S. "Organizing the Black Community in the San Francisco Bay Area, 1915-1930." ArW 23 (Winter, 1981), 335-354.

9061. Buczek, Daniel S. "Ethnic to American: Holy Name of Jesus Parish, Stamford, Connecticut." PAS 37 (Autumn, 1980), 17-60.

9062. Calhoun, John B. "Population Density and Social Pathology." Scientific American 206 (February, 1962), 139-148.

9063. Caplow, Theodore and Bruce A. Chadwick. "Inequality and Lifestyles in Middletown, 1920-1978." SSQ 60 (December, 1979), 367-386.

9064. Choldin, Harvey M. and Michael J. McGinty. "Bibliography: Population Density, Crowding, and Social Relations." Man-Environment Systems 2 (May, 1972), 131-158.

9065. Cohen, Miriam. "Changing Education Strategies among Immigrant Generations: New York Italians in Comparative Perspective." JSH 15 (Spring, 1982), 443-466.
9066. Coles, Robert. "Minority Dreams, American Dreams." Daedalus 110 (Spring, 1981), 29-41.

9067. Conk, Margo A.   "Social Mobility in Historical Perspective." Marxist Perspectives 1 (Fall, 1978), 52-69.

9068. Deloria, Vine, Jr. "Identity and Culture." Daedalus 110 (Spring, 1981), 13-27.

9069. Dinnerstein, Leonard, Roger L. Nichols, and David M. Reimers. Natives and Strangers: Ethnic Groups and the Building of America. (New York, Oxford University Press, 1979)

9070. Dobkowski, Michael N. The Tarnished Dream: the Basis of American Anti-Semitism. (Westport, Connecticut, Greenwood Press, 1979)

9071. Duncan, James, S., Jr. "Landscape Taste as a Symbol of Group Identity: a Westchester County Village." GR 63 (July, 1973), 334-355.

9072. Ellsworth, Scott. Death in a Promised Land: the Tulsa Race Riot of 1921. (Baton Rouge, Louisiana University Press, 1982)

9073. Ewen, Elizabeth. "City Lights: Immigrant Women and the Rise of the Movies." Signs 5, supplement (Spring, 1980), 45-65.

9074. Fite, Gilbert C. American Farmers: the New Minority. (Bloomington, Indiana University Press, 1981)

9075. Fligstein, Neil D. "Who Served in the Military, 1940-1973." Armed Forces and Society 6 (Winter, 1980), 297-312.

9076. Flores, Juan, John Attinasi, and Pedro Pedraza, Jr. "La Carreta Made a U-Turn: Puerto Rican Language and Culture in the United States." Daedalus 110 (Spring, 1981), 193-217.

9077. Foner, Philip Sheldon. Organized Labor and the Black Worker, 1619-1973. (New York, Praeger, 1974)

9078. Fujimoto, Tetsuya. "Social Class and Crime: the Case of the Japanese-Americans." Issues in Criminology 10 (Spring, 1975), 73-93.

9079. Gastil, Raymond D. Cultural Regions of the United States. (Seattle, University of Washington Press, 1975)

9080. Gerlach, Larry R. Blazing Crosses in Zion: the Ku Klux Klan in Utah. (Logan, Utah State University Press, 1982)

9081. Gleason, Philip. "American All: World War II and the Shaping of American Identity." Review of Politics 43 (October, 1981), 483-518.

9082. Gleason, Philip. "In Search of Unity: American Catholic Thought, 1920-1960." CHR 65 (April, 1979), 185-205.

9083. Goldberg, Robert Alan. "Beneath the Hood and the Robe: a Socioeconomic Analysis of Ku Klux Klan Membership in Denver, Colorado, 1921-1925." WestHQ 11 (April, 1980), 181-198.

9084. Goldberg, Robert Alan. Hooded Empire: the Ku Klux Klan in Colorado. (Urbana, University of Illinois Press, 1981)

9085. Hansen, Chadwick. "Social Influences on Jazz Style: Chicago, 1920-1930." AQ 12 (Winter, 1960), 493-507.

9086. Hellwig, David J. "Black Meets Black: Afro-American Reactions to West Indian Immigrants in the 1920's." SAQ 77 (Spring, 1978), 206-224.

9087. Herberg, Will. Protestant, Catholic, Jew: an Essay in American Religous Sociology. (Garden City, New York, Doubleday, 1955)

9088. Hollinger, David A. "Ethnic Diversity, Cosmopolitanism, and the Emergence of the American Liberal Intelligentsia." AQ 27 (May, 1975), 133-151.

9089. Ingham, John N. The Iron Barons: a Social Analysis of an American Urban Elite, 1874-1965. (Westport, Connecticut, Greenwood Press, 1978)

9090. Interrante, Joseph. "The Road to Autopia: the Automobile and the Spatial Transformation of American Culture." Michigan Quarterly Review 19/20 (Fall, 1980/Winter, 1981), 502-517.

9091. Jaret, Charles. "The Greek, Italian, and Jewish American Ethnic Press: a Comparative Analysis." JES 7 (Summer, 1979), 47-70.

9092. Jenkins, William D. "The Ku Klux Klan in Youngstown, Ohio: Moral Reform in the Twenties." Historian 41 (November, 1978), 76-93.

9093. Kashima, Tetsuden. "Japanese American Internees Return, 1945 to 1955: Readjustment and Social Amnesia." Phylon 41 (June, 1980), 107-115.

9094. Kauffman, Christopher J. Faith and Fraternalism: the History of the Knights of Columbus, 1882-1982. (New York, Harper and Row, 1982)

9095. Kemper, Donald J. "Catholic Integration in St. Louis, 1935-1947." MoHR 73 (October, 1978), 1-22.

9096. Kingston, Maxine Hong. China Men. (New York, Knopf, 1980)

9097. Klein, Marcus. Foreigners: the Making of American Literature, 1900-1940. (Chicago, University of Chicago Press, 1981)

9098.   Knoles,   George   H.   "'My   American   Impressions':
English Criticism of American Civilization since 1919." AQ 2
(Summer, 1953), 113-120.

9099. Kolko, Gabriel. "Working Wives: Their Effects on the
Structure of the Working Class."   Science and Society 42
(Fall, 1978), 257-277.

9100. Kopf, Edward. "Untarnishing the Dream: Mobility,
Opportunity, and Order in Modern America." JSH 11 (Winter,
1977), 206-227.

9101.   Laguerre,   Michael   S.   "Internal   Dependency: the
Structural Position of the Black Ghetto in American Society."
JES 6 (Winter, 1979), 29-44.

9102. Loomis, Charles Prince.   "El Cerrito, New Mexico: a
Changing Village." NMHR 33 (January, 1958), 53-75.

9103.   McBride,   David   and   Monroe   H.   Little.   "The
Afro-American Elite, 1930-1940: a Historical and Statistical
Profile." Phylon 42 (June, 1981), 105-119.

9104. McCluskey, John, Jr. "Paradise Valley: Black Writers
and Midwestern Cities, 1910-1950." JAC 5 (Summer, 1982),
93-103.

9105. McGuire, Phillip. Taps for a Jim Crow Army: Letters
from Black Soldiers in World War II.   (Santa Barbara,
California, ABC-Clio, 1983)

9106. Mann, Arthur. The One and the Many: Reflections
on the American Identity. (Chicago, University of Chicago
Press, 1979)

9107. Martensen, Katherine.   "Region, Religion, and Social
Action: the Catholic Committee of the South, 1939-1956."
CHR 68 (April, 1982), 249-267.

9108. Melone, Albert P. and Thomas D. McDonald. "Lawyers
in a Rural Setting: Community Size and the Sociology of the
Bar." NDQ 46 (Autumn, 1978), 21-39.

9109. Miller, Randall M., ed. The Kaleidoscopic Lens: How Hollywood Views Ethnic Groups. (Englewood, New Jersey, Ozer, 1980)

9110. Moberg, David O. "Baptists in a Pluralistic Society." Foundations 21 (July-September, 1978), 198-210.

9111. Mohl, Raymond A. "Cultural Pluralism in Immigrant Education: the International Institutes of Boston, Philadelphia, and San Francisco, 1920-1940." JAEH 1 (Spring, 1982), 35-58.

9112. Mondello, Salvatore. "The Integration of Japanese Baptists in American Society." Foundations 20 (July-September, 1977), 254-263.

9113. Montero, Darrel. "The Japanese Americans: Changing Patterns of Assimilation over Three Generations." ASR 46 (December, 1981), 829-839.

9114. Muller, Peter O. "Everyday Life in Suburbia: a Review of Changing Social and Economic Forces That Shape Daily Rhythms Within the Outer City." AQ 34 (no. 3, 1982), 262-277.

9115. Okamura, Jonathan Y. "Aloha Kanaka Me Ke Aloha 'Aina: Local Culture and Society in Hawaii." AJ 7 (Fall/Winter, 1980), 119-137.

9116. Okamura, Raymond Y. "The American Concentration Camps: a Cover-up Through Euphemistic Terminology." JES 10 (Fall, 1982), 95-109.

9117. O'Leary, Timothy and Sandra Schoenberg. "Ethnicity and Social Class Convergence in an Italian Community: the Hill in St. Louis." MoHSB 33 (January, 1977), 77-86.

9118. Parot, Joseph. "The Racial Dilemma in Chicago's Polish Neighborhoods, 1920-1970." PAS 32 (Autumn, 1975), 27-37.

9119. Pienkos, Donald. "Ethnic Orientations among Polish Americans." IMR 11 (Fall, 1977), 350-362.

9120. Plumley, William. "The Need to Reconsider Notions of Folk Culture in Contemporary America." NDQ 46 (Summer, 1978), 22-26.

9121. Polenberg, Richard. One Nation Divisible: Class, Race, and Ethnicity in the United States since 1938. (New York, Viking Press, 1980)

9122. Posadas, Barbara M. "Crossed Boundaries in Interracial Chicago: Pilipino American Families since 1925." AJ 8 (Fall/Winter, 1981), 34-52.

9123. Pratt, Henry J. The Gray Lobby. (Chicago, University of Chicago Press, 1976)

9124. Raitz, Karl B. and Cotton Mather. "Norwegians and Tobacco in Western Wisconsin." AAG 61 (December, 1971), 684-696.

9125. Saloutos, Theodore. "Cultural Persistence and Change: Greeks in the Great Plains and Rocky Mountain West, 1890-1970." PHR 49 (February, 1980), 76-103.

9126. Scott, Clifford H. "Assimilation in a German-American Community: the Impact of World War I." NOQ 52 (Winter, 1980), 153-167.

9127. Scott, James F. "Beat Literature and the American Teen Cult." AQ 14 (Summer, 1962), 150-160.

9128. Sharma, Miriam. "Pinoy in Paradise: Environment and Adaptation of Pilipinos in Hawaii, 1906-1946." AJ 7 (Fall/Winter, 1980), 91-117.

9129. Sherman, Caroline B. "The Development of American Rural Fiction." AgH 12 (1938), 67-76.

9130. Sims, Robert C. "The Japanese American Experience in Idaho." IY 22 (Spring, 1978), 2-10.

9131. Smith, Norman W. "The Ku Klux Klan in Rhode Island." RIH 37 (May, 1978), 34-45.

9132. Spengler, Joseph J. Population and America's Future. (San Francisco, Freeman, 1975)

9133.   Stack, John E., Jr.   International Conflict in an
American City: Boston's Irish, Italians, and Jews, 1935-1944.
(Westport, Connecticut, Greenwood Press, 1979)

9134.   Stone, Kirk H.   "The Geographical Inheritance of
Current Rural House Densities in Eastern Georgia." GHQ 66
(Summer, 1982), 196-216.

9135.   Synnott, Marcia G.   "The Admission and Assimilation
of Minority   Students at Harvard, Yale, and Princeton,
1900-1950." HEQ 19 (Fall, 1979), 285-304.

9136. Szasz, Margaret. Education and the American Indian:
the Road to Self-Determination, 1928-1973.   (Albuquerque,
University of New Mexico, 1974)

9137.   Takahashi, Jere.   "Japanese American Responses to
Race Relations: the Formation of Nisei Perspectives." AJ 9
(1982), 29-58.

9138.   Taylor, David G.   "Cultural Pluralism Versus
Assimilation: New Perpsectives on the American Indian in
the Twentieth Century." MA 64 (January, 1982), 3-16.

9139.   Toll, William.   "Mobility, Fraternalism and Jewish
Cultural Change: Portland, 1910-1930." AJ 68 (June, 1979),
459-491.

9140. Toll, William. "Progress and Piety: the Ku Klux Klan
and Social Change in Tillamook, Oregon." PNQ 69 (April,
1978), 75-85.

9141.   Toll, William.   The Resurgence of Race: Black Social
Theory from Reconstruction to the Pan-African Conferences.
(Philadelphia, Temple University Press, 1979)

9142.   Tower, J. Allen and Walter Wolf.   "Ethnic Groups in
Cullman County, Alabama." GR 33 (April, 1943), 276-285.

9143.   Tucker, Charles Jackson.   "Changes in Age
Composition of the Rural Black Population of the South, 1950
to 1970." Phylon 25 (September, 1974), 268-275.

9144.   Vanek, Joann.   "Household Technology and Social
Status: Rising Living Standards and Status and Residence

Differences in Housework." Technology and Culture 19 (July, 1978), 361-375.

9145. Vogt, Evon Zartman. Modern Homesteaders: the Life of a Twentieth-Century Frontier Community. (Cambridge, Massachusetts, Harvard University Press, 1955)

9146. Vogt, Evon Zartman and Ethel M. Albert. People of Rimrock: a Study of Values in Five Cultures. (New York, Atheneum, 1966)

9147. Wang, Peter H. "The Immigration Act of 1924 and the Problem of Assimilation." JES 2 (Fall, 1974), 72-75.

9148. Weinberg, Daniel E. "The Ethnic Technician and the Foreign-Born: Another Look at Americanization Ideology and Goals." Societas 7 (Summer, 1977), 209-227.

9149. Western, John. "Social Groups and Activity Patterns in Houma, Louisiana." GR 63 (July, 1973), 301-321.

9150. Williams, Beverly S. "Anti-Semitism and Shreveport, Louisiana: the Situation in the 1920's." LH 21 (Fall, 1980), 387-398.

9151. Woodrum, Eric. "An Assessment of Japanese American Assimilation, Pluralism, and Subordination." AJS 87 (July, 1981), 157-169.

Author Index

Place Index

Subject Index

abolitionists, 8782
Acadians, 4250, 5057, 7171
adolescents, 7054, 7063, 7065, 7111, 7134, 7380, 7383, 7396, 7519, 7591, 7592, 7648, 7819, 7845, 7864, 7866, 7886
Africans, 3183, 4090, 4160, 8123, 8845
Afro-Americans, 4008, 4820, 6104, 7008, 7146, 7346, 7839, 7895,   8104, 8130, 8708, 8744, 8823-8826, 9086, 9103
aged, 2012, 3410, 7046, 7067, 7094, 7106, 7117, 7121, 7123, 7300, 7301, 7387, 7402, 7630, 7808, 7835, 7852, 8233, 9011, 9123
Aleuts, 3207
Amish, 2136, 2212, 2216, 4104
Anglo-Americans, 5152, 8128, 8691, 8730
architects, 8147
artisans, 8746
Asian-Americans, 4720, 4721
Asians, 4550, 4755, 8242, 8436, 8461
Australians, 4693
auto workers, 7868, 8767

Baptists, 7049, 8700, 8832, 8847, 9110, 9112
Blacks, 1213, 2000, 2029, 2100, 2103-2106, 2110-2113, 3007, 3182, 3184, 3185, 3190, 3191, 3194, 3195, 3254, 3522, 3526, 3579, 3721, 3729, 3752, 4012, 4028, 4029, 4033, 4060, 4101, 4111, 4146, 4157-4160, 4168, 4170, 4219, 4248, 4505, 4508, 4528, 4725, 4802, 4803, 4808, 4809, 4813, 4816, 4818, 4819, 4822, 4958, 4968, 5136, 5250-5335, 5809, 5903, 5926, 5958, 5963, 5975, 6000, 6004, 6065, 6069, 6070, 6073, 6076, 6077,

6094, 6097, 6102, 6112, 7001, 7019, 7048, 7075, 7132, 7306-
7309, 7327, 7328, 7340, 7354, 7357, 7360, 7361, 7370, 7373,
7385, 7392, 7399, 7401, 7556, 7561, 7577, 7617, 7630, 7843,
7898, 8003, 8007, 8012, 8014, 8068, 8114, 8119, 8148, 8202,
8219, 8237, 8240, 8266, 8287, 8289, 8300, 8301, 8308, 8320,
8368, 8375, 8379, 8392, 8396, 8397, 8404, 8410, 8419, 8437,
8442, 8460, 8462, 8474, 8499, 8513, 8517, 8642, 8643, 8647,
8654, 8659, 8660, 8665, 8668, 8679, 8680, 8685, 8688, 8709-
8712, 8732, 8736, 8749, 8751, 8755, 8780, 8785, 8803, 8804,
8807, 8809, 8816, 8827, 8839, 8844, 8856, 8903, 8905, 8906,
8914, 8918, 8952, 8954, 8959, 8960, 8963, 8970, 8979-8981,
8987, 8997, 9005, 9013, 9022, 9023, 9060, 9072, 9077, 9086,
9101, 9104, 9105, 9135, 9141, 9143
British, 4051, 4054, 4098, 4518, 4521, 4536, 4537, 4570, 5078,
8150, 8738
British-Americans, 4812
business people, 3662, 4969, 5600, 8142, 8228, 8230, 8243

Californios, 7600
Catholics, 4560, 4608, 4640, 4685, 4703, 4744, 4746, 7409,
8386, 8393, 8422, 8447, 8475, 8512, 8610, 8662, 8689, 8750,
8806, 8848, 8957, 9001, 9051, 9061, 9082, 9087, 9095, 9107
Central Asians, 5904
children, 3205, 3303, 3310, 3387, 3394, 3397-3400, 3403, 3416,
3418, 3424, 3446, 3453, 3659, 3758, 3821, 3828, 4022, 7020,
7026, 7042, 7061, 7065, 7073, 7102, 7108, 7111, 7119, 7125,
7131, 7136, 7137, 7143, 7144, 7151, 7160, 7162, 7167, 7177,
7216, 7325, 7326, 7383, 7393, 7400, 7509, 7519, 7528, 7556,
7559, 7587, 7588, 7591, 7592, 7613, 7614, 7622, 7623, 7633,
7634, 7654, 7664, 7667, 7683, 7822, 7824, 7826, 7836, 7843,
7853, 7875, 7878, 7886, 7897, 7905, 7909, 7913, 8269, 8430,
8615, 8624, 8665, 8781, 8803, 8820, 8965
Chinese, 3667, 4510, 4523, 4539, 4544, 4581, 4599, 4617, 4628,
4642, 4646, 4647, 4654, 4661, 4673, 4690, 4704, 4706, 4725,
4737, 4752, 5040, 5937, 7847, 8275, 8276, 8335, 8344, 8426,
8451, 8464, 8491, 8535, 8536, 8711, 8732, 8836, 8915, 9095
Chinese-Americans, 8825, 8862, 9006
clergy, 3055, 3758, 4154, 8435
clubwomen, 7516
college students and graduates, 2020, 2025, 2226, 3054, 3161,
4140, 4141, 7000, 7335, 7508, 7511, 7896, 8603, 9135
Communists, 8999
Confederates, 4807, 4824, 4827, 7415
Congregationalists, 7234
Cornish, 4699

About the Compilers

DAVID R. GERHAN is Associate Professor and Head of Information Services at Union College Library, Schenectady, New York. He is the author of an American Studies masters thesis, consulting reports to the New York State Library, an ERIC document on multinational business, and co-author of a newspaper bibliography for the Capital District Library Council. His articles have appeared in *Reference Quarterly* and *Journal of Academic Librarianship.*

ROBERT V. WELLS is Washington Irving Professor of Modern Literary and Historical Studies at Union College, Schenectady, New York. He is the author of *The Population of the British Colonies in America Before 1776* (1975), *Revolutions in Americans' Lives* (Greenwood, 1982), and *Uncle Sam's Family* (1985). His most recent articles have appeared in *Journal of Interdisciplinary History.*